This book is the property of
The Cumberland Valley School District
R. D. #1, Mechanicsburg, Pennsylvania
Please try to keep it in as good condition as when you
received it.
Book No.......896044

| Sign your name here | Date | Condition when you received it | | | | Cond t on when you returned it | | |
|---|---|---|---|---|---|---|---|---|
| | | New | Good | Fair | Poor | Good | Fair | Poor |
| | | | | | | | | |
| | | | | | | | | |
| | | | | | | | | |
| | | | | | | | | |
| | | | | | | | | |
| | | | | | | | | |

If you misuse this book you will be asked to pay for the
damage. If you lose it you will be charged for it according
to the condition when you received it.

# Ecce Romani

A Latin Reading Program
Revised Edition

## 4
### Pastimes
### and Ceremonies

---

## 5
### Public Life
### and Private Lives

---

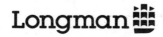
Longman

Ecce Romani Part 4 Pastimes and Ceremonies
Ecce Romani Part 5 Public Life and Private Lives
First Printing 1987
5 4 3 2
ISBN 0-582-99857-3

*Illustrated by Trevor Parkin. Cover illustration by Judy Hans Price.*

This edition of *Ecce Romani* is based on *Ecce Romani: A Latin Reading Course,*
originally prepared by the Scottish Classics Group © copyright The Scottish Classics
Group 1971, 1982, and published in the United Kingdom by Oliver and Boyd, a
division of Longman Group. This edition has been prepared by a team of American and
Canadian educators:

Authors: Professor Gilbert Lawall, University of Massachusetts, Amherst,
Massachusetts; Ron Palma, Holland Hall School, Tulsa, Oklahoma;
Professor Carol Esler, College of William and Mary
Consultants: Dr. Rudolph Masciantonio, Philadelphia Public Schools, Pennsylvania;
Ronald Palma, Holland Hall School, Tulsa, Oklahoma; Dr. Edward
Barnes, C. W. Jefferys Secondary School, Downsview, Ontario; Shirley
Lowe, Wayland Public Schools, Wayland, Massachusetts

Longman Inc.
95 Church Street
White Plains, N.Y. 10601
Associated companies:
Longman Group Ltd., London
Longman Cheshire Pty., Melbourne
Longman Paul Pty., Auckland
Copp Clark Pitman, Toronto
Pitman Publishing Inc., New York

Printed in the U.S.A.

# CONTENTS

# 41
# At the Baths

One of the main entertainments of the Roman was his daily visit to the baths—either to the public **thermae** or to the smaller, private **balneae**. He would expect to find three basic rooms: a warm room (**tepidārium**) which he would enter after undressing in the changing-room (**apodytērium**); a hot room (**caldārium**) where hot water would be provided in a specially heated room which might also incorporate a steam bath; and a cold room (**frīgidārium**) where he could plunge into a cold bath after the heat of the **caldārium**. To clean himself, the Roman would have himself rubbed down with oil (**unguentum**) which was then scraped off with a special metal instrument (**strigilis**). He would also expect to find an exercise ground (**palaestra**), often in the open air, with a covered portico around it, where he could take exercise by playing with a ball (**pilā lūdere**), by wrestling (**luctārī**), by fencing at a post (**pālus**), or by weightlifting. There was a great variety of ball games including **harpastum**, a game involving the "snatching" (**rapere**) of a heavy ball, and **trigōn**, a throwing and catching game played by three people. At the end of it all he would be rubbed down with a towel (**linteum**). The baths were regarded as a social club, and people went there to exercise, play games, and meet each other, as well as to wash.

Iam hōra sexta erat. Titus Cornēlius, ut cōtīdiē solēbat, domō ēgressus, in Campum Martium ad Thermās Nerōnēās dēscendit, nam eō amīcī eius conveniēbant et dē rēbus urbānīs colloquēbantur.

Quō cum Titus pervēnisset, pecūniā datā, in vestibulum ingressus est. Ibi complūrēs ex amīcīs eum salūtāvērunt atque ūnā in apodytērium ini- 5 ērunt. Vestīmenta exūta trādidērunt servīs suīs, quī unguenta et strigilēs portābant.

Iam ūnctī in palaestram exiērunt ubi multī cīvēs variīs modīs sē exercēbant. Aliī harpastum rapiēbant, aliī trigōne lūdēbant, aliī luctābantur, aliī pālum gladiō petēbant. Titus cum duōbus amīcīs trigōne lūdēbat. Cum 10 satis sē ita exercuissent, ā servīs plūs unguentī poposcērunt et strigilibus dēfrictī sunt. Mox tepidārium, deinde caldārium iniērunt. Hīc, cum calōrem et vapōrem vix patī possent, haud multum morābantur. Cum in tepidārium regressī essent, statim inde frīgidārium intrāvērunt et in aquam frīgidam dēsiluērunt. Posteā linteīs tersī, vestīmenta rūrsus induērunt. 15

Nē tum quidem domum discessērunt sed, vīnō sūmptō, inter sē colloquī coepērunt. Titum, cum ille semper vidērētur omnia audīvisse et vīdisse, dē rēbus urbānīs omnēs rogābant. Maximē enim cupiēbant cognōscere quid in senātū agerētur, cūr prīnceps ipse senātōrēs omnēs Rōmam arcessīvisset, quae scelera lībertī Caesaris admitterent.                                         20

"Nīl novī," respondit Titus, "sed herī in Balneīs Palātīnīs rem rīdiculam vīdī; senex calvus, tunicā russātā indūtus, inter puerōs capillātōs pilā lūdēbat. Eās pilās, quae ad terram cecīderant, nōn repetēbat, nam servus follem habēbat plēnum pilārum quās lūdentibus dabat. Tandem hic senex digitōs concrepuit et aquam poposcit. Tum, cum manūs lāvisset, in capite ūnīus  25 ē puerīs tersit!"

| | |
|---|---|
| **Campus Martius**, the Plain of Mars on the outskirts of Rome | **haud**, not |
| | **posteā**, afterwards |
| **Nerōnēus, -a, -um**, of Nero | **vīnō sūmptō**, after a drink of wine |
| **quō cum**, when . . . there | **scelus, sceleris** (n), crime |
| **pecūniā datā**, after paying his entrance fee | **senex, senis** (m), old man |
| | **calvus, -a, -um**, bald |
| **vestibulum, -ī** (n), entrance passage | **capillātus, -a, -um**, with long hair |
| **vestīmenta, -ōrum** (n pl), clothes | **follis, follis** (m), bag |
| **exerceō** (2), to exercise, train | **digitus, -ī** (m), finger |
| **calor, calōris** (m), heat | |

**exuō, exuere** (3), **exuī, exūtum**, to take off
**unguō, unguere** (3), **ūnxī, ūnctum**, to anoint, smear with oil
**dēfricō, dēfricāre** (1), **dēfricuī, dēfrictum**, to rub down
**tergeō, tergēre** (2), **tersī, tersum**, to dry, wipe
**cognōscō, cognōscere** (3), **cognōvī, cognitum**, to find out, learn
**admittō, admittere** (3), **admīsī, admissum**, to commit (a crime)
**repetō, repetere** (3), **repetīvī, repetītum**, to pick up, recover
**concrepō, concrepāre** (1), **concrepuī**, to snap (the fingers)

## Exercise 41a

*Using story 41 as a guide, give the Latin for:*

1. When Titus had arrived there, several of his friends greeted him.
2. When they had exercised enough, they entered the warm room.
3. Since they were scarcely able to endure the heat of the hot room, they returned to the warm room.
4. Since Titus seemed to know everything, they asked him about affairs of the town.
5. They wanted to learn why the Emperor had summoned the senators to Rome and what the senators were doing in the senate.

A bronze oil flask and two strigils. (Reproduced
by courtesy of the Trustees of the British Museum)

## VERBS: Subjunctive Mood I

Look at these sentences:

Pīrātae rogābant quī **essēmus,** unde **vēnissēmus,** quō iter **facerēmus.**
*The pirates kept asking who we were, where we had come from, and
where we were traveling.*

Cum sē **exercuissent,** in tepidārium ingressī sunt.
*When they had exercised, they went into the warm room.*

Grammaticus tamen, cum ego **ignōrārem,** ferulam rapuit et mē crūdē-
lissimē verberāvit.
*The teacher, however, since I didn't know, snatched his cane and beat
me very cruelly.*

Cum nāvis in īnsulam ventīs **acta esset,** nōs in terram ēvāsimus.
*When the ship had been driven on to the island by the winds, we escaped
ashore.*

The verbs in bold type are examples of the *subjunctive mood* which frequently occurs in Latin in subordinate clauses.

9

# Imperfect Subjunctive

This tense of the subjunctive is formed from the present active infinitive by the addition of the personal endings:

|   |   | esse |
|---|---|------|
|     | 1 | esse**m** |
| S | 2 | essē**s** |
|     | 3 | esse**t** |
|     | 1 | essē**mus** |
| P | 2 | essē**tis** |
|     | 3 | esse**nt** |

So also the irregular verbs **posse, velle, nōlle, īre,** and **ferre.**

| ACTIVE VOICE | | | | | |
|---|---|---|---|---|---|
|   |   | *1st Conjugation* | *2nd Conjugation* | *3rd Conjugation* | | *4th Conjugation* |
|     | 1 | portāre**m** | movēre**m** | mitterе**m** | iacere**m** | audīre**m** |
| S | 2 | portārē**s** | movērē**s** | mitterē**s** | iacerē**s** | audīrē**s** |
|     | 3 | portāre**t** | movēre**t** | mittere**t** | iacere**t** | audīre**t** |
|     | 1 | portārē**mus** | movērē**mus** | mitterē**mus** | iacerē**mus** | audīrē**mus** |
| P | 2 | portārē**tis** | movērē**tis** | mitterē**tis** | iacerē**tis** | audīrē**tis** |
|     | 3 | portāre**nt** | movēre**nt** | mittere**nt** | iacere**nt** | audīre**nt** |

| PASSIVE VOICE | | | | | |
|---|---|---|---|---|---|
|     | 1 | portāre**r** | movēre**r** | mittere**r** | iacere**r** | audīre**r** |
| S | 2 | portārē**ris** | movērē**ris** | mitterē**ris** | iacerē**ris** | audīrē**ris** |
|     | 3 | portārē**tur** | movērē**tur** | mitterē**tur** | iacerē**tur** | audīrē**tur** |
|     | 1 | portārē**mur** | movērē**mur** | mitterē**mur** | iacerē**mur** | audīrē**mur** |
| P | 2 | portārē**minī** | movērē**minī** | mitterē**minī** | iacerē**minī** | audīrē**minī** |
|     | 3 | portāre**ntur** | movēre**ntur** | mittere**ntur** | iacere**ntur** | audīre**ntur** |

| DEPONENT VERBS | | | | |
|---|---|---|---|---|
| S  1 | cōnāre**r** etc. | verēre**r** etc. | loquere**r** etc. | regredere**r** etc. | experīre**r** etc. |

Note in the 1st person singular sample of deponent verbs given above that deponents form the imperfect subjunctive by adding the passive endings to a form that would be the *active infinitive* if deponent verbs had an active infinitive, thus cōnāre- + -r = cōnārer.

## Pluperfect Subjunctive

The *active* of all verbs is made up of the perfect active infinitive plus the personal endings.

The *passive* is made up in the same way as the indicative passive (see Chapter 30), but **essem** is substituted for **eram**.

|   |   | ACTIVE VOICE | PASSIVE VOICE | | DEPONENT | |
|---|---|---|---|---|---|---|
| S | 1 | audīvisse*m* | audītus, -a | essem | cōnātus, -a | essem |
|   | 2 | audīvissē*s* | audītus, -a | essēs | cōnātus, -a | essēs |
|   | 3 | audīvisse*t* | audītus, -a, -um | esset | cōnātus, -a, -um | esset |
| P | 1 | audīvissē*mus* | audītī, -ae | essēmus | cōnātī, -ae | essēmus |
|   | 2 | audīvissē*tis* | audītī, -ae | essētis | cōnātī, -ae | essētis |
|   | 3 | audīvisse*nt* | audītī, -ae, -a | essent | cōnātī, -ae, -a | essent |

Be sure to learn all of the subjunctive forms above thoroughly.

## Some Uses of the Subjunctive: Circumstantial and Causal Clauses and Indirect Questions

The examples of the subjunctive you have met so far have been in subordinate clauses beginning with **cum** ("when," "since") or a question word. When **cum** means "when," its clause describes the *circumstances* in which the action of the main clause took place. When **cum** means "since," its clause describes the *cause* or the reason why the action of the main clause took place. When the subordinate clause begins with a question word, the clause is said to express an *indirect question*.

In all of these clauses the subjunctive is translated into English as the corresponding tense of the indicative. The imperfect subjunctive indicates an action going on at the *same time* as that of the main verb of the sentence. Translate with ". . . was . . ." or ". . . were . . . ," e.g.:

Pīrātae rogābant quō iter facerēmus.
*The pirates were asking where we were traveling.*

The pluperfect subjunctive expresses an action that took place *before* that of the main verb. Translate with ". . . had . . . ," e.g.:

Pīrātae rogābant unde vēnissēmus.
*The pirates were asking where we had come from.*

## Exercise 41b

In the Latin sentences on page 9 under VERBS: Subjunctive Mood I, locate two circumstantial clauses, one causal clause, and three indirect questions.

## Exercise 41c

Read aloud and translate each sentence, and then identify each subordinate clause by type (circumstantial, causal, indirect question). Comment on the temporal relationship between the actions of the subordinate clauses and those of the main clauses.

1. Pīrātae rogābant quis esset meus dominus et quō īret.
2. Cum nōllem dominum relinquere, cōnātus sum eum servāre.
3. Cum prīmā lūce profectī essēmus, iam dēfessī erāmus.
4. Lūdī magister rogāvit unde Aenēās vēnisset et quō nāvigāre in animō habēret.
5. Cum multōs annōs nāvigāvissēmus, tandem ad Italiam pervēnimus.
6. Grammaticus mē rogāvit quandō domō abiissem.
7. Māter fīlium rogāvit cūr īrātus esset.
8. Cum diū ambulāvissent, dēfessī erant.
9. Cum lupum cōnspexissem, quam celerrimē aufūgī.
10. Ego nesciēbam cūr Rōmam proficīscerēmur.

The women's changing-room (**apodytērium**) of the baths at Herculaneum. (Photograph: the Mansell Collection)

# The Baths

In addition to the many references to baths in Roman literature, much information about the **balneae** and **thermae** can be deduced from the archaeological remains of bathing establishments still evident today. In Rome, the great Thermae of Diocletian now house the National Museum, its extensive grounds having been laid out by Michelangelo centuries after the baths were built. Grand opera is performed during the summer months in the Baths of Caracalla.

At Pompeii, both public and private bathing establishments have been found, and even in many of the houses there are full suites of bathrooms—warm, hot, and cold rooms—which were apparently used only by the family. On country estates and in town houses, in addition to the suites of baths for the owner, there were bath houses for slaves.

Hadrian's Baths at Lepcis Magna (A.D. 126-7). Open-air swimming-bath (*a*), **frīgidārium** (*b*), plunge-baths (*c*), **tepidārium** (*d*), with a large central and two smaller baths (*e*), **caldārium** (*f*), super-heated rooms (*g*), furnaces (*h*), and latrines (*j*).

13

The first public baths in Rome were built in the second century B.C.; they were small, practical wash-houses for men only. Later, bathing establishments called **balneae** began to be built at private expense and run for profit by individuals or a consortium. As the practice of bathing became more and more popular, huge baths (**thermae**) were built by the state. These were increased in size and splendor under the emperors, e.g., the Thermae of Caracalla (A.D. 217) and of Diocletian (A.D. 303).

Romans of all social classes could spend an hour or more in the luxury of such complexes for only a **quadrāns**, the smallest Roman coin. Children were admitted free. The management of the state **thermae** was awarded for a fixed sum to a contractor. Sometimes a rich citizen or magistrate undertook to pay him the equivalent of the total entrance fees for a certain period, during which entry to the baths was entirely free.

So attached were the Romans to their daily hot steam-bath that they built baths in most communities throughout their Empire. Where there were hot springs, as in Bath, England, they used these and built gymnasia and dressing-rooms around them. Where there were no hot springs, they heated the air by "hypocausts," a system whereby hot air from a furnace circulated under the raised floor and through ducts and vents in the walls. The fuel for the furnace, which was stoked by slaves, was wood and charcoal. Huge reservoirs were built near the baths to provide a constant and plentiful supply of water.

In Rome, the baths opened at noon and remained open till dusk. The opening and closing times were indicated by the striking of a gong.

Many establishments had separate facilities for men and women bathers; others fixed different hours for the two sexes. Mixed bathing, however, was usual in the open-air swimming pools that formed part of the larger baths. Ladies who cared for their reputation did not frequent the baths.

Bathers would take various articles with them to the baths, including towels, bottles of oil, and strigils. All but the poor would bring their own slaves to attend them, but it was possible to hire the services of others at the baths (e.g., masseur, barber). Attendants would guard clothes for a small fee.

Roman baths varied considerably in size and layout, but in all of them the following series of rooms was to be found:

1. **apodytērium:** a changing room with stone benches and rows of deep holes in the walls for holding clothes.

2. **frīgidārium:** cold room, with cold plunge bath at one side.

3. **tepidārium:** warm room, to acclimatize bathers to the difference in temperature between the cold and hot rooms.

4. **caldārium:** hot room, with hot bath and hot air like the modern Turkish bath. It was the best-lit room and was equipped with basins and tubs. Its ceiling was usually domed to allow condensation to run off.

14

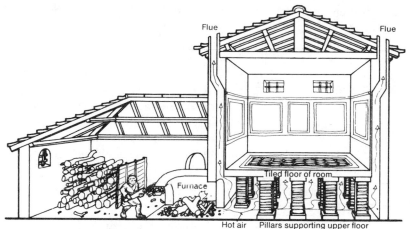

Diagram of a hypocaust

In addition, some baths had a "Spartan" room (**Lacōnicum**), where people sweated in dry heat as in a sauna. It had a dome on top with a round opening closed by a bronze disc on a chain. The bather could thus regulate the heat himself.

Remains of the Baths of Caracalla

The bathers could take the three stages of bathing in any order, but it was usual to end up with a cold plunge. Medicinal and perfumed baths were also available.

The baths became a suitable place for taking exercise. A large complex would have a court for ball games and an area for gymnastics and wrestling, in addition to the swimming pool. There were various ball games, each using a different type of ball and sometimes a racquet as well. Hoops or a dumbbell were also used for exercising.

The Roman baths were centers for recreation and relaxation in the fullest sense, and in the largest establishments the amenities could include gardens, reading-rooms, and even libraries. "Snack-bars" (**popīnae**) were numerous inside the building or near by, while vendors of every type advertised their wares on all sides.


## A Graffito from the Baths at Rome

**Balnea, vīna, Venus corrumpunt corpora nostra; at vītam faciunt—balnea, vīna, Venus.**

balnea = balneae                    Venus = amor
    **corrumpō, corrumpere** (3), **corrūpī, corruptum,** to spoil, harm, ruin

# 42
# *Stop Thief!*

Marcus et Sextus ē lūdō ēgressī ūnā cum Eucleide et alterō servō domum
ībant. Subitō Eucleidēs puerīs, "Vultisne ad thermās īre?" inquit.

Quibus verbīs audītīs, puerī maximē gaudēbant. Mox ad thermās ad-
vēnērunt et in apodytērium intrāvērunt, quod iam erat plēnum puerōrum
quī ē lūdō ēgressī eō cum paedagōgīs vēnerant. Ibi vestīmenta exuēbant.     5

Marcus, vestīmentīs exūtīs, "Nunc in palaestram exeāmus," inquit. At
Eucleidēs, "Minimē!" inquit. "Pater tuus mē iussit vōs ante nōnam hōram
redūcere." Deinde alterī servō, cui nōmen erat Asellus, "Hīc manē!" inquit.
"Vestīmenta dīligenter custōdī! Hīc enim solent esse multī fūrēs quī vestīmenta surrepta in urbe vēndunt."                                            10

Cui Asellus respondit, "Ego semper vestīmenta dīligenter custōdiō. Nēmō
vestīmenta, mē custōde, surripere potest."

Tum puerī, vestīmentīs trāditīs, in tepidārium intrāvērunt et inde in
caldārium, ubi erat magna turba hominum. Subitō tamen exclāmāvit Sextus, "Aeger sum. Hunc calōrem patī nōn possum. Exībō et ad apodytērium  15
regrediar."

Dum ē tepidāriō exit, Asellum prope vestīmenta sedentem cōnspexit.
Dormiēbat Asellus. Eō ipsō tempore vestīmenta ā servō quōdam surripiē-
bantur. Quod ubi vīdit Sextus, "Prehende fūrem!" exclāmāvit. Simul fūr
clāmōrem Sextī audīvit, simul Asellus ē sellā exsiluit, simul Sextus ad   20
iānuam cucurrit. Fūr in palaestram cōnfūgit, nam sē in turbā cēlāre in
animō habēbat. Cum tamen inde in viam ēvādere nōn posset, in frīgidārium
fūgit.

Sextus tamen fūrem cōnspectum subsequēbātur. Fūr, Sextō vīsō, iam
valdē timēbat. In pavīmentō lāpsus in aquam frīgidam cecidit. Statim in   25
aquam dēsiluit Sextus. Fūrem ex aquā trahere cōnābātur, sed frūstrā. Cum
tamen adiūvissent adstantēs, fūr ā Sextō captus ex aquā extractus est. Quem
captum Sextus dominō trādidit.

| | |
|---|---|
| **quibus verbīs audītīs,** on hearing these words, when they heard this | **mē custōde,** while I am on guard |
| **exeāmus,** let us go out | **turba, -ae** (*f*), crowd |
| **fūr, fūris** (*m*), thief | **pavīmentum, -ī** (*n*), tiled floor |

**surripiō, surripere** (3), **surripuī, surreptum,** to steal
**prehendō, prehendere** (3), **prehendī, prehēnsum,** to seize
**exsiliō, exsilīre** (4), **exsiluī,** to leap out
**cōnfugiō, cōnfugere** (3), **cōnfūgī,** to flee for refuge
**subsequor, subsequī** (3), **subsecūtus sum,** to follow (up)
**lābor, lābī** (3), **lāpsus sum,** to slip, stumble

aeger, aegra, aegrum -ill

> **Iūs et fūrī dīcitur.** *Justice is granted even to the thief.* (Seneca, *On Benefits* IV.28)
>
> lapsus calami *a slip of the pen*
>
> lapsus linguae *a slip of the tongue*

### Exercise 42a

*Respondē Latīnē:*

1. Cūr puerī maximē gaudēbant?
2. Ubi vestīmenta exuēbant?
3. Cūr vestīmenta dīligenter custōdīrī dēbent?
4. Quid Sextus patī nōn potest?
5. Ubi sedēbat Asellus et quid faciēbat?
6. Cūr fūr in frīgidārium fūgit?
7. Quī fūrem ā Sextō captum ex aquā extrāxērunt?
8. Cui trāditus est fūr?

# VERBS: Perfect Passive Participles

You have already translated sentences like the following:

**Coquus vocātus** ab omnibus laudātus est.
   *The cook, **having been summoned**, was praised by all.*
   *The cook **was summoned and** was praised by all.*

The first perfect passive participle may be translated by a main verb: "was summoned and. . . ."

Similar participial phrases appear in other cases, and the meaning of the sentence may be expressed in exactly the same way, e.g.:

Accusative:
**Coquum vocātum** omnēs laudāvērunt.
   *The cook **was summoned and** they all praised (him).*

Dative:
**Coquō vocātō** omnēs grātiās ēgērunt.
   *The cook **was summoned and** they all gave thanks (to him).*

There are several ways of translating sentences such as those above, e.g.:

Coquum vocātum omnēs laudāvērunt.
   *The cook was summoned and they all praised him.*
   *When the cook was summoned, they all praised him.*
   *After the cook was summoned, they all praised him.*

Active translations are also possible, e.g.:

> *They all summoned the cook and praised him.*
> *Having summoned the cook, they all praised him.*
> *After summoning the cook, they all praised him.*

## VERBS: *Ablative Absolute*

Another arrangement is also possible:

**Coquō vocātō,** omnēs cēnam laudāvērunt.
*The cook **was summoned** and *they all praised the dinner.*

Here the words **coquō vocātō** are an example of a Latin construction known as the *ablative absolute,* in which a noun (or pronoun) and a participle are in the ablative case and make up a clause which is separate from the rest of the sentence and usually set off by commas.

In addition to the translation given above, the ablative absolute **coquō vocātō** could be translated "when the cook was summoned" or "after the cook was summoned." Other clauses of this sort may best be translated with "although" or "since" or "if," depending on the context.

The participle of an ablative absolute may also be in the present tense, e.g.:

**Fūre vestīmenta surripiente,** Sextus in apodytērium ingreditur.
**While the thief is stealing the clothes,** *Sextus enters the changing room.*

The present active participle is used for an action going on at the *same time* as the action of the main verb of the sentence; the perfect passive participle is used for an action that was completed *before* the action of the main verb. Often the present participle will be translated with a past tense in English because it describes an action going on in the past at the same time as the action of the main verb in a past tense, e.g.:

**Fūre vestīmenta surripiente,** Sextus in apodytērium ingrediēbātur.
**While the thief was stealing the clothes,** *Sextus was entering the changing room.*

Since classical Latin has no present participle for the verb **esse,** ablative absolute clauses sometimes consist only of two nouns in the ablative case, e.g., **Titō prīncipe,** literally, "Titus (being) Emperor," i.e., when Titus is (was) Emperor.

### Exercise 42b

*Locate 5 examples of ablative absolute clauses in story 42.*

19

## Exercise 42c

*Read aloud and translate the following sentences, giving two or three possible translations of the participial phrases:*

1. Amīcī Titum cōnspectum salūtāvērunt.
2. Titus rogātus quid in senātū agerētur, "Nihil novī," respondit.
3. Vestīmenta exūta servō trādita sunt.
4. Vestīmenta exūta Marcus servō trādidit.
5. In palaestram ingressī trigōne lūdēbant.
6. Strigilibus dēfrictī tepidārium ingressī sunt.
7. Ibi nōn diū morātī in caldārium prōcessērunt.
8. Sextus Asellum dormientem cōnspexit.
9. Clāmōribus adstantium perterritus fūr effugere cōnātus est.
10. Vestīmenta ā servō accepta puerī induērunt.

## Exercise 42d

*Read aloud and translate each sentence, and then identify ablative absolute clauses. Comment on the temporal relationship between the participle of the ablative absolute and the action of the verb in the main clause:*

1. Puerīs in lūdō clāmantibus, magister īrātus fiēbat.
2. Magistrō īrātō, puerī ē lūdō missī sunt.
3. Lūdō relictō, puerī ad thermās īvērunt.
4. Titō salūtātō, puerī in apodytērium iniērunt.
5. Vestīmentīs Asellō trāditīs, in palaestram iniērunt.
6. Lūdō cōnfectō, in tepidārium intrāvērunt.
7. Marcō in caldāriō morante, Sextus ad apodytērium regressus est.
8. Asellō dormiente, fūr vestīmenta surripuit.
9. Fūre cōnspectō, Sextus magnā vōce clāmāvit.
10. Vestīmentīs ā fūre trāditīs, puerī domum īvērunt.

> **Quid rīdēs? Mūtātō nōmine dē tē fābula nārrātur.** *Why do you laugh? Just change the name and the tale is told about you.* (Horace, *Satires* I.1.69-70)

# Linking quī

In story 42 you met the following:

| | |
|---|---|
| **Quibus** verbīs audītīs. . . . (3) | *When they heard* **these** *words.* . . . |
| **Cui** Asellus respondit. . . . (11) | *Asellus replied* **to him**. . . . |
| **Quod** ubi vīdit. . . . (19) | *When he saw* **this**. . . . |
| **Quem** captum. . . . (27-28) | *Now that he had caught* **him**. . . . |

The relative pronoun at the beginning of a sentence provides a link with a person, thing, or action in the previous sentence, e.g.:

Quibus verbīs refers to what Eucleides said in the previous sentence.
Cui refers to Eucleides who had just finished speaking.
Quod refers to the theft Sextus had just seen.
Quem refers to the thief mentioned in the previous sentence.

## The Difficulty of Guarding Clothes at the Baths

Etiam quī it lavātum in balneās, cum ibi sēdulō sua vestīmenta servat, tamen surripiuntur, quippe quī quem adstantium observct falsus est. Fūr facile quī observat videt: custōs quī fūr sit nescit.

Even one who goes to the baths to bathe and watches his clothes carefully there has them stolen all the same, since he's confused as to which of the crowd to watch. The thief easily sees the one who's watching; the guard doesn't know who the thief is.

Plautus, *Rudens* 382-85 (adapted)

## The Plight of a Slave from Whom His Master's Clothes Were Stolen

The following story was told by a guest at Trimalchio's dinner party:

We were just about to step into the dining room when a slave, utterly naked, landed on the floor in front of us and implored us to save him from a whipping. He was about to be flogged, he explained, for a trifling offense. He had let someone steal the steward's clothing, worthless stuff really, in the baths. Well, we pulled back our right feet, faced about and returned to the entry where we found the steward counting a stack of gold coins. We begged him to let the servant off. "Really, it's not the money I mind," he replied with enormous condescension, "so much as the idiot's carelessness. It was my dinner-suit he lost, a birthday present from one of my dependents. Expensive too, but then I've already had it washed. Well, it's a trifle. Do what you want with him." We thanked him for his gracious kindness, but when we entered the dining room up ran the same slave whom we'd just begged off. He overwhelmed us with his thanks and then, to our consternation, began to plaster us with kisses. "You'll soon see whom you've helped," he said. "The master's wine will prove the servant's gratitude."

Petronius, *Satyricon* 30-31, tr., William Arrowsmith

# Versiculī: "The Thief's Accomplice," page 117.

21

# 43
# Pyramus and Thisbe

In ancient Rome, the first contact the public was likely to have with a new poem or a completed section of a longer poem would be, not through reading it in a book, but through listening to it at a public reading (**recitātiō**) given by the poet in a private house or theater or recital room. Some enterprising poets even tried to gather an audience in the forum, at the Circus, or in the public baths. The large public baths often contained, in fact, libraries and reading rooms and thus catered to the minds as well as the bodies of their patrons. Martial complained of a boorish poet who pursued him wherever he went, reciting his verses: "I flee to the baths; you echo in my ear. I seek the swimming pool; you don't allow me to swim."

After the adventure with the thief, Marcus, Sextus, and Eucleides relax and enjoy listening to a recitation of one of the most famous love stories of the ancient world. The story of Pyramus and Thisbe, set in ancient Babylon and made familiar to English readers by Shakespeare's A *Midsummer Night's Dream*, was originally part of a long narrative poem called *Metamorphoses* by the Latin poet Ovid (43 B.C.–A.D. 17).

Olim Babylōne habitābat adulēscēns quīdam pulcherrimus, nōmine Pȳramus. In vīcīnā domō habitābat virgō cui nōmen erat Thisbē. Pȳramus hanc virginem in viā forte cōnspectam statim amāvit. Et Thisbē, Pȳramō vīsō, amōre capta est. Sed ēheu! Parentēs et virginis et adulēscentis, quoniam multōs iam annōs inter sē rixābantur, eōs convenīre vetuērunt. Pȳramō 5
Thisbēn nē vidēre quidem licēbat. Valdē dolēbant et adulēscēns et virgō.

Erat mūrus domuī utrīque commūnis. Parva tamen rīma, ā nūllō anteā vīsa, ab amantibus inventa est. (Quid nōn sentit amor?) Quam ad rīmam sedentēs inter sē sēcrētō colloquēbantur, alter alterī amōrem exprimēns. Sed mox, ōsculīs mūrō datīs, valedīcēbant invītī. 10

Tandem novum cōnsilium cēpērunt. Cōnstituērunt enim, parentibus īnsciīs, domō nocte exīre, in silvam convenīre, sub arbore quādam cōnsīdere. Itaque Thisbē silentiō noctis, cum vultum vēlāmine cēlāvisset, fūrtim ēgressa ad silvam festīnāvit. Quō cum advēnisset, sub illā arbore cōnsēdit. Ecce tamen vēnit leō saevus, ōre sanguine bovis aspersō. Quō cōnspectō, 15
Thisbē perterrita in spēluncam, quae prope erat, cōnfūgit. Et dum fugit, vēlāmen relīquit. Quod vēlāmen leō ōre sanguineō rapuit, sed mox dēposuit.

Haud multō post Pȳramus ex urbe ēgressus, dum ad arborem eandem progreditur, vestīgia leōnis vīdit. Subitō puellae vēlāmen sanguine aspersum cōnspexit. Timōre tremēns, "Quid accidit?" clāmāvit. "Ēheu! Ego tē occīdī, 20 mea Thisbē, quod tē iussī in silvam noctū sōlam venīre, nec prior vēnī. Sine tē vīvere nōlō." Gladiō igitur strictō, sē vulnerāvit atque ad terram cecidit moriēns.

Ecce! Metū nōndum dēpositō, Thisbē ē spēluncā timidē exit, Pȳramum quaerit. Subitō corpus eius humī iacēns cōnspicit; multīs cum lacrimīs, 25 "Pȳrame," clāmat, "quis hoc fēcit?" Deinde, suō vēlāmine cōnspectō, iam moritūra, "Ō mē miseram!" clāmat. "Vēlāmen meum tē perdidit. Sine tē vīvere nōlō." Et gladiō Pȳramī ipsa sē occīdit.

Parentēs, dolōre commōtī, eōs in eōdem sepulcrō sepelīvērunt.

Babylōn, Babylōnis (*f*), Babylon
Pȳramus, -ī (*m*), Pyramus
virgō, virginis (*f*), maiden
Thisbē, Thisbēs (*f*), Thisbe
forte, by chance
rixor (1), to quarrel
uterque, utraque, utrumque, each (of two)
rīma, -ae (*f*), crack
ōsculum, -ī (*n*), kiss
cōnsilium, -ī (*n*), plan
cōnsilium capere, to adopt a plan
īnscius, -a, -um, not knowing

vultus, -ūs (*m*), face
vēlāmen, vēlāminis (*n*), veil, shawl
saevus, -a, -um, fierce, savage
ōre sanguine aspersō, his mouth spattered with blood
spēlunca, -ae (*f*), cave
haud multō post, not much later
nec, another form of neque, and . . . not
prior, priōris, first (of two)
humī, on the ground
moritūra, intending to die, determined to die

sentiō, sentīre (4), sēnsī, sēnsum, to feel, notice
exprimō, exprimere (3), expressī, expressum, to express
valedīcō, valedīcere (3), valedīxī, valedictum, to say goodbye
aspergō, aspergere (3), aspersī, aspersum, to sprinkle, splash
occīdō, occīdere (3), occīdī, occīsum, to kill
vīvō, vīvere (3), vīxī, vīctum, to live
perdō, perdere (3), perdidī, perditum, to destroy

## Exercise 43a

*Respondē Latīnē:*

1. Ubi habitābant Pȳramus et Thisbē?
2. Quandō Pȳramus Thisbēn amāvit?
3. Placuitne amor Pȳramī et Thisbēs parentibus?
4. Quid erat inter duās domūs?
5. Quid faciēbant amantēs ad rīmam mūrī sedentēs?
6. Quid faciēbat Thisbē antequam ad silvam festīnāvit?
7. Quid Thisbē in silvā vīdit?
8. Quid vīdit Pȳramus ex urbe ēgressus?
9. Cūr Pȳramus sē occīdit? Cūr Thisbē?
10. Cūr parentēs Pȳramum Thisbēnque in eōdem sepulcrō sepelīvērunt?

# VERBS: *Future Active Participles*

The future active participle is usually formed by adding **-ūrus, -a, -um** to the supine stem, e.g., **portāt-: portātūrus, -a, -um**. The future active participle of some verbs ends instead in **-itūrus, -a, -um**, e.g., **moritūrus, -a, -um** (from **morior, morī, mortuus sum**):

> Thisbē . . . **iam moritūra,** "Ō mē miseram!" clāmāvit.
> *Thisbe . . .* **now about to die,** *cried, "Oh dear me!"*

The following is a tabulation of the participles in conjugations 1–4:

| TENSE | ACTIVE VOICE | PASSIVE VOICE |
|---|---|---|
| *Present* | 1. portāns, portantis<br>   *carrying*<br>2. movēns, moventis<br>   *moving*<br>3. mittēns, mittentis<br>   *sending*<br>   iaciēns, iacientis<br>   *throwing*<br>4. audiēns, audientis<br>   *hearing* | |
| *Perfect* | | 1. portātus, -a, -um<br>   *(having been) carried*<br>2. mōtus, -a, -um<br>   *(having been) moved*<br>3. missus, -a, -um<br>   *(having been) sent*<br>   iactus, -a, -um<br>   *(having been) thrown*<br>4. audītus, -a, -um<br>   *(having been) heard* |
| *Future* | 1. portātūrus, -a, -um<br>   *about to carry*<br>2. mōtūrus, -a, -um<br>   *about to move*<br>3. missūrus, -a, -um<br>   *about to send*<br>   iactūrus, -a, -um<br>   *about to throw*<br>4. audītūrus, -a, -um<br>   *about to hear* | |

# Notes

1. The present and future participles are active in form and meaning.

2. The present participle of **īre** (*to go*) is **iēns, euntis**. The participles of the other irregular verbs are formed regularly, e.g., **volēns, volentis**. There is no present participle of **esse** (*to be*).

3. The future participle of **īre** is **itūrus, -a, -um**.

4. The future participle of **esse** is **futūrus, -a, -um**.

5. Other possible translations of the future participle include: "going to," "likely to," "intending to," "determined to," "on the point of . . . -ing."

6. The perfect participle is passive in form and meaning.

7. Although the participles of deponent verbs have the same endings as those of non-deponent verbs, all the meanings are active:

| | |
|---|---|
| Present Participle | 1. cōnāns, cōnantis, *trying* <br> 2. verēns, verentis, *fearing* <br> 3. loquēns, loquentis, *speaking* <br> moriēns, morientis, *dying* <br> 4. oriēns, orientis, *rising* |
| Perfect Participle | 1. cōnātus, -a, -um, *having tried* <br> 2. veritus, -a, -um, *having feared* <br> 3. locūtus, -a, -um, *having spoken* <br> mortuus, -a, -um, *having died* <br> 4. ortus, -a, -um, *having risen* |
| Future Participle | 1. cōnātūrus, -a, -um, *about to try* <br> 2. veritūrus, -a, -um, *about to fear* <br> 3. locūtūrus, -a, -um, *about to speak* <br> moritūrus, -a, -um, *about to die* <br> 4. oritūrus, -a, -um, *about to rise* |

Be sure you know all of the forms of the participles given above.

## Exercise 43b

*Read aloud and translate:*

1. Multīs hominibus subsequentibus, fūr effugere nōn potuit.
2. Sextus fūrem effugere cōnantem subsequēbatur.
3. Puerī calōrem vix passī haud diū in caldāriō morābantur.
4. Sextus domum profectūrus ab omnibus laudātus est.
5. Thisbē moritūra ad terram cecidit.
6. Asellō custōde, vestīmenta puerōrum surrepta sunt.
7. Pȳramus ad arborem illam progrediēns vestīgia leōnis vīdit.
8. Vēlāmine relictō, Thisbē in spēluncam cōnfūgit.
9. Ad rīmam inter sē sēcrētō colloquentēs amōrem exprimēbant.
10. Pȳramus Thisbēn secūtūrus ex urbe profectus est.
11. Sōle oriente, mercātōrēs profectī sunt ad Āfricam nāvigātūrī.
12. Multa virginī pollicitus, Pȳramus eī valedīxit.

- **orior, orīrī** (4), **ortus sum,** to rise
- **polliceor, pollicērī** (2), **pollicitus sum,** to promise

# The Fine Art of Poetry

Not all poets pursued an audience as boorishly as the versifier about whom Martial complained (see preface to this chapter). Horace (65-8 B.C.) had a far more dignified conception of his art:

Saepe stilum vertās, iterum quae digna legī sint
scrīptūrus, neque tē ut mīrētur turba labōrēs,
contentus paucīs lectōribus.

*Often must you turn your pencil to erase, if you hope to write something worth a second reading, and you must not strive to catch the wonder of the crowd, but be content with the few as your readers.*

Horace, *Satires* I.10.72-74

## Lovers' Graffiti

### I

Rōmula hīc cum Staphylō morātur.

*Romula hangs around here with Staphylus.*

### II

Secundus cum Prīmigeniā conveniunt.

*Secundus and Primigenia are going together.*

### III

Restitūtus multās saepe dēcēpit puellās.

*Restitutus has often deceived many girls.*

### IV

Vibius Restitūtus hīc sōlus dormīvit et Urbānam suam dēsīderābat.

*Vibius Restitutus slept here—alone—and longed for his Urbana.*

### V

Successus textor amat caupōniae ancillam, nōmine Hīredem, quae quidem
illum nōn cūrat. Sed ille rogat illa commiserētur. Scrībit rīvālis. Valē.

*Successus the weaver is in love with the hostess's maid, Iris by name, who
of course doesn't care about him. But he asks that she take pity (on him).
His rival is writing (this). Farewell.*

### VI

Quisquis amat, valeat; pereat quī nescit amāre!
  Bis tantō percat, quisquis amāre vetat!

*Whoever's in love, may he succeed; whoever's not, may he perish!
  Twice may he perish, whoever forbids me to love!*

**Versiculī:** *"A Difference of Opinion," page 117.*

# *Word Study XI*

## *Diminutive Suffixes*

When added to the base (occasionally the nominative singular) of a Latin noun or adjective, the suffixes *-ulus* (*-olus* after a vowel), *-(i)culus*, and *-ellus* (sometimes *-illus*) alter the meaning of the word by diminishing its size or importance, e.g.:

| Noun or Adjective | Base (or Nom. Sing.) | Suffix | Diminutive |
|---|---|---|---|
| puer, -ī (*m*), *boy* | puer- | + *-ulus* | = puerulus, -ī (*m*), *little boy, young slave-boy* |
| parvus, -a, -um, *small* | parv- | + *-ulus* | = parvulus, -a, -um, *little, tiny* |

Diminutives were sometimes used affectionately, e.g.:

| filia, -ae (*f*), *daughter* | fili- | + *-ola* | = filiola, -ae (*f*), *little daughter, darling daughter* |
|---|---|---|---|

but they could also be disparaging, e.g.:

| mulier, -is (*f*), *woman* | mulier- | + *-cula* | = muliercula, -ae (*f*), *a little, weak, foolish woman* |
|---|---|---|---|

Some diminutives had special meanings, e.g.:

| ōs, ōris (*n*), *mouth* | ōs- | + *-culum* | = ōsculum, -ī (*n*), *a kiss* |
|---|---|---|---|

Adjectives formed with diminutive suffixes have endings of the 1st and 2nd declensions; diminutive nouns are in either the 1st or 2nd declension, and the gender is usually the same as that of the original noun, e.g.:

| novus, -a, -um, *new* | nov- | + *-ellus* | = novellus, -a, -um, *young, tender* |
|---|---|---|---|
| pars, partis (*f*), *part* | part- | + *-icula* | = particula, -ae (*f*), *a little part* |

28

English words derived from these Latin diminutives usually end in -*le*, -*ule*, -*ole*, -*cle*, -*cule*, -*el*, or -*il*, e.g., *particle, novel.*

## Exercise 1

Give the meaning of the following Latin diminutives. Consult a Latin dictionary to determine what (if any) special meanings these diminutives may have had for the Romans.

1. servulus, -ī (m)
2. oppidulum, -ī (n)
3. amīcula, -ae (f)
4. lectulus, -ī (m)
5. capitulum, -ī (n)
6. cistella, -ae (f)
7. ancillula, -ae (f)
8. libellus, -ī (m)
9. lapillus, -ī (m)
10. puellula, -ae (f)

## Exercise 2

Give the English word derived from each of the following Latin diminutives:

1. **mūsculus, -ī** (*m*), little mouse
2. **circulus, -ī** (*m*), a round figure
3. **corpusculum, -ī** (*n*), a little body
4. **rīvulus, -ī** (*m*), a little stream
5. **minusculus, -a, -um,** somewhat small
6. **tabernāculum, -ī** (*n*), tent

## Exercise 3

Look up the Roman emperor Caligula in an encyclopedia and find out why he was known by this diminutive nickname.

# Frequentative Verbs

Frequentative verbs are formed from other Latin verbs and denote repeated or intensified action. (They are also called intensive verbs.) They are usually in the first conjugation, e.g., **dictō, -āre,** *to say often, repeat* (from **dīcō, -ere,** *to say*). Often the special frequentative meaning has been lost and the frequentative verb has nearly the same meaning as the original verb, e.g., **cantō, -āre,** *to sing* (from **canō, -ere,** *to sing*). Frequentative verbs are formed from other verbs in one of two ways:

1. by adding -*ō* to the supine stem, e.g., **acceptō, -āre,** *to receive* (from **acceptum,** supine of **accipiō**)

29

2. by adding *-itō* to the base of the present infinitive (occasionally to the supine stem), e.g., **rogitō, -āre,** *to ask frequently or earnestly* (from **rogāre**), and **ēmptitō, -āre,** *to buy up* (from **ēmptum,** supine of **emō**)

## Exercise 4

Give the original Latin verb to which each of the following frequentative verbs is related:

1. iactō, -āre
2. cessō, -āre
3. habitō, -āre
4. ventitō, -āre
5. haesitō, -āre
6. cursō, -āre
7. vīsitō, -āre

8. scrīptitō, -āre
9. exercitō, -āre
10. dormitō, -āre
11. clāmitō, -āre
12. ductō, -āre
13. tractō, -āre
14. agitō, -āre

## Exercise 5

Look up each of the frequentative verbs in Exercise 4 in a Latin dictionary. Identify each frequentative verb whose meaning differs significantly from the meaning of the original verb.

## Exercise 6

Form a frequentative verb from each of the following Latin verbs by adding *-ō* to the supine stem. Look up the frequentative verb in a Latin dictionary and compare its meaning with that of the original verb.

1. excipiō
2. reprehendō
3. olfaciō
4. expellō

5. adiuvō
6. terreō
7. gerō
8. capiō

# Review X

## Exercise Xa

*Read aloud and translate:*

**Caesar Visits Britain**

Gāius Iūlius Caesar, dux praeclārus Rōmānōrum, in Galliā pugnāns multa
dē Britanniā cognōvit. Mercātōrēs enim ē Britanniā ad Galliam trānsgressī
multa emēbant ac vēndēbant; et Britannī auxilium Gallīs Caesarī resistentibus
semper mittēbant. Caesar igitur, Gallīs victīs et nāvibus parātīs, in Britanniam
trānsgredī cōnstituit. Profectūrī tamen mīlitēs, magnā tempestāte coortā, nāvēs 5
cōnscendere vix poterant. Complūribus post diēbus, cum tempestāte nāvēs
paene dēlētae essent, Rōmānī Britanniae appropinquantēs incolās in omnibus
collibus īnstructōs cōnspexērunt. Ēgredientēs Rōmānōs Britannī, pīlīs con-
iectīs, dēpellere cōnātī sunt; sed, quamquam multōs Rōmānōrum vulnerāvērunt, tandem superātī sunt.                                                    10

dux, ducis (*m*), general      īnstructus, -a, -um, drawn up, de-
pugnō (1), to fight            ployed
collis, collis (*m*), hill      pīlum, -ī (*n*), javelin

cōnscendō, cōnscendere (3), cōnscendī, cōnscēnsum, to board (ship)
dēpellō, dēpellere (3), dēpulī, dēpulsum, to drive away

## Exercise Xb

*Choose the clause that could be substituted for the words quoted from
the passage above and that would keep the same sense. Then translate
the sentence, substituting the new clause for the original words:*

1. in Galliā pugnāns
   a. in Galliā pugnātūrus
   b. quī in Galliā pugnābat
   c. in Galliā pugnātus
2. ē Britanniā ad Galliam trānsgressī
   a. quī ē Britanniā ad Galliam trānsgredientur
   b. ē Britanniā ad Galliam trānsgressūrī
   c. quī ē Britanniā ad Galliam trānsgressī sunt
3. Gallīs victīs et nāvibus parātīs
   a. cum Gallī victī essent et nāvēs essent parātae
   b. Gallōs victūrus et nāvēs parātūrus
   c. Gallōs vincēns et nāvēs parāns

31

4. profectūrī tamen mīlitēs
   a. profectīs tamen mīlitibus
   b. mīlitēs tamen quī proficīscī in animō habēbant
   c. mīlitēs tamen quī profectī essent
5. cum tempestāte nāvēs paene dēlētae essent
   a. tempestāte nāvēs paene dēlente
   b. quod tempestāte nāvēs paene dēlētae sunt
   c. nāvibus tempestāte paene dēlētīs
6. quamquam multōs Rōmānōrum vulnerāvērunt
   a. multīs Rōmānīs vulnerātīs
   b. multōs Rōmānōrum vulnerātūrī
   c. multī Rōmānōrum vulnerātī

## Exercise Xc

Read the following passage and answer the questions below in English:

### The Sabine Women

Rōmulus, cum urbem Rōmam condidisset, quod in urbe erant paucī modo
cīvēs, plūrimōs praedōnēs hominēsque scelestōs sine discrīmine ē vīcīnīs po-
pulīs in urbem accēpit. Sed pēnūria erat mulierum. Virī igitur, īrātī quod
nūllās uxōrēs habēbant, cum ad Rōmulum adiissent, "Nisi nōbīs," inquiunt,
"uxōrēs invēneris, urbem relinquēmus." Tum ē cōnsiliō senātōrum Rōmulus 5
nūntiōs circā vīcīnōs populōs mīsit, quī societātem cōnūbiumque petēbant.
Nusquam tamen cōmiter acceptī sunt.

Deinde Rōmulus, cōnsiliō callidō captō, in magnō agrō quī haud longē
ab urbe aberat lūdōs Neptūnō magnificōs parāvit. Sabīnōrum omnis multitūdō
invītāta cum līberīs ac uxōribus vēnit. Quī cum mūrōs et multās domōs urbis 10
vīdissent, mīrātī sunt quod urbs Rōma tam brevī tempore crēverat.

Cum spectāculī tempus vēnisset dēditaeque eō mentēs cum oculīs essent,
subitō Rōmānī, signō datō, in multitūdinem adstantium incurrērunt. Virginēs
abripuērunt. Ubīque erat clāmor et tumultus. Fīliae Sabīnōrum raptae in
urbem tractae sunt lacrimantēs. Parentēs virginum perterritī et trīstissimī fūgē- 15
runt. Iam tandem Rōmānī uxōrēs habēbant.

| | |
|---|---|
| pēnūria, -ae (f), shortage | Sabīnī, -ōrum (m pl), the Sabines, |
| ē cōnsiliō, following the advice | a people to the north-east of |
| circā (+ acc.), around | Rome |
| societātem cōnūbiumque, alliance | dēditae eō, concentrated on it |
| and right to intermarry | mēns, mentis (f), mind |
| callidus, -a, -um, cunning, ingen- | ubīque, everywhere |
| ious | |

mīror, mīrārī (1), mīrātus sum, to be amazed, marvel (at)
crēscō, crēscere (3), crēvī, crētum, to grow, develop

1. When and why did Romulus receive thieves and wicked men from neighboring peoples into his city?
2. Why were these men angry?
3. What did they threaten to do?
4. Whose advice did Romulus take?
5. What did his messengers seek?
6. Who formed an ingenious plan?
7. Whom did Romulus invite to the games in honor of Neptune?
8. What amazed the Sabines? When?
9. At what moment did the Romans rush upon the Sabines?
10. What were the feelings of the Sabine girls and of their parents?


## Exercise Xd

*In the passage in Exercise Xc, locate the following in sequence:*

1. All verbs in the pluperfect active subjunctive.
2. All ablative absolutes.
3. Linking **quī**.

# 44
# A Rainy Day

Many of the games that children play today were also played by Roman children. They built toy houses and rode on long sticks; they had spinning tops, hoops that they bowled along with a stick, and dolls (**pūpae**); they tossed coins, calling out "heads or ships" (**capita aut nāvia**); and they played at being soldiers or judges or consuls. They also used to harness mice to toy carts.

Nuts were used in several children's games. One nut was balanced on three others, and children competed at knocking them down with a fruit stone. The winner got all the nuts. They also competed at throwing nuts into a narrow-necked vase that had been placed some distance away from them. A very popular game was to ask your partner to guess whether the number of nuts or pebbles or other similar objects that you had in your hand was odd or even (**pār impār**). In another popular game two players each showed (or "flashed") a number of fingers on their right hands (**digitīs micāre**) and simultaneously called out how many fingers altogether they believed had been shown. The round was won by the player who first guessed correctly five times. This game is still played in Italy under the name of *morra*.

Both adults and children played a game that resembled checkers or chess (**lūdus latrunculōrum**, "game of bandits"), in which they moved two sets of pieces on a checkered board. They also played a game of chance with knucklebones or dice (**tālī**). Older children and young men took exercise on the Campus Martius—wrestling, riding, and driving chariots—followed possibly by a swim across the Tiber.

As we rejoin our story, Marcus and Sextus are spending a rainy day at home.

"Ēheu!" mussāvit Marcus. "Cūr 'ēheu'?" rogāvit Sextus.

"Semper pluit!" respondit Marcus. "Ego in animō habēbam ad Campum Martium hodiē dēscendere et ad palaestram īre, sed pater nōs domī manēre iussit. Putō patrem esse crūdēlem."

Eō ipsō tempore Eucleidēs ingressus puerōs rogāvit cūr tam trīstēs essent.  5
"In palaestram īre cupiēbāmus," inquit Marcus, "sed pater hoc vetuit."

Cui Eucleidēs, "Bonō animō este!" inquit. "Ego vōs docēbō latrunculīs lūdere. Putō hunc lūdum esse optimum."

Duās ferē hōrās ita lūdēbant. Postrēmō Sextus exclāmāvit, "Hic lūdus mē nōn iam dēlectat. Ego putō hunc lūdum esse pessimum. Age, Marce!  10
Nōnne vīs pār impār lūdere vel digitīs micāre?"

Statim clāmāre coepērunt ambō. Simul Marcus, "Quīnque!," simul Sextus, "Novem!" deinde Marcus, "Octō!," Sextus, "Sex!"

"Tacēte, puerī!" interpellāvit Eucleidēs. "Nōlīte clāmōribus vestrīs vexāre mātrem et Cornēliam! Putō vōs esse molestissimōs hodiē." At puerī eī nōn 15
pārēbant. Itaque Cornēlia, clāmōribus audītīs, in ātrium ingressa rogāvit quid facerent.

"Nōlī nōs vexāre!" inquit Sextus. "Abī! Sed cūr pūpam in manibus habēs? Num pūpā lūdis?"

"Stultus es, Sexte! Pūpa nōn est mea. Num crēdis mē pūpā lūdere? Hanc 20
pūpam, quam ego ipsa fēcī, filiae Dāvī dōnō dabō. Hodiē est diēs nātālis eius."

Subitō Sextus, pūpā abreptā, in peristȳlium aufūgit. Quō vīsō, Eucleidēs Sextō clāmāvit. "Nōlī pūpam laedere! Statim eam refer!"

Eō ipsō tempore ingressus est Cornēlius. Cum audīvisset quid Sextus 25
fēcisset, "Sexte!" clāmāvit. "Venī hūc!" Puer, iam timidus, in ātrium regressus pūpam Cornēliae reddidit. Tum Cornēlius Sextum sēcum ex ātriō ēdūxit.

Quō factō, Marcus rogāvit, "Quid pater faciet? Quid Sextō fiet?"

Cui Cornēlia, "Putō," inquit, "patrem in animō habēre Sextum verberāre." 30

---

- putō (1), to think, consider
  Bonō animō es (este)! Cheer up!
- lūdus, -ī (m), game
- ferē, almost, approximately
- postrēmō, finally
- ambō, ambae, ambō, both
- pūpa, -ae (f), doll

Num . . . ? Surely . . . not . . . ?
dōnō dare, to give as a gift
diēs nātālis, birthday
- peristȳlium, -ī (n), peristyle, courtyard surrounded with a colonnade
Quid Sextō fiet? What will happen to Sextus?

- laedō, laedere (3), laesī, laesum, to harm

## Exercise 44a

*Using story 44 as a guide, give the Latin for:*

1. Marcus intended to go to the exercise ground today.
2. Eucleides will teach the boys to play "bandits."
3. He thinks that this is a very good game.
4. Both boys began to shout and annoy their mother and Cornelia.
5. Eucleides thinks that the boys are very annoying today.
6. The boys do not obey the slave.
7. Sextus believes that Cornelia is playing with a doll.
8. Cornelia is going to give the doll as a gift to the daughter of Davus.
9. Sextus snatches the doll and flees into the courtyard.
10. Cornelia believes that her father intends to beat Sextus.

35

# Accusative and Infinitive (Indirect Statement) I

The following sentences occurred in the story:

Putō **hunc lūdum esse** optimum.
*I think* **that this game is** *a very good one.*

Putō **vōs esse** molestissimōs.
*I think* **that you are** *very annoying.*

Num crēdis **mē** pūpā **lūdere?**
*Surely you do not believe* **that I am playing** *with a doll?*

In such sentences, you are being given two pieces of information:

| (1) I think | (2) what I think |
|---|---|
| **Putō** | **hunc lūdum esse optimum.** |
| | *(that) this game is a very good one.* |

You will see that, in the second part, the Latin subject is expressed in the *accusative* case and the verb is in the *infinitive*, where English says "that this game" and "is." Similarly:

| **Sciō** | | **vōs esse molestissimōs.** |
|---|---|---|
| *I know* | *that* | *you are very troublesome.* |
| **Vidēmus** | | **Dāvum in agrīs labōrāre.** |
| *We see* | *that* | *Davus is working in the fields.* |
| **Audiō** | | **eum domī morārī.** |
| *I hear* | *that* | *he is staying at home.* |

Other verbs which may be followed by the *accusative and infinitive* construction include **dīcō** (I say), **spērō** (I hope), and **sentiō** (I feel).

Sextus sentit **sē** aegrum **esse.**
*Sextus feels* **that he is** *ill.*

In translating this Latin construction, the next English word after verbs such as "I think," "I know," "I see," "I hear," and "I feel" will most often be "that."

This accusative and infinitive construction in which something is being reported indirectly is known as *indirect statement*.

## Exercise 44b

*Read aloud and translate:*

1. Eucleidēs dīcit lūdum latrunculōrum esse optimum.
2. Sciō Cornēlium esse senātōrem Rōmānum.
3. Nōs omnēs scīmus Cornēliam esse puellam Rōmānam.
4. Putō Sextum puerum temerārium esse.
5. Audiō Cornēlium ad Cūriam festīnāre.
6. Scit ancillās cēnam parāre.
7. Videō haud longam esse viam.
8. Audiō caupōnem esse amīcum Eucleidis.
9. Putāmus in agrīs labōrāre servōs.
10. Crēdō Aurēliam ad urbem proficīscī.
11. Dīcunt Marcum dormīre.
12. Scīmus semper ēsurīre puerōs.
13. Audiō Titum mappam nōn habēre.
14. Cornēlia putat pūpam esse pulcherrimam.

## Exercise 44c

*Select, read aloud, and translate:*

1. Aliī putant (Sextus/Sextum) esse bonum, aliī putant eum (est/erat/esse) molestum.
2. Dāvus quidem scit omnēs (puerōs/puerum/puerī) saepe esse (molestum/ molestī/molestōs).
3. At Aurēlia putat Marcum et Sextum semper bonōs (sunt/esse/erant).
4. Sextus Marcō dīcit Dāvum (esse/est/sum) īrācundum.
5. Semper respondet Marcus (Dāvī/Dāvō/Dāvum) nōn (esse/est) īrācundum.
6. Dīcit Dāvum in agrīs dīligenter (labōrāre/labōrāvit/labōrat).
7. Sextus respondet Dāvum sub arbore cotīdiē post merīdiem (dormīs/dor-miēbat/dormīre).
8. Cornēlia putat (puerī/puerīs/puerōs) haud dīligenter (labōrāvērunt/labōr-ant/labōrāre).
9. Dīcit Cornēlia Marcum et (Sextī/Sextum/Sextus) saepe in lectō diū (ia-cēre/iacent/iacēmus).
10. Flāvia, amīca Cornēliae, putat (Cornēlia/Cornēliam/Cornēliae) puellam pulcherrimam (esse/sunt/est).

# Games Played by Children and Adults

A poet describes games boys play with nuts (**nucēs**):

Hās puer aut certō rēctās dīlāminat ictū
  aut prōnās digitō bisve semelve petit.
*These (nuts), as they stand upright, a boy splits with certain aim,*
  *or, as they lie on their side, strikes with his finger once or twice.*

Quattuor in nucibus, nōn amplius, ālea tōta est,
  cum sibi suppositīs additur ūna tribus.
*In four nuts, and no more, is all his hazard,*
  *when one is added to the three beneath it.*

Per tabulae clīvum lābī iubet alter et optat
  tangat ut ē multīs quaelibet ūna suam.
*Another has them roll down a sloping board, and prays*
  *that one out of many, whichever it may be, may touch his own.*

Est etiam, pār sit numerus quī dīcat an impār,
  ut dīvīnātās auferat augur opēs.
*Then there is (a boy) who guesses whether the number be odd or even,*
  *that the augur may bear away the wealth he has divined.*

Fit quoque dē crētā, quālem caeleste figūram
  sīdus et in Graecīs littera quarta gerit.
*Then too there is drawn in chalk a shape, such as a heavenly*
  *constellation or the fourth Greek letter bears.*

Haec ubi distincta est gradibus, quae cōnstitit intus
  quot tetigit virgās, tot capit ipsa nucēs.
*When this has been marked with stages, the nut that stops within it*
  *gains itself as many nuts as it has touched lines.*

Women playing knucklebones.

Vās quoque saepe cavum spatiō distante locātur,
    in quod missa levī nux cadat ūna manū.

*Often too a hollow vessel is placed at a distance,*
    *into which a nut flung by a skillful hand may fall.*

Ovid, *Nux* 73-86

The next two passages refer to playing **pār impār** by flashing the fingers
(**micāre**):

> When they praise a man's honesty, they say, "He is a man with whom you
> can safely play at odd and even in the dark."

Cicero, *De officiis* III.77

> "Suppose there were two men to be saved from a sinking ship—both of
> them wise men—and only one small plank. Should both seize it to save
> themselves? Or should one give way to the other?"
> "Why, of course one should give way to the other, but that other must
> be the one whose life is more valuable, either for his own sake or for that
> of his country."
> "But what if these considerations are of equal weight in both?"
> "Then there will be no contest, but one will give place to the other, as
> if the point were decided by lot or at a game of odd and even."

Cicero, *De officiis* III.90

## *Gambling with Dice* (tālī—compare Chapter 32)

From a personal letter of the Emperor Augustus:

> I dined, dear Tiberius, with the same company; we had besides as guests
> Vinicius and the elder Silius. We gambled like old men during the meal
> both yesterday and today. When the dice were thrown, whoever turned up
> the "dog" or the six put a denarius in the pool for each one of the dice
> and the whole was taken by anyone who threw the "Venus."

From a personal letter of the Emperor Augustus to his daughter:

> I send you two hundred and fifty denarii, the sum that I gave each of my
> guests, in case they wished to play at dice or at odd and even during the
> dinner.

Suetonius, *Augustus* LXXI.2, 4

## *The Last Move in a Game of Chess* (lūdus latrun-culōrum)

Julius Canus, after a long dispute with the Emperor Caligula, was ordered
by the capricious emperor to be executed. Seneca the moralist praises the
bravery of Canus under sentence of death:

Will you believe that Canus spent the ten intervening days before his execution in no anxiety of any sort? What the man said, what he did, how tranquil he was, passes all credence. He was playing chess when the centurion who was dragging off a whole company of victims to death ordered that he also be summoned. Having been called, he counted the pawns and said to his partner: "See that after my death you do not claim falsely that you won." Then nodding to the centurion, he said, "You will bear witness that I am one pawn ahead."

Seneca, De tranquillitate XIV.6-7

---

**Quid est tam incertum quam tālōrum iactus?** *What is so uncertain as a cast of dice?* (Cicero, *De divinatione* II.121)

**nucēs relinquere** *to leave childhood behind* (Persius, *Satires* I.10)

---

## The Irregular Verb *fīō, fierī, factus sum*

This irregular verb, meaning "to become," "to be made," or "to happen," serves as the passive of **faciō**. Some of its forms were introduced in Exercise 32e. Its forms in the present, imperfect, and future tenses are as follows:

|   |   | *Present* | *Imperfect* | *Future* |
|---|---|-----------|-------------|----------|
|     | 1 | fīō   | fīē*bam*   | fīam   |
| S | 2 | fīs   | fīē*bās*   | fīēs   |
|     | 3 | fīt   | fīē*bat*   | fīet   |
|     | 1 | fī*mus* | fīē*bāmus* | fīē*mus* |
| P | 2 | fī*tis* | fīē*bātis* | fīē*tis* |
|     | 3 | fīu*nt* | fīē*bant*  | fīe*nt*  |

Learn the above forms thoroughly.

### Exercise 44d

*Read aloud and translate:*

1. Titus vīnum bibit et paulātim ēbrius fit.
2. Sī Titus plūs vīnī bibet, magis ēbrius fīet.
3. Aurēlia Titum in diēs molestiōrem fierī putat.
4. Quid Titō fīet sī etiam plūs vīnī nunc bibet?
5. Aliquid malī certē eī fīet.

# Versiculī: *"Sextus Reproved," page 118.*

# Circus and Arena

The Romans did not have regular sporting events as we have at weekends, or organized entertainment available every day as we have in the theater or cinema. Instead, to celebrate religious festivals, commemorate great national victories, or honor the emperor, there were public holidays. These lasted a varying number of days, during which entertainments were presented in the circus and the arena. The number of these festivals increased as time went on until, by the reign of Claudius, 159 days of the year were holidays.

Admission to the shows was free, and all the emperors made sure there was plenty of entertainment. According to Fronto:

> Trajan sensibly always paid attention to the idols of the theater, the circus, or the arena because he knew that the entertainment of the people was very important to the government; doling out corn or money might keep individuals quiet, but shows were necessary to keep the mob happy.
>
> Fronto, *Preamble to History* 17

Juvenal, too, refers to the demand of the Roman mob for **pānem et circēnsēs**—the bread-dole and games in the Circus.

The cost of the public games was met by the state. Often, magistrates added to the grant from their own pockets in order to increase their popularity and the chance of success in their careers. To do this they even ran into debt:

> Julius Caesar spent money so recklessly that many thought he was paying a high price to create a short-lived sensation, but really he was buying very cheaply the most powerful position in the world. Before entering politics he was thirteen hundred talents in debt. As aedile he staged games with 320 pairs of gladiators fighting in single combat. In this and his other extravagance in presenting theatrical performances, processions, and public banquets, he completely outdid all previous efforts to obtain publicity in this way.
>
> Plutarch, *Caesar* 5

# 45
# *Looking Forward to the Games*

Postrīdiē, dum Gāius Cornēlius in tablīnō scrībit, subitō intrāvit Titus, frāter eius.

"Salvē, Gāī!" clāmāvit Titus. "Quid agis?"

"Bene!" respondit Cornēlius. "Sed semper sum, ut vidēs, negōtiōsus."

Cui Titus, "Prō certō habeō tē crās nōn labōrātūrum esse. Omnēs enim 5 cīvēs Rōmānī ad mūnera itūrī sunt. Spērō tē quoque ad mūnera itūrum esse."

At Cornēlius, "Mūnera?" inquit. "Quid dīcis, mī Tite?"

"Prō dī immortālēs!" exclāmāvit Titus. "Crās Caesar amphitheātrum aperiet novum. Tū tamen rogās quid dīcam?" 10

Cornēlius autem cum rīsū, "Nōnne sentīs mē per iocum hoc dīxisse? Certē hic diēs maximē omnium memorābilis erit. Cōnstat Iūdaeōs dīligenter labōrāvisse et amphitheātrum summā celeritāte cōnfēcisse. Nōs templum illōrum dēlēvimus, illī amphitheātrum aedificāvērunt nostrum."

Cui Titus, "Mehercule! Tōtum populum continēbit hoc amphitheātrum. 15 Crās māne viae erunt plēnae hominum quī ab omnibus partibus ad spectāculum congredientur."

"Ita!" inquit Cornēlius. "Putō tamen Aurēliam eō nōn itūram esse. Scīs enim Aurēliam neque mūnera neque sanguinem amāre. Aurēlia domī manēre māvult. Marcum tamen mēcum sum ductūrus. Iam adulēscēns est et 20 mox togam virīlem sūmet. Sextus autem, quod adhūc puer est, domī manēbit; nam, ut docet Seneca, 'Quō maior populus, eō plūs perīculī.' Quotā hōrā tū ad amphitheātrum crās māne es itūrus?"

"Prīmā lūce," respondit Titus, "nam mātūrē advenīre in animō habeō. Quandō tū et Marcus eō perveniētis?" 25

"Haud mātūrē," inquit Cornēlius, "sed prō certō habeō nōs tē in amphitheātrō vīsūrōs esse. Nunc haec epistula est cōnficienda. Valē!"

"Valē!" inquit Titus. "Nōs abitūrī tē salūtāmus!"

| | |
|---|---|
| **negōtiōsus, -a, -um,** busy | **māvult,** (she) prefers |
| **prō certō habeō,** I am sure | **quō maior . . . , eō plūs . . . ,** the |
| **mūnera, mūnerum** (*n pl*), games | greater . . . , the more . . . |
| **spērō** (1), to hope | **mātūrē,** early |
| **cōnstat,** it is agreed | **epistula est cōnficienda,** the letter |
| **Iūdaeī, Iūdaeōrum** (*m pl*), Jews | must be finished |
| **mālō, mālle, māluī,** to prefer | |

### Exercise 45a

*Respondē Latīnē:*

1. Quandō intrāvit Titus tablīnum Gāiī?
2. Quālis vir est Cornēlius?
3. Quō cīvēs Rōmānī crās ībunt?
4. Quid Caesar crās faciet?
5. Quālis diēs erit crās?
6. Quid Iūdaeī aedificāvērunt?
7. Quid Rōmānī dēlēvērunt?
8. Unde hominēs ad spectāculum congredientur?
9. Cūr Aurēlia domī manēre māvult?
10. Quis cum Cornēliō ad mūnera ībit?
11. Cūr Sextus domī manēbit?
12. Quotā hōrā Titus ad amphitheātrum crās ībit?
13. Quem putat Cornēlius sē in amphitheātrō crās vīsūrum esse?
14. Quid Cornēlius nunc cōnficere vult?

## Accusative and Infinitive (Indirect Statement) II

The future infinitive and the perfect infinitive are also used in indirect statements. Look at the following examples:

Putō Aurēliam eō nōn **itūram esse.**
*I think that Aurelia will not go there.*

Prō certō habeō nōs tē **vīsūrōs esse.**
*I am sure that we will see you.*

The phrases **itūram esse** and **vīsūrōs esse** are *future active infinitives*. You will recognize this form as **esse** with the future participle, which appears in the accusative case agreeing with the subject of the infinitive clause in gender, case, and number. (For the future participle, see Chapter 43.)

Cōnstat Iūdaeōs dīligenter **labōrāvisse** et amphitheātrum summā celeritāte **cōnfēcisse.**
*It is agreed that the Jews have worked hard and finished the amphitheater very quickly.*

The *perfect active infinitive* (**labōrāvisse** and **cōnfēcisse**) can be recognized by the ending **-isse**, which is added to the perfect stem. (See Chapter 40.)

When **sē** is used in the accusative and infinitive construction in indirect statements, it is translated "he," "she," or "they," and refers to the subject of the verb of *saying, thinking,* or *hearing,* e.g.:

Titus dīxit **sē** ad amphitheātrum itūrum esse.
*Titus said that he would go to the amphitheater.*

43

The use of sē in this sentence shows that "he" refers to Titus. If the "he" had referred to someone else, eum would have been used instead of sē.

Puellae puerīs dīxērunt sē eōs adiūtūrās esse.
*The girls told the boys that they would help them.*

In this sentence, sē must refer to puellae, and the future infinitive adiūtūrās esse is feminine accusative plural agreeing with sē, while eōs refers to puerīs.

---

Adulēscēns spērat sē diū vīctūrum esse; senex potest dīcere sē diū vīxisse.
*A young man hopes that he will live a long time; an old man is able to say that he has lived a long time.* (adapted from Cicero, *On Old Age* XIX.68)

---

## Exercise 45b

*Read aloud and translate:*

1. Putāmus servōs dīligenter labōrātūrōs esse.
2. Putāsne patruum tuum ad amphitheātrum pervēnisse?
3. Cōnstat illum diem memorābilem fuisse.
4. Scīs Cornēliam domī mānsūram esse.
5. Cornēlius audit Titum domum nōn vēnisse.
6. Cornēlius putat Aurēliam in peristȳliō ambulātūram esse.
7. Scīmus Sextum ad patrem suum epistulam scrīpsisse.
8. Audīmus Caesarem amphitheātrum novum aperuisse.
9. Scīmus omnēs cīvēs Rōmānōs ad mūnera itūrōs esse.
10. Spērat Aurēlia Cornēlium domum festīnātūrum esse.

## Exercise 45c

*Select, read aloud, and translate:*

1. Prō certō habeō puerum (ventūrus/ventūrum/ventūrōs) esse.
2. Putāmus mīlitēs tribus diēbus (adventūrōs/adventūrās/adventūram) esse.
3. Spērō tē, Cornēlia, mox (reditūrus/reditūram/reditūrum) esse.
4. Scīmus (eam/eōs/eum) mox ingressūram esse.
5. Putat (omnēs/nēminem/paucōs) discessūrum esse.
6. Spērāsne (eōs/eum/eam) secūtūrōs esse?
7. Scīsne puellās crās (abitūrās esse/abīre/abiisse)?
8. Audīvī Iūdaeōs paucīs diēbus amphitheātrum (cōnficere/cōnfectūrum esse/cōnfectūrōs esse).
9. Respondent servī sē herī quam celerrimē (currere/cucurrisse/cursūrōs esse).
10. Eucleidēs dīcit sē epistulam crās (cōnficere/cōnfēcisse/cōnfectūrum esse).

44

# The Colosseum

When the family of Cornelius returned to Rome, the great building of the Colosseum was nearing completion. Until this time, Rome's amphitheaters had usually been temporary wooden structures and these caused some frightful disasters, as at Fidenae near Rome in A.D. 27, when a wooden amphitheater collapsed, killing or maiming 50,000 people. Wooden structures continued to be built even after the completion of the magnificent architectural monument known to its contemporaries as the **Amphitheātrum Flāvium** but familiar to us as the Colosseum, so named from the nearly colossal statue of Nero, converted by Vespasian into a statue of the sun-god.

Begun by Vespasian, the Colosseum was dedicated in June, A.D. 80, by his son Titus, who had used Jewish prisoners to speed up its construction. The massive elliptical building rose in four tiers and measured overall 620 × 512 feet or 189 × 156 meters. With seating space estimated at 45,000, it could be covered over by a massive awning in excessive heat or rain—though Gaius Caligula is said to have taken delight in opening such awnings in times of extreme heat and forbidding anyone to leave! It took 1,000 sailors of the Imperial fleet to raise this awning.

Admission was free and open to men, women, and children, slave or free, so long as places were available. Women were confined to the topmost area and their view must certainly have been restricted.

The floor of the Colosseum was of timber, strewn with sand, and would contain numerous trapdoors. Under the arena, and extending beyond it, was a vast complex of subterranean cells and passages which now lie open and exposed to view. Remains can be seen of lifts and machinery (worked by counterweights) used to raise, at various points in the arena, caged animals, scenery, and other apparatus needed for wild beast hunts.

On the occasion of the dedication of the Colosseum, Emperor Titus held a festival for 100 days and during the celebrations staged a very lavish gladiatorial show.

The interior of the Colosseum as it is today. (Peter Clayton)

# The Irregular Verb mālō, mālle, māluī

The verb **mālō** is a compound of the adverb **magis** and the irregular verb **volō**, and it means "to wish more," "to wish rather," or "to prefer." It has no imperative. Its forms in the present, imperfect, and future tenses are as follows:

|   |   | *Present* | *Imperfect* | *Future* |
|---|---|---|---|---|
|       | 1 | mālō     | mālē*bam*   | māl*am*  |
| **S** | 2 | māvī*s*  | mālē*bās*   | māl*ēs*  |
|       | 3 | māvul*t* | mālē*bat*   | māl*et*  |
|       | 1 | mālu*mus* | mālē*bāmus* | māl*ēmus* |
| **P** | 2 | māvul*tis* | mālē*bātis* | māl*ētis* |
|       | 3 | mālu*nt*  | mālē*bant*  | māl*ent*  |

Learn the above forms thoroughly.

Note carefully which forms contain the letter *l* and which the letter *v* in the present tense. The imperfect and future are regular.

Review the forms of **volō** and **nōlō** in the Forms section at the end of this book before doing the following exercise.

## Exercise 45d

*For each form of the verb* **volō**, *substitute the corresponding form of the verb* **nōlō**, *read aloud, and translate. Then substitute the corresponding forms of* **mālō**, *read aloud, and translate.*

1. Titus trigōne lūdere volēbat.
2. Puerī ad thermās īre volunt.
3. "In silvam convenīre volumus," inquiunt Pȳramus et Thisbē.
4. "Ad amphitheātrum crās īre volam," inquit Marcus.
5. Titus prīmā lūce ad amphitheātrum īre vult.
6. Sciō puerōs prīmā lūce surgere velle.
7. Cūr pār impār lūdere vīs, Marce?
8. "Vultisne latrunculīs lūdere, puerī?" inquit Eucleidēs.
9. "Dormīre volō," inquit Sextus.
10. Cornēliī ad vīllam rūsticam mox redīre volent.
11. Sciō Aurēliam herī domī manēre voluisse.

---

Dīmidium dōnāre Linō quam crēdere tōtum
   quī māvult, māvult perdere dīmidium.

*Whoever prefers to give Linus half rather than trust him*
   *with the whole, prefers to lose the half.* Martial, *Epigrams* I.75

---

# Martial, De spectaculis

Born in Bilbilis, Spain, about A.D. 40, Martial went to Rome in A.D. 64, the year of the Great Fire, when Nero was Emperor. His fame as a keen observer of life in the City and as a composer of biting, satirical epigrams rests on poems he published in great numbers between A.D. 86 and 98. In A.D. 80, the year in which the Flavian Amphitheater was dedicated, Martial wrote a group of epigrams which he published under the title *De spectaculis*, in which he describes many of the memorable combats that took place in the arena that year. The first three poems in the collection are given below. In the first, Martial tries to assess the importance of the Amphitheater as an architectural monument. In the second he describes the joy of the Roman people in the building program of Vespasian and Titus that replaced the hated **Domus Aurea** of Nero with structures of more use to the people. In the third he pictures the influx of people from all over the Roman world who came to the dedication ceremonies.

(*i*)

Do not let barbarian Memphis tell of the wonder of her Pyramids, nor Assyrian toil vaunt its Babylon; let not the soft Ionians be praised for Trivia's temple; let the altar built of many horns keep its Delos hidden; let not Carians exalt to the skies with excessive praise the Mausoleum poised on empty air. The results of all these labors of man yield to Caesar's Amphitheater. One work in place of all shall Fame rehearse.

(*ii*)

Here where, rayed with stars, the Colossus has a close view of heaven, and in the middle of the way tall scaffolds rise, hatefully gleamed the palace of a savage king, and only a single House then stood in all the City. Here, where the far-seen Amphitheater lifts its mass august, was Nero's lake. Here where we admire the warm baths, a gift swiftly built, a proud domain had robbed the poor of their dwellings. Where the Claudian Colonnade extends its outspread shade, the Palace ended in its farthest part. Now Rome is restored to itself, and under your rule, Caesar, what had been the delight of a tyrant is now the delight of the people.

(*iii*)

What nation is so far distant, what people so barbarous, Caesar, that a spectator has not come from one of them to your city? A farmer of Rhodope has come from Orphic Haemus; a Sarmatian fed on draughts of horses' blood has come; and he who drinks at its source the stream of first-found Nile, and he whose shore the wave of farthest Tethys beats; the Arab has hurried here, Sabaeans have hurried, and Cilicians have here been drenched in their own saffron dew. With hair twined in a knot Sygambrians have come, and Aethiopians with their locks twined in other ways. The languages of the peoples are varied, yet they are one when you are acclaimed your country's true father.

48

# 46
# A Day at
# the Colosseum

A day at the Colosseum was a great occasion. Tickets (**tesserae**), shown to the gate-keepers (**appāritōrēs**), were numbered according to the seating areas in the Amphitheater. Seventy-six main entrances and numerous marble plaques illustrating the seating areas enabled the spectators to move swiftly and efficiently through a network of passages, stairs, and ramps to their correct place. The officiating magistrate, usually the Emperor in Rome, would go to the imperial seat of honor (**pulvīnar**); and then the show could begin. The gladiators would parade and stop before the **pulvīnar**; they would greet the emperor with the words: "Hail, Caesar! Those who are about to die give you greetings." (**Avē, Caesar! Moritūrī tē salūtant.**) Next the band (**cornicinēs** and **tubicinēs**) would strike up. Then came the games. Pairs (**paria**) of gladiators would fight, urged on by the trainers (**lanistae**). The people joined in with roars of "Thrash him!" (**Verberā!**), "Murder him!" (**Iugulā!**), "He's hit!" (**Hoc habet!**), "Let him go!" (**Mitte!**). The savagery reached a peak with the midday fighters (**merīdiānī**), usually condemned criminals.

Marcus and his father go to the amphitheater early in the morning as planned.

Prope amphitheātrum omnēs viae erant plēnae hominum quī ad spectāculum veniēbant. Undique clāmor ac strepitus; undique cīvēs, fēminae, servī. Multī tōtam noctem extrā amphitheātrī portās morātī erant. Nunc adfuit hōra spectāculī.

Cornēlius, cum tesserās appāritōribus ostendisset, ad locum magistrātibus 5 reservātum cum Marcō ā servō ductus est. Marcus tot et tam variōs hominēs numquam vīderat. Dum attonitus circumspicit, subitō vīdit Titum iam cōnsēdisse. Patruum rogāre cupiēbat quandō pervēnisset, nam sciēbat Titum sērō ē lectō surgere solēre. Sed, quod pater aderat, Marcus nihil dīxit. Quam ingēns erat amphitheātrum! Quanta erat spectātōrum turba! Marcus coni- 10 ciēbat quot spectātōrēs amphitheātrō continērī possent cum subitō fuit silentium. Omnēs ad pulvīnar oculōs convertērunt.

"Ecce!" clāmāvit Titus. "Iam intrat Caesar, amor ac dēliciae generis hūmānī!"

49

Tum, clāmōre sublātō, spectātōrēs prīncipem ūnā vōce salūtāvērunt. 15
Stupuit Marcus, admīrātiōne captus. Iam gladiātōrēs cūnctī contrā pulvīnar
cōnstiterant. "Avē, Caesar!" clāmāvērunt. "Moritūrī tē salūtant." Exiērunt
gladiātōrēs. Mox tubicinēs et cornicinēs. Postrēmō gladiātōrum paria in
arēnam intrāvērunt.
Nunc undique erat clāmor, tumultus, furor. Lanistae hūc illūc concur- 20
santēs, "Verberā!" "Iugulā!" clāmābant; turba, "Hoc habet!" aut, "Mitte!"
aut, "Iugulā!" Marcus nihil tāle prius vīderat. Complūrēs hōrās ācriter
pugnābātur; haud minus ferōciter ā spectātōribus clāmābātur.
Subitō Cornēlius, "Nunc," inquit, "domum nōbīs redeundum est. Mox
enim pugnābunt merīdiānī, quōs aliās tū, Marce, vidēbis." 25
"Nōnne tū quoque discēdere vīs, patrue?" clāmāvit Marcus.
Cui respondit Titus sē discēdere nōlle; sē nōndum satis vīdisse; merīdiānōs
mox in arēnam ventūrōs esse. Brevī tempore Marcus cum Cornēliō in lectīcā
per urbem portābātur et sēcum cōgitābat, "Quid ego prīmum Sextō nārrābō?"

- **tot,** so many
**coniciēbat,** was trying to guess
**amor ac dēliciae generis hūmānī,**
  the darling and delight of man-
  kind
**admīrātiōne captus,** in utter
  amazement
- **contrā** ( + *acc.*), opposite, in front
  of, facing

- **furor, furōris** (*m*), frenzy
- **prius,** previously
- **ācriter,** fiercely
**pugnābātur,** the fighting went on
**nōbīs redeundum est,** we must return
**aliās,** at another time

- **ostendō, ostendere** (3), **ostendī, ostentum,** to show, point out
- **convertō, convertere** (3), **convertī, conversum,** to turn (around)
- **tollō, tollere** (3), **sustulī, sublātum,** to lift, raise
- **cōnsistō, cōnsistere** (3), **cōnstitī,** to halt, stop, stand

**Quot hominēs, tot sententiae.** *Everyone has his own opinion.* (Terence, *Phormio* 454)

## Exercise 46a

*Read aloud and translate:*

1. Titus respondet sē domum redīre nōlle.
2. Nōs omnēs scīmus Marcum ad amphitheātrum īvisse.
3. Prō certō habēmus Titum sērō perventūrum esse.

# Accusative and Infinitive (Indirect Statement) III

So far, the verbs of *thinking, knowing, saying,* and *seeing* introducing indirect statements have usually been in the present tense. Now look carefully at these sentences and compare them with the three sentences in Exercise 46a:

Titus respondit sē domum redīre **nōlle.**
*Titus replied that he* **was unwilling** *to return home.*

Nōs omnēs sciēbāmus Marcum ad amphitheātrum **īvisse.**
*We all knew that Marcus* **had gone** *to the amphitheater.*

Prō certō habēbāmus Titum sērō **perventūrum esse.**
*We were sure that Titus* **would arrive** *late.*

After the past tenses **respondit, sciēbāmus,** and **habēbāmus,** although the accusative and infinitive clauses are exactly the same in Latin as they were in Exercise 46a, in English

the present infinitive is translated by *was unwilling,*
the perfect infinitive is translated by *had gone,* and
the future infinitive is translated by *would arrive.*

In all indirect statements, whether introduced by verbs in the present or a past tense,

the present infinitive = action going on at the *same time* as the action of the main verb;
thc perfect infinitive = action that was completed *before* the action of the main verb;
the future infinitive = action that will take place *after* thc action of the main verb.

A sestertius of the Emperor Titus, with the Colosseum on the reverse. (Reproduced by courtesy of the Trustees of the British Museum)

51

## Exercise 46b

*Read aloud and translate each sentence, with the main verb first in the present tense and then in the past tense:*

1. Titus spērat (spērāvit) puerōs ad mūnera itūrōs esse.
2. Marcus dīcit (dīxit) patrem epistulam cōnfēcisse.
3. Audiō (audīvī) Cornēlium ad Cūriam festīnāre.
4. Cornēlius dīcit (dīxit) sē Marcum sēcum ductūrum esse.
5. Num crēdis (crēdidistī) Cornēliam pūpā lūdere?
6. Prō certō habeō (habēbam) Aurēliam nōbīscum nōn itūram esse.
7. Aurēlia scit (sciēbat) Cornēliam pūpam fīliae Dāvī dedisse.
8. Patruus meus respondet (respondit) sē manēre mālle.
9. Sextus dīcit (dīxit) Marcum domum mātūrē reditūrum esse.
10. Marcus putat (putāvit) sē numquam tot et tam variōs hominēs vīdisse.

---

**Sōcratēs putābat sē esse cīvem tōtīus mundī.** *Socrates considered himself a citizen of the whole world.* (Cicero)

---

# Gladiators

Criminals sentenced to death could be purchased cheaply and thrown to the beasts or made to fight to the death, unarmed, in the arena. But those convicted of lesser crimes, for which the mines or deportation was the penalty, might instead go to a gladiatorial school. Slaves acquired through war or piracy were another source of recruitment, and occasionally volunteers, including Roman citizens, actually took up the gladiatorial trade. All gladiators bound themselves to their trade by an oath which laid down the severest penalties for backsliders or runaways: "to be burnt with fire, shackled with chains, beaten with rods, and killed with steel" (**ūrī, vincīrī, verberārī, ferrōque necārī**).

After thorough training in the barracks, the gladiator was ready for the arena. Successful gladiators, like chariot drivers, were popular heroes. This is an inscription from Pompeii:

> The girls' heart-throb, the Thracian Celadus, (property) of Octavius, 3 wins out of 3.

Victorious gladiators were richly rewarded and, after a period of service, might win the wooden sword of freedom, even if slaves. Veteran gladiators could also be employed as overseers in the gladiatorial schools.

The fate of a defeated gladiator rested with the spectators. If he had won favor, the spectators might wave their handkerchiefs, and the Emperor or presiding magistrate might then signal for his release. Otherwise, a turn of the thumb indicated that the fallen gladiator should speedily be killed.

There were various classes of gladiators—these included the heavily armed Samnite with oblong shield, visored helmet, and short sword; the Thracian carrying a small round shield and curved scimitar; the **murmillō**, or "fish man," who wore a helmet with a fish emblem on it and was armed with a sword and large shield; and the **rētiārius**, or "net man," who was unarmed but for a great net and sharp trident. Each had his own supporters: the Emperor Titus, for example, supported the Thracians, as did Caligula. Local rivalry, too, was common, as is borne out by this inscription from Pompeii:

> Luck to the people of Puteoli and all those from Nuceria; down with the Pompeians.

Such rivalry could lead to trouble, as this incident in the reign of Nero illustrates:

> About this time there was a serious riot involving the people of Pompeii and Nuceria. It started with a small incident at a gladiatorial show. Insults were being exchanged, as often happens in these disorderly country towns. Abuse changed to stone-throwing, and then swords were drawn. The games were held in Pompeii and the locals came off best. Many badly wounded Nucerians were taken to their city. Many parents and children were bereaved. The Emperor ordered the Senate to inquire into the matter and the Senate passed it on to the consuls. As a result of their report, the Senate banned Pompeii from holding any similar event for ten years.
>
> Tacitus, *Annals* XIV. 17

---

**Gladiātor in arēnā cōnsilium capit.** *The gladiator adopts a plan in the arena.* (Seneca, *Epistulae Morales* XXII)

**Nōn tē petō, piscem petō. Quid mē fugis, Galle?** *It is not you I am aiming at, but the fish. Why do you flee from me, Gallus?* (spoken by the adversary of a **murmillō**; quoted by Festus, 285M, 358L)

---

## Exercise 46c

### Marcus reports back

*Read the following passage aloud and answer the questions that follow with full sentences in Latin:*

Marcus iam domum regressus omnia quae vīderat Sextō nārrābat:
"Cum amphitheātrō appropinquārēmus, vīdimus magnam hominum multitūdinem per portās intrāre. Nōs ipsī ingressī vīdimus multa mīlia cīvium
iam consēdisse. Ego nōn crēdidissem tot hominēs amphitheātrō continērī
posse. Patruum exspectāre voluī, sed pater mihi dīxit Titum sine dubiō iam     5
adesse. Et rēctē dīxit; nam, cum ad locum magistrātibus reservātum vēnissēmus, vīdimus Titum eō iam ductum esse.
    Subitō undique clāmātum est. Deinde vīdī prīncipem ā gladiātōribus salū-
tārī. Quam fortiter incēdēbant hī gladiātōrēs! Multī tamen eōrum moritūrī
erant. Ubi pugnam commīsērunt, spectābam obstupefactus. Nihil tāle prius     10
vīderam. Vīdī multōs vulnerārī atque complūrēs quidem occīdī. Quam fortēs
erant gladiātōrēs!
    Maximē dolēbam quod ante merīdiem domum nōbīs redeundum erat.
Titus dīxit sē mālle manēre, cum cuperet merīdiānōs vidēre. Spērō patrem
mē ad amphitheātrum iterum ductūrum esse. Fortasse tē quoque dūcet."     15

crēdidissem, I would have believed    pugnam committere, to join battle
clāmātum est, there was shouting    obstupefactus, -a, -um, astounded

incēdō, incēdere (3), incessī, to march

## Exercise 46d

*Respondē Latīnē:*

1. Quandō Marcus hominum multitūdinem vīdit?
2. Quid Marcus vīdit postquam amphitheātrum intrāvit?
3. Quid Marcus nōn crēdidisset?
4. Quid Cornēlius Marcō dīxit?
5. Quem ad locum Marcus vīdit Titum ductum esse?
6. Quōmodo Marcus pugnam spectābat?
7. Quid Marcus in gladiātōrum pugnā fierī vīdit?
8. Cūr Marcus dolēbat?
9. Quid Titus dīxit?
10. Quid Marcus spērat?

# Accusative and Infinitive (Indirect Statement) IV

Passive infinitives are also used in this construction:

Vīdī multōs **vulnerārī** atque complūrēs quidem **occīdī.**
*I saw that many **were being wounded** and several actually **were being killed.***

The present passive infinitive is already familiar from Chapter 29. It can be recognized by the ending **-rī** in the 1st, 2nd, and 4th conjugations and the ending **-ī** in the 3rd conjugation.

For the perfect tense, the passive infinitive consists of the perfect passive participle and **esse.**

Vīdimus Titum eō iam **ductum esse.**
*We saw that Titus **had** already **been taken** there.*

Note that the perfect passive participle in this sentence agrees in gender, case, and number with the subject of the infinitive, **Titum.**

## Exercise 46e

*Read aloud and translate:*

1. Eucleidēs vīdit Cornēliam ā puerīs vexārī.
2. Sextus nescīvit vōcem suam audītam esse.
3. Vīdimus complūrēs nāvēs iam dēlētās esse.
4. Putāvērunt vestīmenta ā servō custōdīrī.
5. Scīvī mīlitēs in Britanniam mittī.
6. Fūrēs scīvērunt sē in apodytēriō cōnspectōs esse.

# VERBS: Infinitives

You have now met the following forms of the infinitive:

| | PRESENT | | PERFECT | |
|---|---|---|---|---|
| | *Active* | *Passive* | *Active* | *Passive* |
| 1 | portāre | portārī | portāvisse | portātus, -a, -um esse |
| 2 | movēre | movērī | mōvisse | mōtus, -a, -um esse |
| 3 | mittere | mittī | mīsisse | missus, -a, -um esse |
| 4 | audīre | audīrī | audīvisse | audītus, -a, -um esse |

| | FUTURE |
|---|---|
| | *Active* |
| 1 | portātūrus, -a, -um esse |
| 2 | mōtūrus, -a, -um esse |
| 3 | missūrus, -a, -um esse |
| 4 | audītūrus, -a, -um esse |

## Deponent Verbs

The present and perfect infinitives of deponent verbs are passive in form; the future infinitive is active in form. For example,

| PRESENT | PERFECT | FUTURE |
|---|---|---|
| cōnārī | cōnātus, -a, -um esse | cōnātūrus, -a, -um esse |
| sequī | secūtus, -a, -um esse | secūtūrus, -a, -um esse |

## Notes

1. The infinitives of 3rd conjugation verbs in *-iō* are not listed in the charts above because they are formed in the same way as the infinitives of **mittō** that are given.

2. The future passive infinitive rarely appears in Latin and will not be taught in this course.

3. Translations of the various forms of the infinitive are not given in the charts above because they will vary according to the use of the infinitive in the sentence. The infinitives of deponent verbs in all three tenses are active in meaning.

# Graffiti and Inscriptions on Gladiators

Written at night on the facade of a private house in Pompeii:

**D. Lucrētī Satrī Valentis flāminis Nerōnis Caesaris Aug. fīlī perpetuī gladiātōrum paria XX et D. Lucrētiō Valentis fīlī glad. paria X, pug. Pompēīs VI V IV III pr. Īdūs Apr. Vēnātiō legitima et vēla erunt.**

*Twenty pairs of gladiators provided by Decimus Lucretius Satrius Valens priest for life of Nero, son of Caesar Augustus, and ten pairs of gladiators provided by the son of Decimus Lucretius Valens, will fight at Pompeii on April 8, 9, 10, 11, and 12. There will be a regular hunt and awnings.*

Scratched on the columns in the peristyle of a private house in Pompeii:

**Suspīrium puellārum Tr. Celadus Oct. III III.**

*The girls' heart-throb, the Thracian Celadus, (property) of Octavius, 3 wins out of 3.*

A curse against a **bēstiārius**:

**Occīdite extermināte vulnerāte Gallicum, quem peperit Prīma, in istā hōrā in amphiteātrī corōnā. Oblīgā illī pedēs membra sēnsūs medullam; oblīgā Gallicum, quem peperit Prīma, ut neque ursum neque taurum singulīs plāgīs occīdat neque bīnīs plāgīs occīdat neque ternīs plāgīs occīdat taurum ursum; per nōmen deī vīvī omnipotentis ut perficiātis; iam iam citō citō allīdat illum ursus et vulneret illum.**

*Kill, destroy, wound Gallicus whom Prima bore, in this hour, in the ring of the amphitheater. Bind his feet, his limbs, his senses, his marrow; bind Gallicus whom Prima bore, so that he may slay neither bear nor bull with single blows, nor slay (them) with double blows, nor slay with triple blows bear (or) bull; in the name of the living omnipotent god may you accomplish (this); now, now, quickly, quickly let the bear smash him and wound him.*

Sepulchral inscription of a **rētiārius**:

**D. M. Vītālis invictī rētiārī, nātiōne Bataus, hīc suā virtūte pariter cum adversāriō dēcidit, alacer fu. pugnīs III. Convīctor eius fēcit.**

*To the deified spirits of Vitalis, a net-fighter who was never beaten; a Batavian by birth, he fell together with his opponent as a result of his own valor; he was a keen competitor in his 3 fights. His messmate erected (this monument).*

**Versiculī:** *"Hermes the Gladiator," pages 118–119*

# Other Shows
# in the Arena

The Emperor Titus also held a sea fight (**naumachia**) on the old artificial
lake of Augustus and afterwards used the empty basin of the lake for still
more gladiatorial bouts and a wild-beast hunt (**vēnātiō**) in which over 5,000
animals of different kinds died in a single day. His brother and imperial
successor, Domitian, was not to be outdone; he even used the Colosseum
itself as a lake! Suetonius, in his life of Domitian, writes:

> Domitian constantly gave lavish entertainments both in the Amphitheater
> and in the Circus. As well as the usual races with two-horse and four-horse
> chariots, he put on two battles, one with infantry and one with cavalry; he
> also exhibited a naval battle in his amphitheater. He gave hunts of wild
> beasts and gladiatorial fights at night by torchlight, and even fights between
> women.
>
> He staged sea battles with almost full-sized fleets. For these he had a
> pool dug near the Tiber and seats built around it. He even went on watching
> these events in torrential rain.
>
> Suetonius, *Domitian* 4

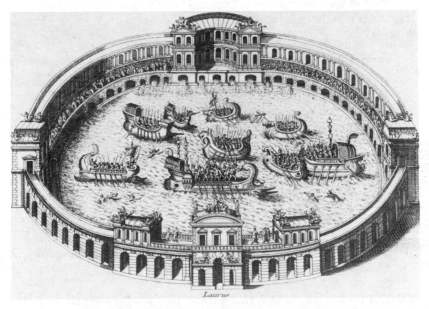

A drawing of a sea fight staged in an arena. Notice the rams on the front of the boats.
(Photograph: The Mansell Collection).

58

Gladiators were not used to fight animals (**bēstiae**) in the wild-beast hunts. For this, special fighters, **bēstiāriī**, were employed. In these shows, such animals as lions, tigers, bears, bulls, hippopotami, elephants, crocodiles, deer, pigs, and even ostriches were made to fight each other or the **bēstiāriī**, or else driven to attack condemned criminals, who were sometimes chained or nailed to stakes. When Trajan held four months of festivities to celebrate his Dacian wars, some 10,000 gladiators and over 11,000 animals appeared in the arena over this period.

Vēnātiō

Even before the time of the emperors we read of the provinces being scoured for animals for these shows. Caelius, in a letter to his friend Cicero, wrote:

> Curio is very generous to me and has put me under an obligation; for if he had not given me the animals which had been shipped from Africa for his own games, I would not have been able to continue with mine. But, as I must go on, I should be glad if you would do your best to let me have some animals from your province—I am continually making this request.
>
> Cicero, *Epistulae ad Familiares* VIII.8

# 47
# *Androcles*
# *and the Lion*

Ōlim in Circō Maximō lūdus bēstiārius populō dabātur. Omnēs spectātōribus admīrātiōnī fuērunt leōnēs, sed ūnus ex eīs vidēbātur saevissimus.
Ad pugnam bēstiāriam introductus erat inter complūrēs servus quīdam cui
Androclēs nōmen fuit. Quem cum ille leō procul vīdisset, subitō quasi
admīrāns stetit ac deinde lentē et placidē hominī appropinquābat. Tum 5
caudam clēmenter et blandē movēns, manūs hominis, prope iam metū
exanimātī, linguā lambit. Androclēs, animō iam recuperātō, leōnem atten-
tius spectāvit. Tum, quasi mūtuā recognitiōne factā, laetī ibi stābant et
homō et leō.

Ea rēs tam mīrābilis turbam maximē excitāvit. Androclem ad pulvīnar 10
arcessītum rogāvit Caesar cūr ille saevissimus leō eī sōlī pepercisset. Tum
Androclēs rem mīrābilem nārrāvit:

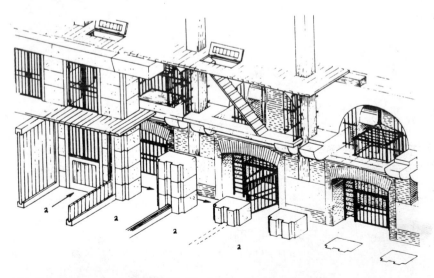

This diagram shows the cages for wild animals under the floor of the Colosseum. The animals
were brought in through an entry (marked a). The cages were hoisted to a higher floor directly
below the arena and from there the animals were driven up a gangway and into the arena
through a hatch.

"Dum ego in Āfricā cum dominō meō habitō," inquit, "propter eius crūdēlitātem fugere coāctus in spēluncam cōnfūgī. Haud multō post ad eandem spēluncam vēnit hic leō gemēns et dolēns, ūnō pede claudus. Atque 15 prīmō quidem terrōris plēnus latēbam. Sed leō, cum mē cōnspexisset, mītis et mānsuētus appropinquāvit atque pedem mihi ostendit, quasi auxilium petēns. Stirpem ingentem, quae in eius pede haerēbat, ego extrāxī ac iam sine magnō timōre vulnus lāvī. Tum ille, pede in manibus meīs positō, recubuit et dormīvit. Trēs annōs ego et leō in eādem spēluncā habitābāmus, 20 eōdem cibō vescentēs. Posteā captus ā mīlitibus, reductus sum ad dominum quī mē statim ad bēstiās condemnāvit."

Prīnceps, fābulā servī audītā, maximē admīrābātur. Androclēs omnium cōnsēnsū līberātus est, datusque eī leō.

admīrātiōnī esse, to be a source of wonder or surprise (to)
quasi, as if
placidē, quietly, tamely
clēmenter et blandē, in a gentle, friendly way
metū exanimātus, paralysed with fear
mūtuā recognitiōne factā, recognising one another

crūdēlitās, crūdēlitātis (f), cruelty
claudus, -a, -um, lame
lateō (2), to lie in hiding
mītis, -is, -e, gentle
mānsuētus, -a, -um, tame
stirps, stirpis (f), thorn
omnium cōnsēnsū, by general agreement

admīror, admīrārī (1), admīrātus sum, to wonder (at)
lambō, lambere (3), lambī, to lick
parcō, parcere (3), pepercī, (+ dat.), to spare
cōgō, cōgere (3), coēgī, coāctum, to compel, force
vescor, vescī (3) (+ abl.), to feed (on)

## Building Up the Meaning VII

## What to expect after the verb **audiō**, "to hear"

Look at the following sentences:

Audīvit cūr pater advēnisset.
*He heard why his father had arrived.*

Clāmōrēs servōrum audīvit.
*He heard the shouts of the slaves.*

Audīvit patrem ad urbem advēnisse.
*He heard that his father had reached the city.*

You will see that the sense after *heard* can develop in three different ways:

| | |
|---|---|
| He heard why, who, what, how. . . . | *indirect question* (with verb in the subjunctive) |
| He heard something/someone. | *direct object* (accusative case) |
| He heard that. . . . | *indirect statement* (with accusative and infinitive) |

When you meet **audiō**, you must expect one of these three possibilities:

1. **Audiō cūr, quis, quid, quōmodo . . . :** Translate straight on, e.g.:

   Audīvī quid dīcerēs.
   *I heard what you were saying.*

2. **Audiō** *accusative . . . :* Wait to see if there is also an *infinitive*. If there is no infinitive, the accusative is the direct object of **audiō**, e.g.:

   Audiō servōs.
   *I hear the slaves.*

   Audiō servōs in viīs clāmantēs.
   *I hear the slaves shouting in the streets.*

3. If there is an infinitive, insert *that . . .* and continue with the translation of the accusative, e.g.:

   Audiō servōs cēnam parāvisse.
   *I hear (that) the slaves have prepared dinner.*

The following verbs have to be treated in the same way:

**sciō**, I know    **videō**, I see    **intellegō**, I understand    **sentiō**, I realize

## Exercise 47a

*Read aloud and translate:*

1. Puerī audīvērunt gladiātōrēs prīncipem salūtantēs.
2. Eucleidēs nōn sēnsit ubi essent puerī.
3. Marcus vīdit gladiātōrēs iam in arēnam intrāvisse.
4. Spectātōrēs nōn intellegunt cūr leō manūs servī lambat.
5. Cornēlius sciēbat locum magistrātibus reservātum esse.
6. Androclēs dīxit sē stirpem ē pede leōnis extrāxisse.
7. Pȳramus crēdēbat Thisbēn ā leōne occīsam esse.
8. Nōnne audīs illōs leōnēs strepitum maximum facientēs?
9. Ita vērō! Leōnēs audiō; sed cīvēs maiōrem strepitum facere videntur.
10. Cīvēs intellegēbant servōs saepe fugere cōgī.

### Exercise 47b

*Read aloud and translate:*

1. Puer nesciēbat quot gladiātōrēs vulnerātī essent.
2. Androclēs dīxit leōnem ūnō pede claudum ad spēluncam vēnisse.
3. Scīvistīne bēstiās sub arēnā continērī? Ipse eās audīvī.
4. Cīvēs prō certō habēbant nūllōs gladiātōrēs effugere cōnātūrōs esse.
5. Cīvēs audīre cupiēbant cūr leō hominem nōn necāvisset.
6. Fūr nesciēbat sē ā Sextō cōnspicī.
7. Spectātōrēs vīdērunt leōnem caudam clēmenter moventem.
8. Androclēs nōn intellēxit cūr leō pedem sibi ostenderet.
9. Marcus audīvit patrem domō ēgredientem.
10. Spectātōrēs vīdērunt ūnum leōnem saevissimum esse.

---

quid pro quo *literally,* "something for something," *one thing in exchange for another*

**Manus manum lavat.** *One hand washes the other* or *One good turn deserves another.*

**Ab aliō exspectēs alterī quod fēceris.** *Expect (the same treatment from another) that you give to your neighbor.* (Publilius Syrus 2)

How do these sayings fit the moral of the story of Androcles and the lion?

---

## Versiculī: *"Another Example of Caesar's Leniency,"* page 120.

A gladiator's helmet embossed with figures representing Rome and its provinces. (The Mansell Collection)

63

# 48
# *Audience Reaction*

## Scene I: In the Amphitheater

(Licinius Caeliusque, duo spectātōrēs in amphitheātrō sedentēs, inter sē loquuntur.)

LICINIUS: Ecce! In arēnam veniunt gladiātōrēs! Scīsne quot sint?

CAELIUS: Minimē vērō! Scīsne tū quot leōnēs, quot tigrēs adsint? Ego audīvī multōs leōnēs ingentēs ab Āfricā allātōs esse et sub arēnā in caveīs 5 tenērī.

*(Intrat Postumius quī sērō venīre solet.)*

POSTUMIUS: Videō prīncipem iam advēnisse et ā cīvibus salūtārī.

CAELIUS: Ecce! Iam gladiātōrēs eum salūtant! Ēheu! Sciunt sē moritūrōs esse.

POSTUMIUS: Tacēte! Audiō bēstiās! Vidētisne leōnēs in arēnam immittī? 10

LICINIUS: Ecce bēstia immānis! Servō illī parvō numquam parcet! Iam pugnāre incipiunt. Euge!

POSTUMIUS: Euge! At cōnstitit leō! Mīror cūr leō cōnstiterit!

CAELIUS: Num crēdis eum rē vērā cōnstitisse? Prō certō habeō eum mox impetum ferōciter factūrum esse. 15

LICINIUS: At videō leōnem lentē et placidē hominī appropinquantem. Meher-cule! Vidēsne eum manūs hominis linguā lambentem? Sciō leōnem esse saevissimum. Nesciō cūr hominem nōn occīdat.

CAELIUS: Vidēsne servum leōnem spectantem? Timēre nōn vidētur.

POSTUMIUS: Videō servum ā prīncipe arcessītum esse. Mīror quid dīcat. 20

## Scene II: Leaving the Amphitheater

LICINIUS: Nōn poteram intellegere cūr leō impetum nōn fēcisset. Mīrum qui-dem erat spectāculum.

CAELIUS: Audīvī leōnem ā prīncipe hominī datum esse.

POSTUMIUS: Ita vērō! Sed ecce! Paetus venit. Salvē, Paete!

PAETUS: Cūr hunc tantum clāmōrem facitis? 25

CAELIUS: Hoc vix crēdēs! Vīdimus leōnem, bēstiam saevissimam, servī manūs lambentem! Nescīmus cūr manūs nōn dēvorāverit.

PAETUS: Quid? Nōnne audīvistis causam? Leō ille sēnsit sē hominem anteā vīdisse. Homō prīncipī nārrāvit quōmodo stirpem ōlim ē pede leōnis extrāxisset. Nārrāvit sē et leōnem in Āfricā in eādem spēluncā trēs 30 annōs habitāvisse. Ubi captus est, putāvit sē numquam iterum leō-nem vīsūrum esse. Nesciēbat quō leō īvisset.

POSTUMIUS: Agite! Sērō est. Ēsuriō! Domum redeāmus. Fortasse vidēbimus ser-vum leōnem per viās dūcentem.

64

cavea, -ae (f), cage
immānis, -is, -e, huge
rē vērā, really, actually

impetus, -ūs (m), attack
redeāmus, let us return

immittō, immittere (3), immīsī, immissum, to send in, release
incipiō, incipere (3), incēpī, inceptum, to begin
mīror, mīrārī (1), mīrātus sum, to wonder
intellegō, intellegere (3), intellēxī, intellēctum, to understand, realize

**Versiculī:** *"Androcles' True Bravery," page 121.*

# Gladiatorial Fever

Sometimes high-born Romans were so enthusiastic about the combats in the arena that they took part themselves as gladiators. The Roman poet Juvenal, and Romans generally, strongly disapproved:

> There in the arena you have a disgrace to the city: Gracchus fighting not in the arms of a **murmillō** with shield and saber, for he scorns and rejects such equipment; nor does he hide his face with a visor. Look! It's a trident he sports; he shakes his trailing net in his right hand, casts, and misses. Then he holds up his naked face for all to see and runs frantically around the whole arena, easily recognizable!
>
> Juvenal, *Satires* VIII.199–206

# Opposition to the Games

Some Romans protested the brutality of these shows. Seneca writes about the midday "interval" between the morning and afternoon sessions. In this interval criminals were forced to fight in the arena until everyone was dead:

> Cāsū in merīdiānum spectāculum incidī lūsūs expectāns et salēs et aliquid laxāmentī, quō hominum oculī ab hūmānō cruōre acquiēscant; contrā est. Quicquid ante pugnātum est, misericordia fuit. Nunc omissīs nūgīs mera homicīdia sunt. Nihil habent quō tegantur, ad ictum tōtīs corporibus expositī numquam frūstrā manum mittunt. Hoc plērīque ōrdināriīs paribus et pos- 5 tulātīciīs praeferunt. Quidnī praeferant? Nōn galeā, nōn scūtō repellitur ferrum. Quō mūnīmenta? Quō artēs? Omnia ista mortis morae sunt. Māne leōnibus et ursīs hominēs, merīdiē spectātōribus suīs obiciuntur. Interfectōrēs interfectūrīs iubent obicī et victōrem in aliam dētinent caedem. Exitus pugnantium mors est; ferrō et igne rēs geritur.   10

By chance I attended a midday exhibition, expecting some fun, wit, and relaxation—an exhibition at which men's eyes have respite from the slaughter of their fellow-men. But it was quite the reverse. The previous combats were the essence of compassion; but now all the trifling is put aside and it is pure murder. The men have no defensive armor. They are exposed to blows at all points, and no one ever strikes in vain. Many persons prefer this program to the usual pairs and to the bouts "by request." Of course they do; there is no helmet or shield to deflect the weapon. What is the need of defensive armor, or of skill? All these mean delaying death. In the morning they throw men to the lions and the bears; at noon, they throw them to the spectators. The spectators demand that the slayer shall face the man who is to slay him in his turn; and they always reserve the latest conqueror for another butchering. The outcome of every fight is death, and the means are fire and sword.

Seneca, *Epistulae Morales* VII

After Seneca, others came out against the institution of the games. Among these were Christian writers like Tertullian and Augustine. The Emperor Constantine made a decree of abolition but this seems not to have been enforced. Gladiatorial shows were finally suppressed by Honorius (Emperor of the West, A.D. 395–423), though other blood-sports in the arena continued for several centuries after this.

# Word Study XII

## Suffixes -ārium and -ōrium

The addition of the suffix -ārium (neuter form of the adjectival suffix -ārius; see Word Study V) to the base of a Latin noun or adjective creates a 2nd declension neuter noun meaning "a place for . . . ," e.g., libr- (base of liber, book) + -ārium = librārium, -ī (n), a place for books or a bookcase. English sometimes uses this Latin suffix to create new words, such as aquarium, (literally, "a place for water," from Latin aqua); but most English words derived from Latin words with the suffix -ārium end in -ary, e.g., library.

Similarly, the suffix -ōrium (neuter form of -ōrius, an adjectival suffix similar to -ārius), when added to the supine stem of a Latin verb, forms a 2nd declension neuter noun which denotes a place where the action of the verb takes place, e.g., audīt- (supine stem of audīre, to hear) + -ōrium = audītōrium, -ī (n), "a place for listening," or a lecture-room.

### Exercise 1

Give the meaning of each of the following Latin nouns, using the words in parentheses as guides. Confirm the meanings in a Latin dictionary.

1. caldārium (calidus)
2. repositōrium (repōnere)
3. armārium (arma)
4. aviārium (avis, bird)
5. sōlārium (sōl, sun)
6. Tabulārium (tabula, tablet, record)

### Exercise 2

Give the meaning of each of the following English nouns, and give the Latin root word from which each is derived:

1. dormitory
2. infirmary
3. lavatory
4. terrarium
5. laboratory
6. diary

## Suffix -ūra

The suffix -ūra may be added to the supine stem of a Latin verb to form a 1st declension noun which means the "act of or result of . . . ," e.g., scrīpt- (supine stem of scrībere, to write) + -ūra = scrīptūra, -ae (f), a writing. English words derived from these nouns generally end in -ure, e.g., scripture.

## Exercise 3

Give the Latin noun ending in **-ūra** which is formed from the supine stem of each of the following verbs. Give the English derivative of each noun formed. Consult an English dictionary as needed.

1. colō
2. coniciō
3. adveniō
4. stō
5. pōnō
6. capiō
7. misceō
8. nāscor

## Exercise 4

Give the meaning of each of the following English nouns and give the Latin verb from which each is derived. Consult an English dictionary, as needed.

1. lecture
2. creature
3. pasture
4. aperture
5. rupture
6. stricture

# Suffix -mentum

When the suffix **-mentum** is added to the present stem of a Latin verb, a 2nd declension neuter noun is formed which means the "result of or means of" the action of the verb, e.g., **impedī-** (pres. stem of **impedīre,** *to hinder*) + **-mentum** = **impedīmentum, -ī** (*n*), *a hindrance*; plural, *baggage*. English derivatives of these nouns end in *-ment*, e.g., *impediment*. Latin nouns ending in **-mentum** frequently alter the spelling of the present stem of the root verb, e.g., **documentum**, from **docēre**.

## Exercise 5

Give the Latin noun ending in **-mentum** formed from the present stem of each of the following verbs. Give the meaning of the noun and its English derivative.

1. compleō
2. ligō
3. paviō (4) *to pound, tamp down*

## Exercise 6

Give the meaning of each of the following English words and give the Latin root verb from which each is derived. Consult an English dictionary as needed.

1. sediment
2. monument
3. sentiment
4. regiment
5. momentum
6. augment

# Inceptive Verbs

Latin verbs which end in *-scō* are called *inceptive* (from **incipiō**, *to begin*) since they denote an action in its beginning stages, e.g., **conticēscō**, *to become silent*. Compare the simple verb, **taceō**, *to be silent*. Inceptive verbs are in the 3rd conjugation. Often the inceptive is related to a noun or adjective rather than to another verb, e.g., **advesperāscit**, *it grows dark*, from **vesper**, *evening*.

## Exercise 7

Using the words in parentheses as a guide, give the meaning of each of the following inceptive verbs:

1. quiēscō (**quiēs, quiētis**, *f, rest, quiet*)
2. convalēscō (**valeō**, *to be strong*)
3. senēscō (**senex**, *old*)
4. ingravēscō (**ingravō**, *to burden*: *cf.* **gravis**, *heavy*)
5. aegrēscō (**aeger**, *sick*)
6. stupēscō (**stupeō**, *to be amazed*)
7. proficīscor (**faciō**, *to make, do*)
8. adolēscō (**adulēscēns**, *a young man*)

## Exercise 8

The present participle stem of an inceptive verb often becomes an English word. Give the meaning of the following English words, derived from inceptive verbs in Exercise 7. Consult an English dictionary as needed.

1. convalescent    2. quiescent    3. adolescent    4. senescent

# Review XI

## Exercise XIa

*Read aloud and translate. Identify each indirect statement, indirect question, ablative absolute, and circumstantial clause. Identify the tense and voice of each infinitive, subjunctive, and participle.*

1. Sciēbāmus multōs fūrēs vestīmenta ē balneīs surrepta in urbe vēndere.
2. Pȳramus, vestīgiīs leōnis vīsīs, putāvit puellam necātam esse.
3. Thisbē, corpore Pȳramī vīsō, gladiō strictō dīcit ipsam sē occīsūram esse.
4. Ex urbe profectūrī audīvimus viam Appiam esse clausam. Nesciēbāmus quandō Bāiās perventūrī essēmus.
5. Puerī ex ātriō ēgredientēs, vōce Eucleidis audītā, sē in cubiculum cōnfugitūrōs esse mussāvērunt.
6. Sextus spērāvit sē suum patrem vīsūrum esse. Ē lūdō enim domum missus sciēbat Cornēlium sē pūnītūrum esse.
7. Titō rogantī Cornēlius respondit Aurēliam ad amphitheātrum nōn itūram esse; eam domī manēre mālle.
8. Marcus Titum cōnspectum rogāvit quot spectātōrēs amphitheātrō continērī possent.
9. Gladiātōrēs pugnātūrī Caesarem salūtāre solent. Sciunt multōs esse moritūrōs.
10. Post pugnās in amphitheātrō spectātōrēs multōs gladiātōrēs occīsōs esse vīdērunt.
11. Aurēlia servōs in culīnā loquentēs audīvit.
12. Cornēlia Valerium ad Italiam regressum esse nōn audīverat.
13. Spectātōrēs nōn audīverant cūr servus līberātus esset.
14. Stirpe ē pede extractā, leō recubuit et dormīvit.
15. Prīnceps, fābulā audītā, cōnstituit servō parcere. Negāvit enim sē umquam prius tālem fābulam audīvisse.
16. Audīvimus spectātōrēs, cum leōnem hominis manūs lambentem vīdissent, attonitōs fuisse.
17. Cornēlius putāvit Titum domum sē secūtum esse; sed mox intellēxit eum in amphitheātrō morātum esse.
18. Sextō vīsō, fūr effugere cōnāns in pavīmentō lāpsus est.
19. "Ēheu!" inquit Thisbē. "Putō meum vēlāmen tē perdidisse." Quibus verbīs dictīs, sē occīdere cōnāta est.

    **negō** (1), to say that . . . not

## Exercise XIb

Read the following passage and answer the questions below in English:

### Tale of a Tyrant

Dionӯsius, ille Syrācūsānōrum tyrannus, ōlim dēmōnstrābat tyrannōs nōn semper esse beātōs. Nam cum quīdam ex assentātōribus eius, Dāmoclēs nō-mine, dīvitiās eius et magnificentiam rēgnī commemorāret, "Vīsne igitur," inquit, "ō Dāmoclē, quoniam haec tē vīta dēlectat, ipse eam vītam dēgustāre?"

Cum sē ille cupere dīxisset, Dionӯsius iussit hominem, pulcherrimīs ves- 5
tibus indūtum, in lectō aureō recumbere. Tum ad mēnsam puerōs pulcher-rimōs iussit cōnsistere et eī dīligenter ministrāre. Aderant unguenta, corōnae; incendēbantur odōrēs; mēnsae cibō ēlegantissimō onerābantur. Fortūnātus sibi Dāmoclēs vidēbātur.

At Dionӯsius gladium ingentem, ā lacūnārī saetā equīnā aptum, suprā 10
caput illīus beātī dēmittī iussit. Quō vīsō, neque pulchrōs illōs puerōs neque ōrnāmenta aurea Dāmoclēs spectābat, neque manum ad mēnsam porrigēbat. Dēnique ōrāvit tyrannum ut sibi abīre licēret, quod iam beātus esse nōllet.

Hōc modō Dionӯsius dēmōnstrāvit nēminem esse beātum, cui semper aliquī terror impendeat. 15

Syrācūsānī, -ōrum (m pl), the citizens of Syracuse, a city in Sicily
beātus, -a, -um, happy, blessed
assentātor, -ōris (m), flatterer
dīvitiae, -ārum (f pl), riches
commemorō (1), to mention, com-ment on
dēgustō (1), to taste, have a taste of

ministrō (1), to attend to
ā lacūnārī sactā equīnā aptum, hanging from the ceiling by a horse-hair
dēnique, at last
ōrō (1), to beg

porrigō, porrigere (3), porrēxī, porrēctum, to stretch out
impendeō, impendēre (2) (+ dat.), to hang over

1. What was the tyrant's name?
2. What did he wish to demonstrate?
3. What is the first thing we are told about Damocles?
4. In the phrase dīvitiās eius, to whom does eius refer?
5. Translate the words in which Dionysius makes an offer to Damocles.
6. Did Damocles accept?
7. What did Dionysius order Damocles to do?
8. Name five things that suggest the luxury of the situation.
9. Translate suprā caput illīus beātī.
10. In the phrase quō vīsō to what does quō refer?
11. What put an end to Damocles' feeling of happiness and what particularly alarmed him?
12. What request did Damocles make?

13. With reference to the last two lines, express in your own words the lesson Dionysius was illustrating.
14. "Although he had built up a successful business, the threat of exposure hung over the escaped war criminal like the sword of Damocles." Explain the significance of the final phrase.

## Exercise XIc

*In the passage in Exercise XIb, locate the following in sequence:*

1. Examples of indirect statement.
2. Infinitives used with the verb **iussit.**
3. Imperfect and pluperfect subjunctives.
4. An ablative absolute.

# 49
# *Nothing Ever Happens*

Sōl caelō serēnō lūcēbat. Cantābant avēs. Nātūra ipsa gaudēre vidēbātur.
Trīstī vultū tamen sedēbat Cornēlia sōla in peristȳliō. Sēcum cōgitābat: "Mē
taedet sōlitūdinis. Cūr nēmō mē observat? Cūr mēcum nēmō loquitur?
Pater tantum temporis in tablīnō agit ut eum numquam videam. Māter tam
occupāta est ut mēcum numquam loquātur. Marcus et Sextus suīs lūdīs     5
adeō dēditī sunt ut nihil aliud faciant. Nōn intellegō cūr nūper etiam servae
mē neglēxerint, cūr Eucleidēs ille verbōsus verbum nūllum mihi dīxerit.
Ō mē miseram!"

Cornēliae haec cōgitantī, "Heus tū, Cornēlia!" clāmāvit Marcus quī tum
intrāvit in peristȳlium. "Pater iubet tē in tablīnō statim adesse. Festīnāre tē   10
oportet."

Cornēlia, cum in tablīnum intrāvisset, vīdit adesse et patrem et mātrem,
id quod erat eī admīrātiōnī et cūrae.

Tum pater gravī vultū, "Ōlim, Cornēlia," inquit, "Publius Cornēlius
Scīpiō Āfricānus, vir praeclārissimus gentis nostrae, dīcitur inter epulās   15
senātōrum fīliam suam Tiberiō Gracchō dēspondisse. Post epulās, cum
Scīpiō domum regressus uxōrī dīxisset sē fīliam dēspondisse, illa maximā
īrā erat commōta. 'Nōn decet patrem,' inquit, 'dēspondēre fīliam, īnsciā
mātre.' At pater tuus nōn est Publiō Cornēliō similis, nam ūnā cōnstituimus
et ego et māter tua iuvenī cuidam nōbilī tē dēspondēre. Quīntus Valerius,   20
adulēscēns ille optimus, vult tē in mātrimōnium dūcere, id quod nōbīs
placet. Placetne tibi, Cornēlia?"

Cornēlia adeō perturbāta erat ut vix loquī posset, sed tandem submissā
vōce, "Mihi quoque placet," respondit.

Cui Cornēlius, "Crās aderit Valerius ipse."        25

sōl, sōlis (m), sun
serēnus, -a, -um, clear, bright
avis, avis (m/f), bird
mē taedet (+ gen.), I am tired (of)
observō (1), to pay attention to
adeō, so much, to such an extent
dēditus, -a, -um, devoted, dedi-
    cated
nūper, recently
Heus! Ho there!
tē oportet (+ infinitive), you must

id quod, (a thing) which
cūrae esse, to be a cause of anxiety
    (to)
gēns, gentis (f), family, clan
epulae, -ārum (f pl), banquet, feast
nōn decet patrem, a father should
    not
similis, -is, -e (+ dat.), like, similar
    (to)
iuvenis, -is (m), young man
submissā vōce, in a subdued voice

neglegō, neglegere (3), neglēxī, neglēctum, to neglect, ignore
dēspondeō, dēspondēre (2), dēspondī, dēspōnsum, to betroth, promise in
    marriage

## Exercise 49a

*Using story 49 as a guide, give the Latin for:*

1. Cornelia's mother is so busy that she never talks with her.
2. Marcus and Sextus are so devoted to their games that they do nothing
   with Cornelia.
3. Cornelia does not understand why the slave-girls have neglected her.
4. She does not understand why Eucleides has said nothing to her.
5. Cornelia was so happy that she could scarcely speak.

# Result Clauses

When you meet these words—

adeō, so much, to such an extent
ita, thus, in such a way
sīc, thus, in this way
tālis, such

tam, so
tantus, so great
tantum, so much
tot, so many

—you will often find the word **ut** later in the sentence meaning "that,"
followed by a clause indicating result, e.g.:

**Adeō** perturbāta erat **ut** vix loquī posset.
*She was so confused that she could hardly speak.*

**Tam** occupāta est **ut** mēcum numquam loquātur.
*She is so busy that she never speaks to me.*

74

A negative result clause is introduced by **ut** and uses **nōn,** e.g.:

**Adeō** perturbāta est **ut** loquī **nōn** possit.
*She is so confused that she cannot speak.*

The verb in the result clause is in the subjunctive and is translated into the equivalent tense of the English indicative. The verbs **loquātur** and **possit** in the examples above are in the *present subjunctive.*

## VERBS: Subjunctive Mood II

The imperfect and pluperfect subjunctives were tabulated on pages 10–11. The following is the tabulation of the other two tenses of the subjunctive, the present and perfect:

### Present Subjunctive

| ACTIVE VOICE | | | | | |
|---|---|---|---|---|---|
| | *1st Conjugation* | *2nd Conjugation* | *3rd Conjugation* | | *4th Conjugation* |
| S 1 | port*em* | move*am* | mitt*am* | iaci*am* | audi*am* |
| S 2 | port*ēs* | move*ās* | mitt*ās* | iaci*ās* | audi*ās* |
| S 3 | port*et* | move*at* | mitt*at* | iaci*at* | audi*at* |
| P 1 | port*ēmus* | move*āmus* | mitt*āmus* | iaci*āmus* | audi*āmus* |
| P 2 | port*ētis* | move*ātis* | mitt*ātis* | iaci*ātis* | audi*ātis* |
| P 3 | port*ent* | move*ant* | mitt*ant* | iaci*ant* | audi*ant* |

| PASSIVE VOICE | | | | | |
|---|---|---|---|---|---|
| S 1 | port*er* | move*ar* | mitt*ar* | iaci*ar* | audi*ar* |
| S 2 | port*ēris* | move*āris* | mitt*āris* | iaci*āris* | audi*āris* |
| S 3 | port*ētur* | move*ātur* | mitt*ātur* | iaci*ātur* | audi*ātur* |
| P 1 | port*ēmur* | move*āmur* | mitt*āmur* | iaci*āmur* | audi*āmur* |
| P 2 | port*ēminī* | move*āminī* | mitt*āminī* | iaci*āminī* | audi*āminī* |
| P 3 | port*entur* | move*antur* | mitt*antur* | iaci*antur* | audi*antur* |

| DEPONENT VERBS | | | | |
|---|---|---|---|---|
| S 1 | cōn*er* etc. | ver*ear* etc. | loqu*ar* etc. | regredi*ar* etc. | experi*ar* etc. |

| esse | | So also |
|---|---|---|
| **1** | si**m** | So also |
| **S 2** | sī**s** | **possim** |
| **3** | si**t** | **velim** |
| | | **nōlim** |
| | | **mālim** |
| **1** | sī**mus** | |
| **P 2** | sī**tis** | |
| **3** | si**nt** | |

| īre | | So also |
|---|---|---|
| **1** | ea**m** | So also |
| **S 2** | eā**s** | **feram** |
| **3** | ea**t** | **fiam** |
| **1** | eā**mus** | |
| **P 2** | eā**tis** | |
| **3** | ea**nt** | |

# Perfect Subjunctive

| ACTIVE VOICE | | | | | |
|---|---|---|---|---|---|
| **1** | portāv**erim** | mōv**erim** | mīs**erim** | iēc**erim** | audīv**erim** |
| **S 2** | portāv**eris** | mōv**eris** | mīs**eris** | iēc**eris** | audīv**eris** |
| **3** | portāv**erit** | mōv**erit** | mīs**erit** | iēc**erit** | audīv**erit** |
| **1** | portāv**erimus** | mōv**erimus** | mīs**erimus** | iēc**erimus** | audīv**erimus** |
| **P 2** | portāv**eritis** | mōv**eritis** | mīs**eritis** | iēc**eritis** | audīv**eritis** |
| **3** | portāv**erint** | mōv**erint** | mīs**erint** | iēc**erint** | audīv**erint** |

| PASSIVE VOICE | | | | | |
|---|---|---|---|---|---|
| **S 1** | portātus sim etc. | mōtus sim etc. | missus sim etc. | iactus sim etc. | audītus sim etc. |

| DEPONENT VERBS | | | | | |
|---|---|---|---|---|---|
| **S 1** | cōnātus sim etc. | veritus sim etc. | locūtus sim etc. | regressus sim etc. | expertus sim etc. |

| **S 1** | fu**erim** etc. |
|---|---|

So also **potuerim, voluerim, nōluerim, māluerim, īverim,** and **tulerim.** The perfect subjunctive of **fīō** is **factus sim.**

Be sure to learn the above forms thoroughly.

# Sequence of Tenses

Compare the following pairs of sentences containing indirect questions:

1. a. Nōn intellegō cūr servae mē **neglegant.**
   *I do not understand why the slave-girls* **neglect** *me.*

   b. Nōn intellegō cūr servae mē **neglēxerint.**
   *I do not understand why the slave-girls* **neglected** *me.*

2. a. Nōn intellegēbam cūr servae mē **neglegerent.**
   *I did not understand why the slave-girls* **were neglecting** *me.*

   b. Nōn intellegēbam cūr servae mē **neglēxissent.**
   *I did not understand why the slave-girls* **had neglected** *me.*

When the verb in the main clause is in the *present tense* (as in 1.a and 1.b above), a *present subjunctive* in the indirect question (as in 1.a above) indicates an action going on at the same time as that of the main verb, and a *perfect subjunctive* in the indirect question (as in 1.b above) indicates an action that took place before that of the main verb.

When the verb in the main clause is in the *past tense* (as in 2.a and 2.b above), an *imperfect subjunctive* in the indirect question (as in 2.a above) indicates an action going on at the same time as that of the main verb, and a *pluperfect subjunctive* in the indirect question (as in 2.b above) indicates an action that took place before that of the main verb.

This relationship between the tense of the verb in the main clause and the tense of the subjunctive in the subordinate clause is called *sequence of tenses*. The sequence is said to be *primary* when the verb in the main clause is in a primary tense, i.e., *present* or *future* or *future perfect*, as in 1.a and 1.b above. The sequence is said to be *secondary* when the verb in the main clause is in a secondary tense, i.e., *imperfect* or *perfect* or *pluperfect*, as in 2.a and 2.b above.

## PRIMARY SEQUENCE

| *Verb of Main Clause* | *Verb of Subordinate Clause* |
| --- | --- |
| present, future, or future perfect indicative | present subjunctive (for action going on at the *same time* as that of the main verb) |
| | perfect subjunctive (for action that took place *before* that of the main verb) |

| Verb of Main Clause | Verb of Subordinate Clause |
|---|---|
| imperfect, perfect, or pluperfect indicative | imperfect subjunctive (for action going on at the *same time* as that of the main verb) |
| | pluperfect subjunctive (for action that took place *before* that of the main verb) |

## Sequence of Tenses in Result Clauses

In result clauses a *present subjunctive* will be used in primary sequence, and the *imperfect subjunctive* may be used in secondary sequence. (See the examples in the note on result clauses on pages 74–5.) In practice, however, the Romans were more flexible in choosing the tenses of result clauses, and fairly regularly the *perfect subjunctive* is found in result clauses after main verbs in *secondary tenses*. This puts a special emphasis on the result that took place.

### Exercise 49b

*Read aloud and translate each sentence, and then explain the sequence of tenses between the main and the subordinate clauses:*

1. Tam laetae cantant avēs ut nātūra ipsa gaudēre videātur.
2. Leō tantus et tam ferōx erat ut servus metū exanimātus ceciderit.
3. Tot spectātōrēs ad lūdōs convēnerant ut Circus vix omnēs continēret.
4. Cornēliī fīlia adeō perturbāta erat ut submissā vōce respondēret.
5. Tanta tempestās coorta erat ut sērō Brundisium advēnerimus.
6. Cornēlia nōn rogāvit cūr pater sē Valeriō dēspondisset.
7. Tālis iuvenis erat Valerius ut Cornēliō placēret fīliam eī dēspondēre.
8. Cornēlia tam laeta subitō fit ut omnia Flāviae nārrāre cupiat.
9. Cornēlia, "Tam laeta sum," inquit, "ut vix loquī possim."
10. Pater tam gravī vultū locūtus est ut Cornēlia mīrārētur quid accidisset.

# Roman Weddings I

When a Roman girl reached marriageable age—somewhere between twelve and fourteen—her father set about finding her a husband.

When a friend asked the writer Pliny to help him find a suitable match for his niece, Pliny wrote back to say that a certain Acilianus would be just the man. After speaking highly of Acilianus' father, his grandmother on his mother's side, and his uncle, he describes the prospective bridegroom as follows:

> Acilianus himself is a person of very great energy and application, but at the same time exceedingly modest. He has held the offices of quaestor, tribune, and praetor with very great distinction, and this relieves you of the need to canvass on his behalf. His expression is frank and open; his complexion is fresh and he has a healthy color; his whole bearing is noble and handsome, with the dignity of a senator. I don't know whether I should add that his father has ample means; for, when I picture you and your brother for whom we are seeking a son-in-law, I think there is no need for me to say more on that subject; and yet, when I consider the attitudes of people nowadays and even the laws of the country, which judge a man's income as of primary importance, I'm probably right in thinking that even a reference to his father's means should not be omitted. Certainly, if one thinks of the children of the marriage and their children, one must take the question of money into account when making a choice.
>
> Pliny, *Letters* I.14

When we remember that a Roman would be nearly forty before he attained the praetorship, Pliny's candidate (if we read between the lines) was probably red-faced, stout, and middle-aged, but Pliny seems to consider these points less important than having good family connections and plenty of money.

So our thirteen-year-old Cornelia might find herself engaged to a mere boy (minimum age fourteen) or to someone three times her age, but she was not expected to raise any objections to what was simply a legal contract between families.

Before the actual wedding, a betrothal ceremony (**spōnsālia**) often took place, witnessed by relatives and friends. The father of the girl was asked formally if he "promised" his daughter and replied that he did. (Question: **Spondēsne?** Answer: **Spondeō**.) Gifts were then given to the bride-to-be, including a ring (**ānulus**) either of gold or of iron set in gold. This was worn on the third finger of the left hand, from which it was believed a nerve ran straight to the heart.

79

Usually, the two families had already discussed the terms of the dowry (**dōs, dōtis**, given by the bride's father along with the girl), which was returnable in the event of a divorce.

## Exercise 49c

Omnia iam diū ad spōnsālia parāta erant, īnsciā Cornēliā. Valerius enim, cum prīmum Brundisī ē nāve ēgressus est, ad Cornēlium scrīpserat sē velle Cornēliam in mātrimōnium dūcere; deinde Cornēlius rescrīpserat sē libenter fīliam Valeriō dēspōnsūrum esse; tum Aurēlia Vīniam, mātrem Flāviae, invītāverat ut prōnuba esset. Ad spōnsālia igitur Valerius et Vīnia et Flāvia 5 Rōmam iam advēnerant.

Aderat diēs spōnsālium. Quīntā hōrā omnēs Cornēliī atque propinquī amīcīque in ātrium convēnērunt. Deinde, silentiō factō, Cornēlia vultū dēmissō ingressa in ātrium dēducta est. Tum Valerius, quī contrā Cornēlium in mediō ātriō stābat, eī, "Spondēsne," ait, "tē fīliam tuam mihi uxōrem 10 datūrum esse?"

Cui Cornēlius, "Spondeō."

Quō dictō, Valerius ad Cornēliam conversus ānulum aureum tertiō digitō sinistrae manūs eius aptāvit. Tum ōsculum eī dedit. Omnēs spōnsō et spōnsae grātulātī sunt. 15

ad spōnsālia, for the betrothal
prōnuba, -ae (*f*), bride's attendant
propinquus, -ī (*m*), relative
vultū dēmissō, with eyes lowered
ait, (he, she) says, said

conversus, -a, -um, having turned,
  turning
ānulus, -ī (*m*), ring
sinister, -tra, -trum, left
aptō (1), to place, fit

spondeō, spondēre (2), spopondī, spōnsum, to promise solemnly, pledge
grātulor, grātulārī (1), grātulātus sum ( + *dat.*), to congratulate

**Sīqua volēs aptē nūbere, nūbe parī.** *If you wish a suitable marriage, marry an equal.* (Ovid, *Heroides* IX.32)

# The Ring Finger

Aulus Gellius, a Roman scholar and writer of the second half of the second century A.D., gives the following explanation of why the Greeks and Romans wore rings on the third finger of the left hand.

Veterēs Graecōs ānulum habuisse in digitō accēpimus sinistrae manūs quī minimō est proximus. Rōmānōs quoque hominēs aiunt sīc plērumque ānulīs ūsitātōs. Causam esse huius reī Apiōn in librīs *Aegyptiacīs* hanc dīcit, quod insectīs apertīsque hūmānīs corporibus, ut mōs in Aegyptō fuit, quās Graecī ἀνατομάς appellant, repertum est nervum quendam tenuissimum   5 ab eō ūnō digitō dē quō dīximus, ad cor hominis pergere ac pervenīre; proptereā nōn īnscītum vīsum esse eum potissimum digitum tālī honōre decorandum, quī continēns et quasi conēxus esse cum prīncipātū cordis vidērētur.

I have heard that the ancient Greeks wore a ring on the finger of the left hand which is next to the little finger. They say, too, that the Roman men commonly wore their rings in that way. Apion in his *Egyptian History* says that the reason for this practice is, that upon cutting into and opening human bodies, a custom in Egypt which the Greeks call ἀνατομαί, or "dissection," it was found that a very fine nerve proceeded from that finger alone of which we have spoken, and made its way to the human heart; that it therefore seemed quite reasonable that this finger in particular should be honored with such an ornament, since it seems to be joined, and as it were united, with that supreme organ, the heart.

Aulus Gellius, *Attic Nights* X.10

A betrothal ring.
(Reproduced by courtesy of
the Trustees of the British Museum)

# 50
# *Marcus Comes of Age*

Coming of age was an important occasion for a Roman boy and it was marked both by an official ceremony (**officium togae virīlis**) and by family celebrations. The ceremony usually took place when the boy had reached the age of sixteen but not on his birthday. It was common for it to be celebrated at the festival called the **Līberālia** on March 17. It began with the boy dedicating (**cōnsecrāre**) the lucky charm (**bulla**) which he had worn since he was a baby and the toga with the purple edge (**toga praetexta**) which boys wore. These he placed before the shrine of the household gods (**larārium**) which was usually in the atrium of the house. From this time on he wore the plain white toga (**toga virīlis** or **toga pūra**) indicating that he was no longer a boy but a man. After the ceremony members of his family and friends escorted him to the forum (**in forum dēdūcere**). There, in the building where the public records were housed (**Tabulārium**), his name was entered in the records (**tabulae**, literally, "tablets"). The official ceremony was now completed, and the family entertained their friends at a private celebration.

The time has now come for Marcus to assume the **toga virīlis**.

Iam aderat mēnsis Martius. Erat diēs Līberālium quō diē adulēscentēs Rōmānī togam pūram sūmere solēbant. Abhinc complūrēs mēnsēs Marcus sēdecim annōs complēverat; nunc togam virīlem sumptūrus erat. Itaque Cornēlius amīcōs clientēsque omnēs invītāverat ut eō diē apud sē convenīrent. Omnēs sciēbant patrem Marcī dīvitissimum esse; omnēs prō certō 5 habēbant eum optimam cēnam amīcīs datūrum esse.

Domus Gāī Cornēliī plēna erat tumultūs, strepitūs, clāmōris. Tot et tam variī hominēs eō conveniēbant ut iānitor, ab iānuā prōgressus, in ipsō līmine sollicitus stāret. Sī quis appropinquābat, eum magnā vōce rogābat quis esset et quid vellet. Aliōs rogābat ut in domum prōcēderent, aliīs praecipiēbat ut 10 in viā manērent. Nōnnūllī autem, quī neque amīcī Cornēliī erant neque

clientēs, domuī appropinquāvērunt, quod spērābant Cornēlium sē ad cēnam invītātūrum esse. Hī iānitōrem ōrābant nē sē dīmitteret; ille autem eīs imperābat ut statim discēderent.

Tandem, omnibus rēbus parātīs, Cornēlius tōtam familiam rogāvit ut in 15 ātrium convenīrent. Aderant propinquī; aderant multī amīcī; aderant plūrimī clientium; aderant omnēs servī lībertīque Cornēliōrum. Cūnctī inter sē colloquēbantur, cūnctī gaudēbant quod ad hoc officium togae virīlis invītātī erant.

In ātriō ante larārium stābat Marcus togam praetextam bullamque auream 20 in manibus tenēns. Sēnsit oculōs omnium in sē conversōs esse. Conticuērunt omnēs. Marcus prīmum togam praetextam atque bullam ante larārium dēpositās Laribus familiāribus cōnsecrāvit. "Nunc," inquit, "hās rēs puerīlēs hīc dēpōnō. Nunc vōbīs, ō Larēs familiārēs, haec libenter cōnsecrō."

Quō factō, pater servō cuidam imperāvit ut togam pūram Marcō indueret. 25 Deinde parentēs eum amplexī sunt et cēterī eī grātulātī sunt. Nunc Marcus, multīs comitantibus, in Forum ā patre est dēductus.

Quō cum pervēnissent, Marcō ad Tabulārium ductō, pater eōs quī comitābantur rogāvit ut extrā Tabulārium manērent. Ipse ūnā cum fīliō et paucīs propinquīs in Tabulārium ingressus est, nam ibi nōmen Marcī in tabulīs 30 pūblicīs erat īnscrībendum.

83

Quibus rēbus cōnfectīs, omnēs adstantēs Marcum iam ēgressum magnō clāmōre salūtāvērunt. Deinde cum Marcus omnibus grātiās ēgisset propter tantam ergā sē benevolentiam, omnēs domum Cornēliōrum rediērunt, nam Cornēlius multōs invītāverat ut apud sē eō diē cēnārent.                                      35

sūmere, to assume (i.e., put on for the first time)
invītāverat ut, he had invited (them) to
līmen, līminis (n), threshold, doorway
sī quis, if anyone
nōnnūllī, -ae, -a, some
ōrō (1), to beg
nē sē dīmitteret, not to send them away

imperō (1) (+ dat.), to order
Larēs, Larum (m pl), household gods
familiāris, -is, -e, (belonging to the) family or household
erat īnscrībendum, had to be registered
grātiās agere (+ dat.), to thank
ergā (+ acc.), towards
benevolentia, -ae (f), kindness

praecipiō, praecipere (3), praecēpī, praeceptum (+ dat.), to instruct, order
conticēscō, conticēscere (3), conticuī, to fall silent
amplector, amplectī (3), amplexus sum, to embrace
comitor, comitārī (1), comitātus sum, to accompany

## Exercise 50a

*Respondē Latīnē:*

1. Quid iānitor rogābat ut aliī appropinquantēs facerent?
2. Quid aliīs praecipiēbat?
3. Quid iānitor imperābat eīs quī neque amīcī Cornēliī neque clientēs erant?
4. Quid Cornēlius servō cuidam imperāvit?
5. Postquam nōmen Marcī in tabulīs īnscrīptum est, quid Cornēlius adstantēs invītāvit ut facerent?

## Exercise 50b

*Using story 50 as a guide, give the Latin for:*

1. Cornelius invited all his relatives, friends, and clients to come together at his house.
2. Some who were not friends of Cornelius were begging the doorkeeper not to send them away.
3. Cornelius asked his whole household to come together in the atrium.
4. Cornelius asked his friends and clients to stay outside the Tabularium.
5. When Marcus had thanked everyone, they all returned to Cornelius' house.

# Telling to, Asking to: Indirect Commands

Compare the following pairs of sentences:

1. a. Aliōs rogat **ut** in domum **prōcēdant**.
      *He asks some* **to** *go on* **into** *the house.*

   b. Aliōs rogāvit **ut** in domum **prōcēderent**.
      *He asked some* **to** *go on* **into** *the house.*

2. a. Hī iānitōrem ōrant **nē** sē **dīmittat**.
      *They keep begging the doorkeeper* **not to send** *them* **away**.

   b. Hī iānitōrem ōrābant **nē** sē **dīmitteret**.
      *They kept begging the doorkeeper* **not to send** *them* **away**.

In these sentences **ut** is translated by *to*. **nē** is translated by *not to*.

In the story you have also seen **praecipiō** (I instruct), **imperō** (I order), and **invītō** (I invite) used to introduce **ut** clauses. Other verbs are also used in this manner, with **ut** and **nē** followed by the subjunctive, e.g.:

>  **moneō** (I advise, warn); **persuādeō** (I persuade); **hortor** (I urge); and **obsecrō** (I beg, beseech).

These subordinate clauses with the subjunctive, introduced by **ut** or **nē**, are called *indirect commands*.

Note that most of the verbs that introduce indirect commands are followed by a direct object in the accusative case, e.g.:

>  **Aliōs** rogābat ut in domum prōcēderent. (See above.)

The verbs **imperō** and **persuādeō**, however, are followed by the dative case, e.g.:

>  **Coquō** imperāvit (persuāsit) ut in ātrium venīret.
>  *He ordered (persuaded)* **the cook** *to come into the atrium.*

Another arrangement is also possible, e.g.:

>  Imperāvit (persuāsit) ut coquus in ātrium venīret.
>  *He ordered (persuaded) the cook to come into the atrium.*

In this latter case, "that" may be used in translation, e.g.:

>  *He ordered that the cook come into the atrium.*

A *present subjunctive* will be used in primary sequence (examples 1.a and 2.a above), and an *imperfect subjunctive* will be used in secondary sequence (examples 1.b and 2.b above).

## Exercise 50c

*In story 50, locate 9 subordinate clauses that express indirect commands.*

1. Translate the sentences in which these indirect commands occur.
2. Tell in English what the direct command (or request) was or would have been that is being reported indirectly in each case.
3. Locate one example of a subordinate clause with *indirect questions* (rather than indirect commands or requests) in story 50, and tell in English what the direct questions were that are here being reported indirectly.

## Exercise 50d

*Read aloud and translate each sentence, identify the type of each subordinate clause, and then identify the tense of each verb in the subjunctive.*

1. Cornēlius convīvās omnēs invītat ut in ātrium prōcēdant.
2. Tum Cornēlius Marcō imperāvit ut rēs puerīlēs Laribus cōnsecrāret.
3. Cornēlius Marcum togā pūrā indūtum rogāvit ut ad Forum sēcum proficīscerētur.
4. In Tabulāriō pater rogat ut nōmen Marcī in tabulīs pūblicīs īnscrībātur.
5. Cornēlius omnēs convīvās invītāvit ut apud sē cēnārent.
6. Tē ōrō atque obsecrō ut domum veniās.
7. Iānitor iam iānuam claudēbat: tam dēfessus erat ut dormīre cuperet.
8. Asellus iānitōrem vīsum rogāvit quid eō diē fēcisset.
9. "Tibi dīcō," inquit iānitor, "plūrimōs hominēs ā mē aut ad iānuam acceptōs esse aut dīmissōs."
10. "Nōlī ibi morārī," inquam, "nam dominus imperāvit ut iānua claudātur."

Note that in sentence 10 present time is clearly in the speaker's mind when using the verb **imperāvit,** "has ordered." When the perfect tense is used in this way, the sequence is primary, and therefore a present subjunctive is used in the indirect command.

## Exercise 50e

*Select, read aloud, and translate:*

1. Nōlī mē hortārī ut ad illam urbem (īrem/eam).
2. Tē semper moneō nē in mediā viā (ambulēs/ambulārēs).
3. Abhinc multōs mēnsēs Valerius Cornēliō persuāsit ut Cornēliam sibi (spondēret/spondeat).
4. Plūrimī hominēs domum Cornēliī pervenientēs rogābant ut intrāre (possint/possent).

86

5. Prīmō omnēs hominēs hortor ut in viā (maneant/manērent).
6. Deinde amīcōs propinquōsque Cornēliī rogāvī ut (intrārent/intrent).
7. Clientibus praecēpī nē statim in domum (prōcēderent/prōcēdant).
8. Nōnnūllī, quōs nōn prius vīdī, mē ōrant nē sē (dīmitterem/dīmittam).
9. Eōs monuī nē ad iānuam (morārentur/morentur).
10. Tandem coāctus sum servōs rogāre ut eōs baculīs (repellant/repellerent).

Ego vōs hortor tantum possum ut amīcitiam omnibus rēbus hūmānīs antepōnātis. *As much as I am able, I urge you to set friendship before all other human affairs.* (Cicero, *On Friendship* V.17)

## Cicero: Coming of Age Ceremonies for Nephew and Son

When Cicero, the great statesman and orator (106-43 B.C.), was governor of Cilicia, an area of southern Asia Minor, he wrote the following in a letter to his friend Atticus (50 B.C.) about his nephew Quintus and his son Marcus:

Cicerōnēs puerī amant inter sē, discunt, exercentur, sed alter frēnīs eget, alter calcāribus. Quīntō togam pūram Līberālibus cōgitābam dare; mandāvit enim pater.

My son and nephew are fond of one another, learn their lessons, and take their exercise together; but the one needs the rein and the other the spur. I intend to celebrate Quintus' coming of age on the feast of Bacchus. His father asked me to do this.

Cicero, *Letters to Atticus* VI.1

The following year Cicero planned to give the **toga pūra** to his own son, Marcus, in his hometown of Arpinum to the south-east of Rome:

Volō Cicerōnī meō togam pūram dare, Arpīnī putō.

I wish to celebrate my son's coming of age. Arpinum, I think, will be the place.

Cicero, *Letters to Atticus* IX.17

On 31 March, 49 B.C., Cicero, barred from Rome for political reasons, wrote with pride from Arpinum:

Ego meō Cicerōnī, quoniam Rōmā carēmus, Arpīnī potissimum togam pūram dedī, idque mūnicipibus nostrīs fuit grātum.

Since Rome was out of bounds, I celebrated my son's coming of age at Arpinum in preference to any other place, and so doing delighted my fellow-townsmen.

Cicero, *Letters to Atticus* IX.19

## Versiculī: *"Nucēs Relinquere," pages 121–122.*

# *Augury*

Like the ancient Greeks, the Romans laid great stress upon augury, the "science" of "taking the omens." They would not contemplate taking any important step until it was clear from the omens that the gods were in favor of it.

First of all, they would offer a sacrifice to some appropriate god or gods. For example, for an important family event, they would offer a sacrifice to their household gods, called the **Larēs** and **Penātēs**, at the family shrine in the **ātrium**; someone planning to go on a journey might offer a sacrifice to Mercury, a soldier going into battle a sacrifice to Mars or Mithras, and a young man in love an offering to Venus or Fortuna. The Romans worshiped many gods, both native and foreign; all of them would have their own temples, each with a sacrificial altar outside in the open air.

At home, the sacrifice could be small cakes, honey, cheese, or fruit which would be burnt upon the altar. At a temple, an animal such as a pig, a sheep, or a bull (or all three, the **suovetaurīlia**) would be sacrificed.

In the latter case, once the animal had been killed, the vital organs—heart, liver, and intestines—were inspected by the **haruspicēs**, who claimed to be able to tell from the spots or marks on these organs whether the omens were favorable or not. If the omens were bad, the ordinary Roman simply put off the undertaking to another day. More sceptical Romans usually dismissed all this as mumbo-jumbo and, in fact, the Elder Cato said, "How can one **haruspex** look at another without laughing?"

The most popular form of augury, **auspicium** ("taking the auspices"), can be described quite accurately as "bird watching" (from **avis**, a bird, and **spectāre**, to watch). The **auspex** based his predictions upon the number of birds seen at a particular time, the direction of flight, and so on. Astrology, dreams, thunder and lightning, and strange events of any kind were all taken very seriously by those engaged in augury.

A procession on its way to the altar to sacrifice a pig, a sheep, and a bull. (The Mansell Collection)

# How Numa Pompilius Became the Second King of Rome (715-673 B.C.)

The senators unanimously voted to offer the kingship to Numa Pompilius. When he was summoned to Rome, he ordered that, just as Romulus had obeyed the augural omens in building his city and assuming regal power, so the gods should be consulted in his case, too. Accordingly, an augur conducted him to the citadel and arranged for him to sit down on a stone, facing the south. The augur seated himself on Numa's left, with his head covered, and holding in his right hand the crooked staff with no knots which they call a **lituus**. Then, looking out over the city and the fields beyond, the augur prayed to the gods and marked off the heavens by a line from east to west, designating as "right" the regions to the south, as "left" those to the north, and fixing in his mind a landmark opposite to him and as far away as the eye could see. Next, shifting the crook to his left hand and laying his right hand on Numa's head, the augur made the following prayer: "Father Jupiter, if it is Heaven's will that this man Numa Pompilius, whose head I am touching, should be king of Rome, show us unmistakable signs within those limits which I have set." He then specified the auspices which he desired should be sent, and upon their appearance Numa was declared king and so descended from the augural station.

Livy, I.18

# On the Importance of Consulting the Auspices

In ancient times scarcely any matter out of the ordinary was undertaken, even in private life, without first consulting the auspices. Clear proof of this is seen even at the present time by our custom of having "nuptial auspices," though they have lost their former religious significance and only preserve the name.

Cicero, *On Divination* I.16

**Auspex** with **lituus**

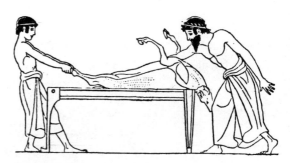

**Haruspex** with sacrificial victim

# 51
# *Papirius*
# *Praetextatus*

Now that Marcus has assumed the **toga virīlis**, Cornelius will begin to consider his public career. In the early Republic, boys began their training for public life when they were much younger than Marcus is now. In those days fathers took their sons with them while they carried out their public duties. This story shows that Papirius, though still wearing the **toga praetexta,** had already learned how to be discreet.

Mōs anteā senātōribus Rōmae fuit in Cūriam cum praetextātīs filiīs introīre. Ōlim in senātū rēs maior agēbātur et in diem posterum prōlāta est. Placuit nē quis eam rem ēnūntiāret. Māter Papīriī, puerī quī cum parente suō in Cūriā fuerat, rogāvit filium quid in senātū patrēs ēgissent. Puer tamen respondit nōn licēre eam rem ēnūntiāre. Eō magis mulier audīre cupiēbat; 5 silentium puerī animum eius adeō incitāvit ut vehementius quaereret.

91

Tum puer, mātre urgente, prūdēns cōnsilium cēpit. Dīxit āctum esse in senātū utrum ūnus vir duās uxōrēs habēret an ūna uxor duōs virōs. Hoc ubi illa audīvit, domō trepidāns ēgressa est. Ad cēterās mātrōnās rem pertulit. Vēnit ad senātum postrīdiē mātrōnārum caterva. Lacrimantēs atque ob- 10 secrantēs ōrāvērunt ut ūna uxor duōs virōs habēret potius quam ut ūnus vir duās uxōrēs. Senātōrēs ingredientēs in Cūriam mīrābantur quid mātrōnae vellent.

Puer Papīrius in medium prōgressus nārrāvit quid māter audīre cupīvisset et quid ipse mātrī dīxisset. Senātus fidem atque ingenium puerī laudāvit ac 15 cōnsultum fēcit nē posteā puerī cum patribus in Cūriam introīrent praeter illum ūnum Papīrium. Puerō posteā cognōmen honōris causā *Praetextātus* datum est quod tantam prūdentiam praebuerat.

mōs, mōris (*m*), custom
posterus, -a, -um, next, following
placuit, it was decided
nē quis, that no one
ēnūntiō (1), to reveal, divulge
patrēs, patrum (*m pl*), senators
eō magis, all the more
dīxit āctum esse, he said that there
  had been a debate
utrum . . . an . . . , whether . . .
  or . . .
habēret, should have

trepidāns, trepidantis, in a panic
caterva, -ae (*f*), crowd
potius quam, rather than
fidēs, fideī (*f*), good faith, reliability, trust
ingenium, -ī (*n*), intelligence, ingenuity
cōnsultum, -ī (*n*), decree
cognōmen, cognōminis (*n*), nickname
honōris causā, as an honor
praebeō (2), to display, show

agō, agere (3), ēgī, āctum, (here) to discuss, debate
prōferō, prōferre (*irreg.*), prōtulī, prōlātum, to carry forward, continue
urgeō, urgēre (2), ursī, to press, insist

mōs maiōrum literally, "the custom of the ancestors," *inherited custom, tradition* (used respectfully of the old ways as a guide for present conduct)

Mōribus antīquīs rēs stat Rōmāna virīsque. *On customs and men of olden times the Roman state stands firm.* (Ennius)

Ō tempora! Ō mōrēs! *How times and customs have changed!* (Cicero, *Orations against Catiline* I.2; spoken by the orator in indignation over the open conspiracy of Catiline against the Roman state)

mōs prō lēge *A long established custom has the force of law.*

mōre suō *in one's own way*

nūllō mōre *without precedent, unparalleled*

## Exercise 51a

*Using story 51 as a guide, give the Latin for:*

1. It was the custom for Roman boys wearing the **toga praetexta** to enter the Senate House with their fathers.
2. Once, the senators were debating a rather important matter.
3. It was decided that the matter should be put off until the following day.
4. The senators ordered that the matter not be revealed.
5. The mother of Papirius asked her son what had been debated by the senators.
6. The boy replied that he would not reveal the matter.
7. The boy's silence aroused his mother all the more.
8. At his mother's insistence, the boy revealed that the senators were discussing whether a husband should have one wife or two.
9. Upon hearing this, Papirius' mother left the house.
10. She discussed the matter with other matrons.
11. It was decided that a crowd of matrons should go to the senate the next day.
12. In a panic they begged that one husband should have one wife rather than two.
13. The senators wondered why the women were saying this.
14. Papirius revealed what he had said to his mother.
15. The boy's ingenuity aroused the senators so much that they made a decree that afterwards only Papirius could enter the Senate House with his father.
16. As an honor they gave him the nickname *Praetextatus*.

# Roman Names

In the earliest days, most Romans had only two names, that of the clan or **gēns** to which they belonged (**nōmen**), and their personal name by which they would be addressed by relatives and friends (**praenōmen**). Later, as families divided, branches of the same **gēns** were distinguished by a third name (**cognōmen**), e.g.:

Gaius (personal name) **praenōmen**
Julius (name of **gēns**) **nōmen**
Caesar (branch of Julian **gēns**) **cognōmen**

The **cognōmen** frequently started off as a nickname given to one member of the family, and it was handed down to his descendants as part of their name even though the nickname did not apply to them personally, e.g.:

P. Ovidius Naso ("big nose")
L. Domitius Ahenobarbus ("bronze beard")
M. Junius Brutus ("the stupid one")
C. Licinius Calvus ("bald")

A few Romans, who had earned some special distinction, were granted a fourth name (**agnōmen**) which was usually connected with the event which had made them famous, e.g., Publius Cornelius Scipio, who conquered the Carthaginians in North Africa, was called Publius Cornelius Scipio Africanus.

It is usual in Latin to find the **praenōmen** abbreviated. This is not the same as our practice of giving someone's initials. In Latin each abbreviation stands for a particular **praenōmen**. The following list contains most of the **praenōmina** in common use:

| | | | | | |
|---|---|---|---|---|---|
| A. | = Aulus | L. | = Lūcius | S(er). | = Servius |
| App. | = Appius | M. | = Marcus | S(ex). | = Sextus |
| C. | = Gāius | M'. | = Mānius | Sp. | = Spurius |
| Cn. | = Gnaeus | P. | = Pūblius | T. | = Titus |
| D. | = Decimus | Q. | = Quīntus | Ti(b). | = Tiberius |

Women usually had no **praenōmen**, but only the feminine form of the **nōmen** of their **gēns**, i.e., the **nōmen** of their father. Thus Cornelius' daughter is called **Cornēlia**. Sometimes the adjectives **Prīma, Secunda** or **Minor**, and **Tertia** were added to indicate the order of birth.

# Roman Weddings II

In spite of the unromantic pre-arrangements, the wedding itself was celebrated with great festivity by the families and guests. The second half of June was considered to be the luckiest time for a wedding.

On the evening before her marriage, the girl dedicated her toys to the household gods to show that her childhood had ended, just as a boy dedicated his **toga praetexta** and **bulla** at the coming-of-age ceremony. At the same time, she received her **mundus muliebris**—the jewelry, perfumes, toilet articles, and attire of the grown-up woman.

On her wedding day the bride wore a **tunica rēcta** which was plain white and over it a cloak (**palla**) which was saffron-yellow, as were her sandals. Her hair was specially styled for the occasion, and over it she wore a bright orange veil (**flammeum**). Her attendant was a married woman (**prōnuba**). The bride's house, where the wedding ceremony (**nūptiae**) was performed, was also decorated for the occasion.

The bride and her family and friends assembled in the **ātrium** and received the bridegroom and his guests. The ceremony began with a sacrifice, usually of a pig, the entrails of which were carefully examined by the **auspex** to make sure that the omens were favorable. If they were unfavorable, the marriage was postponed. The ceremony also included the signing of the marriage contract (**tabulās nūptiālēs obsignāre**) by ten witnesses, the joining of the couple's right hands (**dextrās iungere**) by the **prōnuba**, and the repetition of the formula **Ubi tū Gāius, ego Gāia** by the bride. Then the guests all shouted, "Good luck!" (**Fēlīciter!**).

The ceremony was followed by a banquet and then, after nightfall, the couple prepared to go to their new home. The bridegroom pretended to carry off the bride by force just as the Romans once carried off the Sabine women. Then the bride and groom were escorted home by a procession of guests (**dēductiō**) carrying torches (**taedae**) and singing songs to Hymen, god of marriage. Some guests threw nuts (**nucēs**) to children for luck. On arrival at the house, the bride was carried over the threshold (**super līmen tollere**) to avoid an unlucky stumble.

# Word Study XIII

## Latin and the Romance Languages

Although Latin has influenced the development of many languages (including English, of course), there are five modern languages which are so universally derived from Latin as to be called "Romance" (i.e., Roman) languages. These languages are Italian, French, Spanish, Portuguese, and Rumanian. The following examples show clearly the relationship of the Romance languages to Latin:

| Latin | French | Italian | Spanish | Portuguese | Rumanian |
|-------|--------|---------|---------|------------|----------|
| arbor, *tree* | arbre | albero | arbol | árvore | arbore |
| dulcis, *sweet* | doux | dolce | dulce | doce | dulce |

Rome's conquering legions brought Latin to lands as far apart as Britain and Egypt. In those places with well-established civilizations, such as Egypt, Latin did not displace the native languages; when the Romans left, Latin left with them. However, in areas such as Gaul (France) where civilization in Roman times was relatively primitive, Latin took hold and became the language of the people. The Romans also sent many colonists to these less-developed and less-populated provinces, further insuring the dominance of Latin as the accepted tongue in these lands.

In the evolution of provincial Latin into the Romance languages, these major developments (as well as many others) took place:

1. In general, the importance of word endings (inflection) in classical Latin was greatly reduced in the Romance languages. Nouns were usually reduced to two forms: a singular and a plural, e.g., the French *homme*, *hommes*, from the Latin **hominem**; and endings such as those of the comparative and superlative of adjectives were often replaced by words meaning "more" and "most," e.g., the Latin **dīligentior** became in Italian, *più diligente*. (*Più* is derived from the Latin **plus**.)

2. The definite article developed from the demonstrative pronoun and adjective **ille**. For example, the Latin **ille lupus** became "the wolf" in each of the Romance languages, as follows:

| French | Italian | Spanish | Portuguese | Rumanian |
|--------|---------|---------|------------|----------|
| le loup | il lupo | el lobo | o lobo | lupul* |

(*The article is attached as a suffix in Rumanian.)

3. Pronunciation developed separately in each language, diverging greatly from that of classical Latin, e.g., the Latin word **caelum** (*c* pronounced *k*) became *cielo* in Italian (*c* pronounced *ch*), and *ciel* in French (*c* pronounced *s*).

96

## Exercise 1

Next to each number below are words of equivalent meaning from each of three Romance languages. Give the Latin word from which each trio of Romance language words is derived and give the English meaning. Consult a French, Spanish, or Italian dictionary, as needed.

| | Italian | Spanish | French | Latin | Meaning |
|---|---|---|---|---|---|
| | | | NOUNS | | |
| 1. | acqua | agua | eau | _____ | _____ |
| 2. | amico | amigo | ami | _____ | _____ |
| 3. | libro | libro | livre | _____ | _____ |
| 4. | lingua | lengua | langue | _____ | _____ |
| 5. | madre | madre | mère | _____ | _____ |
| 6. | ora | hora | heure | _____ | _____ |
| 7. | pane | pan | pain | _____ | _____ |
| 8. | tempo | tiempo | temps | _____ | _____ |
| 9. | terra | tierra | terre | _____ | _____ |
| | | | VERBS | | |
| 10. | abitare | habitar | habiter | _____ | _____ |
| 11. | amare | amar | aimer | _____ | _____ |
| 12. | dormire | dormir | dormir | _____ | _____ |
| 13. | scrivere | escribir | écrire | _____ | _____ |
| | | | ADJECTIVES | | |
| 14. | buono | bueno | bon | _____ | _____ |
| 15. | breve | breve | bref | _____ | _____ |
| 16. | facile | fácil | facile | _____ | _____ |
| 17. | male | malo | mal | _____ | _____ |
| | | | NUMBERS | | |
| 18. | quattro | cuatro | quatre | _____ | _____ |
| 19. | sette | siete | sept | _____ | _____ |
| 20. | dieci | diez | dix | _____ | _____ |

## Exercise 2

In which of the following places is French spoken? In which is Spanish spoken? In which is Portuguese spoken? Consult an encyclopedia as needed.

1. Brazil
2. Haiti
3. Guatemala
4. Belgium
5. Madagascar
6. Angola
7. Quebec
8. Argentina
9. Switzerland
10. Mexico

# 52
# *Cornelia's Wedding*

Ubi diēs nūptiālis vēnit, omnēs mātūrē surrēxērunt. Aurēlia Marcum Sextumque hortābātur ut festīnārent. Ancillae hūc illūc concursābant ut omnia parārent.

Flāvia et Vīnia, māter eius, iam diū aderant. Mox adveniēbant cēterī amīcī et propinquī. Appropinquantēs laetī vīdērunt iānuam et postēs vittīs 5 et corōnīs myrtī laurīque ōrnātōs esse. Domum ingressī in ātrium ductī sunt ubi Cornēlia, tunicam albam indūta, flammeum gerēns, eōs exspectābat. Paulō post clāmor rīsusque maximus audītus est. Valerius cum propinquīs amīcīsque suīs intrābat.

Cornēlia cum prōnubā ad āram stābat. Sacrīs rīte parātīs, auspex prōcessit 10 ut porcum sacrificāret. Deinde tabulae nūptiālēs obsignātae sunt. Vīnia prōnuba dextrās Valeriī et Cornēliae iūnxit. Valeriō rogantī, "Quid nōmen tibi est?" Cornēlia, "Ubi tū Gāius ego Gāia," respondit. Quō factō, cūnctī, "Fēlīciter!" exclāmābant.

Cēnā iam parātā, omnēs convīvae accubuērunt, atque optimam post 15 cēnam cōnsecūta est commissātiō hilaritātis plēna.

Iam advesperāscēbat. Cornēlia ad mātrem haerēbat; Valerius simulābat sē eam ē manibus mātris vī abripere. Mox illa domum novam multīs comitantibus dēdūcēbātur. Praecēdēbant quīnque puerī quī taedās ardentēs ferēbant; subsequēbantur cēterī rīdentēs et cantantēs; nucēs ad līberōs, quī 20 undique concurrerant, coniciēbant. Cum domum vēnissent, nova nūpta super līmen sublāta est nē lāberētur.

"Quam fēlīx est Cornēlia!" exclāmāvit Flāvia.

vitta, -ae (f), ribbon
myrtus, -ī (f), myrtle
laurus, -ī (f), bay (tree), laurel
ōrnō (1), to decorate
albus, -a, -um, white
paulō post, a little later
āra, -ae (f), altar
sacra, -ōrum (n pl), sacrifice

rīte, properly
auspex, auspicis (m), augur, officiating priest
dextra, -ae (f), right hand
nova nūpta, bride
nē lāberētur, so she wouldn't stumble

iungō, iungere (3), iūnxī, iūnctum, to join
ardeō, ardēre (2), arsī, to burn
nūbō, nūbere (3), nūpsī, nūptum (+ dat.), to marry

99

### Exercise 52a

*Respondē Latīnē:*

1. Cūr ancillae hūc illūc concursābant?
2. Quandō clāmor rīsusque maximus audītus est?
3. Quandō prōcessit auspex?
4. Cūr auspex prōcessit?
5. Quid Valerius rogāvit cum dextrae iūnctae essent?
6. Quid Cornēlia respondit?
7. Quid Valerius simulābat?
8. Cūr nova nūpta super līmen sublāta est?

## Purpose Clauses

In addition to the uses of the subjunctive described on page 11 (circumstantial and causal clauses and indirect questions), pages 74–5 (result), and page 85 (indirect commands), the subjunctive is used with **ut** to express *purpose*. Here, it is usually most naturally translated by "to" or "so that." The corresponding negative, **nē**, can be translated in various ways, e.g., "so that . . . not," "in case," "to avoid," or "to prevent." For example:

Auspex prōcessit **ut** porcum **sacrificāret**.
*The priest stepped forward **to** sacrifice a pig.*

Super līmen sublāta est **nē lāberētur**.
*She was carried over the threshold **so she wouldn't stumble**.*

The imperfect subjunctive is used in secondary sequence (as in the examples above). The present subjunctive is used in primary sequence (as below):

Auspex prōcēdit **ut** porcum **sacrificet**.
*The priest steps forward **to** sacrifice a pig.*

Super līmen tollētur **nē lābātur**.
*She will be carried over the threshold **so she won't stumble**.*

**Ut amēris, amābilis estō!** *To be loved, be lovable!* (Ovid, *The Art of Love* II.107)

**Lēgum omnēs servī sumus, ut līberī esse possīmus.** *We are all slaves of law so that we may be free.* (Cicero, *Pro Cluentio* 146)

**Cūr nōn mitto meōs tibi, Pontiliāne, libellōs?**
**nē mihi tū mittās, Pontiliāne, tuōs!**

*Why don't I send you my little books of verse, Pontilianus?*
*So that you, Pontilianus, won't send me yours!* (Martial, *Epigrams* VII.3)

## Exercise 52b

*Read aloud and translate each sentence, identify the tenses of all verbs, and determine whether the subordinate clauses are in primary or secondary sequence:*

1. Multī amīcī convēnērunt ut novae nūptae grātulārentur.
2. Iānitor baculum habet ut clientēs repellat.
3. Marcus ante Larārium stābat ut bullam Laribus cōnsecrāret.
4. Cavēte nē cadātis, amīcī!
5. Ancilla in cubiculum festīnāvit ut Cornēliae speculum daret.
6. Servus vestīmenta custōdit nē quis ea surripiat.
7. Flāvia Rōmam veniet ut Cornēliam adiuvet.
8. Eucleidēs per viās festīnāvit nē ā praedōnibus caperētur.
9. Pater Sextī Rōmam redībit ut filium sēcum domum dūcat.
10. Marcus ad Tabulārium dēductus est ut nōmen eius in tabulīs pūblicīs īnscrīberētur.

# Versiculī: "Bridal Hymn," page 122–123.

## A Noble Wife

There is much evidence to show that husbands and wives loved each other and lived as happily as if they had themselves chosen each other. When a bride repeated the words **Ubi tū Gāius ego Gāia** at the wedding ceremony, she was promising to be a faithful wife. The following story, adapted from Pliny (*Letters* III.16), tells us how Arria, during the illness of her husband, concealed the death of her son from him to avoid aggravating his illness.

Aegrōtābat Caecina Paetus, marītus Arriae; aegrōtābat et filius, uterque mortiferē, ut vidēbātur. Fīlius dēcessit, puer eximiā pulchritūdine et parentibus cārissimus. Huic Arria ita fūnus parāvit, ita dūxit exsequiās ut ignōrāret marītus. Praetereā cum cubiculum eius intrāverat, simulābat vīvere filium atque etiam convalēscere; ac Paetō saepe interrogantī quid ageret 5 puer, respondēbat, "Bene quiēvit; libenter cibum sūmpsit." Deinde cum lacrimae prōrumperent, ē cubiculō ēgrediēbātur. Tum sē dolōrī dabat. Tandem siccīs iam oculīs, vultū iam compositō redībat; atque dum marītus aegrōtābat, sīc lacrimās retinēbat, dolōrem operiēbat.

| | |
|---|---|
| **marītus, -ī** (*m*), husband | **dūxit exsequiās**, (she) carried out |
| **mortiferē**, mortally, critically | the funeral rites |
| **eximius, -a, -um**, outstanding | **cum**, whenever |
| **cārus, -a, -um**, dear, beloved | **quid ageret**, how he was |
| **fūnus, fūneris** (*n*), funeral | **siccus, -a, -um**, dry |

**dēcēdō, dēcēdere** (3), **dēcessī, dēcessum**, to die
**quiēscō, quiēscere** (3), **quiēvī, quiētum**, to rest
**compōnō, compōnere** (3), **composuī, compositum**, to compose
**operiō, operīre** (4), **operuī, opertum**, to hide, cover

# Another Story about Arria

The culmination of Arria's devotion is described in the following story of her death, also told in the letter of Pliny (III.16), from which the passage above is adapted.

Many years later Scribonianus in Illyria took up arms against the Emperor Claudius, and Paetus took part in the revolt. Scribonianus was killed, and Paetus was captured and put on board a ship to be taken to Rome. When he was about to go on board, Arria pleaded with the soldiers to be allowed to go with him. "Surely a man of senatorial rank is entitled to have some slaves to prepare his food, dress him, and put on his shoes? I will do all of these tasks on my own." Her request was refused, however. She therefore hired a small fishing boat and followed the larger vessel. When they reached Rome, Paetus was condemned to death, but he was told that he might take his own life, if he wished. At that point, Arria, who had no desire to go on living after the death of her husband, drew a dagger, plunged it into her breast, drew it out, and, as she held it out to her husband, uttered the immortal words, **Paete, nōn dolet** ("Paetus, it does not hurt").

Martial wrote the following epigram on Arria's death:

Casta suō gladium cum trāderet Arria Paetō
    quem dē visceribus trāxerat ipsa suīs,
"Crēde mihī, vulnus quod fēcī nōn dolet," inquit.
    "Sed quod tū faciēs, hoc mihi, Paete, dolet."

Martial, Epigrams I.13

castus, -a, -um, virtuous, chaste
dē ( + abl.), (here) from
viscera, viscerum (n pl), the inner organs of the body, the womb

# Roman Funerals

When a death occurred in a Roman family, it was the custom to display grief more than is common today. Tears and lamentations were expected, and it was usual, for female mourners at least, to beat the breast (**pectus plangere**) and go about with torn clothing (**scissā veste**) and dishevelled hair (**capillīs solūtīs**). Some families even hired professional mourners to do this for them.

In the case of an important family, like the Cornelii in our story, the actual funeral procession (**pompa**) was a very elaborate affair. After the body had lain in state, feet towards the door, in the **ātrium** of the house surrounded by lamps (**lucernae**) and candles (**candēlae**), there would be a procession through the city to the Forum and then on to the family tomb. It would be headed by trumpet players (**tubicinēs**) followed by the litter on which the body lay. Then, after professional mourners, singers of dirges (**nēniae**), and torch-bearers (a reminder of the days when all funerals had taken place at night), came members of the family wearing masks of famous ancestors (**imāginēs maiōrum**), and, in the case of a magistrate, even the public attendants (**līctōrēs**) carrying his symbol of office, the bundles of rods (**fascēs**). Family and friends followed. A halt was made in the Forum where a speech of praise (**laudātiō**) was made in honor of the dead man.

At the family tomb outside the walls, the body was usually placed on a funeral pyre (**rogus**) which was set alight by a member of the family after some of the deceased's possessions had been placed on it. Flowers and spices were also thrown on the fire.

After the body had been cremated, the ashes were cooled with wine and were collected with the bones in an urn and placed in the family tomb. The last farewell was then uttered, and after nine days of mourning a food offering was made at the tomb to the spirit of the dead man (**mānēs**).

Slaves and the very poor, who could not afford even to hire the four bearers to carry the bier, were usually buried in public cemeteries in simple coffins. Some, however, would join one of the guilds or societies that were formed to ensure a respectable funeral for their members and spare them the indignity of being flung into a common grave. The poor were buried on the day they died, and their funerals, like those of children, usually took place after dark with a minimum of ceremony. Death among children was common, both in the early vulnerable years and in later childhood, as is proved by many inscriptions found on tombstones in various parts of the Roman world.

# 53
# *A Sad Occasion*

Mēnse Iūliō tantus erat calor in urbe ut omnēs ad vīllam redīre vellent. Gāius Cornēlius igitur omnia parāre coepit ut Bāiās redīrent. Antequam profectī sunt, accidit rēs trīstissima.

Cornēlius, ut solēbat, cum Titō frātre ad balneās īverat. Per tōtam domum erat silentium. Subitō audītae sunt vōcēs atque clāmor. Cornēlius servōs 5 hortābātur ut lectīcam in domum maximā cum cūrā ferrent. Aurēlia, vōcibus audītīs, in ātrium irrūpit. "Quid factum est, Gāī? Cūr servōs iubēs lectīcam in domum ferre?" Cui Cornēlius, "Titus noster aliquid malī accēpit. Frīgidāriī pavīmentum tam lēve et lūbricum erat ut ille lāpsus ceciderit. Putō eum coxam frēgisse. Medicus statim est arcessendus." 10

Multōs diēs Titus in lectō iacēbat. Prīmō convalēscere vidēbātur; mox tamen fiēbat īnfirmior, nam in febrem subitō inciderat. In diēs morbus ingravēscēbat.

Tandem tam īnfirmus erat ut vix loquī posset. Haud multō post ē vītā excessit. Cornēlius maximō dolōre affectus est. Tōta domus sē dolōrī dedit. 15 Aurēlia et Cornēlia et omnēs ancillae, scissā veste capillīsque solūtīs, pectora plangēbant. Corpus Titī, togā praetextā opertum, in ātriō in lectō fūnebrī positum est. Circum lectum ardēbant lucernae et candēlae.

Postrīdiē corpus Titī summō honōre ēlātum est. Praecēdēbant tubicinēs. Subsequēbantur in pompā virī taedās tenentēs, mulierēs nēniās cantantēs, 20 propinquī imāginēs maiōrum gerentēs, līctōrēs fascēs ferentēs; postrēmī incēdēbant familiārēs.

Cum in Forum vēnissent, Gāius Cornēlius prōcessit ut frātrem mortuum laudāret. Commemorāvit quālis vir Titus fuisset, quot merita in prīncipem cīvēsque contulisset.

Quō factō, corpus Titī ad sepulcra Viae Flāminiae in pompā lātum est. Ibi rogus exstrūctus erat. In rogum impositum est corpus et super corpus vestēs atque ōrnāmenta. Appropinquāvit Gāius Cornēlius taedam manū tenēns. Quam taedam oculīs āversīs in rogum iniēcit.

Exsequiīs cōnfectīs, Cornēliī trīstēs domum regressī sunt. Multa dē Titō loquēbantur. Commemorābant quam hilaris fuisset, quantum līberōs amāvisset. "Maximē," inquiunt, "nōs omnēs eum dēsīderābimus."

lēvis, -is, -e, smooth
coxa, -ae (f), hipbone
est arcessendus, must be sent for
febris, febris (f), fever
morbus, -ī (m), illness
fūnebris, -is, -e, funeral
familiārēs, familiārium (m pl), close friends
commemorō (1), to mention, comment on, recount

merita cōnferre, to render services (to)
Via Flāminia, a road from Rome leading through the Campus Martius and north to Ariminum on the Adriatic Sea
hilaris, -is, -e, cheerful

hortor, hortārī (), hortātus sum, to encourage, urge
frangō, frangere (3), frēgī, frāctum, to break
ingravēscō, ingravēscere (3), to grow worse
exstruō, exstruere (3), exstrūxī, exstrūctum, to build

## Exercise 53a

*Using story 53 as a guide, give the Latin for:*

1. In summer the heat is so great in the city that everyone wishes to return to the farmhouse.
2. Therefore Gaius Cornelius intends to prepare everything so that they may return to Baiae.
3. Cornelius as usual goes to the baths with his brother Titus.
4. "Watch out! The pavement is so smooth and slippery that you may fall."
5. Suddenly he urges slaves to bring a litter into the house.
6. Titus is now so weak that he can scarcely speak.
7. In the Forum Cornelius recounts how many services Titus rendered to the emperor and the citizens.
8. After the funeral the Cornelii recount how cheerful Titus was, how much he loved the children.

Statue of a man carrying funeral
busts of his ancestors

# An Account
# of Roman Funerals

The following account of Roman funerals was given by Polybius, a historian of the second century B.C.

Whenever an important citizen dies, they have a funeral procession, in which his body is carried into the Forum to the Rostra, sometimes upright so as to be conspicuous, less often in a reclining position. There, surrounded by the whole populace, a grown-up son mounts the rostrum and delivers a speech about the virtues and achievements of the deceased. As a result, the majority of those present are so deeply affected that the loss seems not merely a private one affecting the relatives only, but a public loss involving everyone.

Then, after he is buried with the usual ceremonies, they place a likeness of the deceased in a part of the house where everyone can readily see it, and they enclose it in a little wooden shrine. This likeness is a mask which reproduces with remarkable faithfulness the features and complexion of the deceased.

On the death of any important member of the family, these likenesses are taken to the Forum, worn by those members of the family who seem most nearly to resemble them in height and bearing. These people wear togas with a purple border if the deceased was a consul or praetor, totally purple if he was a censor, and edged with gold if he had celebrated a triumph or had any similar distinction. They all ride in chariots preceded by the **fascēs**, axes, and other emblems appropriate to the official positions held by each during his life; and when they arrive at the Rostra, they all sit down in their proper order on chairs of ivory.

It would be difficult to imagine a sight more inspiring to an ambitious young man than to see the likenesses of men who had once been famous for their goodness all together and as if alive and breathing. What sight could be finer than this?

Besides, the person who makes the speech over the deceased, after speaking of the deceased himself, goes on to tell of the successful exploits of the other ancestors whose likenesses are present, beginning from the earliest. In this way, by constantly refreshing their memories about the fame of good men, the glory of those who performed noble deeds becomes immortal, and the fame of those who served their country well is passed on to future generations.

Polybius, *Histories* VI. 3

# Epitaphs

Roman tombs ranged from the very simple to the extremely elaborate. There was usually an inscription on the tomb and many of these have survived. The following five are in some cases slightly modified. The fifth preserves the original spellings of the inscription.

(i)
Pontia Prīma hīc est sita. Nōlī violāre!

situs, -a, -um, buried                              violō (1), to do harm

(ii)
Est hoc monumentum Marcī Vergileī Eurysacis pistōris redemptōris appāritōris.

pistor, pistōris (*m*), baker
redemptor, redemptōris (*m*), contractor
appāritor, appāritōris (*m*), public servant

(iii)
Carfinia Marcī līberta vīxit annōs XX. Iūcunda suīs, grātissima amīcīs, omnibus officiōsa fuit.

iūcundus, -a, -um, delightful
grātus, -a, -um, loved by, pleasing to
officiōsus, -a, -um, ready to serve, obliging

Funeral relief of Aurelius Hermia and his wife, a freedwoman.

108

## (iv)

Dīs Mānibus. C. Tullius Hesper āram fēcit sibi ubi ossa sua coniciantur. Quae sī quis violāverit aut inde exēmerit, optō eī ut cum dolōre corporis longō tempore vīvat et, cum mortuus fuerit, īnferī eum nōn recipiant.

**Dīs Mānibus,** to the spirits of the dead
**optō** (1), to wish

    **eximō, eximere** (3), **exēmī, exēmptum,** to remove

## (v)

Hospes, quod dcicō paullum est; astā ac pellege.
Heic est sepulcrum hau pulcrum pulcrai fēminae:
nōmen parentēs nōminārunt Claudiam.
Suom mareitum corde deilēxit souō:
gnātōs duōs creāvit: hōrunc alterum           5
in terrā linquit, alium sub terrā locat.
Sermōne lepidō, tum autem incessū commodō,
domum servāvit. Lānam fēcit. Dīxī. Abei.

**cor, cordis** (*n*), heart
**(g)nātus, -ī** (*m*), son
**sermō, sermōnis** (*m*), conversation, talk

**lepidus, -a, -um,** charming
**incessus, -ūs** (*m*), bearing, walk(ing)
**commodus, -a, -um,** pleasant

    **dīligō (dei-), dīligere** (3), **dīlēxī, dīlēctum,** to love
    **linquō, linquere** (3), **līquī,** to leave

# *Funeral Customs*

## Two Laws Concerning Burial

Law of the XII Tables:

Hominem mortuum in urbe nē sepelītō nēve ūritō.
*No one must bury or burn a dead man in the city.*

Law of the Colony of Julia Genetiva in Spain:

No person shall bring a dead person or bury one or burn one inside the boundaries of the town or the area marked around by the plough or build a monument to a dead person there. Any person breaking this law shall be fined 5,000 sesterces.

# The Crier's Words at a Ceremonial Funeral

———*, a citizen, has died; it is now time for those for whom it is convenient to go to his funeral. ———* is being brought from his house for burial.

(*name of deceased)

## Building Up the Meaning VIII

### Translating ut

You have now met the following uses of ut:

A. With an indicative verb, e.g.:

Semper, ut vidēs, negōtiōsus sum.
*As you see, I am always busy.*

Sextus, ut lupum cōnspexit, arborem ascendit.
*When Sextus caught sight of the wolf, he climbed the tree.*

Clue: ut followed by an indicative verb should be translated by "as" or "when."

B. With a subjunctive verb:

1. To indicate *result*, e.g.:

Tam īnfirmus erat ut vix loquī posset.
*He was so weak that he could scarcely speak.*

Clue: a word like tam, tantus, tālis, tot, or adeō suggests that the translation will be "so . . . that."

2. In an *indirect command*, e.g.:

Cornēlius servōs hortābātur ut lectīcam maximā cum cūrā ferrent.
*Cornelius was urging the slaves to carry the litter very carefully.*

Ōrāvērunt ut ūna uxor duōs virōs habēret.
*They begged that one wife should have two husbands.*

Clue: the ut clause depends on a verb of "telling," "ordering," "begging," "urging," "persuading," etc.

110

3. To indicate *purpose*, e.g.:

Gāius Cornēlius prōcessit ut frātrem mortuum laudāret.
*Gaius Cornelius came forward to praise his dead brother.*

This type of **ut** clause is very common after verbs which suggest that someone went somewhere *to do* something.

## Exercise 53b

*What would you expect* **ut** *to mean in the following sentences?*

1. Cornēlius Cornēliae praecēpit ut . . . .
2. Tantus erat terror in urbe ut . . . .
3. Marcus, ut vidēs, est filius senātōris.
4. Iānitor servīs impcrāvit ut . . . .
5. In urbem dēscendit ut . . . .
6. Aurēlia tam īrāta erat ut . . . .
7. Puerī ut vōcem patris audīvērunt . . . .
8. Senātōrēs nūntium mīsērunt ut . . . .
9. Sextus adeō ēsuriēbat ut . . . .
10. Eucleidēs, ut nōs omnēs scīmus, est ērudītissimus.

## Exercise 53c

*Read aloud and translate each of the following sentences, and then identify each use of* **ut** *and explain the sequence of tenses for all subjunctives:*

1. Magister Sextō imperāvit ut domum statim redīret.
2. Sextus, ut imperāverat eius magister, domum statim rediit.
3. Marcus nōs rogat ut sēcum ad theātrum eāmus.
4. Puerī, ut Titum vīdērunt, eum laetī salūtāvērunt.
5. Amīcō meō persuāsī ut mēcum ad Circum venīret.
6. Eucleidēs, ut vōs omnēs scītis, fābulās puerīs semper nārrāre vult.
7. Servō imperāvī ut pānem emeret.
8. Cornēliī ex urbe Rōmā discēdent ut Bāiās redeant.
9. In balneīs paulīsper morābantur ut cum amīcīs colloquerentur.
10. Eucleidēs, "Ut fēriātī estis," inquit, "vōs moneō ut multōs librōs legātis."

## At a Brother's Grave

The poet Catullus was very devoted to his brother who died far away from home in Asia Minor. Catullus visited the tomb and wrote these lines. He does not tell us what he sees for his brother beyond the grave. He merely seeks comfort from the age-old Roman ritual for the dead.

Multās per gentēs et multa per aequora vectus,
    adveniō hās miserās, frāter, ad īnferiās,
ut tē postrēmō dōnārem mūnere mortis
    et mūtam nēquīquam alloquerer cinerem.
Quandoquidem fortūna mihī tētē abstulit ipsum,    5
    heu miser indignē frāter adēmpte mihi,
nunc tamen intereā haec, priscō quae mōre parentum
    trādita sunt trīstī mūnere ad īnferiās,
accipe frāternō multum mānantia flētū,
    atque in perpetuum, frāter, avē atque valē!    10

gentēs, peoples
aequora, seas
vectus, having been carried, having traveled
īnferiae, -ārum (*f pl*), offerings and rites in honor of the dead at the tomb
dōnō (1), to present
mūnus, mūneris (*n*), gift, service
mūtus, -a, -um, silent
nēquīquam, in vain
cinis, cineris (*m*), ashes, dust (of the cremated body)
5 quandoquidem, since
tētē = emphatic tē
indignē, undeservedly
priscus, -a, -um, of olden times, ancient
   priscō . . . mōre, by the ancient custom
trīstī mūnere, through (my) sad service (to the dead)
multum, abundantly
mānantia flētū, flowing with tears
10 in perpetuum, forever

# Versiculī: *"Martial Laughs over Illness and Death,"* pages 123–124.

# Review XII

## Exercise XIIa

*Read aloud and translate. Identify each subordinate clause and tell what type it is. Identify the tense and voice of each subjunctive and say whether it is in primary or secondary sequence.*

1. Cornēlia tam dēfessa erat ut paene lacrimāret.
2. Cornēlius Sextum monuit nē iterum in lūdō tam ignāvus esset.
3. Iānitor eīs imperābat ut statim abīrent.
4. Matrōnae ad senātum lacrimantēs vēnērunt ut senātōribus persuādērent.
5. Servus in aquam dēsiluit nē fūr effugeret.
6. Eucleidēs puerīs persuāsit ut vēra dīcerent.
7. Cornēlia nescit cūr pater sē adesse in tablīnō iusserit.
8. Puerōs rogāvit ut extrā tablīnum manērent.
9. Gāius puerōs monet nē ē cubiculō exeant.
10. Ancillae in cubiculum festīnāvērunt ut crīnēs Aurēliae cūrārent.
11. Servus arborem ascendit nē caperētur.
12. Ille liber est tālis ut Aurēlia eum legere nōlit.
13. Tanta multitūdō ad domum convenit ut omnibus intrāre nōn liceat.
14. Tam longum erat iter ut Valerius dēfessus esset.
15. Sextum Marcus rogāvit ut sibi nārrāret quid in amphitheātrō āctum esset.
16. Prīnceps imperāvit nē servus occīderētur.
17. Cīvēs in palaestram excēdēbant ut sē exercērent.
18. Aenēās ad Hesperiam nāvigābat ut urbem novam conderet.
19. Servus casam pīrātārum celerrimē petīvit ut dominum servāret.
20. Grammaticus ferulam rapit ut Sextum verberet.
21. Praedōnēs tam celeriter cucurrērunt ut Eucleidem facile cōnsequerentur.
22. Tot et tanta erant incendia ut cīvēs aedificia servāre nōn possent.
23. Tanta tempestās coorta est ut mīlitēs nāvem cōnscendere vix possent.
24. Eucleidēs Sextō imperat nē pūpam laedat.
25. Cornēlia mātrem rogāvit ut servum arcesseret ut cum eō loquerētur.

114

## Exercise XIIb

*Read the following passage and answer the questions below in English:*

At a dinner party given by Trimalchio, one of his guests, Niceros, tells the strange story of a werewolf.

Cum adhūc servus essem, in urbe Brundisiō habitābāmus. Ibi amāre coepī Melissam, mulierem pulcherrimam quae in vīllā rūsticā habitābat. Forte dominus meus Capuam discesserat. Occāsiōne datā, igitur, Melissam vīsitāre cōnstituī, sed sōlus īre nōluī. Itaque amīcō cuidam persuāsī ut mēcum ad quīntum mīliārium venīret. Ille autem erat mīles, homō audācissimus. 5
Nōs mediā nocte profectī sumus. Lūna lūcēbat tamquam merīdiē. Vēnimus inter monumenta. Homō meus coepit ad stēlās īre; sedeō ego cantābundus et stēlās numerō. Deinde, ut respexī ad comitem, ille omnia vestīmenta exūta humī prope viam posuit. Dī immortālēs! Nōlīte mē iocārī putāre! Ille subitō lupus est factus. Mihi anima in nāsō erat; stābam tamquam mortuus. 10
Postquam lupus factus est, ululāre coepit et in silvās fūgit. Ego prīmō nesciēbam ubi essem. Deinde ad stēlās prōcessī ut vestīmenta eius tollerem. Illa autem lapidea facta sunt. Paulīsper stābam immōbilis. Gladium tamen strīnxī et umbrās cecīdī, donec ad vīllam amīcae meae pervēnī. Melissa mea mīrābātur quod tam sērō ambulārem: "Sī ante vēnissēs, nōs adiuvāre potuistī. 15
Lupus enim vīllam intrāvit et omnia pecora tamquam lanius necāvit. Servus tamen noster lanceā collum eius vulnerāvit."
Haec ut audīvī, tam dēfessus eram ut statim obdormīverim. Prīmā lūce fūgī. Postquam vēnī in illum locum in quō lapidea vestīmenta erant facta, nihil invēnī nisi sanguinem. Ut domum vēnī, iacēbat mīles meus in lectō 20 tamquam bōs, et collum illīus medicus cūrābat. Intellēxī illum versipellem esse, nec posteā cum illō pānem esse potuī, nōn sī mē occīdissēs.

---

| | |
|---|---|
| **mīliārium, -ī** (*n*), milestone | **lancea, -ae** (*f*), lance |
| **lūna, -ae** (*f*), moon | **collum, -ī** (*n*), neck |
| **tamquam**, as, just as, just like | **versipellis, versipellis** (*m*), were- |
| **stēla, -ae** (*f*), tombstone | wolf (**vertō**, to change + **pel-** |
| **nāsus, -ī** (*m*), nose | **lis**, skin) |
| **donec**, until | **esse**, to eat |
| **vēnissēs**, you had come | **occīdissēs**, you had killed |
| **pecus, pecoris** (*n*), animal, cattle | |

**caedō, caedere** (3), **cecīdī, caesum,** to strike out at, slash at

1. What were Niceros' feelings for Melissa?
2. What details are we given about her?
3. Why was Niceros able to leave the house to visit her?
4. Who was to be his companion for part of the way?
5. Why did this man seem a suitable companion for the journey?
6. When did they set out?
7. How were they able to see their way in the dark?
8. Using your knowledge of Roman life and customs, indicate what stage in the journey the two men had reached when they came to the tombs.
9. What did Niceros do when they reached the tombs?
10. What strange behavior did he first observe in his companion?
11. Why had Niceros good reason to be scared?
12. What further details does he add about his companion's unnatural behavior?
13. What did Niceros now attempt to do, and why was he prevented from doing so?
14. What steps did he now take to defend himself?
15. Why do you think he "slashed at shadows" on the road?
16. Why was Melissa surprised to see him?
17. What had happened at the farm?
18. On the way home, what did Niceros find at the spot where his companion had deserted him?
19. Describe what he saw when he arrived home.
20. What conclusion did Niceros draw about his former companion, and how did he feel about him now?
21. In what way does the last sentence throw light on the derivation of the English word *companion*?
22. Find the phrase in the passage that would be equivalent to the English expression "My heart was in my mouth."

## Exercise XIIc

*In the passage in Exercise XIIb, locate in sequence all clauses of the following types:*

1. Circumstantial **cum**.
2. Ablative absolute.
3. Indirect command.
4. Ut + indicative.
5. Indirect question.
6. Purpose.
7. Result.

# *VERSICULĪ*

## 22 The Thief's Accomplice
### (after Chapter 42)

"Vestīmenta malus quis mē custōde valēbit
  surripere?" Haec semper dīcere, serve, solēs.
Num nescīs furtum quam rārō fīat ab ūnō?
  Somnifer auxilium fert deus ipse suum!

**valēbit**, will be able
**Num . . . ?** Surely . . . not? (introduces a question that expects the answer
  "no"; note the implied double negative in the sentence)
**furtum, -ī** (*n*), theft
**fīat**, is committed
**somnifer, somnifera, somniferum**, sleep-bringing

## 23 A Difference of Opinion
### (after Chapter 43)

Tē iuvenīlis amor, iam tē, Cornēlia, sanguis
  dēlectat causā sparsus amōris humī.
Vēmenter cum tē dissentit Sextus. "Amōris
  quis causā sānus caeditur," inquit, "homō?"

**iuvenīlis, -is, -e**, youthful    **causā** (+ *gen.*), for the sake of

  **spargō, spargere** (3), **sparsī, sparsum,** to sprinkle
  **dissentiō, dissentīre** (4), **dissēnsī, dissēnsum,** to disagree
  **caedō, caedere** (3), **cecīdī, caesum,** to kill (*here passive in reflexive sense*,
    to kill oneself)

117

## 24   Sextus Reproved
### (after Chapter 44)

Dīcimus haec omnēs, "Annōs tot, pessime, nātō
pūpa puellāris nūlla ferenda tibi."

   annōs tot . . . nātō, so many years old
   ferenda (est) tibi, ought to be carried away by you

## 25   Hermes the Gladiator
### (after Chapter 46)

The poet Martial, whose epigrams you have already met, found much to write about
in the contests taking place in the amphitheater. In the following poem he praises
the gladiator Hermes, who excelled in no fewer than three fighting roles: as a **vēles**
lightly armed with a spear, as a **rētiārius** with net and trident, and as a **Samnīs**
heavily armed and with visored helmet. This explains why he is called **ter ūnus** in
the last line. The meter is hendecasyllabic.

Hermēs Martia saeculī voluptās,
Hermēs omnibus ērudītus armīs,
Hermēs et gladiātor et magister,
Hermēs turba suī tremorque lūdī,
Hermēs quem timet Hēlius, sed ūnum,   5
Hermēs cui cadit Advolāns, sed ūnī,
Hermēs vincere nec ferīre doctus,
Hermēs suppositīcius sibi ipse,
Hermēs dīvitiae locāriōrum,
Hermēs cūra laborque lūdiārum,                10
Hermēs belligerā superbus hastā,
Hermēs aequoreō mināx tridente,
Hermēs casside languidā timendus,
Hermēs glōria Martis ūniversī,
Hermēs omnia sōlus, et ter ūnus.            15

—Martial, *Epigrams* V.24

**Hermēs:** the gladiator has adopted the name of the god.

**Martius, -a, -um,** connected with Mars, the god of war and combat

**saeculum, -ī** (*n*), age, era

**voluptās, voluptātis** (*f*), pleasure, delight

**turba, -ae** (*f*), crowd, (here) confusion

**suī . . . lūdī,** of his school (of gladiators)

5 **Hēlius,** "Sun," and **Advolāns,** literally, "Flying to (the Attack)," were two distinguished gladiators.

**sed ūnum,** but the only one

**feriō, ferīre** (4), to strike, kill

**suppositīcius sibi ipse,** himself his only substitute

**dīvitiae, -ārum** (*f pl*), wealth, riches

**locārius, -ī** (*m*), a person who buys up seats (**loca**) in the amphitheater and then sells them for as high a price as he can get, a scalper

10 **cūra, -ae** (*f*), care, (here) the favorite

**labor lūdiārum,** the heart-throb of the female fans

**belliger, belligera, belligerum,** warlike (cf. the phrase **bellum gerere,** to wage war)

**hasta, -ae** (*f*), spear

**aequoreō . . . tridente,** with his sea trident (cf. **aequor, aequoris,** *n*, the sea)

**mināx, minācis,** menacing

**cassis, cassidis** (*f*), a plumed metal helmet

**languidus, -a, -um,** drooping (here perhaps describing the crest of the helmet drooping down over his eyes)

**Martis ūniversī,** of every kind of combat

15 **ter,** three times

119

# 26  Another Example of Caesar's Leniency (after Chapter 47)

In this epigram of Martial we find the Emperor refusing to decide the fate of two gladiators until one or the other makes the formal sign of surrender—by raising a hand and lowering his shield (**ad digitum levātum pōnere parmam**). He awards them trophies (**lancēs**) in abundance as the fight proceeds, and on their simultaneous surrender he awards to both an honorable discharge from the arena.

Cum traheret Priscus, traheret certāmina Vērus,
    esset et aequālis Mars utriusque diū,
missiō saepe virīs magnō clāmōre petīta est;
    sed Caesar lēgī pāruit ipse suae:
lēx erat ad digitum positā concurrere parmā:    5
    quod licuit, lancēs dōnaque saepe dedit.
Inventus tamen est fīnis discrīminis aequī:
    pugnāvēre parēs, succubuēre parēs.
Mīsit utrīque rudēs et palmās Caesar utrīque:
    hoc pretium virtūs ingeniōsa tulit.    10
Contigit hoc nūllō nisi tē sub prīncipe, Caesar:
    cum duo pugnārent, victor uterque fuit.

*—De spectaculis* XXIX

**traheret . . . certāmina,** was drawing out the contest
**aequālis, -is, -e,** equal
**utriusque,** *gen.* of **uterque**
**missiō, missiōnis** (*f*), release
**lēx, lēgis** (*f*), law
5 **concurrere,** (here) to fight
**parma, -ae** (*f*), a small, round shield
**quod licuit,** as the rules allowed
**lanx, lancis** (*f*), a metal dish, (here) a trophy
**discrīmen, discrīminis** (*n*), decision, test, combat
**aequus, -a, -um,** equal
**pugnāvēre = pugnāvērunt**
**succumbō, succumbere** (3), **succūbuī, succūbitum,** to give up, collapse
**utrīque,** *dat.* of **uterque**
**rudis, rudis** (*f*), a wooden sword given to a successful gladiator on his final discharge
10 **pretium, -ī,** (*n*), (here) reward
**virtūs, virtūtis** (*f*), courage
**ingeniōsus, -a, -um,** talented
**contingō, contingere** (3), **contigī, contactum,** to touch, (here) to happen
**nisi,** (here) except

# 27   Androcles' True Bravery
## (after Chapter 48)

"Hoc volumus magnō cognōscere in Amphitheātrō—
   fortis quam sit homō, bēstia quamque ferōx.
Mānsuētum nēmō māvult spectāre leōnem
   lambere, quā vescī dēbuit ille, manum!"
Tālia cōniciō sentīre, ō Caesar, inānēs,                              5
   parcente et cēnae tē simul atque ferae;
nec meminisse queunt audācia quanta fuisset
   illīus, nūllō cōnspiciente, virī;
quī laesum, gemitū resonante per antra, leōnem—
   fortiter (ā!) mītis—mulsit, opemque tulit!          10

   **sit,** present subjunctive of the verb **esse**, in an indirect question, "how brave a
        man is"
   5 **inānis, -is, -e,** empty, foolish
        **inānēs, -ium** (*m pl*), foolish folk
      **simul atque,** at the same time as
      **nec meminisse queunt,** nor can they remember
      **gemitus, -ūs** (*m*), groaning
      **antrum, -ī** (*n*), cave (often used in the plural of a single cave)
   10 **ā!,** exclamation
      **mulceō, mulcēre** (2), **mulsī,** to soothe
      **ops, opis** (*f*), help

# 28   Nucēs Relinquere
## (middle of Chapter 50)

Nōn modo, Marce, togam, iuvenis formōse, relinquēs
   praetextam, multīs testibus, ante Larēs.
Praecipit ipse pater, sēcum ut, quodcunque virīlēs
   annōs nōn deceat, bulla sacrāta trahat.
"Pār!"-ne "impār!" clāmāre iuvat? Digitīsque micāre?  5
   Cūnctās illa nucēs abstulit ūna diēs!

formōsus, -a, -um, handsome
testis, testis (*m*), witness
   multīs testibus, before many witnesses
quodcunque, whatsoever
decet, decēre (2), decuit, is right or fitting for, appropriate to (used with accusative)
sacrō (1), to consecrate, dedicate
trahat: (here) should take (along with it)
5  iuvō (1), to please, delight. (Supply tē as direct object.)


# 29  Bridal Hymn
## (middle of Chapter 52)

This is part of a longer poem by Catullus. It is meant to be sung as the bride is accompanied on the evening of her wedding from her father's house to her new home. The bride's name on this occasion is Aurunculeia. In the first two stanzas she is told to dry her tears. After all, she is very beautiful! The meter is glyconic.

Flēre dēsine! Nōn tibi, Aurunculeia, perīculum est
nē qua fēmina pulchrior
clārum ab Ōceanō diem
        vīderit venientem.        5

Tālis in variō solet
dīvitis dominī hortulō
stāre flōs hyacinthinus.
Sed morāris! Abit diēs!
        Prōdeās, nova nūpta!        10

At last the chorus see the bright veil of the bride appearing. It is time for the hymn and the distribution of nuts.

Tollite, ō puerī, facēs!
Flammeum videō venīre.
Īte, concinite in modum
"Iō Hymēn Hymenaee iō,
        iō Hymēn Hymenaee!"        15

Da nucēs puerīs, iners
concubīne: satis diū
lūsistī nucibus. Lubet
iam servīre Talassiō.
   Concubīne, nucēs da!   20

—Catullus LXI.86–95, 121–125, and 131–135

    fleō, flēre (2), flēvī, flētum, to weep, cry
    dēsinō, dēsinere (3), dēsiī, dēsitum, to stop
    nōn . . . perīculum est nē qua, there is no danger that any
    clārus, -a, -um, bright
  6 varius, -a, -um, many-hued
    hortulus, -ī (m), diminutive of hortus
10 prōdeō, prōdīre (irreg.), prōdiī, prōditum, to come forth. The present sub-
      junctive prōdeās expresses a command.
    fax, facis (f), wedding-torch
    concinō, concinere (3), concinuī, to sing together (cf. cantō, 1, to sing)
    modus, -ī (m), (here) rhythmic, harmonious manner
    Iō! a ritual exclamation. (The i is consonantal, and the word is pronounced as
      one syllable.)
    Hymēn (m), an exclamation chanted at weddings; later thought of as the god
      of weddings
    Hymenaeus, -ī (m), another form of Hymēn (see above)
16 Da nucēs puerīs . . . : during the procession the bridegroom threw nuts to the
      children at the side of the road.
    iners, inertis, lazy
    concubīnus, -ī (m), bridegroom
    lubet = libet, libēre (2), libuit or libitum est, it is pleasing (to someone, dat.)
      to do something (infin.). Supply tibi.
    serviō (4) (+ dat.), to serve
    Talassius, -ī (m), god of marriage

# 30  Martial Laughs over Illness and Death
## (after Chapter 53)

    In these epigrams, Martial sees the funny side of illness and death. The first two
poems make observations on the medical profession of 1,900 years ago.

## (i) Symmachus Takes the Students Around

Languēbam: sed tū comitātus prōtinus ad mē
vēnistī centum, Symmache, discipulīs.
Centum mē tetigēre manūs aquilōne gelātae;
nōn habuī febrem, Symmache: nunc habeō.

—V.9

## (ii) Hermocrates Who Cures All

Lōtus nōbīscum est, hilaris cēnāvit, et īdem
inventus māne est mortuus Andragorās.
Tam subitae mortis causam, Faustīne, requīris?
In somnīs medicum vīderat Hermocratem!

—VI.53

## (iii) Epitaph with a Difference!

Sit tibi terra levis, mollīque tegāris harēnā
nē tua nōn possint ēruere ossa canēs!

—IX.29.11–12

**langueō, languēre** (2), to be ill in bed
**comitātus, -a, -um,** accompanied
**prōtinus,** immediately
**tangō, tangere** (3), **tetigī, tactum,** to touch. **tetigēre** = **tetigērunt**
**aquilōne gelātae,** chilled by the north wind
**febris, febris** ( *f* ), fever

**lōtus** = **lavātus,** one form of the perfect passive participle of **lavō,** to wash.
  **lōtus est,** he bathed
**subitus, -a, -um,** sudden
**requīrō, requīrere** (3), **requīsīvī, requīsītum,** to ask, inquire

**sit,** may (it) be
**levis, -is, -e,** light
**mollis, -is, -e,** soft
**tegāris,** may you be covered
**harēna, -ae** ( *f* ), sand
**nē . . . nōn possint,** so that (they) may not be unable
**ēruo, ēruere** (3), **ēruī, ērutum,** to dig up

# FORMS

## I. Nouns

| Number / Case | 1st Declension<br>Fem. | 2nd Declension<br>Masc. | 2nd Declension<br>Masc. | 2nd Declension<br>Neut. | 3rd Declension<br>Masc. | 3rd Declension<br>Fem. | 3rd Declension<br>Neut. | 4th Declension<br>Fem. | 4th Declension<br>Neut. | 5th Declension<br>Masc. |
|---|---|---|---|---|---|---|---|---|---|---|
| **Singular** | | | | | | | | | | |
| Nom. | puélla | sérvus | púer | báculum | páter | vōx | nōmen | mánus | génū | diḗs |
| Gen. | puéllae | sérvī | púerī | báculī | pátris | vōcis | nōminis | mánūs | génūs | diḗī |
| Dat. | puéllae | sérvō | púerō | báculō | pátrī | vōcī | nōminī | mánuī | génū | diḗī |
| Acc. | puéllam | sérvum | púerum | báculum | pátrem | vōcem | nōmen | mánum | génū | diem |
| Abl. | puéllā | sérvō | púerō | báculō | pátre | vōce | nōmine | mánū | génū | diḗ |
| **Plural** | | | | | | | | | | |
| Nom. | puéllae | sérvī | púerī | bácula | pátrēs | vōcēs | nōmina | mánūs | génua | diḗs |
| Gen. | puellárum | servốrum | puerốrum | baculốrum | pátrum | vōcum | nōminum | mánuum | génuum | diḗrum |
| Dat. | puéllīs | sérvīs | púerīs | báculīs | pátribus | vōcibus | nōminibus | mánibus | génibus | diḗbus |
| Acc. | puéllās | sérvōs | púerōs | bácula | pátrēs | vōcēs | nōmina | mánūs | génua | diḗs |
| Abl. | puéllīs | sérvīs | púerīs | báculīs | pátribus | vōcibus | nōminibus | mánibus | génibus | diḗbus |

## II. Adjectives

| Number Case | 1st and 2nd Declension | | | 3rd Declension | | |
|---|---|---|---|---|---|---|
| | *Masc.* | *Fem.* | *Neut.* | *Masc.* | *Fem.* | *Neut.* |
| *Singular* | | | | | | |
| Nominative | mágnus | mágna | mágnum | ómnis | ómnis | ómne |
| Genitive | mágnī | mágnae | mágnī | ómnis | ómnis | ómnis |
| Dative | mágnō | mágnae | mágnō | ómnī | ómnī | ómnī |
| Accusative | mágnum | mágnam | mágnum | ómnem | ómnem | ómne |
| Ablative | mágnō | mágnā | mágnō | ómnī | ómnī | ómnī |
| *Plural* | | | | | | |
| Nominative | mágnī | mágnae | mágna | ómnēs | ómnēs | ómnia |
| Genitive | magnṓrum | magnárum | magnṓrum | ómnium | ómnium | ómnium |
| Dative | mágnīs | mágnīs | mágnīs | ómnibus | ómnibus | ómnibus |
| Accusative | mágnōs | mágnās | mágna | ómnēs | ómnēs | ómnia |
| Ablative | mágnīs | mágnīs | mágnīs | ómnibus | ómnibus | ómnibus |

# III. Numerical Adjectives or Numbers

| Case | Masc. | Fem. | Neut. |
|---|---|---|---|
| Nom. | trēs | trēs | tría |
| Gen. | tríum | tríum | tríum |
| Dat. | tríbus | tríbus | tríbus |
| Acc. | trēs | trēs | tría |
| Abl. | tríbus | tríbus | tríbus |

| Case | Masc. | Fem. | Neut. |
|---|---|---|---|
| Nom. | dúo | dúae | dúo |
| Gen. | duórum | duárum | duórum |
| Dat. | duóbus | duábus | duóbus |
| Acc. | dúōs | dúās | dúo |
| Abl. | duóbus | duábus | duóbus |

| Case | Masc. | Fem. | Neut. |
|---|---|---|---|
| Nom. | únus | úna | únum |
| Gen. | úníus | úníus | úníus |
| Dat. | únī | únī | únī |
| Acc. | únum | únam | únum |
| Abl. | únō | únā | únō |

## Cardinal

| | | |
|---|---|---|
| I | ūnus, -a, -um, | one |
| II | duo, -ae, -o, | two |
| III | trēs, trēs, tria, | three |
| IV | quattuor, | four |
| V | quīnque, | five |
| VI | sex, | six |
| VII | septem, | seven |
| VIII | octō, | eight |
| IX | novem, | nine |
| X | decem, | ten |
| XI | ūndecim, | eleven |
| XII | duodecim, | twelve |
| XX | vīgintī, | twenty |
| L | quīnquāgintā, | fifty |
| C | centum, | a hundred |
| D | quīngentī, -ae, -a, | five hundred |
| M | mīlle, | a thousand |

## Ordinal

prīmus, -a, -um, first
secundus, -a, -um, second
tertius, -a, -um, third
quārtus, -a, -um
quīntus, -a, -um
sextus, -a, -um
septimus, -a, -um
octāvus, -a, -um
nōnus, -a, -um
decimus, -a, -um
ūndecimus, -a, -um
duodecimus, -a, -um
vīcēsimus, -a, -um
quīnquāgēsimus, -a, -um
centēsimus, -a, -um
quīngentēsimus, -a, -um
mīllēsimus, -a, -um

N.B. The cardinal numbers from **quattuor** to **centum** do not change their form to indicate case and gender.

## IV. Comparative Adjectives

| Number Case | Masculine | Feminine | Neuter |
|---|---|---|---|
| **Singular** | | | |
| Nom. | púlchrior | púlchrior | púlchrius |
| Gen. | pulchrióris | pulchrióris | pulchrióris |
| Dat. | pulchriórī | pulchriórī | pulchriórī |
| Acc. | pulchriórem | pulchriórem | púlchrius |
| Abl. | pulchrióre | pulchrióre | pulchrióre |
| **Plural** | | | |
| Nom. | pulchriórēs | pulchriórēs | pulchrióra |
| Gen. | pulchriórum | pulchriórum | pulchriórum |
| Dat. | pulchrióribus | pulchrióribus | pulchrióribus |
| Acc. | pulchriórēs | pulchriórēs | pulchrióra |
| Abl. | pulchrióribus | pulchrióribus | pulchrióribus |

Adjectives have *positive, comparative,* and *superlative* forms. You can usually recognize the comparative by the letters **-ior(-)** and the superlative by **-issimus, -errimus,** or **-illimus,** e.g.:

| | | |
|---|---|---|
| ignāvus, *lazy* | ignāvior | ignāvissimus, -a, -um |
| pulcher, *beautiful* | pulchrior | pulcherrimus, -a, -um |
| facilis, *easy* | facilior | facillimus, -a, -um |

Some adjectives are irregular in the comparative and superlative, e.g.:

| | | |
|---|---|---|
| bonus, *good* | melior, *better* | optimus, *best* |
| malus, *bad* | peior, *worse* | pessimus, *worst* |
| magnus, *big* | maior, *bigger* | maximus, *biggest* |
| parvus, *small* | minor, *smaller* | minimus, *smallest* |
| multus, *much* | plūs, *more* | plūrimus, *most, very much* |
| multī, *many* | plūrēs, *more* | plūrimī, *most, very many* |

# V. Present Active Participles

| Number<br>Case | Masculine | Feminine | Neuter |
|---|---|---|---|
| **Singular** | | | |
| Nom. | párāns | párāns | párāns |
| Gen. | parántis | parántis | parántis |
| Dat. | parántī | parántī | parántī |
| Acc. | parántem | parántem | párāns |
| Abl. | paránte | paránte | paránte |
| **Plural** | | | |
| Nom. | parántēs | parántēs | parántia |
| Gen. | parántium | parántium | parántium |
| Dat. | parántibus | parántibus | parántibus |
| Acc. | parántēs | parántēs | parántia |
| Abl. | parántibus | parántibus | parántibus |

For all tenses and forms of participles, see Chapter 43, pages 24–5.

# VI. Demonstrative Adjectives and Pronouns

| Number<br>Case | Masc. | Fem. | Neut. | Masc. | Fem. | Neut. |
|---|---|---|---|---|---|---|
| **Singular** | | | | | | |
| Nom. | hic | haec | hoc | ílle | ílla | íllud |
| Gen. | húius | húius | húius | illíus | illíus | illíus |
| Dat. | húic | húic | húic | íllī | íllī | íllī |
| Acc. | hunc | hanc | hoc | íllum | íllam | íllud |
| Abl. | hōc | hāc | hōc | íllō | íllā | íllō |
| **Plural** | | | | | | |
| Nom. | hī | hae | haec | íllī | íllae | ílla |
| Gen. | hórum | hárum | hórum | illórum | illárum | illórum |
| Dat. | hīs | hīs | hīs | íllīs | íllīs | íllīs |
| Acc. | hōs | hās | haec | íllōs | íllās | ílla |
| Abl. | hīs | hīs | hīs | íllīs | íllīs | íllīs |

| Number<br>Case | Masc. | Fem. | Neut. | Masc. | Fem. | Neut. |
|---|---|---|---|---|---|---|
| **Singular** | | | | | | |
| Nom. | is | éa | id | ídem | éadem | ídem |
| Gen. | éius | éius | éius | eiúsdem | eiúsdem | eiúsdem |
| Dat. | éī | éī | éī | eídem | eídem | eídem |
| Acc. | éum | éam | id | eúndem | eándem | ídem |
| Abl. | éō | éā | éō | eódem | eádem | eódem |
| **Plural** | | | | | | |
| Nom. | éī | éae | éa | eídem | eaédem | éadem |
| Gen. | eórum | eárum | eórum | eōrúndem | eārúndem | eōrúndem |
| Dat. | éīs | éīs | éīs | eísdem | eísdem | eísdem |
| Acc. | éōs | éās | éa | eósdem | eásdem | éadem |
| Abl. | éīs | éīs | éīs | eísdem | eísdem | eísdem |

# VII. Indefinite Adjective

| Number Case | Masc. | Fem. | Neut. |
|---|---|---|---|
| **Singular** | | | |
| Nom. | quídam | quaédam | quóddam |
| Gen. | cuiúsdam | cuiúsdam | cuiúsdam |
| Dat. | cúidam | cúidam | cúidam |
| Acc. | quéndam | quándam | quóddam |
| Abl. | quódam | quádam | quódam |
| **Plural** | | | |
| Nom. | quídam | quaédam | quaédam |
| Gen. | quōrúndam | quārúndam | quōrúndam |
| Dat. | quibúsdam | quibúsdam | quibúsdam |
| Acc. | quósdam | quásdam | quaédam |
| Abl. | quibúsdam | quibúsdam | quibúsdam |

# VIII. Intensive Adjective

| Number Case | Masc. | Fem. | Neut. |
|---|---|---|---|
| **Singular** | | | |
| Nom. | ípse | ípsa | ípsum |
| Gen. | ipsíus | ipsíus | ipsíus |
| Dat. | ípsī | ípsī | ípsī |
| Acc. | ípsum | ípsam | ípsum |
| Abl. | ípsō | ípsā | ípsō |
| **Plural** | | | |
| Nom. | ípsī | ípsae | ípsa |
| Gen. | ipsórum | ipsárum | ipsórum |
| Dat. | ípsīs | ípsīs | ípsīs |
| Acc. | ípsōs | ípsās | ípsa |
| Abl. | ípsīs | ípsīs | ípsīs |

# IX. Adverbs

Latin adverbs may be formed from adjectives of the 1st and 2nd declensions by adding *-ē* to the base of the adjective, e.g., **strēnuē**, "strenuously," from **strēnuus, -a, -um.** To form an adverb from a 3rd declension adjective, add *-iter* to the base of the adjective or *-ter* to bases ending in **-nt-**, e.g., **breviter,** "briefly," from **brevis, -is, -e,** and **prūdenter,** "wisely," from **prūdēns, prūdentis.**

The comparative ends in *-ius.*
The superlative ends in *-issimē, -errimē,* or *-illimē,* e.g.:

| | | |
|---|---|---|
| lentē, *slowly* | lentius | lentissimē |
| fēlīciter, *luckily* | fēlīcius | fēlīcissimē |
| dīligenter, *carefully* | dīligentius | dīligentissimē |
| celeriter, *quickly* | celerius | celerrimē |
| facile, *easily* | facilius | facillimē |

Some adverbs are irregular:

| | | |
|---|---|---|
| bene, *well* | melius, *better* | optimē, *best* |
| male, *badly* | peius, *worse* | pessimē, *worst* |
| magnopere, *greatly* | magis, *more* | maximē, *most* |
| paulum, *little* | minus, *less* | minimē, *least* |
| multum, *much* | plūs, *more* | plūrimum, *most* |

Some adverbs are not formed from adjectives:

| | | |
|---|---|---|
| diū, *for a long time* | diūtius | diūtissimē |
| saepe, *often* | saepius | saepissimē |
| sērō, *late* | sērius | sērissimē |

# X. Personal and Demonstrative Pronouns

| | | | Singular | | | | | Plural | | |
|---|---|---|---|---|---|---|---|---|---|---|
| Case | *1st* | *2nd* | *3rd* | | | *1st* | *2nd* | *3rd* | | |
| | | | *Masc.* | *Fem.* | *Neut.* | | | *Masc.* | *Fem.* | *Neut.* |
| Nom. | égo | tū | is | éa | id | nōs | vōs | éī | éae | éa |
| Gen. | | | éius | éius | éius | | | eórum | eárum | eórum |
| Dat. | míhi | tíbi | éī | éī | éī | nóbīs | vóbīs | éīs | éīs | éīs |
| Acc. | mē | tē | éum | éam | id | nōs | vōs | éōs | éās | éa |
| Abl. | mē | tē | éō | éā | éō | nóbīs | vóbīs | éīs | éīs | éīs |

## XI. Reflexive Pronoun

|       | Singular | Plural |
|-------|----------|--------|
| Nom.  | --------- | ------ |
| Gen.  | súī      | súī    |
| Dat.  | síbi     | síbi   |
| Acc.  | sē       | sē     |
| Abl.  | sē       | sē     |

## XII. Relative and Interrogative Pronouns and Adjectives

|       | Singular | | | Plural | | |
|-------|----------|------|-------|--------|-------|-------|
|       | Masc. | Fem. | Neut. | Masc. | Fem. | Neut. |
| Nom.  | quī   | quae  | quod  | quī    | quae  | quae  |
| Gen.  | cúius | cúius | cúius | quórum | quárum | quórum |
| Dat.  | cúi   | cúi   | cúi   | quíbus | quíbus | quíbus |
| Acc.  | quem  | quam  | quod  | quōs   | quās  | quae  |
| Abl.  | quō   | quā   | quō   | quíbus | quíbus | quíbus |

The interrogative pronoun **Quis** . . . ? has the same forms as the relative pronoun except for the nominative masculine singular **Quis** . . . ? and the nominative and accusative neuter singular **Quid** . . . ? In the singular, the feminine has the same forms as the masculine. In the plural, all forms are the same as those of the relative pronoun.

# XIII. Regular Verbs Active: Infinitive, Imperative, Indicative

| | | 1st Conjugation | 2nd Conjugation | 3rd Conjugation | | 4th Conjugation |
|---|---|---|---|---|---|---|
| Present Infinitive | | parā́re | habḗre | míttere | iácere (-iō) | audī́re |
| Imperative | Present — Singular | párā | hábē | mítte | iáce | áudī |
| | Present — Plural | parā́te | habḗte | míttite | iácite | audī́te |
| Present | Singular 1 | párō | hábeō | míttō | iáciō | áudiō |
| | Singular 2 | párās | hábēs | míttis | iácis | áudīs |
| | Singular 3 | párat | hábet | míttit | iácit | áudit |
| | Plural 1 | parā́mus | habḗmus | míttimus | iácimus | audī́mus |
| | Plural 2 | parā́tis | habḗtis | míttitis | iácitis | audī́tis |
| | Plural 3 | párant | hábent | míttunt | iáciunt | áudiunt |
| Imperfect | Singular 1 | parā́bam | habḗbam | mittḗbam | iaciḗbam | audiḗbam |
| | Singular 2 | parā́bās | habḗbās | mittḗbās | iaciḗbās | audiḗbās |
| | Singular 3 | parā́bat | habḗbat | mittḗbat | iaciḗbat | audiḗbat |
| | Plural 1 | parābā́mus | habēbā́mus | mittēbā́mus | iaciēbā́mus | audiēbā́mus |
| | Plural 2 | parābā́tis | habēbā́tis | mittēbā́tis | iaciēbā́tis | audiēbā́tis |
| | Plural 3 | parā́bant | habḗbant | mittḗbant | iaciḗbant | audiḗbant |

# XIII. Regular Verbs Active: Indicative, Infinitive (continued)

| | | | parō | habeō | mittō | iaciō | audiō |
|---|---|---|---|---|---|---|---|
| **Future** | *Singular* | 1 | parábō | habēbō | míttam | iáciam | aúdiam |
| | | 2 | parábis | habēbis | míttēs | iáciēs | aúdiēs |
| | | 3 | parábit | habēbit | míttet | iáciet | aúdiet |
| | *Plural* | 1 | parábimus | habēbimus | mittēmus | iaciēmus | audiēmus |
| | | 2 | parábitis | habēbitis | mittētis | iaciētis | audiētis |
| | | 3 | parábunt | habēbunt | míttent | iácient | aúdient |
| | Perfect Infinitive | | parāvísse | habuísse | mīsísse | iēcísse | audīvísse |
| **Perfect** | *Singular* | 1 | parávī | hábuī | mísī | iēcī | audívī |
| | | 2 | parāvístī | habuístī | mīsístī | iēcístī | audīvístī |
| | | 3 | parávit | hábuit | mísit | iécit | audívit |
| | *Plural* | 1 | parávimus | habúimus | mísimus | iécimus | audívimus |
| | | 2 | parāvístis | habuístis | mīsístis | iēcístis | audīvístis |
| | | 3 | parāvérunt | habuérunt | mīsérunt | iēcérunt | audīvérunt |

135

# XIII. Regular Verbs Active: Indicative (continued)

|  |  |  | parō | habeō | mittō | iaciō | audiō |
|---|---|---|---|---|---|---|---|
| **Pluperfect** | *Singular* | 1 | paráveram | habúeram | míseram | iéceram | audíveram |
|  |  | 2 | paráverās | habúerās | míserās | iécerās | audíverās |
|  |  | 3 | paráverat | habúerat | míserat | iécerat | audíverat |
|  | *Plural* | 1 | parāverámus | habuerámus | mīserámus | iécerámus | audīverámus |
|  |  | 2 | parāverátis | habuerátis | mīserátis | iécerátis | audīverátis |
|  |  | 3 | paráverant | habúerant | míserant | iécerant | audíverant |
| **Future Perfect** | *Singular* | 1 | paráverō | habúerō | míserō | iécerō | audíverō |
|  |  | 2 | paráveris | habúeris | míseris | iéceris | audíveris |
|  |  | 3 | paráverit | habúerit | míserit | iécerit | audíverit |
|  | *Plural* | 1 | parāvérimus | habuérimus | mīsérimus | iécérimus | audīvérimus |
|  |  | 2 | parāvéritis | habuéritis | mīséritis | iécéritis | audīvéritis |
|  |  | 3 | paráverint | habúerint | míserint | iécerint | audíverint |

# XIV. Regular Verbs Passive: Indicative

| | | | 1st Conjugation | 2nd Conjugation | 3rd Conjugation | | 4th Conjugation |
|---|---|---|---|---|---|---|---|
| **Present** | Singular | 1 | pórtor | móveor | míttor | iácior | audíor |
| | | 2 | portáris | movéris | mítteris | iáceris | audíris |
| | | 3 | portátur | movétur | míttitur | iácitur | audítur |
| | Plural | 1 | portámur | movémur | míttimur | iácimur | audímur |
| | | 2 | portáminī | movéminī | mittíminī | iacíminī | audíminī |
| | | 3 | portántur | movéntur | mittúntur | iaciúntur | audiúntur |
| **Imperfect** | Singular | 1 | portábar | movébar | mittébar | iaciébar | audiébar |
| | | 2 | portābáris | movēbáris | mittēbáris | iaciēbáris | audiēbáris |
| | | 3 | portābátur | movēbátur | mittēbátur | iaciēbátur | audiēbátur |
| | Plural | 1 | portābámur | movēbámur | mittēbámur | iaciēbámur | audiēbámur |
| | | 2 | portābáminī | movēbáminī | mittēbáminī | iaciēbáminī | audiēbáminī |
| | | 3 | portābántur | movēbántur | mittēbántur | iaciēbántur | audiēbántur |

# XIV. Regular Verbs Passive: Indicative (continued)

**Future**

| | | | | | |
|---|---|---|---|---|---|
| *Singular* | 1 | portábor | movébor | míttar | iáciar | aúdiar |
| | 2 | portáberis | movéberis | mittéris | iaciéris | audiéris |
| | 3 | portábitur | movébitur | mittétur | iaciétur | audiétur |
| *Plural* | 1 | portábimur | movébimur | mittémur | iaciémur | audiémur |
| | 2 | portābíminī | movēbíminī | mittéminī | iaciéminī | audiéminī |
| | 3 | portābúntur | movēbúntur | mitténtur | iaciéntur | audiéntur |

| | | PERFECT PASSIVE | | PLUPERFECT PASSIVE | | FUTURE PERFECT PASSIVE | |
|---|---|---|---|---|---|---|---|
| *Singular* | 1 | portátus, -a | sum | portátus, -a | éram | portátus, -a | érō |
| | 2 | portátus, -a | es | portátus, -a | érās | portátus, -a | éris |
| | 3 | portátus, -a, -um | est | portátus, -a, -um | érat | portátus, -a, -um | érit |
| *Plural* | 1 | portátī, -ae | súmus | portátī, -ae | erámus | portátī, -ae | érimus |
| | 2 | portátī, -ae | éstis | portátī, -ae | erátis | portátī, -ae | éritis |
| | 3 | portátī, -ae, -a | sunt | portátī, -ae, -a | érant | portátī, -ae, -a | érunt |

# XV. Irregular Verbs: Infinitive, Imperative, Indicative

| Infinitive | | ésse | pósse | vélle | nólle |
|---|---|---|---|---|---|
| Imperative | | es<br>éste | —<br>— | —<br>— | nólī<br>nólíte |

| | | | ésse | pósse | vélle | nólle |
|---|---|---|---|---|---|---|
| **Present** | *Singular* | 1<br>2<br>3 | sum<br>es<br>est | póssum<br>pótes<br>pótest | vólō<br>vīs<br>vult | nólō<br>nōn vīs<br>nōn vult |
| | *Plural* | 1<br>2<br>3 | súmus<br>éstis<br>sunt | póssumus<br>potéstis<br>póssunt | vólumus<br>vúltis<br>vólunt | nólumus<br>nōn vúltis<br>nólunt |
| **Imperfect** | *Singular* | 1<br>2<br>3 | éram<br>érās<br>érat | póteram<br>póterās<br>póterat | volébam<br>volébās<br>volébat | nōlébam<br>nōlébās<br>nōlébat |
| | *Plural* | 1<br>2<br>3 | erámus<br>erátis<br>érant | poterámus<br>poterátis<br>póterant | volēbámus<br>volēbátis<br>volébant | nōlēbámus<br>nōlēbátis<br>nōlébant |
| **Future** | *Singular* | 1<br>2<br>3 | érō<br>éris<br>érit | póterō<br>póteris<br>póterit | vólam<br>vólēs<br>vólet | nólam<br>nóles<br>nólet |
| | *Plural* | 1<br>2<br>3 | érimus<br>éritis<br>érunt | potérimus<br>potéritis<br>póterunt | volémus<br>volétis<br>vólent | nōlémus<br>nōlétis<br>nólent |

# XV: Irregular Verbs: Infinitive, Imperative, Indicative (continued

| Infinitive | | | málle | íre | férre | férrī | fíerī |
|---|---|---|---|---|---|---|---|
| Imperative | | | — | ī | fer | férre | — |
| | | | — | íte | férte | ferímínī | — |
| **Present** | *Singular* | 1 | málō | éō | férō | féror | fíō |
| | | 2 | mávīs | īs | fers | férris | fīs |
| | | 3 | mávult | it | fert | fértur | fit |
| | *Plural* | 1 | málumus | ímus | férimus | férimur | fímus |
| | | 2 | mávúltis | ítis | fértis | ferímínī | fítis |
| | | 3 | málunt | éunt | férunt | ferúntur | fíunt |
| **Imperfect** | *Singular* | 1 | mālébam | íbam | ferébam | ferébar | fiébam |
| | | 2 | mālébās | íbās | ferébās | ferēbáris | fiébās |
| | | 3 | mālébat | íbat | ferébat | ferēbátur | fiébat |
| | *Plural* | 1 | mālēbámus | íbámus | ferēbámus | ferēbámur | fiēbámus |
| | | 2 | mālēbátis | íbátis | ferēbátis | ferēbámínī | fiēbátis |
| | | 3 | mālébant | íbant | ferébant | ferēbántur | fiébant |
| **Future** | *Singular* | 1 | málam | íbō | féram | férar | fíam |
| | | 2 | málēs | íbis | férēs | feréris | fíēs |
| | | 3 | málet | íbit | féret | ferétur | fíet |
| | *Plural* | 1 | mālémus | íbimus | ferémus | ferémur | fiémus |
| | | 2 | mālétis | íbitis | ferétis | feréminī | fiétis |
| | | 3 | málent | íbunt | férent | feréntur | fíent |

Note: perfect, pluperfect, and future perfect tenses are formed regularly from the perfect stem plus the regular endings for each tense. These tenses of **fíō** are made up of the participle **factus, -a, -um** plus **sum, eram,** and **erō** respectively.

## XVI. Subjunctive

For the present subjunctive of all verbs, see Chapter 49, pages 75–76.

For the imperfect subjunctive of all verbs, see Chapter 41, pages 10–11.

For the perfect subjunctive of all verbs, see Chapter 49, page 76.

For the pluperfect subjunctive of all verbs, see Chapter 41, page 11.

## XVII. Infinitives

For all tenses and forms of the infinitive, see Chapter 46, page 56.

## XVIII. Participles

For all tenses and forms of the participle, see Chapter 43, pages 24–5.

# Vocabulary

## A

ā, ab (+ *abl.*), by, from, away from

ábeō, -íre (*irreg.*), -iī, -itum, to go away

abhínc (+ *acc.*), ago, previously

abrípiō, -ípere (3), -ípuī, -éptum, to snatch away

ábsum, abésse (*irreg.*), áfuī, to be away, be distant from

ac, and

áccidit, -ere (3), -it, to happen

accípiō, -ípere (3), -épī, -éptum, to receive, get, welcome

accúmbō, -mbere (3), -buī, -bitum, to recline (at table)

46  ácriter, fiercely

ad (+ *acc.*), to, towards, at, near

49  ádeō, so much, to such an extent

ádeō, -íre (*irreg.*), -iī, -itum, to come to, approach

adhúc, still, as yet

ádimō, -ímere (3), -émī, -émptum (+ *dat.*), to take away (from)

49

ádiuvō, -iuváre (1), -iúvī, -iútum, to help

46  admīrátiō, -ónis (*f*), amazement

46  admīrātióne cáptus, in utter amazement

47  admīrātiónī ésse, to be a source of wonder or surprise (to)

47  admíror, -árī (1), -átus sum, to wonder (at)

41  admíttō, -íttere (3), -ísī, -íssum, to commit (a crime)

adstántēs, -ntium (*m pl*), bystanders

ádstō, -áre (1), -itī, to stand near, stand by

ádsum, -ésse (*irreg.*), -fuī, to be present, near

aduléscēns, -ntis (*m*), young man, youth

advéniō, -veníre (4), -vénī, -véntum, to come to, reach, arrive at

advesperáscit, -áscere (3), -ávit, it is getting dark

aedifícium, -ī (*n*), building

aedíficō (1), to build

aéger, aégra, aégrum, ill

aegrótō (1), to be ill

afféctus, -a, -um, affected, moved, overcome

áfferō, -rre (*irreg.*), áttulī, allátum, to bring, bring to, bring in

Áge! Ágite! Come! Come on!

áger, ágrī (*m*), field, territory, land

ágō, ágere (3), égī, áctum, to do, drive, discuss, debate

50  grátiās ágere (+ *dat.*), to thank

Quid ágis? How are you?

49  áit, (he, she) says, said

52  álbus, -a, -um, white

46  áliās, at another time

áliquī, áliqua, áliquod, some (or other)

áliquis, áliquid, someone, something

44  áliquid málī, some harm

51  nē quis (quis = áliquis), that no one

50  sī quis (quis = áliquis), if anyone

álius, ália, áliud, other, another, different, one . . . another

áliī . . . áliī . . . , some . . . others . . .

álter, áltera, álterum, the one, the other (of two), the second

4 ámbō, ámbae, ámbō, both
ámbulō (1), to walk
amíca, -ae (f), friend
amícus, -ī (m), friend
ámō (1), to like, love
ámor, -óris (m), love
amphitheátrum, -ī (n), amphitheater

0 ampléctor, -ctī (3), -xus sum, to embrace

1 an, or

1 útrum . . . an . . . ,
whether . . . or . . .
ancílla, -ae (f), slave-woman
ánimus, -ī (m), mind, spirit, will
ánimum recuperáre, to regain one's senses
in ánimō habére, to intend

4 Bónō ánimō es (éste)! Cheer up!
ánnus, -ī (m), year
ánte (+ acc.), before, in front of
ánte (adverb), before
ánteā, previously, before
ántequam, before

9 ánulus, -ī (m), ring
apériō, -íre (4), -uī, -tum, to open

1 apodytérium, -ī (n), changing-room

6 appáritor, -óris (m), gate-keeper, public servant
appropínquō (1) (+ dat.), to approach, draw near to

9 áptō (1), to place, fit
ápud (+ acc.), at the house of
áqua, -ae (f), water

2 ára, -ae (f), altar
árbor, -oris (f), tree
arcéssō, -ere (3), -ívī, -ítum, to summon, send for

2 árdeō, -dére (2), -sī, to burn, blaze
aréna, -ae (f), arena, sand
ascéndō, -dere (3), -dī, -sum, to climb

3 aspérgō, -gere (3), -sī, -sum, to sprinkle, splash, spatter
at, but

átque, and, also
átrium, -ī (n), atrium, main room
atténtē, attentively, closely
attónitus, -a, -um, astonished, astounded
aúdāx, -ácis, bold
aúdiō (4), to hear, listen to
aúferō, -rre (irreg.), ábstulī, ablátum, to carry away, take away
aufúgiō, -fúgere (3), -fúgī, to run away, escape
aúreus, -a, -um, golden

52 aúspex, -icis (m), augur, officiating priest
aut, or
aut . . . aut . . . , either . . . or . . .
aútem, however, but, moreover
auxílium, -ī (n), help
Ávē! Avéte! Hail! Greetings!

53 āvértō, -tere (3), -tī, -sum, to turn away, divert

49 ávis, -is (m/f), bird


# B

báculum, -ī (n), stick

41 bálneae, -árum (f pl), baths
béne, well

50 benevoléntia, -ae (f), kindness

48 béstia, -ae (f), beast

47 bēstiárius, -a, -um, involving wild beasts
bíbō, -ere (3), -ī, to drink
blándē, in a friendly way
bónus, -a, -um, good
Bónō ánimō es (éste)! Cheer up!
bōs, bóvis (m/f), ox, cow
brévis, -is, -e, short
brévī témpore, in a short time
Británnī, -órum (m pl), Britons
Británnia, -ae (f), Britain

50 búlla, -ae (f), luck-charm, locket


143

# C

cádō, -ere (3), cécidī, cásum, to fall
caélum, -ī (n), the sky, heaven
41 caldárium, -ī (n), hot room (at
baths)
41 calor, -óris (m), heat
41 cálvus, -a, -um, bald
41 cámpus, -ī (m), plain, field
41 Cámpus Mártius, the Plain of
Mars on the outskirts of Rome
53 candéla, -ae (f), candle
cántō (1), to sing
41 capillátus, -a, -um, with long hair
53 capíllī, -órum (m pl), hair
53 capíllīs solútīs, with dishevelled
hair
cápiō, -ere (3), cépī, -tum, to take,
capture
43 cōnsílium cápere, to adopt a plan
cáput, -itis (n), head
52 cárus, -a, -um, dear, beloved
cása, -ae (f), hut
51 catérva, -ae (f), crowd
caúda, -ae (f), tail
caúpō, -ónis (m), innkeeper
caúsa, -ae (f), cause, reason
51 genitive + causā, for the sake of,
as
48 cávea, -ae (f), cage
cáveō, -ére (2), cávī, caútum, to
watch out, be careful
celéritās, -átis (f), speed
súmmā celeritáte, with the greatest speed, as fast as possible
celériter, quickly
quam celérrimē, as quickly as
possible
célō (1), to hide, conceal
céna, -ae (f), dinner
cénō (1), to dine, eat dinner
cértus, -a, -um, certain
cértē, certainly, at least
45 prō cértō hábeō, I am sure
céterī, -ae, -a, the rest, the others,
other

cíbus, -ī (m), food
círcum (+ acc.), around
46 circumspíciō, -ícere (3), -éxī,
-éctum, to look around
Círcus, -ī (m), Circus Maximus
císta, -ae (f), trunk, chest
cívis, -is (m), citizen
clámō (1), to shout
clámor, -óris (m), shout, shouting
claúdō, -dere (3), -sī, -sum, to shut,
close
47 claúdus, -a, -um, lame
47 cléménter, quietly, gently
clíēns, -ntis (m), client, dependent
coépī, I began
cógitō (1), to think, consider
51 cognómen, -inis (n), nickname
41 cognóscō, -óscere (3), -óvī, -itum,
to find out, learn, hear of
47 cógō, -ere (3), coégī, coáctum, to
compel, force
cólloquor, -quī (3), -cútus sum, to
speak together, converse
cómes, -itis (m/f), companion
50 comitor, -árī (1), -átus sum, to accompany
53 commémorō (1), to mention, comment on, recount
commissátiō, -ónis (f), drinking
party
46 committō, -íttere (3), -ísī, -íssum,
to bring together, entrust
46 púgnam commíttere, to join
battle
53 cómmodus, -a, -um, pleasant
commótus, -a, -um, moved, excited
írā commótus, in a rage, made
angry
43 commúnis, -is, -e, common
cómpleō, -ére (2), -évī, -étum, to
fill, complete
complúrēs, -ēs, -a, several
52 compónō, -ónere (3), -ósuī,
-ósitum, to compose

144

cóncrepō, -áre (1), -uī, to snap (the fingers)

concúrrō, -rere (3), -rī, -sum, to run together, rush up ... 49

concúrsō (1), to run to and fro, run about ... 46

condémnō (1), to condemn

cóndō, -ere (3), -idī, -itum, to found, establish

(mérita) cónferō, -rre (irreg.), cóntulī, collátum, to render (services to)

confíciō, -ícere (3), -écī, -éctum, to accomplish, finish ... 53 ... 46

cōnfúgiō, -úgere (3), -úgī, to flee for refuge

congrédior, -dī (3), -ssus sum, to come together

coníciō, -ícere (3), -iécī, -iéctum, to throw, guess ... 53

cónor, -árī (1), -átus sum, to try

cónsecrō (1), to dedicate

cōnséusus, -ūs (m), agreement

cónsequor, -quī (3), -cútus sum, to follow, catch up to, overtake

cōnsídō, -sídere (3), -sédī, to sit down ... 47

cōnsílium, -ī (n), plan
    cōnsílium cápere, to adopt a plan

cōnsístō, -sístere (3), -stitī, to halt, stop, stand

cōnspíciō, -ícere (3), -éxī, -éctum, to catch sight of

cónstat, it is agreed

cōnstítuō, -úere (3), -uī, -útum, to decide

cōnsúltum, -ī (n), decree ... 49

conticéscō, -éscere (3), -uī, to become silent

contíneō, -inére (2), -ínuī, -éntum, to confine, hold

cóntrā (+ acc.), opposite, in front of, facing

convaléscō, -éscere (3), -uī, to grow stronger, get well

convéniō, -enīre (4), -énī, -éntum, to come together, meet, assemble

convérsus, -a, -um, having turned, turning

convértō, -tere (3), -tī, -sum, to turn (around)

convíva, -ae (m), guest (at a banquet)

coórior, -írī (4), -tus sum, to rise up, arise

cóquus, -ī (m), cook

cor, córdis (n), heart

córnicen, -inis (m), horn-player, bugler

coróna, -ae (f), garland, crown

córpus, -oris (n), body

cotídiē, daily, every day

cóxa, -ae (f), hipbone

crās, tomorrow

crédō, -ere (3), -idī, -itum (+ dat.), to trust, believe

creō (1), to appoint, create

crínis, -is (m), hair

crūdélis, -is, -e, cruel

crūdélitas, -átis (f), cruelty

cubículum, -ī (n), bedroom

culína, -ae (f), kitchen

cum (+ abl.), with

cum, when, since, whenever
    cum prímum, as soon as

cúnctī, -ae, -a, all

cúpiō, -ere (3), -ívī, -ítum, to desire, want

Cūr . . . ? Why . . . ?

cúra, -ae (f), care, anxiety
    cúrae ésse, to be a cause of anxiety (to)

Cúria, -ae (f), Senate House

cúrō (1), to look after, take care of

cúrrō, -rere (3), cucúrrī, -sum, to run

custódiō (4), to guard

cústōs, -ódis (m), guard

145

# D

dē (+ *abl.*), down from, concerning, about
52 dēcḗdō, -dere (3), -ssī, -ssum, to die
49 décet (+ *acc.*), (someone) should
49 dḗditus, -a, -um, devoted, dedicated
49 dēdūcō, -cere (3), -xī, -ctum, to
  show into, bring, escort
dēfḗssus, -a, -um, weary, tired
41 dḗfricō, -ā́re (1), -uī, -tum, to rub
  down
deínde, then
dēlḗctō (1), to delight
dḗleō, -ḗre (2), -ḗvī, -ḗtum, to
  destroy
46 dēlíciae, -ā́rum (*f pl*), delight
49 dēmíssus, -a, -um, downcast, lowered
49 vúltū dēmíssō, with eyes lowered
dēmíttō, -íttere (3), -ísī, -íssum, to
  let down, suspend
depṓnō, -ṓnere (3), -ósuī, -ósitum,
  to lay down, put aside, set
  down
dēscéndō, -dere (3), -dī, -sum, to
  climb down, go down
dēsī́derō (1), to long for, desire,
  miss
dēsī́liō, -ī́re (4), -uī, to leap down
49 dēspóndeō, -dḗre (2), -dī, -sum, to
  betroth, promise in marriage
déus, déī (*m*), (*dat.* and *abl. pl.*
  dīs), god
  Dī immortā́lēs! Immortal gods!
  Good heavens!
  Prō dī immortā́lēs! Good heavens!
  dī mā́nēs, the spirits of the dead
dḗvorō (1), to devour
52 déxtra, -ae (*f*), right hand
dī́cō, -cere (3), -xī, -ctum, to say,
  tell
díēs, -ḗī (*m*), day
  in díēs, every day, day by day

44 diēs nātā́lis, birthday
41 dígitus, -ī (*m*), finger
44 dígitīs micā́re, to play morra
dīligénter, carefully
53 dī́ligō, -ígere (3), -ḗxī, -ḗctum, to
  love, have special regard for
50 dīmíttō, -íttere (3), -ísī, -íssum, to
  send away, let go
discḗdō, -dere (3), -ssī, -ssum, to
  depart, leave, go away
discrī́men, -inis (*n*), distinction
díū, for a long time
dī́ves, -itis, rich
dō, dā́re (1), dédī, dátum, to give
44 dṓnō dā́re, to give as a gift
dóceō, -ḗre (2), -uī, -tum, to teach
dóleō (2), to be sorry, be sad, to
  hurt
dolor, -ṓris (*m*), grief, pain
dóminus, -ī (*m*), master, owner
dómus, -ūs (*f*), house, home
  dómī, at home
  dómō, from home
  dómum, (to) home, to the home
44 dṓnum, -ī (*n*), gift
44 dṓnō dā́re, to give as a gift
dórmiō (4), to sleep
dúbium, -ī (*n*), doubt
dū́cō, -cere (3), -xī, -ctum, to lead,
  take
52 exséquiās dū́cere, to carry out the
  funeral rites
dum, while, as long as
dúo, dúae, dúo, two

# E

ē, ex (+ *abl.*), from, out of, of
ḗbrius, -a, -um, drunk
Écce! Look at . . . ! Look!
édō, ésse (*irreg.*), ḗdī, ḗsum, to eat
ēdū́cō, -cere (3), -xī, -ctum, to lead
  out
éfferō, -rre (*irreg.*), éxtulī, ēlā́tum,
  to bring out, carry out (for
  burial)

146

effúgiō, -úgere (3), -úgī, to escape 52
égo, I
ēgrédior, -edī (3), -éssus sum, to go 42
out, leave, disembark
Éheu! Alas!
élegāns, -ntis, elegant, tasteful 53
émo, émere (3), émī, émptum, to
buy
énim (postpositive), for
51 ēnúntiō (1), to reveal, divulge
éō, íre (irreg.), ívī, ítum, to go 41
éō (adverb), there, to that place
51 éō mágis, all the more
epístula, -ae (f), letter
9 épulae, -árum (f pl), banquet, feast
0 érgā (+ acc.), towards
ērudítus, -a, -um, learned, schol-
arly
ēsúriō (4), to be hungry
et, and, also 50
et . . . et, both . . . and 53
étiam, also, even 50
Eúge! Hurray!
ēvádō, -dere (3), -sī, -sum, to 53
escape
ex, ē (+ abl.), from, out of 53
7 exanimátus (métū), paralyzed (with 52
fear)
3 excédō, -dere (3), -ssī, -ssum, to go 46
out, leave
3 ē vítā excédere, to die
éxcitō (1), to stir up, excite, rouse,
wake up
exclámō (1), to shout out
éxeō, -íre (irreg.), -iī, -itum, to go
out
1 exérceō (2), to exercise, train
7 exímius, -a, -um, outstanding
3 éximō, -ímere (3), -émī, -émptum, 51
to remove
expérior, -írī (4), -tus sum, to test,
try
3 éxprimō, -ímere (3), -éssī, -éssum,
to press out, express
2 exséquiae, -árum (f pl), funeral rites

exséquiās dúcere, to carry out the 52
funeral rites
exsíliō, -íre (4), -uī, to leap out 42
exspéctō (1), to look out for, wait
for
éxstruō, -ere (3), -xī, -ctum, to 53
build
éxtrā (+ acc.), outside
éxtrahō, -here (3), -xī, -ctum, to
pull out, drag out
éxuō, -úere (3), -uī, -útum, to take 41
off

# F

fábula, -ae (f), story
fácile, easily
fáciō, -ere (3), fécī, fáctum, to
make, do
família, -ae (f), family, household 50
familiárēs, -ium (m pl), close friends 53
familiáris, -is, -e, (belonging to the) 50
family or household
fáscēs, -ium (m pl), rods (symbol of 53
office)
fébris, -is (f), fever 53
Féliciter! Good luck! 52
félīx, -ícis, happy, lucky, fortunate
fémina, -ae (f), woman 46
férē, almost, approximately 44
fēriátus, -a, -um, celebrating a holiday
férō, -rre (irreg.), túlī, látum, to
carry, bring, bear
feróciter, fiercely
férōx, -ócis, fierce
férula, -ae (f), cane
festínō (1), to hurry
fídēs, -eī (f), good faith, reliability, 51
trust
fília, -ae (f), daughter
fílius, -ī (m), son
fíō, fíerī (irreg.), fáctus sum, to
become, be made, be done,
happen

147

52 flámmeum, -ī (n), orange (bridal)
  veil
41 fóllis, -is (m), bag
  fortásse, perhaps
43 fórte (adverb), by chance
  fórtis, -is, -e, brave
  fortūnắtus, -a, -um, happy, lucky
  Fórum, -ī (n), Forum, market place
53 frángō, -ngere (3), frḗgī, -ctum, to
  break
  fráter, -tris (m), brother
  frīgidắrium, -ī (n), cold room (at
  baths)
  frīgidus, -a, -um, cold
  frústrā, in vain
  fúgiō, -ere (3), fū́gī, to flee
53 fū́nebris, -is, -e, funeral
52 fū́nus, -eris (n), funeral
42 fūr, -ris (m), thief
46 fúror, -ṓris (m), frenzy
  fū́rtim, stealthily


G

  Gállī, -ṓrum (m pl), Gauls
  Gállia, -ae (f), Gaul
  gaúdeō, -dḗre (2), gāvī́sus sum, to
  rejoice
  gémō, -ere (3), -uī, -itum, to groan
49 gēns, -tis (f), family, clan
46 génus, -eris (n), kind, race
  gérō, -rere (3), -ssī, -stum, to wear,
  carry on
46 gladiátor, -ṓris (m), gladiator
  gládius, -ī (m), sword
53 gnắtus (nắtus), -ī (m), son
  grammáticus, -ī (m), teacher
50 grắtiās ágere (+ dat.), to thank
49 grátulor, -ắrī (1), -ắtus sum (+
  dat.), to congratulate
53 grắtus, -a, -um, pleasing, dear (to),
  loved (by)
  grávis, -is, -e, heavy, serious

H

  hábeō (2), to have, hold
45 prō cértō hábeō, I am sure
  hábitō (1), to live, dwell
  haéreō, -rḗre (2), -sī, -sum, to stick,
  cling
41 harpástum, -ī (n), ball game, hand
  ball
41 haud, not
  héri, yesterday
  Heu! = É̄heu!
49 Heús! Ho there!
  hic, haec, hoc, this
  hīc (adverb), here
53 hílaris, -is, -e, cheerful
52 hiláritās, -ắtis (f), good humor,
  merriment
  hódiē, today
  hómō, -inis (m), man, fellow
  hóminēs, -inum (m pl), people
51 honṓris caúsā, as an honor
  hṓra, -ae (f), hour
50 hórtor, -ắrī (1), -ắtus sum, to encourage, urge
  hóspes, -itis (m), friend, guest
  hūc, here, to here
  hūc illū́c, here and there, this
  way and that
46 hūmắnus, -a, -um, human
43 húmī, on the ground


I

  iáceō (2), to lie, be lying down
  iáciō, -ere (3), iḗcī, -ctum, to throw
  iam, now, already
  iánitor, -ṓris (m), doorkeeper
  iánua, -ae (f), door
  íbi, there
  id quod, (a thing) which
  ídem, éadem, ídem, the same
  ígitur, therefore
  ignắvus, -a, -um, cowardly, lazy

ignṓrō (1), to be ignorant, not to know

ílle, ílla, íllud, that, he, she, it

illúc, there, to that place  51

 hūc illúc, here and there, this way and that

imágō, -inis (f), likeness, mask  53

immánis, -is, -e, huge

immíttō, -íttere (3), -ísī, -íssum, to send in, hurl at, hurl into, let loose, release  53

immóbilis, -is, -e, motionless

immortális, -is, -e, immortal  43

 Dī immortálēs! Immortal gods! Good heavens!  50

 Prō dī immortálēs! Good heavens!  48

ímpar (see pār)

ímperō (1) (+ dat.), to order

ímpetus, -ūs (m), attack

impónō, -ónere (3), -ósuī, -ósitum, to place on, put  52

in (+ abl.), in, on, among

in (+ acc.), into, towards, until  47

 in díēs, every day, day by day

incḗdō, -dere (3), -ssī, to march, go  51

incéndium, -ī (n), fire

incéndō, -dere (3), -dī, -sum, to burn, set on fire

incéssus, -ūs (m), bearing, walk(ing)

íncidō, -ere (3), -ī, incásum, to fall into (on to)

incípiō, -ípere (3), -épī, -éptum, to begin

íncitō (1), to spur on, urge on, rouse

íncola, -ae (m/f), inhabitant, tenant

incúrrō, -rere (3), -rī, -sum, to run into

índe, from there, then

índuō, -úere (3), -uī, -útum, to put on

íneō, -íre (irreg.), -iī, -itum, to go in

Ínferī, -órum (m pl), the underworld, gods of the underworld

īnfírmus, -a, -um, weak, shaky, frail

ingénium, -ī (n), intelligence, ingenuity

íngēns, -ntis, huge, big

ingravḗscō, -ere (3), to grow worse

ingrédior, -dī (3), -ssus sum, to go in, enter

iníciō, -ícere (3), -iḗcī, -iéctum, to throw into, thrust

ínquit, he (she) says, said

ínscius, -a, -um, not knowing

īnscríbō, -bere (3), -psī, -ptum, to write in, register

ínsula, -ae (f), island, tenement

intéllegō, -gere (3), -xī, -ctum, to understand, realize

ínter (+ acc.), between, among

intéreā, meanwhile

interpéllō (1), to interrupt

intérrogō (1), to ask

íntrō (1), to enter

introdúcō, -cere (3), -xī, -ctum, to bring in

intróeō, -íre (irreg.), -iī, -itum, to enter

invéniō, -eníre (4), -énī, -éntum, to come upon, find

invítō (1), to invite

invítus, -a, -um, unwilling

iócor, -árī (1), -átus sum, to joke

iócus, -ī (m), joke, funny story

ípse, ípsa, ípsum, -self

íra, -ae (f), anger

 írā commótus, made angry, in a rage

īrācúndus, -a, -um, irritable, in a bad mood

īrátus, -a, -um, angry

irrúmpō, -úmpere (3), -úpī, -úptum, to burst in, attack

is, ea, id, he, she, it, this, that

 id quod, (a thing) which

149

íta, thus, in this way
Íta vérō! Yes!
ítaque, and so, therefore
íter, itíneris (n), journey, road
íterum, again, a second time
iúbeō, -bére (2), -ssī, -ssum, to order
53 iucúndus, -a, -um, pleasant, a delight
45 Iudaéus, -ī (m), Jew
46 iúgulō (1), to kill, murder
Iúlius, -ī (m), July
52 iúngō, -gere (3), -xī, -ctum, to join
49 iúvenis, -is (m), young man

## L

42 lábor, -bī (3), -psus sum, to slip, stumble
labórō (1), to work
43 lácrima, -ae (f), tear
lácrimō (1), to weep, cry
44 laédō, -dere (3), -sī, -sum, to harm
laétus, -a, -um, joyful, happy
laétē, joyfully
47 lámbō, -ere (3), -ī, to lick
lána, -ae (f), wool
lánius, -ī (m), butcher
46 lanísta, -ae (m), trainer
lapídeus, -a, -um, of stone, stony
50 larárium, -ī (n), shrine of household gods
50 Lárēs, -um (m pl), household gods
47 láteō (2), to lie in hiding, hide
44 latrúnculus, -ī (m), robber, (pl) pawns (a game like chess)
44 lúdus latrunculórum, game of bandits
laúdō (1), to praise
52 laúrus, -ī (f), bay (tree), laurel
lávō, -áre (1), lávī, -átum or lótum, to wash
lectíca, -ae (f), litter
léctus, -ī (m), bed, couch
légō, -ere (3), légī, léctum, to read

léntē, slowly
43 léō, -ónis (m), lion
53 lépidus, -a, -um, charming
53 lévis, -is, -e, smooth
libénter, gladly
líber, -brī (m), book
50 Līberália, -ium (n pl), the Liberalia (Festival of Liber)
líberī, -órum (n pl), children
47 líberō (1), to set free
53 lībérta, -ae (f), freedwoman
lībértus, -ī (m), freedman
lícet, -ére (2), -uit (+ dat.), it is allowed
53 líctor, -óris (m), lictor, officer
50 límen, -inis (n), threshold, doorway
língua, -ae (f), tongue, language
53 línquō, -ere (3), líquī, to leave
41 línteum, -ī (n), towel
53 lócō (1), to place
lócus, -ī (m; n in pl), place
lóngus, -a, -um, long
lóngē, far
lóquor, -ī (3), locútus sum, to speak, talk
53 lúbricus, -a, -um, slippery
53 lucérna, -ae (f), lamp
lúcet, -ére (2), lúxit, to be light, to shine
41 lúctor, -árī (1), -átus sum, to wrestle
lúdō, -dere (3), -sī, -sum, to play
lúdus, -ī (m), game, school
lúdī, -órum (m pl), games (as in the Circus)
lúpus, -ī (m), wolf
lūx, lúcis (f), light
príma lūx, dawn

## M

mágis, more
51 éō mágis, all the more
magíster, -trī (m), schoolmaster, master
46 magistrátus, -ūs (m), magistrate

150

**magníficus, -a, -um,** magnificent
**mágnus, -a, -um,** great, big, large, loud (voice)
**máior, -óris,** greater     44
    **maiórēs, -um** (*m pl*), ancestors
**málō, -lle** (*irreg.*), **-luī,** to prefer     44
**málus, -a, -um,** bad, evil
**máne,** early in the day, in the morning
**máneō, -ére** (2), **-sī, -sum,** to remain, stay
**mánēs, -ium** (*m pl*), spirits of the dead
**mānsuḗtus, -a, -um,** tame     47
**mánus, -ūs** (*f*), hand, band (of men)
**máppa, -ae** (*f*), napkin
**marītus, -ī** (*m*), husband
**máter, -tris** (*f*), mother
**mātrimónium, -ī** (*n*), marriage     47
    **in mātrimónium dúcere,** to marry
**mātróna, -ae** (*f*), married woman
**mātúrē,** early
**máximus, -a, -um,** very great, greatest, very large
    **máximē,** very much, very, most
**mécum,** with me
**médicus, -ī** (*m*), doctor
**médius, -a, -um,** mid-, middle of
**Mehércule!** By Hercules! Goodness me!
**memorábilis, -is, -e,** memorable
**ménsa, -ae** (*f*), table
**ménsis, -is** (*m*), month
**mercátor, -óris** (*m*), merchant
**merīdiánī, -órum** (*m pl*), midday fighters
**merídiēs, -éī** (*m*), noon, midday
**méritum, -ī** (*n*), good deed, (*pl*) services
    **mérita cōnférre,** to render services (to)
**métus, -ūs** (*m*), fear

**métū exanimátus,** paralyzed with fear
**méus, -a, -um,** my, mine
**mícō, -áre** (1), **-uī,** to move quickly to and fro, flash     44
    **dígitīs micáre,** to play *morra*
**míles, -itis** (*m*), soldier
**mílle,** a thousand
**mília,** thousands     46
**mínimē,** least, no
**mínuō, -úere** (3), **-uī, -útum,** to lessen, reduce, decrease
**mínus,** less
**mīrábilis, -is, -e,** wonderful     47
**míror, -árī** (1), **-átus sum,** to wonder     48
**mírus, -a, -um,** wonderful, marvelous, strange
**míser, -era, -erum,** unhappy, miserable, wretched
**mítis, -is, -e,** gentle     47
**míttō, -ere** (3), **mísī, míssum,** to send, let go
**módo,** only
**módus, -ī** (*m*), way, method
**moléstus, -a, -um,** troublesome, annoying
**móneō** (2), to advise, warn
**monuméntum, -ī** (*n*), monument, tomb     53
**mórbus, -ī** (*m*), illness     53
**mórior, -ī** (3), **-tuus sum,** to die
**moror, -árī** (1), **-átus sum,** to delay, remain, stay
**mors, -tis** (*f*), death
**mortíferē,** mortally, critically     52
**mórtuus, -a, -um,** dead
**mōs, mǒris** (*m*), custom     51
**móveō, -ére** (2), **móvī, mótum,** to move, shake
**mox,** soon, presently
**muliébris, -is, -e,** womanly, female, of a woman
**múlier, -eris** (*f*), woman
**multitúdō, -inis** (*f*), crowd

151

**múltus, -a, -um,** much, *(pl)* many
47    **múltō,** by much, much
   **múltum** *(adverb)*, much, long
45 **múnus, -eris** *(n)*, gladiatorial show,
   *(pl)* games
**múrus, -ī** *(m)*, wall
**mússō** (1), to mutter
47 **mútuus, -a, -um,** mutual, common, of each other
52 **mýrtus, -ī** *(f)*, myrtle

# N

**nam,** for
**nárrō** (1), to tell (a story)
44 **nātális, -is, -e** (belonging to) birth
44    **díēs nātális,** birthday
**nātúra, -ae** *(f)*, nature
53 **nātus (gnátus), -ī** *(m)*, son
**nāvigō** (1), to sail
**návis, -is** *(f)*, ship
**-ne,** (indicates a question)
50 **nē** ( + *subjunctive*), in case, to prevent, not to
**nē . . . quídem,** not even
51 **nē quis,** that no one
43 **nec,** and . . . not
   **nec . . . nec . . . ,**
   neither . . . nor
**nécō** (1), to kill
49 **néglegō, -gere** (3), **-xī, -ctum,** to
   neglect, ignore
45 **negōtiósus, -a, -um,** busy
**némō, -inis** *(m)*, no one
53 **nénia, -ae** *(f)*, lament, dirge
**néque,** and . . . not
   **néque . . . néque . . . ,**
   neither . . . nor . . .
41 **Nerōnéus, -a, -um,** of Nero
**nésciō** (4), to be ignorant, not know
**níhil,** nothing
**nīl,** nothing
**nísi,** unless, if . . . not, except
49 **nóbilis, -is, -e,** noble
**nócte,** at night

43 **nóctū,** by night, at night
**nólō, -lle, -luī,** to be unwilling, not
   wish, refuse
**nómen, -inis** *(n)*, name
**nóminō** (1), to name, call by name
**nōn,** not
**nóndum,** not yet
**Nónne . . . ?** (introduces a question
   that expects the answer "yes")
50 **nōnnúllī, -ae, -a,** some
**nónus, -a, -um,** ninth
**nōs,** we, us
**nóster, -tra, -trum,** our
**nóvem,** nine
**nóvus, -a, -um,** new
**nox, -ctis** *(f)*, night
52 **núbō, -bere** (3), **-psī, -ptum** ( +
   *dat.*), to marry
**núllus, -a, -um,** no, none
44 **Num . . . ? Surely . . . not . . . ?**
   (introduces a question that expects the answer "no")
**númerō** (1), to count
**númquam,** never
**nunc,** now
**núntius, -ī** *(m)*, messenger
49 **núper,** recently
52 **(nóva) núpta, -ae** *(f)*, bride
52 **nūptiális, -is, -e,** wedding
   (adjective)
**núsquam,** nowhere
52 **nux, núcis** *(f)*, nut

# O

**obdórmiō** (4), to go to sleep
**óbsecrō** (1), to beseech, beg
49 **obsérvō** (1), to watch, pay attention
   to
52 **obsígnō** (1), to sign
46 **obstupefáctus, -a, -um,** astounded
**occásiō, -ónis** *(f)*, opportunity
43 **occídō, -dere** (3), **-dī, -sum,** to kill
**occupátus, -a, -um,** busy
**óctō,** eight

óculus, -ī (m), eye
officiósus, -a, -um, ready to serve, obliging
officium, -ī (n), official ceremony, duty
ōlim, once upon a time, one day
ómnis, -is, -e, all, the whole, every, each — 52
ónerō (1), to load — 42
opériō, -íre (4), -uī, -tum, to hide, — 53
cover — 53
opórtet tē (+ infin.), you must
óptimus, -a, -um, best, very good, excellent
óptō (1), to wish — 43
órior, -írī (4), -tus sum, to rise
ōrnāméntum, -ī (n), decoration — 51
órnō (1), to decorate, equip
órō (1), to beg
ōs, óris (n), mouth, face, expression — 44
os, óssis (n), bone
ósculum, -ī (n), kiss
osténdō, -dere (3), -dī, -tum, to — 53
show, point out

# P

paedagógus, -ī (m), tutor
paéne, almost
palaéstra, -ae (f), exercise-ground — 49
Palātínus, -a, -um, belonging to the Palatine Hill
pálus, -ī (m), post
pánis, -is (m), bread
pār ímpār, odds or evens (a game)
párcō, -cere (3), pepércī (+ dat.), to spare
párēns, -ntis (m/f), parent — 41
páreō (2) (+ dat.), to obey
pária, -ium (n pl), pairs — 53
párō (1), to prepare
pars, -tis (f), part — 47
párvus, -a, -um, small — 51
páter, -tris (m), father — 53
pátrēs, -um (m pl), senators

pátior, -tī (3), -ssus sum, to suffer, endure
pátruus, -ī (m), uncle
paúcī, -ae, -a, few
paulátim, gradually, little by little
paulísper, for a short time
paúlō post, a little later
paúlum, a little, little
pavīméntum, -ī (n), tiled floor
péctus, -oris (n), chest, breast
péctus plángere, to beat the breast
pecúnia, -ae (f), money
per (+ acc.), through, along, over
pérdō, -ere (3), -idī, -itum, to destroy
pérferō, -rre (irreg.), pértulī, perlátum, to report
perículum, -ī (n), danger
peristýlium, -ī (n), peristyle, courtyard surrounded with a colonnade
pérlegō, -égere (3), -égī, -éctum, to read through
persuádeō, -dére (2), -sī, -sum (+ dat.), to persuade
pertérritus, -a, -um, frightened, terrified
perturbátus, -a, -um, confused
pervéniō, -eníre (4), -énī, -éntum (ad + acc.), to reach, arrive (at)
pēs, pédis (m), foot
péssimus, -a, -um, worst
pétō, -ere (3), -ívī, -ítum, to seek, aim at, attack
píla, -ae (f), ball
pīráta, -ae (m), pirate
místor, -óris (m), baker
pláceō (2), (+ dat.), to please
plácidē, quietly, tamely
plácuit, it was decided
plángō, -gere (3), -xī, -ctum, to beat

53     péctus plángere, to beat the
        breast
    plḗnus, -a, -um, full
    plúit, -úere (3), plúit, it is raining
    plū́rimus, -a, -um, most, very
        much
    plūs, plū́ris, more
43     pollíceor, -érī (2), -itus sum, to
        promise
53     pómpa, -ae (f), funeral procession
    pṓnō, pṓnere (3), pósuī, pósitum,
        to put, place
    pópulus, -ī (m), people
    pórcus, -ī (m), pig
    pórta, -ae (f), gate
    pórtō (1), to carry
    póscō, -ere (3), popóscī, to ask for,
        demand
    póssum, pósse (irreg.), pótuī, to be
        able
    post (adverb), after(wards), later
52     paúlō post, a little later
    post (+ acc.), after
41     pósteā, afterwards
51     pósterus, -a, -um, next, following
    póstis, -is (m), door-post
44     postrḗmō, finally
53     postrḗmus, -a, -um, last
    postrídiē, on the following day
51     pótius quam, rather than
51     praébeō (2), to display, show,
        provide
52     praecḗdō, -ḗdere (3), -éssī, -éssum,
        to go in front
50     praecípiō, -ípere (3), -épī, -éptum
        (+ dat.), to instruct, order
    praeclárus, -a, -um, distinguished,
        famous
    praédō, -ónis (m), robber
    praéter (+ acc.), except, beyond
    praetéreā, besides, moreover
    praetéxta (toga), with purple edge
51     praetextátus, -a, -um, wearing the
        toga praetexta

42     prehéndō, -dere (3), -dī, -sum, to
        seize
    prī́mus, -a, -um, first
    prī́ma lūx, dawn
    prī́mō, at first, first
    prī́mum (adverb), first
    prī́nceps, -cipis (m), emperor,
        leader, leading citizen
43     príor, -óris, first (of two), previous
46     príus, previously
45     prō cértō hábeō, I am sure
    Prō dī immortálēs! Good heavens!
42     prōcḗdō, -dere (3), -ssī, -ssum, to
        step forward
    prócul, in the distance, far off
51     prṓferō, -férre (irreg.), -tulī, -látum,
        to carry forward, continue
    proficíscor, -icíscī (3), -éctus sum,
        to set out
    prōgrédior, -dī (3), -ssus sum, to go
        forward, advance
49     prṓnuba, -ae (f), bride's attendant
43     própe (adverb), near, nearly
    própe (+ acc.), near
49     propínquus, -ī (m), relative
    própter (+ acc.), on account of
52     prōrúmpō, -úmpere (3), -ū́pī,
        -úptum, to burst forth, burst
        out
    prū́dēns, -ntis, wise, sensible
51     prūdéntia, -ae (f), good sense, dis-
        cretion, skill
50     pū́blicus, -a, -um, public
    puélla, -ae (f), girl
    púer, -erī (m), boy
50     puerílis, -is, -e, childish, of child-
        hood
46     púgna, -ae (f), battle
46     púgnam commíttere, to join
        battle
46     púgnō (1), to fight
    púlcher, -chra, -chrum, beautiful,
        handsome
52     pulchritū́dō, -inis (f), beauty

**pulvīnar, -āris** (*n*), imperial seat (at games)
**pūniō** (4), to punish
**pūpa, -ae** (*f*), doll
**pūrus, -a, -um**, spotless, clean, plain white
**putō** (1), to think, consider

# Q

**quaérō, -rere** (3), **-sīvī, -sītum**, to seek, look for, ask (for)
**Quālis** . . . ? What sort of . . . ? In what state (or condition) . . . ?    53
**Quam** . . . ! How . . . !
**quam**, than    47
  **pótius quam**, rather than
**quam** (+ *superlative*), as . . . as possible
**quámquam**, although
**Quándō** . . . ? When . . . ?
**Quántus, -a, -um** . . . ? How big . . . ? How much . . . ?    53
**quási**, as if
**-que**, and
**quī, quae, quod**, who, which, that
**quídam, quaédam, quóddam**, a certain, (*pl*) some    44
**quídem**, indeed
  **nē** . . . **quídem**, not even
**quiéscō, -ere** (3), **quiévī, quiétum**, to rest, keep quiet
**quínque**, five
**quíntus, -a, -um**, fifth
**Quis** . . . ? **Quid** . . . ? Who . . . ? What . . . ? Which . . . ?
  **Quid agis?** How are you?    41
**(sī) quis** (see **aliquis**)
**(nē) quis** (see **aliquis**)
**quō**, there, to that place
**Quō** . . . ? Where . . . to?
**quō** . . . **eō** . . . , the (more) . . . the (more)
**quod**, because    48

# R

**rápiō, -ere** (3), **-uī, -tum**, to snatch, seize
**rē vérā**, really, actually
**recípiō, -ípere** (3), **-ḗpī, -éptum**, to receive
**recognítiō, -ōnis** (*f*), recognition
**recúmbō, -mbere** (3), **-buī**, to recline, lie down
**réctē**, rightly, properly
**réddō, -ere** (3), **-idī, -itum**, to give back, return
**redḗmptor, -ōris** (*m*), contractor
**rédeō, -īre** (*irreg.*), **-iī, -itum**, to return, go back
**redúcō, -cere** (3), **-xī, -ctum**, to lead back, take back
**réferō, -rre** (*irreg.*), **réttulī, relátum**, to bring back
**régnum, -ī** (*n*), kingdom
**regrédior, -dī** (3), **-ssus sum**, to go back, return
**relínquō, -ínquere** (3), **-íquī, -íctum**, to leave
**repéllō, -ere** (3), **réppulī, rcpúlsum**, to drive off, drive back, beat back
**répetō, -ere** (3), **-īvī, -ítum**, to pick up, fetch, recover
**reprehéndō, -dere** (3), **-dī, -sum**, to blame, scold, reprimand
**rēs, réī** (*f*), thing, matter, affair, situation
  **rēs urbánae**, affairs of the town
  **rē vérā**, really, actually

155

49 rescríbō, -bere (3), -psī, -ptum, to write back, reply
46 reservátus, -a, -um, reserved
resístō, -ístere (3), -titī (+ *dat.*), to resist
respíciō, -ícere (3), -éxī, -éctum, to look back, look around at
respóndeō, -dére (2), -dī, -sum, to answer, reply
retíneō, -ére (2), -uī, retentum, to hold back, keep
48 rē vérā, really
rídeō, -dére (2), -sī, -sum, to laugh, laugh at, smile
41 rīdículus, -a, -um, absurd, laughable
43 ríma, -ae (*f*), crack
rísus, -ūs (*m*), laughter, laugh, smile
52 ríte, properly
43 ríxor, -árī (1), -átus sum, to quarrel
rógō (1), to ask
53 rógus, -ī (*m*), funeral pyre
Róma, -ae (*f*), Rome
Rōmánus, -a, -um, Roman
rúrsus, again
russátus, -a, -um, red
rústicus, -a, -um, of or belonging to the country or farm

# S

sácer, -cra, -crum, sacred, religious, holy
52 sácra, -órum (*n pl*), sacrifice
52 sacríficō (1), to sacrifice
saépe, often
43 saévus, -a, -um, fierce, savage
salútō (1), to greet, welcome
Sálvē! Salvéte! Greetings! Good morning! Hello!
43 sanguíneus, -a, -um, bloodstained
sánguis, -inis (*m*), blood
sátis, enough
sceléstus, -a, -um, wicked

41 scélus, -eris (*n*), crime
scíndō, -ere (3), scídī, scíssum, to cut, split, carve
53 scíssā véste, with torn clothing
scíō (4), to know
scríbō, -bere (3), -psī, -ptum, to write
sē, himself, herself, oneself, itself, themselves
43 sēcrétō, secretly
sécum, with him (her, it, them) (-self, -selves)
sed, but
50 sédecim, sixteen
sédeō, -ére (2), sédī, séssum, to sit
sélla, -ae (*f*), sedan chair, seat, chair
sémper, always
senátor, -óris (*m*), senator
41 senátus, -ūs (*m*), senate
41 sénex, -is (*m*), old man
43 séntiō, -tíre (4), -sī, -sum, to feel, notice, realize
sepéliō, -elíre (4), -elívī, -últum, to bury
sepúlc(h)rum, -ī (*n*), tomb
séquor, -quī (3), -útus sum, to follow
49 serénus, -a, -um, clear, bright
53 sérmo, -ónis (*m*), conversation, talk
sérō, late
49 sérva, -ae (*f*), slave-woman, slave-girl
sérvō (1), to save, keep, protect
sérvus, -ī (*m*), slave
sex, six
séxtus, -a, -um, sixth
sī, if
50 sī quis (= áliquis), if anyone
sīc, thus, in this way
52 síccus, -a, -um, dry
sígnum, -ī (*n*), signal, sign
siléntium, -ī (*n*), silence
sílva, -ae (*f*), woods

**símilis, -is, -e** ( + *dat.*), like, similar (to)  49

**símul**, together, at the same time  42

**símulō** (1), to pretend

**síne** ( + *abl.*), without

**siníster, -tra, -trum**, left

**sítus, -a, -um**, placed, buried

**sōl, sōlis** (*m*), sun

**sóleō, -ére** (2), -**itus sum**, to be accustomed, in the habit

**sōlitū́dō, -inis** (*f*), loneliness, solitude

**sollícitus, -a, -um**, anxious, worried

**sólus, -a, -um**, alone  42

**sóror, -ōris** (*f*), sister

**spectáculum, -ī** (*n*), sight, spectacle

**spectátor, -ōris** (*m*), spectator, onlooker

**spéctō** (1), to watch, look at

**spéculum, -ī** (*n*), mirror

**spēlúnca, -ae** (*f*), cave  50

**spḗrō** (1), to hope

**spóndeō, -dére** (2), **spopóndī, -sum**, to promise solemnly, pledge  50

**spónsa, -ae** (*f*), betrothed woman, bride  52

**spōnsália, -ium** (*n pl*), betrothal  49

**spónsus, -ī** (*m*), betrothed man, bridegroom  49

**státim**, immediately

**stírps, -pis** (*f*), thorn

**stō, stáre** (1), **stétī, státum**, to stand

**strépitus, -ūs** (*m*), noise, din, clattering

**strígilis, -is** (*f*), strigil, scraper  49

**stríngō, -ngere** (3), -**nxī, -ctum**, to draw (a sword)

**stúltus, -a, -um**, stupid, foolish

**stúpeō** (2), to be amazed, gape

**sub** ( + *abl.*), under, beneath

**súbitō**, suddenly

**submíssus, -a, -um**, quiet, subdued, soft  41

**submíssā vóce**, in a subdued voice

**súbsequor, -quī** (3), -**cútus sum**, to follow (up)

**sum, ésse** (*irreg.*), **fúī**, to be

**súmmus, -a, -um**, very great, the greatest, the top of . . .

**súmō, -mere** (3), -**mpsī, -mptum**, to take, pick out, pick up, assume, put on

**súperō** (1), to overcome, defeat

**súrgo, -rgere** (3), -**rréxī, -rréctum**, to get up, rise

**surrípiō, -ípere** (3), -**ípuī, -éptum**, to steal

**súus, -a, -um**, his, her, one's, its, their (-own)

# T

**tablínum, -ī** (*n*), study (room)

**tábulae, -árum** (*f pl*), tablets, records

**Tabulárium, -ī** (*n*), Public Records Office

**táceō** (2), to be quiet

**taéda, -ae** (*f*), torch

**taédet**, it bores, makes one (*acc.*) tired of something (*gen.*)

**mē taédet** ( + *gen.*), I am bored (with), tired (of)

**tális, -is, -e**, such, of this kind

**tam**, so

**támen**, however, nevertheless

**tándem**, at last, at length

**tántus, -a, -um**, so great

**tántum**, so much

**temerárius, -a, -um**, rash, reckless, bold

**tempéstās, -átis** (*f*), storm

**témplum, -ī** (*n*), temple

**témpus, -oris** (*n*), time

**téneō, -ére** (2), -**uī, -tum**, to hold

**tepidárium, -ī** (*n*), warm room (at baths)

41 **térgeō, -gére** (2), **-sī, -sum,** to dry, wipe
**térra, -ae** (*f*), earth
**térror, -ṓris** (*m*), terror, fear
**tértius, -a, -um,** third
46 **téssera, -ae** (*f*), ticket
41 **thérmae, -árum** (*f pl*), public baths
43 **Thísbē, -ēs** (*f*), Thisbe
48 **tígris, -is** (*m/f*), tiger
**tímeō** (2), to fear
**tímidus, -a, -um,** afraid, fearful, timid
43 **tímidē,** fearfully, timidly
**tímor, -ṓris** (*m*), fear
**tóga, -ae** (*f*), toga
   **tóga praetéxta,** toga with purple edging
50    **tóga pū́ra,** plain white toga
   **tóga virī́lis,** toga worn by adult male (plain white)
46 **tóllō, -ere** (3), **sústulī, sublátum,** to lift, raise
46 **tot,** so many
**tṓtus, -a, -um,** all, the whole
**trā́dō, -ere** (3), **-idī, -itum,** to hand over
**tráhō, -here** (3), **-xī, -ctum,** to drag, pull
**trānsgrédior, -dī** (3), **-ssus sum,** to cross
**trémō, -ere** (3), **-uī,** to tremble
51 **trépidāns, -ntis,** in a panic
**trēs, trēs, tría,** three
41 **trígōn, -ṓnis** (*m*), ball game involving three people
**trístis, -is, -e,** sad
**tū,** you (sing.)
46 **túbicen, -inis** (*m*), trumpet-player
**tum,** at that moment, then
**tumúltus, -ūs** (*m*), uproar, din, commotion
**túnica, -ae** (*f*), tunic
**túrba, -ae** (*f*), crowd
**túus, -a, -um,** your (sing.)

# U

**Úbi . . . ?** Where . . . ?
**úbi,** where, when
**úlulō** (1), to howl
**úmbra, -ae** (*f*), shadow, shade (of the dead)
**úmquam,** ever
**ū́nā,** together
**Únde . . . ?** Where . . . from?
**úndique,** on all sides, from all sides
41 **unguéntum, -ī** (*n*), ointment, perfume, oil
41 **únguō, -guere** (3), **-xī, -ctum,** to anoint, smear with oil
**ū́nus, -a, -um,** one
**urbā́nus, -a, -um,** of the city or town
   **rēs urbā́nae,** affairs of the town
**urbs, -bis** (*f*), city
51 **úrgeō, -ḗre** (2), **úrsī,** to press, insist
**ut** (+ *indicative*), when, as
49 **ut** (+ *subjunctive*), so that, that, to
43 **utérque, útraque, utrúmque,** each (of two), both
51 **útrum . . . an . . . ,** whether . . . or . . .
**úxor, -ṓris** (*f*), wife

# V

**váldē,** very, very much
**Válē! Valḗte!** Goodbye!
43 **valedī́cō, -cere** (3), **-xī, -ctum,** to say goodbye, bid farewell
41 **vápor, -ṓris** (*m*), steam
41 **várius, -a, -um,** different, various, varied
**veheménter,** violently, furiously, insistently
**vel,** or
   **vel . . . vel . . . ,** either . . . or . . .
43 **vēlā́men, -inis** (*n*), veil, shawl, head-scarf

vēnátiō, -ónis (f), hunting, animal hunt

vēndō, -ere (3), -idī, -itum, to sell

véniō, venīre (4), vénī, véntum, to come

véntus, -ī (m), wind

vérberō (1), to beat

verbósus, -a, -um, talkative    53

vérbum, -ī (n), word, verb

véreor, -érī (1), -itus sum, to be afraid, fear    43

vérus, -a, -um, true

rē vérā, really, actually

vérō, truly, really, actually    53

Íta vérō! Yes!    52

véscor, -ī (3) (+ abl.), to feed (on)    43

véster, -tra, -trum, your (pl.)

vestíbulum, -ī (n), entrance passage

vestígium, -ī (n), track, footprint, trace

vestīménta, -órum (n pl), clothes

véstis, -is (f), clothing, garment

scíssā véste, with torn clothing

vétō, -áre (1), -uī, -itum, to forbid, tell not to    49

véxō (1), to annoy, tease

vía, -ae (f), road, street

viátor, -óris (m), traveler    43

vīcínus, -a, -um, neighboring    49

vídeō, vidére (2), vídī, vísum, to see

vídeor, vidérī (2), vísus sum, to seem, be seen

vílla, -ae (f), farmhouse

víncō, -ere (3), vícī, víctum, to win, conquer, overcome

vínum, -ī (n), wine

víolō (1), to do harm to

vir, vírī (m), man

vírgō, -inis (f), maiden

virílis, -is, -e, a man's, of a man

vīs, vim (acc.), vī (abl.) (f), force

vísitō (1), to visit

víta, -ae (f), life

vítta, -ae (f), ribbon, headband

vívō, -vere (3), -xī, -ctum, to live

vix, scarcely, with difficulty, only just

vócō (1), to call, invite

vólō, vélle (irreg.), vóluī, to wish, want, be willing

vōs, you (pl.)

vōx, vócis (f), voice

submíssā vōce, in a subdued voice

vúlnerō (1), to wound

vúlnus, -eris (n), wound

vúltus, -ūs (f), face, expression

vúltū dēmíssō, with eyes lowered

159

# ACKNOWLEDGMENTS

For providing us with photographs, drawings or permission to publish extracts from their publications, we would like to thank:

Page 9: Reproduced by Courtesy of the Trustees of the British Museum, photograph of a bronze oil flask and two strigils. Page 12: The Mansell Collection, photograph of the women's changing room. Page 13: Reprinted by the publisher, George Braziller, Inc., drawing of Hadrian's Baths at Lepcis Magna. Page 16: The Mansell Collection, photograph of Baths of Caracalla. Page 38: Scala/Art Resource, NY, photograph of women playing knucklebones. Page 46: Photograph, Peter Clayton, photograph of the Colosseum. Page 51: The Trustees of the British Museum, photograph of a sestertius. Page 58: The Mansell Collection, a drawing of a sea fight. Page 63: The Mansell Collection, photograph of a gladiator's helmet. Page 81: The Trustees of the British Museum, photograph of a betrothal ring. Pages 88–89: The Mansell Collection, photograph of a procession on its way to the altar. Page 106: Claudia Karabaic Sargent, drawing of statue of a man carrying funeral busts. Page 108: Claudia Karabaic Sargent, drawing of funeral relief.

The extract on page 21: From *The Satyricon* by Petronius, translated by William Arrowsmith. Copyright © 1959 by William Arrowsmith. Reprinted by arrangement with New American Library, New York, New York.

The extract on page 57: *Roman Voices: Everyday Latin in Ancient Rome* by Carol Clemeau Esler and *Teacher's Guide to Roman Voices: Everyday Latin in Ancient Rome*, published by Gilbert Lawall, 71 Sand Hill Road, Amherst, MA 01002.

The extracts on the following pages are reprinted by permission of Harvard University Press and The Loeb Classical Library, Cambridge, Mass.:

Page 21: *Plautus*, Volume IV, translated by Paul Nixon, (1965).

Page 26: *Satires, Epistles, and Ars Poetica* by Horace, translated by H. Rushton Fairclough, (1978).

Page 38–39: *The Art of Love, and Other Poems* by Ovid, translated by J. H. Mozley, (1962).

Page 39: *De Officiis*, Volume XXI by Cicero, translated by Walter Miller, (1975).

Page 39: *Suetonius*, Volume I, translated by J. C. Rolfe, (1979).

Page 40: *Moral Essays*, Volume II by Seneca, translated by John W. Basore, (1965).

Page 48: *Martial Epigrams*, Volume I, translated by Walter C. A. Ker, (1979).

Page 66: *Ad Lucilium Epistulae Morales*, Volume I by Seneca, translated by Richard M. Gummere, (1967).

Page 81: *The Attic Nights of Aulus Gellius*, Volume II, translated by John C. Rolfe, (1982).

Page 87: *Letters of Atticus*, Volume I by Cicero, translated by E. O. Winstedt, (1962).

Page 87: *Letters of Atticus*, Volume II by Cicero, translated by E. O. Winstedt, (1966).

Page 90: *Livy*, Volume I, translated by B. O. Foster, (1957).

Page 90: *De Senectute, De Amicitia, De Diviniatione*, Volume XX by Cicero, translated by William Armistead Falconer, (1979).

Page 102: *Pliny the Younger: Letters and Panegyricus*, Volume I, translated by Betty Radice, (1969).

# Ecce Romani

A Latin Reading Program
Revised Edition

## 5

## Public Life
## and Private Lives

Longman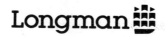

Ecce Romani Part 5 Public Life and Private Lives

*Illustrated by Claudia Karabaic Sargent. Cover illustration by Judy Hans Price.*

# CONTENTS

5

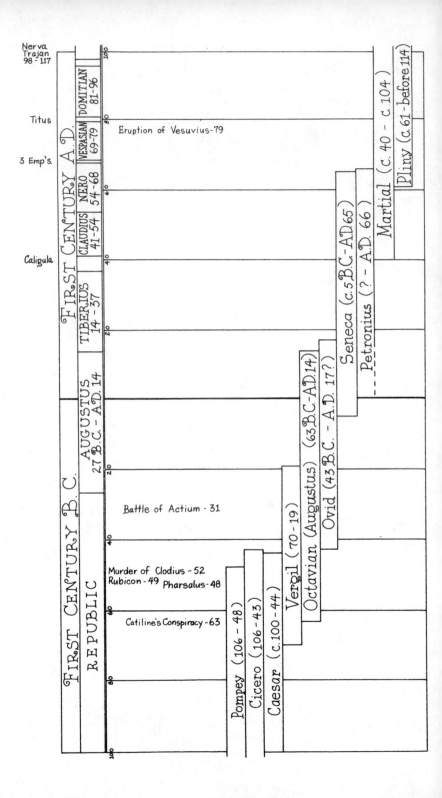

# PART I
# A Satirist's View of Life in the Early Empire

The readings for Chapters 54–56 are taken from a comic novel of the first century a.d. known as the *Satyricon*. Its author is usually identified with the C. Petronius described by Tacitus as a man who held a privileged but dangerous position as unofficial "Arbiter of Elegance" at the court of Nero. Yet as governor of Bithynia, and later consul, he showed himself a capable and energetic administrator. Eventually he aroused Nero's suspicions and died by suicide (a form of imperial execution), surrounded by friends who comforted him "not with philosophical doctrines but frivolous songs and light verse."

The longest and most famous of the surviving fragments of the *Satyricon* is the *Cena Trimalchionis* (*Banquet of Trimalchio*). It describes an elaborate dinner party given by the ex-slave and self-made millionaire Trimalchio. An army of slaves serves a vast array of dishes, most of them disguised as something other than what they are: glowing "coals" made of sliced damsons and pomegranates, a roast boar with sausages for entrails, a sow with pastry "piglets." From time to time the guests are entertained by musicians, actors, or singing waiters of various degrees of awfulness. But some of the most interesting and amusing passages of the *Cena* are those in which Petronius lets us eavesdrop on the conversations of Trimalchio and his guests. These conversations, from which our selections are taken, are unique in Latin literature for the vividness with which they portray the habits of speech and thought of ordinary people in the ancient Roman world.

The readings for this and the next chapter consist of monologues by two of Trimalchio's freedmen guests. Both are concerned with local politics, its relationship to the high cost of living, and the "bread and circuses" that were the Roman politician's key to popularity and re-election. Their philosophy is echoed by the Pompeian campaign posters shown below.

---

"SERVA ME, SERVABO TE" "*You take care of me, I'll take care of you.*"

Sabīnum aed(īlem), Procule, fac et ille tē faciet. *Elect Sabinus aedile, Proculus, and he'll elect you.*

Popidium Secundum aed(īlem), Rufine, favē et ille tē faciet. *Support Popidius Secundus for aedile, Rufinus, and he'll elect you.*

(Pompeian campaign posters)

---

7

1  **is:** the previous speaker, who has been gossiping about personal matters that Ganymedes regards as trivial and irrelevant (**nec . . . pertinet**).

    **quod:** the antecedent is omitted: "He's talking about what. . . ."

2  **quid:** "how much."

    **mordet:** we say the "pinch" of inflation. Why would **mordeat** be more correct?

4  **Aedīlēs . . . ēveniat:** more correctly, **aedīlibus** (dat.), "Damn the aediles!" (literally, "May it go badly for the aediles!").

5  **labōrat:** not just "work hard" but "suffer," "are oppressed."

    **maiōrēs māxillae:** slang for "the greedy rich," "the fat cats"; **istī** used loosely for **istae** as if in apposition rather than agreement with the noun.

6  **habērēmus:** subjunctive expressing a wish, "if only we had. . . ."

    **leōnēs:** i.e., bold and aggressive men, like Safinius in the next line.

7  **Asiā:** many Roman slaves came from the East, especially Asia Minor (Turkey).

8  **piper, nōn homō:** another slang expression, "(he wasn't) a man, he was a walking pepperbox," i.e., fiery-tempered.

10  **pilābat:** literally, "removed their hair," i.e., "gave them a scalping."

11  **schēmās:** "(fancy) figures of speech"; **schēma, schēmatis** (*n*) is here treated by an uneducated speaker as if it belonged to the 1st declension.

13  **nesciō quid Asiādis:** "something Asiatic (about him)"; to Ganymedes this is presumably a compliment, referring to Safinius' cool urbanity. **nesciō quid:** "something," often followed by a partitive genitive.

    **resalūtāre . . . reddere:** infinitives loosely used to complete the meaning of **benīgnus:** "gracious in returning your greeting. . . ."

15  **prō lutō:** "equivalent to (i.e., as cheap as) mud," "dirt-cheap."

    **Asse:** abl. of price, "for an **ās**," i.e., very cheaply.

    **ēmissēs:** "you had bought."

16  **nōn potuissēs:** "you couldn't have."

17  **cōda** = **cauda**, reflecting colloquial pronunciation.

18  **trium cauniārum:** gen. of value, "worth three figs," i.e., worthless.

21  **Quod . . . attinet:** "as for (what concerns) me."

22  **pannōs . . . comēdī:** i.e., sold or pawned them to buy food.

23  **futūrum:** "going to happen."

    **colōniae:** gen. object of **miserentur**.

24  **Ita . . . putō:** literally, "So may I enjoy my (family), as I think," or simply "So help me, I think. . . ."

    **diibus** = **dīs**.

25  **pilī facit:** literally, "values at a hair" (gen. of value), i.e., "cares two cents for."

26  **opertīs oculīs:** Romans covered their heads during prayer; Ganymedes seems to suggest that his contemporaries hypocritically pretend to pray while in reality they are counting their cash.

27  **in clīvum:** "up the hill," i.e., the Capitoline in Rome, at the top of which stood the temple of Jupiter Capitolinus.

28  **urceātim:** "in pitchers" or "by the pitcherful," as we say "in buckets."

    **plovēbat** = **pluēbat**.

29  **diī . . . habent:** the allusion is obscure, but it must mean the gods have turned away from, or been ignored by, the town because of its impiety.

30  **iacent:** i.e., unused, fallow; here Ganymedes is interrupted by the next speaker, whose speech forms the reading for the next chapter.

# 54
# The Cost of Living

*Ganymedes bemoans the sky-high price of food, the corruption of politicians, and the demise of the good old-fashioned virtues.*

Dīxit Ganymēdēs: "Nārrat is quod nec ad caelum nec ad terram pertinet, cum interim nēmō cūrat, quid annōna mordet. Nōn mehercules hodiē buccam pānis invenīre potuī. Et quōmodo siccitās persevērat! Iam annum ēsurītiō fuit. Aedīlēs male ēveniat, quī cum pistōribus collūdunt: 'Servā mē, servābō tē.' Itaque populus minūtus labōrat; nam istī maiōrēs māxillae sem- 5 per Sāturnālia agunt. Ō sī haberēmus illōs leōnēs, quōs ego hīc invēnī, cum prīmum ex Asiā vēnī! Illud erat vīvere.]Sed meminī Safīnium; tunc habitābat ad arcum veterem, mē puerō: piper, nōn homō. Is quācumque ībat, terram adūrēbat. Sed rēctus, sed certus, amīcus amīcō, cum quō audācter possēs in tenebrīs micāre. In cūriā autem quōmodo singulōs pilābat! 10 Nec schēmās loquēbātur sed dīrēctum. Cum ageret porrō in forō, sīc illīus vōx crēscēbat tamquam tuba. Nec sūdāvit umquam nec expuit; putō eum nesciō quid Asiādis habuisse. Et quam benīgnus resalūtāre, nōmina omnium reddere, tamquam ūnus dē nōbīs!

"Itaque illō tempore annōna prō lutō erat. Asse pānem quem ēmissēs, 15 nōn potuissēs cum alterō dēvorāre. Nunc oculum būblum vīdī maiōrem. Heu heu, cotīdiē pēius! Haec colōnia retrōversus crēscit tamquam cōda vitulī. Sed quārē nōs habēmus aedīlem trium cauniārum, quī sibi māvult assem quam vītam nostram? Itaque domī gaudet, plūs in diē nummōrum accipit quam alter patrimōnium habet. Iam sciō unde accēperit dēnāriōs 20 mīlle aureōs. Sed populus est domī leōnēs, forās vulpēs. Quod ad mē attinet, iam pannōs meōs comēdī, et sī persevērat haec annōna, casulās meās vēndam. Quid enim futūrum est, sī nec diī nec homines eius colōniae miserentur? Ita meōs frūniscar, ut ego putō omnia illa ā diibus fierī. Nēmō enim caelum caelum putat, nemō iēiūnium servat, nēmō Iovem pilī facit, 25 sed omnēs opertīs oculīs bona sua computant. Anteā stolātae ībant nūdīs pedibus in clīvum, passīs capillīs, mentibus pūrīs, et Iovem aquam exōrābant. Itaque statim urceātim plovēbat, aut tunc aut numquam, et omnēs redībant ūdī tamquam mūrēs. Itaque diī pedēs lānātōs habent, quia nōs religiōsī nōn sumus. Agrī iacent—"  30

—Petronius, *Satyricon* 44

interim, meanwhile
annōna, -ae (*f*), (price of) grain
bucca, -ae (*f*), cheek, mouthful

siccitās, siccitātis (*f*), drought
ēsurītiō, ēsurītiōnis (*f*), famine
aedīlis, aedīlis (*m*), aedile

minūtus, -a, -um, little, minute
iste, ista, istud, this, that (of yours)
  (often disparaging)
māxilla, -ae (f), jaw
Sāturnālia, -ium (n pl), the Saturnalia, festival of Saturn; Sāturnālia agere, to celebrate the
  Saturnalia
tunc, then, at that time
piper, piperis (n), pepper
quācumque, wherever
audācter, boldly, with confidence
tenebrae, -ārum (f pl), darkness
singulī, -ae, -a, single, individual,
  each and every one
dīrēctum (adverb), directly, simply
porrō, then, furthermore
tamquam, like, as if
tuba, -ae (f), trumpet
sūdō (l), to sweat
benīgnus, -a, -um, kind, friendly
ās, assis (m), as, a small coin com-
  parable to a penny
būb(u)lus, -a, -um, of or belonging
  to an ox

Heu! Alas! Ah me!
colōnia, -ae (f), colony, town
retrōversus (adverb), backwards
vitulus, -ī (m), calf
Quārē . . . ? Why . . . ?
nummus, -ī (m), coin, money
forās (adverb), out of doors
vulpēs, vulpis (f), fox
pannus, -ī (m), cloth, garment
casula, -ae (f), little house, hut
iēiūnium, -ī (n), a fast, fast-day
Iuppiter, Iovis (m), Jupiter, king of
  the gods
computō (l), to add up, count
stolāta, -ae (f), woman dressed in a
  stola (long robe)
passus, -a, -um, disheveled
mēns, mentis (f), mind, heart
exōrō (l), to pray for (implying that
  your prayer will be answered)
ūdus, -a, -um, wet
lānātus, -a, -um, bearing wool,
  wrapped in wool
quia, because

mordeō, mordēre (2), momordī, morsum, to bite
ēveniō, ēvenīre (4), ēvēnī, ēventum, to happen, turn out
collūdō, collūdere (3), collūsī, collūsum, to connive, be in cahoots
meminī, meminisse (perfect with present meaning), to remember
adūrō, adūrere (3), adūssī, adūstum, to set on fire, burn, scorch
crēscō, crēscere (3), crēvī, crētum, to rise, grow, swell
expuō, expuere (3), expuī, expūtum, to spit out, spit
attineō, attinēre (2), attinuī, to concern
comedō, comesse (3), comēdī, comēsum, to eat up, eat
misereor, miserērī (2), miseritus sum (+ gen.), to pity, take pity on
frūniscor, frūniscī (3), frūnītus sum, to enjoy

## Exercise 54a

*Answer the following questions in English, with reference to the specified lines of the reading passage.*

1.  What aspect of politics would you say is uppermost in Ganymedes' mind?
    (2–6, 15–16, 21–23)

2. Judging from Ganymedes' remarks, what did a Roman politician have to do to be popular with the common people? (6–9, 9–10, 10–12, 12–14)
3. Describe the style of political oratory preferred by Ganymedes. (10–12)
4. What does Ganymedes object to in present-day politicians? (4–6, 18–20)
5. How does Ganymedes describe his own condition? (2–3, 21–23)
6. What evidence do you find of a nostalgic view of the past on Ganymedes' part? (6–14, 15–17, 24–29)

## Exercise 54b

1. Have you ever listened to a present-day conversation that reminded you of Ganymedes' speech? What would the similarities be? The differences?
2. Do you share Ganymedes' enthusiasm for Safinius? Why or why not?
3. Do Ganymedes' views on politicians seem to you similar to those of anyone you know or have read about? His views on religion?
4. In what senses is Ganymedes a "true Roman." In what senses is he not?

# Building Up the Meaning IX
## The Subjunctive in Subordinate Clauses

You have already met several types of subordinate clauses that use the subjunctive mood:

1. Indirect Questions:
   Pīrātae rogābant quī essēmus, unde vēnissēmus, quō iter facerēmus.
   *The pirates kept asking who we were, where we had come from, and where we were traveling.*

2. Circumstantial Clauses:
   Cum sē exercuissent, in tepidārium ingressī sunt.
   *When they had exercised, they went into the warm room.*

3. Causal Clauses:
   Grammaticus, cum Sextus ubi Hesperia esset ignōrāret, ferulam rapuit.
   *Since Sextus didn't know where Hesperia was, the teacher snatched up his cane.*

4. Result Clauses:
   Adeō perturbāta erat ut vix loquī posset.
   *She was so confused that she could hardly speak.*

5. Indirect Commands:
   Hī iānitōrem ōrant nē sē dīmittat.
   *They keep begging the doorkeeper not to send them away.*

6. Purpose Clauses:
   Auspex prōcēdit ut porcum sacrificet.
   *The priest steps forward to sacrifice a pig.*

11

## Sequence of Tenses

As you learned in Chapter 49, all of these subjunctive clauses follow the sequence of tenses:

### PRIMARY SEQUENCE

| *Verb of Main Clause* | *Verb of Subordinate Clause* |
|---|---|
| present, future, or future perfect indicative | present subjunctive (for action going on at the *same time* as that of the main verb) |

Nōn intellegō cūr servae mē **neglegant**.
*I do not understand why the slave-girls* **neglect** *me.*

perfect subjunctive (for action that took place *before* that of the main verb)

Nōn intellegō cūr servae mē **neglēxerint**.
*I do not understand why the slave-girls* **neglected** *me.*

### SECONDARY SEQUENCE

| *Verb of Main Clause* | *Verb of Subordinate Clause* |
|---|---|
| imperfect, perfect, or pluperfect indicative | imperfect subjunctive (for action going on at the *same time* as that of the main verb) |

Nōn intellegēbam cūr servae mē **neglegerent**.
*I did not understand why the slave-girls* **were neglecting** *me.*

pluperfect subjunctive (for action that took place *before* that of the main verb)

Nōn intellegēbam cūr servae mē **neglēxissent**.
*I did not understand why the slave-girls* **had neglected** *me.*

## Sequence of Tenses in Result Clauses

In result clauses there often occurs an apparent exception to the usual sequence of tenses. The perfect and pluperfect subjunctive are not used in the usual way, because a result cannot occur before the action that produces it. The *present subjunctive* is used in primary sequence, as you would expect. In secondary sequence, however the *perfect subjunctive* often replaces the expected imperfect. This use of the perfect emphasizes the finality or completeness of the result (**perfectum** = "completed").

Leō tantus et tam ferōx erat ut servus metū exanimātus **ceciderit**.
*The lion was so big and so fierce that the slave* **fell down** *paralyzed with fear.*

12

## Exercise 54c

*Select, read aloud, translate, and identify the type of subordinate clause in each sentence; pay careful attention to sequence of tenses.*

1. Vōx Safīniī crēvit tamquam tuba cum in forō (ēgit, agat, ageret).
2. Safīnius tam benīgnus erat ut omnibus grātissimus (fuit, esset, fuerit).
3. Nesciō quārē nōs (habēmus, habeāmus, habērēmus) aedīlem trium cauniārum.
4. Illī persuāsimus ut casulās suās (vēnderet, vēndidisset, vēndat).
5. Cum nēmō Iovem pilī (faciēbat, fēcit, faceret), diī huius colōniae nōn miseritī sunt.
6. Rōmānae Iovem tantum ōrāvērunt ut statim (pluerit, pluēbat, pluit).
7. Rogās cūr nōs religiōsī nōn (sumus, fuissēmus, sīmus).
8. Nēmō cūrābat quid annōna (mordēret, mordeat, momorderit).
9. Ille tam rēctus, tam certus est ut (potuerās, potueris, possīs) cum eō in tenebrīs micāre.
10. Safīnius nōmina omnium reddēbat ut populō grātus (fuisset, esset, fuerit).

## A Witch Story (Part One)

In addition to personal and political gossip, another kind of conversation enjoyed by Trimalchio and his dinner guests is the exchanging of spooky stories. You have already read Niceros' tale of the werewolf in Review XII. Trimalchio, never one to let himself be upstaged, replies to that story with one from his own experience.

Et ipse vōbīs rem horribilem nārrābō. Cum adhūc capillātus essem (nam ā puerō vītam Chīam gessī), ipsimī nostrī dēlicātus dēcessit, meherculēs margarītum. Cum ergō illum māter misella plangeret et nōs tum plūrēs in trīstimōniō essēmus, subitō strīdēre strīgae coepērunt; putārēs canem le-

---

1 **capillātus:** "a long-haired boy"; handsome young slaves, such as Trimalchio was at the time of this story, were thought to be more attractive if their hair was worn long and curly.
2 **ā puerō:** "from childhood."
   **vītam Chīam:** i.e., a life of luxury like that on the Greek island of Chios.
   **ipsimī:** "master"; **ipsimus** is a shortened form of **ipsissimus,** superlative of **ipse,** "Himself," commonly used to designate the head of a household.
3 **misella:** "poor little"; colloquial speakers were fond of diminutives (see Word Study XI).
   **nōs . . . plūrēs:** "several (of) us."
4 **trīstimōniō:** "sadness," "sorrow," another colloquial word, used instead of the classical **trīstitia.**
   **putārēs:** "you would have thought."

porem persequī. Habēbāmus tunc hominem Cappadocem, longum, valdē 5
audāculum et quī valēbat: poterat bovem īrātum tollere. Hic audācter strictō
gladiō extrā ōstium prōcucurrit, involūtā sinistrā manū cūriōsē, et mulierem
tamquam hōc locō (salvum sit, quod tangō!) mediam trāiēcit. Audīmus
gemitum et (plānē nōn mentiar) ipsās nōn vīdimus.

—Petronius, *Satyricon* 63.2–6

(to be concluded in Chapter 55)

6 **audāculum:** from **audāx**; another diminutive form.
8 **tamquam hōc locō:** "just about here"; Trimalchio apparently points to his own
abdomen as he speaks these words; this is implied by **salvum sit, quod tangō!**:
"heaven preserve what I'm touching!"

**dēlicātus, -ī** (*m*), favorite, pet
**margarītum, -ī** (*n*), pearl
**ergō,** therefore, so
**strīga, -ae** (*f*), witch
**Cappadox, Cappadocis,** Cappadocian, of Cappadocia in Asia Minor

**ōstium, -ī** (*n*), door
**cūriōsē,** carefully
**gemitus, -ūs** (*m*), groan
**plānē,** wholly, absolutely

**gerō, gerere** (3), **gessī, gestum,** to live, spend (time)
**plangō, plangere** (3), **plānxī, planctum,** to beat (especially the breast or head,
in grief), lament
**strīdeō, strīdēre** (2), **strīdī,** to shriek, howl
**persequor, persequī** (3), **persecūtus sum,** to pursue, chase
**prōcurrō, prōcurrere** (3), **prōcucurrī, prōcursum,** to run forth, rush out
**involvō, involvere** (3), **involvī, involūtum,** to wrap in, wrap up
**tangō, tangere** (3), **tetigī, tactum,** to touch
**trāiciō, trāicere** (3), **trāiēcī, trāiectum,** to stab through, pierce
**mentior, mentīrī** (4), **mentītus sum,** to lie, deceive

## Exercise 54d

*Using the witch story as a guide, give the Latin for:*

1. Trimalchio says that he led a "Chian life" from childhood.
2. The poor little mother was lamenting (her) dead son.
3. The witches' shrieking (**strīdor**) was like (**similis** + *dat.*) the voice of a
   dog chasing a rabbit.
4. The Cappadocian was so strong that he could pick up an angry ox.
5. When he had drawn his sword and wrapped up his left hand, he rushed
   out the door.
6. He pierces the shrieking witch with his sword.
7. Trimalchio heard the witches' groans but did not see the women themselves.

# 55
# *Bread and Circuses*

The gossip at Trimalchio's party is continued by another guest, a rag dealer named Echion. He emphasizes a different aspect of local politics: the gladiatorial shows and handouts of food or money that a Roman politician was expected to give his constituents. Echion's political attitudes were shared by real Romans, as is shown by these election posters from Pompeii:

### C. IULIUM POLYBIUM AED(ILEM) O(RO) V(OS) F(ACIATIS): PANEM BONUM FERT!
*I ask you to elect C. Julius Polybius aedile: he provides good bread!*

### M. CASELLIUM MARCELLUM AEDILEM BONUM ET MUNERARIUM MAGNUM.
*M. Casellius Marcellus: a good aedile and a great show-sponsor!*

Another aspect of Echion's attitude toward local officials is echoed by the following inscription in honor of a real-life politician who held office in the Campanian town of Minturnae in the middle of the third century A.D.:

> To Publius Baebius Justus, son of Publius, of the Terentine tribe. To this man the senate (of Minturnae) decreed that a statue be set up, because he had held every office in the city, because to each and every (citizen) he always showed equal respect, and because after holding the splendid office of duumvir, by popular request when his inaugural show was held, he willingly undertook a (second) gladiatorial show by imperial dispensation, consisting of three pairs (of gladiators) plus bears and herbivores. In consideration of the granting of the statue he gave each of the decurions three denarii. Land granted by decree of the decurions.
>
> He sponsored at Minturnae, in four days, eleven pairs (of gladiators): of these he killed eleven of Campania's finest gladiators; he also slaughtered ten bears, and cruelly. As you yourselves recall, excellent citizens, he killed all the herbivores on each of the four days.

"Dē Lucernā Equitēs"

15

1 **centōnārius:** a maker of patchwork, a rag dealer.
  **modo . . . sīc:** "sometimes it's one way, sometimes another": i.e., life has its
  ups and downs. This is also the implication of the spotted pig (2).
3 **patria:** "town": this Campanian town, the setting of the *Cena*, is never named.
4 **habēret:** "if (only) it had."
5 **ubīque . . . est:** proverbial for "things are pretty much the same everywhere."
  **porcōs . . . ambulāre:** i.e., an earthly paradise where life is effortless.
7 **in trīduō:** i.e., three days from now, "in three days"; **excellente = excellēns.**
  **familia . . . lanistīcia:** "troupe (of gladiators) owned by a **lanista,**" a manager-
  trainer. The gladiators provided by Titus are veterans freed (**lībertī**) as a reward
  for skillful fighting, and so presumably of better quality.
8 **Titus:** the current aedile, who is paying for the show.
  **magnum . . . caldicerebrius:** "is generous and impulsive," spares no expense.
10 **miscix:** "mixed," i.e., diluted, wishy-washy; he doesn't do things by halves.
  **sine fugā:** defeated gladiators will be killed, not dismissed to fight another day
  —an expensive policy for the sponsor, but popular with the fans.
11 **unde:** "(the funds) from which (to pay)," as we say "the wherewithal."
12 **trecentiēs:** this is the standard Roman way of expressing millions of sesterces:
  **sēstertiūm** (gen. pl. typical of nouns denoting coins), **centēna mīlia** understood, and a numerical adverb in **-iēs;** here 300 × 100,000 = 30,000,000.
  **male:** probably implying premature rather than unnatural or painful death.
  **Ut:** concessive, with subjunctive, "even if he should . . . ."
  **quadringenta:** supply **mīlia sēstertiūm.**
14 **essedāriam:** "who fights from an **esseda,**" a Celtic war-chariot.
15 **matella:** literally, "chamber-pot"; here, slang for "slut."
  **digna . . . iactāret:** "deserved to be gored by a bull," rather than her lover.
16 **Quid . . . ?:** "Why . . . ?" or more freely, "What made him think . . . ?"
17 **filicem:** a weed that bothered farmers; metaphorically, a worthless person.
  **Ille:** Hermogenes, the wife's father; **milvō volantī** is dative of interest, equivalent
  to a genitive; the phrase is proverbial for a sharp operator.
18 **colubra . . . parit:** another proverb, similar to "like father, like son."
19 **subolfaciō, quia:** "get a whiff (i.e., suspect) that . . . ."
  **epulum:** here not a real dinner but a cash bonus, "two **dēnariī** per person."
20 **Quod sī:** "But if"; **Norbānō:** another local politician.
  **Sciās oportet:** "You must know . . . ," "You better believe . . ."
21 **plēnīs vēlīs:** like a ship with favorable winds, easily, "hands down."
  **vincitūrum:** Echion's illiterate attempt at the future participle of **vincō.**
22 **sēstertiāriōs:** "worth one **sēstertius,**" as we say "two-bit."
  **sī sufflāssēs, cecidissent:** "if you had . . . , they would have . . . ."
23 **Occīdit:** the subject is Norbanus; he did not literally kill the losers himself but
  authorized the **lanista** to have them killed rather than released.
  **dē lucernā equitēs:** "knights off a lamp," i.e., puny, lifeless fighters.
  **gallōs . . . lōripēs:** "barnyard roosters . . . a mere stick . . . a clubfoot."
24 **tertiārius:** a "third man" or substitute sent in to replace a dead fighter.
25 **quī . . . praecīsa:** he moved as if he were hamstrung.
  **quī . . . pugnāvit:** "and even he fought by the rules," without imagination.
27 **'Adhibēte!':** "(shouts of) 'Give it to 'em!' "
28 **plōdō = plaudō,** reflecting colloquial pronunciation.

*Echion, the rag dealer, interrupts Ganymedes: "Look on the bright side of things," he says, "for example, the upcoming gladiatorial show."*

"Ōrō tē," inquit Echion centōnārius, "melius loquere. 'Modo sīc, modo sīc,' inquit rūsticus: varium porcum perdiderat. Quod hodiē nōn est, crās erit: sīc vīta trūditur. Nōn meherculēs patria melior dīcī potest, sī hominēs habēret. Sed labōrat hōc tempore, nec haec sōla. Nōn dēbēmus dēlicātī esse; ubīque medius caelus est. Tū sī aliubi fueris, dīcēs hīc porcōs coctōs 5 ambulāre.

"Et ecce habitūrī sumus mūnus excellente in trīduō diē festā; familia nōn lanistīcia, sed plūrimī lībertī. Et Titus noster magnum animum habet et est caldicerebrius; aut hoc aut illud erit, quid utique. Nam illī domesticus sum, nōn est miscix. Ferrum optimum datūrus est, sine fugā, carnārium 10 in mediō, ut amphitheāter videat. Et habet unde: relictum est illī sēstertiūm treccntics; dēcessit illīus pater male. Ut quadringenta impendat, nōn sentiet patrimōnium illīus, et sempiternō nōminābitur. Iam nannōs aliquot habet et mulierem essedāriam et dispēnsātōrem Glycōnis, quī dēprehēnsus est cum dominam suam dēlectārētur. Magis illa matella digna fuit quam taurus 15 iactāret. Sed quī asinum nōn potest, strātum caedit. Quid autem Glycō putābat Hermogenis filicem umquam bonum exitum factūram? Ille milvō volantī poterat unguēs resecāre; colubra restem nōn parit.

"Sed subolfaciō, quia nōbīs epulum datūrus est Mammaea, bīnōs dēnāriōs mihi et meīs. Quod sī hoc fēcerit, ēripiat Norbānō tōtum favōrem. Sciās 20 oportet plēnīs vēlīs hunc vincitūrum. Et rēvērā, quid ille nōbis bonī fēcit? Dedit gladiātōrēs sēstertiāriōs iam dēcrepitōs, quōs sī sufflāssēs, cecidissent; iam meliōrēs bēstiāriōs vīdī. Occīdit de lucernā equitēs; putārēs eōs gallōs gallīnāceōs: alter burdubasta, alter lōripēs, tertiārius mortuus prō mortuō, quī habēret nervia praecīsa. Ūnus alicuius flatūrae fuit Thraex, quī et ipsc 25 ad dictāta pugnāvit. Ad summam, omnēs posteā sectī sunt; adeō dē magnā turbā 'Adhibēte!' accēperant: plānē fugae merae. 'Mūnus tamen,' inquit, 'tibi dedī': et ego tibi plōdō. Computā, et tibi plūs dō quam accēpī. Manus manum lavat."

—Petronius, *Satyricon* 45

**modo . . . modo,** now . . . now,
   sometimes . . . sometimes
**dēlicātus, -a, -um,** spoiled, fussy
**ubīque,** everywhere
**aliubi,** elsewhere, somewhere else
**trīduum, -ī** (*n*), three-day period
**festus, -a, -um,** festive, holiday
**utique,** at any rate, at least
**domesticus, -a, -um,** of the house
   or family, close, intimate

**fuga, -ae** (*f*), a fleeing, rout
**carnārium, -ī** (*n*), butcher-shop,
   slaughterhouse
**sēstertius, -ī** (*m*) (*gen. pl.* **sēster-**
   **tiūm**), sestertius, a coin worth
   four **assēs**
**trecentiēs** (*adverb*), three hundred
   times
**quadringentī, -ae, -a,** four hundred
**sempiternō,** forever

17

nannus, -ī (m), dwarf
aliquot (indeclinable), some, a few
dispēnsātor, dispēnsātōris (m),
    steward, household manager
dēlector (1), to please, amuse
dignus, -a, -um, worthy, deserving
taurus, -ī (m), bull
asinus, -ī (m), ass, donkey
strātum, -ī (n), blanket, saddle-
    cloth, saddle
exitus, -ūs (m), outcome, end
volō (1), to fly
unguis, unguis (m), nail (of finger
    or toe), claw
colubra, -ae (f), snake
restis, restis (f), rope
epulum, -ī (n), banquet, feast
bīnī, -ae, -a, two each

favor, favōris (m), support
vēlum, -ī (n), sail
sufflō (1), to blow on
bēstiārius, -ī (m), animal-fighter (in
    the arena)
eques, equitis (m), horseman, knight
nervia, -ōrum (n pl), sinews, ten-
    dons
flātūra, -ae (f), breath, fighting spirit
Thraex, Thraecis (m), Thracian,
    native of Thrace in northern
    Greece; a gladiator with Thra-
    cian equipment
dictāta, -ōrum (n pl), things dic-
    tated, rules
ad summam, in sum, in short
merus, -a, -um, pure, nothing but

perdō, perdere (3), perdidī, perditum, to lose
trūdō, trūdere (3), trūsī, trūsum, to push, shove (along)
impendō, impendere (3), impendī, impēnsum, to spend
dēprehendō, dēprehendere (3), dēprehendī, dēprehēnsum, to seize, catch
caedō, caedere (3), cecīdī, caesum, to cut, beat
resecō, resecāre (1), resecuī, resectum, to cut off, clip
pariō, parere (3), peperī, partum, to bear, give birth to
praecīdō, praecīdere (3), praecīdī, praecīsum, to cut off, cut through
secō, secāre (1), secuī, sectum, to cut, beat, flog
plaudō, plaudere (3), plausī, plausum, to applaud, clap the hands

## Exercise 55a

*Answer the following questions in English with reference to the specified
lines of the reading passage.*

1. What qualities does Echion chiefly value in a politician? (8–11, 19–20)
2. Why does Echion think Mammaea is likely to beat Norbanus in the
   coming election? (19–21, 22–25)
3. Does Echion value anything in gladiatorial fighting besides pure blood-
   shed? (25–26)
4. What does Echion mean by "I'm giving you more than I got"? (28)
5. What similarities do you see between the fictional "Titus" and the historical Baebius of Minturnae? (8–13, and inscription, page 15)

## Exercise 55b

1. How would you compare Echion's attitude toward violence in public entertainment with ours today?
2. Echion and Ganymedes are intended to represent the common man. But do you see anything in Petronius' portrayal of them that gives them individual personalities and distinguishes them from each other?
3. Do you find anything to admire in Echion or Ganymedes? Anything to dislike?

# Conditional Sentences

A conditional sentence has two parts:

a subordinate clause (if-clause or *protasis*) introduced by sī (negative **nisi**) expressing a condition

a main clause (*apodosis*) describing the situation that results, or would result, if this condition is, or were, fulfilled; in English this clause may be introduced by "then" (for which there is no equivalent in Latin).

Different kinds of conditional sentences in Latin require different kinds of verbs:

1. **Simple or factual conditions:** the verb of both clauses is in the *indicative*, in the *present* or *past* (imperfect or perfect tense), e.g.:
    a. Sī id dīcit, errat.
       *If* (in fact) *he* **says** *that*, (then) *he* **is wrong**.
    b. Sī id dīxit, errāvit.
       *If* (in fact) *he* **said** *that*, (then) *he* **was wrong**.

This kind of condition should cause no difficulty, because the verbs can be translated directly into English in the usual way.

2. **Future more/less vivid:** in these conditions, the events described in both clauses have not yet occurred; the speaker is speculating about what will, or might, happen if a certain condition is, or should be, fulfilled in the future. Latin distinguishes between
    a. a future situation that seems likely ("more vivid" in the speaker's mind), and
    b. a future situation that seems less likely ("less vivid" in the speaker's mind).
    a. **Future more vivid:** in this kind of condition (which you first encountered in Chapter 25), the verb of both clauses is in the *future indicative* (the verb of the sī-clause often in the *future perfect indicative*), where

English rather illogically puts the verb of the if-clause into the *present*, ignoring the fact that the event referred to has not yet occurred:

Sī quadringenta **impendet**, nōn **sentiet** patrimōnium.
*If he spends (will spend) 400,000, his inheritance will not feel it.*

Sī hoc **fēcerit, ēripiet** Norbānō tōtum favōrem.
*If he does (will have done) this, he will take away all support from Norbanus.*

b. **Future less vivid**: the verb of both clauses is in the *present subjunctive*; the subjunctive, as often in Latin, expresses the idea that something is less than certain or factual; the English equivalent is "should" or "were to" (if-clause) and "would" (main clause); these are often called *should-would conditions*.

Sī hoc **faciat, ēripiat** Norbānō tōtum favōrem.
*If he were to (should) do this, he would take away all support from Norbanus.*

## Exercise 55c

*Read aloud and translate. Pay particular attention to the tenses and moods of the verbs. Identify the type of condition in each sentence.*

1. Sī dēprehēnsus erit, pūniētur.
2. Sī dēprehendātur, pūniātur.
3. Nisi gladiātōrēs bene pugnant, spectātōrēs "Adhibēte!" clāmant.
4. Sī gladiātōrēs bene pugnābunt, spectātōrēs "Optimē!" clāmābunt.
5. Sī gladiātōrēs dēcrepitōs dēs, nōn tibi plaudam.
6. Nisi gladiātōrēs meliōrēs dederis, nōn tibi plaudam.
7. Sī hōs gladiātōrēs sufflēs, cadant.
8. Norbānus, nisi bīnōs dēnāriōs nōbīs dabit, tōtum favōrem perdet.

## Excercise 55d

*Using the reading passage as a guide, give the Latin for:*

1. If you were to go to another town (**patria**), you would say this one is better. (3–5)
2. If they were to spend four hundred (thousand sesterces), they could provide very good gladiators. (10, 12)
3. If his father should die, he would get thirty million. (11–12)
4. If that man's father dies, he will get thirty million. (11–12)
5. If you should do this, you would be talked about forever. (13)
6. If the aedile gives us a good dinner tomorrow, we will all be happy. (19)
7. Unless the aediles give a very good show, the people will be angry. (27–28)

# A Witch Story (Part Two)

Bārō autem noster intrōversus sē prōiēcit in lectum, et corpus tōtum līvidum habēbat quasi flagellīs caesus, quia scīlicet illum tetigerat mala manus. Nōs clūsō ōstiō redīmus iterum ad officium, sed dum māter amplexāret corpus fīliī suī, tangit et videt manuciolum dē strāmentīs factum. Nōn cor habēbat, nōn intestīna, nōn quicquam: scīlicet iam puerum strīgae 5 involāverant et supposuerant strāmenticium vavatōnem. Rogō vōs, oportet crēdātis, sunt mulierēs plussciae, sunt nocturnae, et quod sūrsum est, deorsum faciunt. Cēterum bārō ille longus post hoc factum numquam colōris suī fuit, immō post paucōs diēs frenēticus periit.

—Petronius, *Satyricon* 63.7–10

bārō, bārōnis (*m*), lout
intrōversus (*adverb*), (once) indoors (again)
līvidus, -a, -um, black and blue (as by bruising)
flagellum, -ī (*n*), whip
scīlicet, of course, no doubt
mala manus, (a witch's) evil hand
clūsus, -a, -um, colloquial for clausus
amplexō (1), embrace
manuciolum, -ī (*n*), small bundle
strāmentum, -ī (*n*), straw
quisquam, quicquam, anyone, anything

involō (1), to fly at, attack, carry off
strāmenticius, -a, -um, of straw
vavatō, -ōnis (*m*), doll, puppet
oportet crēdātis, you must believe
plusscius, -a, -um, skilled in witchcraft (literally, who know more than others, from plūs + sciō)
nocturnae, -ārum (*f pl*), nocturnal ones, i.e., witches
sūrsum (*adverb*), up, high
deorsum (*adverb*), down, low
cēterum, but
colōris suī, himself (literally, of his proper color)
frenēticus, -a, -um, raving mad

prōiciō, prōicere (3), prōiēcī, prōiectum, to throw (forward, headlong)
suppōnō, suppōnere (3), supposuī, suppositum, to put in place of
pereō, perīre (*irreg.*), periī, peritum, to perish, die

## Exercise 55e

*Read aloud and translate each of the following sentences, then tell whether it is* **Vērum** *or* **Falsum**; *if* **Falsum**, *give a correct Latin version.*

1. Corpus bārōnis līvidum erat quia flagellīs caesum erat.
2. Cum ōstium clausissēmus, prōiēcimus nōs in lectum.
3. Cum māter corpus fīliī tetigisset, vīdit strāmenticium vavatōnem.
4. Mulierēs plussciae puerum interfēcerant.
5. Bārō longus aliquot mēnsēs vīxit, deinde frenēticus periit.
6. Trimalchiō negat nocturnās esse.

21

# Building Up the Meaning X

## Indirect Statement

You have learned that Latin expresses indirect statement by means of an infinitive with its subject in the accusative. The most important thing to remember about this construction is that the tense of the verb (the infinitive) in the indirect statement is not absolute but *relative* to the tense of the main verb. The present infinitive expresses action at *the same time* as that of the main verb (whatever its tense), the perfect infinitive action *before*, and the future infinitive action *after* that of the main verb.

*Main Vb.*   *Inf.*

Present
{
Pres.   Sciō vōs **esse** molestissimōs.
*I know that you are very troublesome.*

Perf.   Audīmus Caesarem amphitheātrum novum **aperuisse**.
*We hear that Caesar has opened (or opened) a new amphitheater.*

Fut.   Prō certō habeō nōs tē **vīsūrōs esse**.
*I am sure that we will see you.*
}

Past
{
Pres.   Titus respondit sē domum redīre **nōlle**.
*Titus replied that he was unwilling to return home.*

Perf.   Sciēbāmus Marcum ad amphitheātrum **īvisse**.
*We knew that Marcus had gone to the amphitheater.*

Fut.   Prō certō habēbāmus Titum sērō **perventūrum esse**.
*We were sure that Titus would arrive late.*
}

Another important point to remember: the perfect passive and future active infinitives usually consist of **esse** plus a participle, which must agree with the subject of the infinitive in gender, case, and number:

Putō **Aurēliam** eō nōn **itūram** esse.
*I think that Aurelia will not go there.*

## Exercise 55f

*Complete the Latin translations of the following sentences with indirect statements, paying particular attention to the tense of the verb.*

1. We were hoping that Norbanus *would give* a better show.
   Spērābāmus Norbānum mūnus melius _____.
2. Do you know that that man *spent* four hundred (thousand sesterces)?
   Scīsne illum quadringenta _____?
3. They all believed that Norbanus *was making a mistake.* (**errō**)
   Omnēs crēdēbant Norbānum _____.
4. Nobody thought that the steward *had been* deservedly *punished.*
   Nēmō putāvit dispēnsātōrem meritō _____.
5. She was certain that *she was going to win.*
   Prō certō habēbat _____.

22

# 56
# A Millionaire's Tomb

Ganymedes, Echion, and Trimalchio's other guests give us a vivid impression, unique in Latin literature, of the mentality and the speech of ordinary Romans. But the real heart of the *Cena* is the brilliant comic portrait of Trimalchio himself. Every aspect of the banquet reveals some facet of Trimalchio's life and personality: the culinary extravaganzas, the service and entertainment, and the guests' comments concerning their host, his career, and his fabulous wealth. But of all the ways in which Petronius brings to life this great comic figure, Trimalchio's own speeches are the most revealing. The following passage, in which he describes the preparations he has made for his own death, is an example of this kind of self-characterization. As you read it, try to share Petronius' double vision: on the one hand, the way Trimalchio sees himself (i.e., the image he thinks he is presenting to others) and on the other hand the way we the readers see him. It is in the gap between these two ways of looking at the same man that much of the humor and humanity of the *Cena* is to be found.

Relief from the tomb of Q. Haterius Tychicus, a rich building contractor of the late first century A.D. A tomb-temple is shown, every inch of its surface crammed with sculpture. A crane (operated by slaves on a treadwheel) symbolizes the owner's trade. The upper right-hand corner gives an interior view of the temple: Haterius himself reclines on a couch while his three children play on the floor and his old nurse lays a sacrifice on an altar. To their right is a shrine of Venus with ancestor-masks above.

23

1 **et servī:** "slaves, too"; Trimalchio has just invited his slaves to share the dining couches with his guests; as they scramble to accept this offer, the dining room is thrown into confusion; Trimalchio then defends his liberal gesture with bits of ill-digested "philosophy."

    **aequē:** "equally," i.e., with us free men.

2 **lactem** = **lāc:** what is wrong here and in the following phrase **malus fātus?**

    **mē . . . gustābunt:** a humorous confusion of two incompatible ideas, "(they'll be all right) as long as I'm around" and "they'll go free (when I die)."

3 **aquam . . . gustābunt:** "they will taste the water of freedom," a cliché.

4 **ideō:** anticipates **ut;** omit in translating.

6 **oblītus nūgārum:** "getting down to business" (literally, "forgetting trifles").

8 **Habinnam:** Habinnas, one of Trimalchio's friends, a stonemason.

11 **Petraitis:** genitive of **Petraites**, a real gladiator of the 1st century A.D.

12 **ut sint:** continuing the indirect command construction from **rogō** (10).

    **in fronte . . . in agrum:** "frontage . . . deep"; such specifications for the size of a burial plot are common in Roman epitaphs.

13 **Omne genus . . . pōma:** "every kind of fruit tree"; the tombs of the wealthy were sometimes set in orchards or gardens.

    **sint:** supply **ut.**

14 **vīneārum largiter:** "plenty of grapevines."

    **vīvō . . . esse:** "for a living man to have"; **vīvō** is dative of possession, and the infinitives (**esse** and **cūrārī**) are the subjects of **est.**

15 **nōbīs habitandum est:** "we must live."

16 **Hoc . . . sequātur:** a formula often found in Roman epitaphs; it was intended to prevent sale or unauthorized use of the tomb by the heirs of the deceased: it did not "pass to" them (**sequātur**) with the rest of his possessions.

17 **nāvēs:** Trimalchio's vast fortune was founded on merchant shipping.

18 **tribūnālī:** in his epitaph (27) we learn that he was a **sēvir Augustālis**, one of the priests in charge of the worship of the emperor in the towns; a bordered toga, gold ring, and throne were symbols of the office.

19 **quod:** "that," introducing an indirect statement.

20 **Faciātur:** for **fiat;** singular either because Trimalchio mistakes **triclīnia** for a 1st declension noun, or because he is thinking in Greek, in which a neuter plural subject takes a singular verb; either way, his Latin is shaky.

21 **sibi suāviter facientem:** "enjoying themselves."

22 **cicarōnem:** "my little pet," probably his favorite slave.

23 **amphorās cōpiōsās gypsātās:** "large wine jars sealed with gypsum."

    **licet . . . sculpās:** "you may carve."

24 **in mediō:** supply **sit,** "let there be."

25 **velit nōlit:** "whether he wants to or not."

26 **vidē . . . haec:** "consider carefully whether this (inscription) . . . ."

27 **sēvirātus:** "the office of **sēvir**"; see note on line 18 above.

    **absentī:** with **huic,** "in his absence"; an additional honor, implying that he neither campaigned nor paid for the office.

28 **decuriīs:** the "boards" that formed the lower ranks of the Roman civil service.

29 **sēstertium . . . trecentiēs:** see note on 55:12.

30 **Valē. Et tū:** "Farewell (to you, passerby). And (to) you, (Trimalchio)." This and similar formulas are common in Roman epitaphs (see page 129).

24

*Trimalchio describes the elaborate tomb he is having prepared for himself.*

Trimalchiō, "Amīcī," inquit, "et servī hominēs sunt et aequē ūnum lactem bibērunt, etiam sī illōs malus fātus oppresserit. Tamen mē salvō, citō aquam līberam gustābunt. Ad summam, omnēs illōs in testāmentō meō manū mittō. Et haec ideō omnia pūblicō, ut familia mea iam nunc sīc mē amet tamquam mortuum."   5

Grātiās agere omnēs indulgentiae coeperant dominī, cum ille oblītus nūgārum exemplar testāmentī iussit afferrī et tōtum ā prīmō ad ultimum ingemēscente familiā recitāvit. Respiciēns deinde Habinnam, "Quid dīcis," inquit, "amīce cārissime? Aedificās monumentum meum, quemadmodum tē iussī? Valdē tē rogō, ut secundum pedēs statuae meae catellam pingās et   10 corōnās et unguenta et Petraitis omnēs pugnās, ut mihi contingat tuō beneficiō post mortem vīvere; praetereā ut sint in fronte pedēs centum, in agrum pedēs dūcentī. Omne genus enim pōma volō sint circā cinerēs meōs, et vīneārum largiter. Valdē enim falsum est vīvō quidem domōs cultās esse, nōn cūrārī eās, ubi diūtius nōbīs habitandum est. Et ideō ante omnia adicī   15 volō: 'Hoc monumentum hērēdem nōn sequātur.'

"Tē rogō ut nāvēs etiam in monumentō meō faciās plēnīs vēlīs euntēs, et mē in tribūnālī sedentem praetextātum cum ānulīs aureīs quīnque et nummōs in pūblicō dē sacculō effundentem; scīs enim, quod epulum dedī bīnōs dēnāriōs. Faciātur, sī tibi vidētur, et triclīnia. Faciēs et tōtum populum   20 sibi suāviter facientem. Ad dexteram meam pōnēs statuam Fortūnātae meae columbam tenentem, et catellam cingulō alligātam dūcat, et cicarōnem meum, et amphorās cōpiōsās gypsātās, nē effluant vīnum. Et urnam licet frāctam sculpās, et super eam puerum plōrantem. Hōrologium in mediō, ut quisquis hōrās īnspiciet, velit nōlit, nōmen meum legat. Īnscrīptiō quoque   25 vidē dīligenter sī haec satis idōnea tibi vidētur: 'C. Pompeius Trimalchiō Maecēnātiānus hīc requiēscit. Huic sēvirātus absentī dēcrētus est. Cum posset in omnibus decuriīs Rōmae esse, tamen nōluit. Pius, fortis, fidēlis, ex parvō crēvit, sēstertium relīquit trecentiēs, nec umquam philosophum audīvit. Valē. Et tū.' " Haec ut dīxit Trimalchiō, flēre coepit ūbertim. Flēbat   30 et Fortūnāta, flēbat et Habinnas, tōta dēnique familia, tamquam in fūnus rogāta, lāmentātiōne triclīnium implēvit.          —Petronius, *Satyricon* 71

| | |
|---|---|
| **lāc, lactis** (*n*), milk | **quemadmodum,** in what way, as |
| **fātum, -ī** (*n*), fate, destiny | **secundum** ( + *acc.*), by, beside |
| **citō,** quickly, soon | **catella, -ae** (*f*), puppy |
| **līber, -era, -erum,** free | **beneficium, -ī** (*n*), kindness |
| **gustō** (1), to taste | **dūcentī, -ae, -a,** two hundred |
| **ideō,** for this reason, therefore | **pōmum, -ī** (*n*), fruit tree |
| **pūblicō** (1), to make public | **circā** ( + *acc.*), around |
| **nūgae, -ārum** (*f pl*), jokes, trifles | **cinis, cineris** (*m*), ashes |
| **exemplar, exemplāris** (*n*), copy | **vīvus, -a, -um,** alive, living |

25

cultus, -a, -um, cultivated, elegant
diūtius (*adverb*), longer
tribūnal, tribūnālis (*n*), magistrates'
  raised platform, tribunal
sacculus, -ī (*m*), little sack
columba, -ae (*f*), dove
cingulum, -ī (*n*), belt, leash
alligō (1), to tie
super (+ *acc.*), over, above

plōrō (1), to weep
hōrologium, -ī (*n*), clock, sundial
quisquis, quicquid, whoever,
  whatever
idōneus, -a, -um, suitable
pius, -a, -um, dutiful, conscien-
  tious
ūbertim, copiously, abundantly
dēnique, at last, finally

oblīvīscor, oblīvīscī (3), oblītus sum (+ *gen.*), to forget
ingemēscō, ingemēscere (3), to groan
pingō, pingere (3), pinxī, pictum, to paint, portray, represent
contingō, contingere (3), contigī, contāctum, to befall, happen to
adiciō, adicere (3), adiēcī, adiectum, to add
effundō, effundere (3), effūdī, effūsum, to pour out
effluō, effluere (3), effluxī, to flow out, to spill
sculpō, sculpere (3), sculpsī, sculptum, to sculpt, carve
requiēscō, requiēscere (3), requiēvī, requiētum, to rest
dēcernō, dēcernere (3), dēcrēvī, dēcrētum, to decide, decree
fleō, flēre (2), flēvī, flētum, to weep
impleō, implēre (2), implēvī, implētum, to fill

EPITAPH FOR A SON

Lagge fīlī, bene quiēscās, māter tua rogat tē ut mē ad tē recipiās. Valē.
P(edēs) q(uadrātī) XV. *Laggus my son, may you rest well; (I) your mother
ask that you take me to you. Farewell. 15 square feet.*

## Exercise 56a

1. What does Trimalchio intend his guests to think about his will? His tomb?
2. What is his guests' actual reaction to them? What is yours?
3. Would you describe Trimalchio as hypocritical? Generous? Altruistic?
   Humanitarian? Self-centered? How would he describe himself?
4. Is Trimalchio afraid of death?
5. Is it true that Trimalchio "never listened to a philosopher"? What words
   suggest that he has somehow picked up a smattering of philosophy? Why
   does he make this claim? As part of an epitaph, what is the effect of the
   remark?
6. Explain what is humorous about the following phrases: "ut familia . . .
   tamquam mortuum" (4–5); "ingemēscente familiā" (8); "corōnās et unguenta . . . pugnās" (11); "nē effluant vīnum" (23); "velit nōlit" (25).

26

# Jussive and Hortatory Subjunctives

You have studied several kinds of subordinate clauses that require subjunctive verbs: circumstantial and causal clauses introduced by **cum**, result and purpose clauses introduced by **ut**, and indirect questions (see Chapter 54, page 11, "The Subjunctive in Subordinate Clauses").

The *present* subjunctive can also be used in a *main* or *independent* clause to give a command. It is found mainly in the 1st and 3rd persons; for the 2nd person the imperative mood is used. The negative is **nē**. Several examples in the 3rd person occur in the reading:

Hoc monumentum hērēdem nōn (*more correctly,* nē) **sequātur**.
**Let** *this tomb not* **pass** *to (my) heir.*
**Faciātur** (*more correctly,* **fīat**) et triclīnia.
**Let** *a dining room* **be made** *also.*
Catellam cingulō alligātam **dūcat**.
**Let her be leading** *a puppy tied with a leash.*

In line 24 the subjunctive of **esse** is not expressed but has to be supplied:

Hōrologium in mediō [**sit**].
[**Let there be**] *a clock in the middle.*

When the subjunctive is used this way in the 3rd person, it is called *jussive* (from **iubeō, iubēre, 2, iussī, iussum,** *to command*).

When this kind of subjunctive occurs in the 1st person plural, it is called *hortatory* (from **hortor, hortārī, 1, hortātus sum,** *to urge*). Some famous examples of the hortatory subjunctive are:

**Vīvāmus**, mea Lesbia, atque **amēmus**!
**Let us live**, *my Lesbia, and* **let us love**!
**Gaudeāmus** igitur, iuvenēs dum sumus.
**Let us rejoice** *then, while we are young.*


## Exercise 56b

*Read aloud and translate:*

1. "Testāmentum meum," inquit Trimalchiō, "afferātur."
2. Gustēmus omnēs aquam līberam!
3. Omnēs servōs manū mittant dominī.
4. Statua Fortūnātae in monumentō pōnātur.
5. Nē philosophōs audiāmus!
6. Amīcīs cārissimīs grātiās agāmus omnēs!
7. Nē iniūriam accipiat hoc monumentum.
8. Rēs gestae et nōmen Trimalchiōnis ab omnibus legantur.
9. Īnscrīptiōnem idōneam in monumentō meō habeam.
10. Requiēscat in pāce C. Pompēius Trimalchiō Maecēnātiānus.

27

### Exercise 56c

*The following is a love charm laid on a woman named Vettia by a man named Felix; it was found in Tunisia, scratched on a lead tablet. Read it aloud, translate it, and identify nine examples of the jussive subjunctive.*

Faciat quodcumque dēsīderō Vettia quam peperit Optāta; amōris meī causā, nē dormiat neque cibum accipere possit. Amet mē, Fēlīcem quem peperit Frūcta; oblīvīscātur patris et mātris et propinquōrum suōrum et amī-cōrum omnium et aliōrum virōrum. Sōlum mē in mente habeat, dormiēns vigilāns ūrātur frīgeat ardeat Vettia amōris et dēsīderī meī causā.        5

quīcumque, quaecumque, quod-    dēsīderium, -ī (*n*), desire
cumque, whoever, whatever

ūrō, ūrere (3), ūssī, ūstum, to burn
frīgeō, frīgēre (2), to freeze, be cold

## Building Up the Meaning XI

### Commands

You have now studied three ways of expressing a command or request in Latin:

A. Directly, by using the imperative (Chapter 10):
    "**Tacēte**, omnēs!" magnā vōce clāmat. "**Audīte** mē!"
    "**Be quiet**, *everyone!*" *he cries in a loud voice.* "**Listen** *to me!*"
The usual negative is **Nōlī/Nōlīte** + infinitive:
    **Nōlīte** cistam **iacere**, servi!
    **Don't throw** *the trunk, slaves!*
**Nē** + 2nd person of the present or perfect subjunctive can also express a negative command:
    **Nē discēdās!** *Don't go away!*
The *passive* imperative (found mostly in deponents) ends in **-re** (sing.) or **-minī** (pl.) (Chapter 35):
    "Amīcī," inquit, "**ingrediminī** domum meam!"
    "*Friends,*" *he said,* "**come** *into my house!*"

B. Indirectly, by using an **ut**-clause with the subjunctive (negative **nē**) (Chapter 50):
    Tē rogō, ut nāvēs in monumentō meō **faciās**.
    *I ask you* **to make** *some ships on my monument.*

C. By using the jussive or hortatory subjunctive (negative **nē**) (Chapter 56):
    Catellam cingulō alligātam **dūcat**.
    **Let her be leading** *a puppy tied with a leash.*
    **Vīvāmus**, mea Lesbia, atque **amēmus!**
    **Let us live**, *my Lesbia, and* **let us love!**

## Exercise 56d

*Select, read aloud, and translate.*

1. Trimalchiō praecēpit servīs ut exemplar testāmentī (afferunt / afferrent/ afferant).
2. "Amīce," inquit, "(affer / afferant / afferrent) testāmentum meum!"
3. Trimalchiō dīxit, "(Afferāmus / Afferrent / Afferant) servī testāmentum meum."
4. Amīcī, (sequiminī / sequātur / sequī) mē omnēs!
5. (Adiciāmur / adiciātur / adicerētur) H.M.H.N.S. monumentō meō.
6. "(Nōlite / Nōlit / Nōlī) flēre, Fortūnāta," inquit Trimalchiō.
7. Fortūnātae autem nōn persuāsit nē (flēret / flet / flēre).
8. Monēbat convīvās nē philosophōs (audiant / audīrentur / audīrent).
9. "Nōs," inquit, "nē philosophōs (audiant / audiāmus / audīrēmus)."

# The Millionaire's Autobiography: Ex Parvo Crevit

*Having regaled his guests with a detailed account of his preparations for death, Trimalchio next treats them to the story of his life, a classic of the rags-to-riches genre.*

"Ad hanc mē fortūnam frūgālitās mea perdūxit. Tam magnus ex Asiā vēnī, quam hic candēlābrus est. Cēterum, quemadmodum dī volunt, dominus in domō factus sum et ecce cēpī ipsimī cerebellum. Quid multa? Cohērēdem mē Caesarī fēcit, et accēpī patrimōnium lāticlāvium. Nēminī tamen nihil satis est. Concupīvī negōtiārī. Nē multīs vōs morer, quīnque 5 nāvēs aedificāvī, onerāvī vīnum—et tunc erat contrā aurum—mīsī Rōmam. Putārēs mē hoc iussisse: omnēs nāvēs naufragāvērunt. Factum, nōn fābula. Alterās fēcī maiōrēs et meliōrēs et fēlīciōrēs. Citō fit quod dī volunt. Ūnō cursū centiēs sēstertium corrotundāvī. Quicquid tangēbam, crēscēbat tamquam favus. Postquam coepī plūs habēre quam tōta patria mea habet, manum dē 10 tabulā: sustulī mē dē negōtiātiōne. Crēdite mihi: assem habeās, assem valeās. Sīc amīcus vester, quī fuit rāna, nunc est rēx."

—Petronius, Satyricon 75–77 (excerpts)

candēlābrum, -ī (*n*), lampstand
cerebellum, -ī (*n*), brain, heart
Quid multa? to make a long story
 short, to put it briefly
lāticlāvius, -a, -um, fit for a senator,
 princely
Nē . . . morer, to cut a long story
 short

onerō (1), to load
contrā (+ *acc.*), worth its weight
 in . . .
putārēs, you would think
naufragō (1), to be wrecked
cursus, -ūs (*m*), run, voyage
corrotundō (1), to round off, "clear"
favus, -ī (*m*), honeycomb

**manum dē tabulā,** hand(s) off (the tablet, or painting, or gaming-board—exact meaning disputed)

**negōtiātiō, -ōnis** (*f*), business

**assem . . . valeās,** (if you) have an **as,** an **as** is what you're worth

**amīcus vester,** yours truly

**rāna, -ae** (*f*), frog; metaphorically, a nobody

**concupīscō, concupīscere** (3), **concupīvī, concupītum,** to long for
**negōtior, negōtiārī** (1), **negōtiātus sum,** to go into business

# Word Study XIV

## Romance Derivatives: Survival of the Simplest

Many Romance words derive from colloquial, rather than literary ("classical") Latin. Some common literary words were short, irregular, and/or easily confused with other words; ordinary speakers of Latin preferred synonyms that were easier to recognize and to inflect. Hence:

1. **Ōs, ōris** (*n,*), "mouth," was a very short word and liable to be confused with **os, ossis** (*n*), "bone"; it lost out, in popular speech, to **bucca, -ae** (*f*), "cheek," from which derive It. *bocca,* Sp. *boca,* and Fr. *bouche.*

2. **Rēs, reī** (*f*), "thing," another short word and a member of the relatively rare 5th declension, was replaced by **causa,** which eventually produced It. and Sp. *cosa* and Fr. *chose.*

3. Where a classical verb had an alternative form in the 1st conjugation, the latter tended to survive, as being easier to conjugate; hence the Romance verbs for "to sing" derive not from **canere** but from the frequentative form **cantāre:** It. *cantare,* Sp. *cantar,* Fr. *chanter.*

4. Some short words were easier to remember and inflect in their diminutive form: classical **auris, -is** (*f*), "ear" (not to be confused with **aura,** "breeze," or **aurum,** "gold") gave way to its diminutive form **auricula,** from which derive Sp. *oreja* and Fr. *oreille.*

5. Some of the commonest classical words seem to have been rejected by ordinary people as being too literary or "fancy." To them, **equus** sounded something like "steed," and you don't hitch a "steed" to a plow or a wagon; they called the beast a **caballus** ("nag"); hence It. *cavallo,* Sp. *caballo,* and Fr. *cheval.* An amusing illustration of the ordinary person's preference for the slang word over the literary word is the Italian noun *testa* (Fr. *tête*), "head." These words come from **testa, -ae** (*f*), whose literal meaning was "a ceramic pot," but which was used jokingly of the human head until it eventually supplanted the classical **caput** altogether.

These modern Romance words bear eloquent witness to the difficulties and frustrations ordinary Romans experienced in handling their language. Like us, they found look-alike words confusing, they liked simplicity and regularity, and they bypassed "fancy" or "poetic" words.

# PART II
# Public Life, Government, and Politics in the Late Republic

Thus far, you have been reading about the time of the imperial period of Roman history in the 1st century A.D. We now turn to an earlier time, the time of the Republic (509–27 B.C.), which began after the period of the kings (753–509 B.C.). The early Republic saw the extension of Roman power throughout the Italian peninsula and the subsequent expansion of Roman influence throughout the Mediterranean world after the Punic Wars with Carthage (264–146 B.C.). Politically, the period of the Republic was a time of struggle between the noble or senatorial class, which held control of the government, and the middle or equestrian class, which wanted more political control. The last century B.C., known as the late Republic, was a turbulent time of transition between the political orders of Republican and Imperial Rome (27 B.C.–A.D. 476).

At the center of the events of the late Republic was Marcus Tullius Cicero, orator and statesman, philosopher and writer. Always a political idealist, Cicero was often confused by the perplexities of Republican politics and became a pawn of men with more powerful ambitions: first Caesar and Pompey, and then Antony and Octavian. During the final two decades of the Republic, the struggles of these men for control of Rome led to two civil wars, the first between Caesar and Pompey (49–45 B.C.) and the second between Antony and Octavian (44–31 B.C.). These wars led to the final dissolution of the Republic.

The events of 53–52 B.C. serve to illustrate the political forces and public personalities of the late Republic. During the previous decade, political bands, led by P. Clodius Pulcher, agent of Caesar, and T. Annius Milo, henchman of the senatorial faction, opposed each other and disrupted the normal constitutional processes of state. Milo and Clodius themselves became political candidates for the elections of 53; the subsequent postponement of elections due to violence eventually led to the murder of Clodius by Milo. During this crisis, the Senate turned to Pompey while Caesar was fighting in Gaul, and this set up a confrontation between Pompey and Caesar that was to lead to civil war. In 52 B.C., Cicero delivered a courtroom speech of defense on behalf of his friend Milo, a speech which has been preserved and is titled *Pro Milone (For Milo)*. The commentary on this speech by Q. Asconius Pedianus, a scholar of the 1st century A.D., who consulted official records of the trial, gives us a unique perspective on Cicero's courtroom pyrotechnics and on the volatile politics of the late Republic.

31

3 **Milōnī . . . erant inimīcitiae:** the dative with **esse** shows possession; literally, "There were to Milo and Clodius. . . ." A smoother English translation would be "Milo and Clodius had. . . ."

  **inimīcitiae:** literally, "hostility," but here a technical term meaning "political rivalry." Cf. **amīcissimus** (4).

4 **in redūcendōque eō:** Milo had helped to recall Cicero from exile five years earlier, in 57 B.C. Clodius had been responsible for his exile in 58 B.C.

  **tribūnus plēbis:** this officer, one of 10, protected the rights of the plebs, or common people, by interposing his veto when an act, decree, or law proved detrimental to the interests of the plebeians.

8 **erant uterque: uterque** refers to both Clodius and Milo, considered separately, and therefore the verb is plural.

  **audāciā:** ablative of respect, designating the specific way or respect in which Clodius and Milo were equal.

  **prō meliōribus partibus:** these were the Optimates or "best people," that faction of the Senate interested in maintaining senatorial dominance in government. Their rivals were the Populares or those from the middle class who sought the support of the poor in opposition to the control of the Senate.

9 **quam dēbilem futūram cōnsule Milōne:** the praetorship was subordinate to the consulship in status and authority, so Milo would have a political advantage over Clodius.

10 **futūram:** = **futūram esse,** future infinitive of **esse.**

11 **eius:** i.e., Milo's.

12 **T. Munātius Plancus:** tribune of 52 B.C. and archenemy of Cicero, Plancus was later accused by him and condemned for public violence.

  **referrī ad senātum:** technical term, "(that a motion) be put before (referred to) the Senate."

  **patriciīs:** patricians were members of the Roman nobility, whose ancestors had been advisors to the kings during the period of the monarchy. The patricians had originally appointed an **interrēx** to exercise provisional authority upon the death of the king. During the Republic, the patrician members of the Senate would select an **interrēx** as an emergency measure from among their number to serve for five-day periods in the absence of consuls.

13 **quī interrēgem prōderent:** here, as often, the relative pronoun **quī** is equivalent to **ut** in introducing a purpose clause; it links the purpose directly to a particular word, in this case the antecedent **patriciīs,** and introduces a *relative clause of purpose.*

14 **aliī ex aliīs:** "one after another."

16 **senātūs cōnsultum ultimum:** "final decree of the Senate," often abbreviated S.C.U., was passed in times of emergency and granted martial powers to magistrates. Asconius provides the traditional formula of the grant, **ut vidērent nē quid dētrīmentī rēs pūblica caperet,** that the magistrates "see to it that the State should come to no harm." The S.C.U. was invoked 10 times during the final 45 years of the Republic.

32

# 57
# Government in Crisis

Milo and Clodius, deadly political enemies, are both seeking office for the same year, 52 B.C. Milo is a candidate for the consulship, Clodius for a judicial office known as the praetorship. Asconius's vivid account of how the elections were postponed and of the final outcome gives the reader a ringside seat in this political arena.

T. Annius Milō et P. Plautius Hypsaeus et Q. Metellus Scīpiō cōnsulātum petīvērunt, nōn sōlum largītiōne palam profūsā sed etiam factiōnibus armātōrum succinctī. Milōnī et Clōdiō summae erant inimīcitiae, quod Milō Cicerōnis erat amīcissimus, in redūcendōque eō ēnixē operam tribūnus plēbis dederat; et P. Clōdius restitūtō quoque Cicerōnī erat īnfestissimus, 5 ideōque summē studēbat Hypsaeō et Scīpiōnī contrā Milōnem. Ac saepe inter sē Milō et Clōdius cum suīs factiōnibus Rōmae dēpugnāvērunt: et erant uterque audāciā pārēs, sed Milō prō meliōribus partibus stābat. Praetereā eōdem annō cōnsulātum Milō, Clōdius praetūram petēbat, quam dēbilem futūram cōnsule Milōne intellegēbat. 10

Asconius goes on to explain that the elections had to be postponed due to the violence of the candidates. Milo, however, was confident of election for he enjoyed the support of the Optimates, who opposed Clodius, and the favor of the people, whose votes he solicited through lavish expenditures on games and shows.

Competītōrēs eius trahere diem volēbant, ideōque Pompēius gener Scīpiōnis et T. Munātius Plancus tribūnus plēbis referrī ad senātum dē patriciīs convocandīs, quī interrēgem prōderent, nōn sunt passī, cum interrēgem prōdere ob statum rērum opus esset. Fiēbant tandem aliī ex aliīs interrēgēs, quia comitia cōnsulāria propter eōsdem candidatōrum tumultūs et eāsdem 15 manūs armātās habērī nōn poterant. Itaque prīmō factum est senātūs cōnsultum ultimum ut interrēx et tribūnī plēbis et Pompēius, quī prō cōnsule ad urbem erat, vidērent nē quid dētrimentī rēs pūblica caperet atque dīlectūs autem Pompēius tōtā Italiā habēret.

Inter haec cum crēbrēsceret rūmor Cn. Pompēium creārī dictātōrem 20 oportēre neque aliter mala cīvitātis sēdārī posse, vīsum est optimātibus tūtius esse cōnsulem sine collēgā creārī, et cum tractāta ea rēs esset in senātū, factō in M. Bibulī sententiam senātūs. cōnsultō, Pompēius ab interrēge Serviō Sulpiciō cōnsul creātus est statimque cōnsulātum iniit.

—Asconius, *Commentary on Cicero's Speech for Milo* (excerpts)

17 **prō cōnsule ad urbem erat:** a magistrate acting **prō cōnsule**, more commonly known as a **prōcōnsul**, was a former consul who retained military authority as governor of a province. Pompey, although nominally serving as proconsul of Spain, had remained near Rome to protect his political interests.

19 **tōtā Italiā:** = **ā tōtā Italiā,** ablative of place from which.

20 **cum crēbrēsceret rūmor:** "although the rumor grew stronger. . . ."; **cum** here means "although," and the clause with the subjunctive is called a *concessive clause*, because it grants or concedes the truth of what is being maintained.

    **Cn. Pompēium:** Pompey the Great, an earlier political ally of Caesar and the Populares, was now supported by senatorial extremists who wanted him to intercede in the riots provoked by Caesar's henchman Clodius.

21 **oportēre . . . posse:** infinitives after **rūmor crēbrēsceret**, in an indirect statement. **Creārī** and **sēdārī** complement the meanings of these infinitives.

    **vīsum est:** "it seemed (best). . . ." = "they decided. . . ."

22 **cōnsulem sine collēgā:** consuls, regular chief magistrates of state, were usually two in number. Pompey's sole consulship would be sure to hasten his inevitable confrontation with Caesar, since both aspired to the leadership of Rome. Caesar was fighting in Gaul at the time.

23 **in M. Bibulī sententiam:** "on the motion of Bibulus," a technical idiom.

**nōn sōlum . . . sed etiam,** not only, but also

**largītiō, largītiōnis** (*f*), bribery

**palam,** openly, publicly

**factiō, factiōnis** (*f*), gang, political partisans

**inimīcitia, -ae** (*f*), political rivalry

**in redūcendō eō,** in bringing him back

**ēnixē,** eagerly

**operam dare,** to give attention to, work hard to

**tribūnus plēbis,** tribune or representative of the common people

**īnfestus, -a, -um,** hostile to (+ *dat.*)

**studeō** (2) (+ *dat.*), to support, be eager for

**pār, paris,** equal

**prō** (+ *abl.*), for, on behalf of

**praetūra, -ae** (*f*), praetorship, office of praetor, one of eight judges

**dēbilis, -is, -e,** feeble, powerless

**gener, generī** (*m*), son-in-law

**dē patriciīs convocandīs,** about assembling the patricians

**cum** (+ *subjunctive*), although

**interrēx, interrēgis** (*m*), interrex, temporary chief magistrate

**status, -ūs** (*m*), condition, state

**opus est,** it is necessary, there is need to

**comitia cōnsulāria,** assembly to elect consuls and praetors

**manus, -ūs** (*f*), band, gang

**senātūs cōnsultum,** decree of the Senate

**prō cōnsule,** with consular power

**dīlectus, -ūs** (*m*), draft of troops, levy

**dictātor, dictātōris** (*m*), dictator, magistrate with absolute power in emergencies

**aliter,** otherwise

**cīvitās, cīvitātis** (*f*), state, body of citizens

**sēdō** (1), to settle, calm

**tūtus, -a, -um,** safe

**collēga, -ae** (*m*), colleague, partner

**creō** (1), to elect

**tractō** (1), to discuss, handle

**sententia, -ae** (*f*), feeling, opinion

profundō, profundere (3), profūdī, profūsum, to pour forth
succingō, succingere (3), succinxī, succinctum, to equip
restituō, restituere (3), restituī, restitūtum, to restore, reinstate
prōdō, prōdere (3), prōdidī, prōditum, to appoint
crēbrēscō, crēbrēscere (3), crēbuī, to increase, gather strength

## Exercise 57a

Answer the following questions in English, with reference to the specified lines of the reading passage. Questions 4 and 5 refer to the English following line 10.

1. By what means did the consular candidates secure votes during their election campaigns? (2–3)
2. What offices did Clodius and Milo each seek? (1–2, 9–10)
3. What role did Cicero play in the rivalry between the candidates? (3–5)
4. What immediate consequences did the behavior of the candidates have for the election?
5. For what reasons did Milo feel confident about winning?
6. What further measures did Milo's rivals take? (11–14)
7. What were the provisions of the senātūs cōnsultum ultimum? (17–19)
8. How was the crisis temporarily resolved? (20–24)

## Exercise 57b

1. Was Roman society classless? What indications do we have in this passage that it was not? What were the political positions of these classes?
2. What is meant by the term "republic"? What evidence is there in this reading passage that Rome was a republic at this time?
3. To what extent was Rome a government of laws? To what extent was it a government of men? What features of Roman politics and government seem familiar to you? What features seem strange?

---

Virtūs, probitās, integritās in candidātō, nōn linguae volūbilitās, nōn ars, nōn scientia requīrī solet. *Moral courage, honesty, and integrity are usually sought in candidates, not a glib tongue, skill, or knowledge.* (Cicero, *For Plancius,* 62)

---

# Politics in the Late Republic

A candidate for political office, when canvassing for votes in the Forum, an activity termed **ambitiō**, wore a toga of bright white rubbed with chalk (**toga candida**) as a symbol of his purity and fitness for office. The candidate was accompanied by a slave (**nōmenclātor**), who reminded him of voters' names, and by a crowd of partisans (**sectātōrēs**), mostly freedmen clients, whose task it was to secure votes through promises and even bribery.

In 64 B.C., Cicero's brother Quintus wrote a campaign handbook titled *On Being a Candidate for the Consulship*, to assist his elder brother's election bid for the consulship of 63. This political pamphlet lists some things for a candidate to consider during a campaign:

> Take care to have followers at your heels daily, of every kind, class, and age; because from their number people can figure out how much power and support you are going to have at the polls.

> You particularly need to use flattery. No matter how vicious and vile it is on the other days of a man's life, when he runs for office it is indispensable.

> Getting votes among the rank and file requires calling everyone by his name. Make it clear you know people's names; practice, get better at it day to day. Nothing seems to me better for popularity and gaining favor.

> If you make a promise, the matter is not fixed. It's for a future day, and it affects only a few people. But if you say no, you are sure to alienate people right away, and a lot of them.

But, of all the forces at work in determining the outcome of an election, it was usually the character of the candidate himself which was the most influential factor.

> When Scipio Nasica was seeking the office of curule aedile and, in the custom of a campaigner, had firmly grasped the hand of a certain man worn leathery with farm work, to get a laugh he asked the man whether or not he usually walked on his hands. This comment, when heard by bystanders and passed around, was the source of Scipio's downfall: for all the country voters thought that he was laughing at poverty.
>
> Valerius Maximus, VII.5.2

| **Cōnsul:** chief officer of state |
| **Praetor:** presided over courts |
| **Aedilis:** oversaw public works and games |
| **Quaestor:** managed state finances |

**CURSUS HONORUM**

36

# VERBS: The Gerundive or Future Passive Participle

Look at these examples from the reading passage:

> Milō . . . in **redūcendō** . . . eō ēnixē operam . . . dederat. . . . (4–5)
> *Milo had given serious attention to **bringing** him **back**. . . .*
> Pompēius . . . et . . . Plancus . . . referrī ad senātum dē patriciīs **convocandīs** nōn sunt passī. . . . (11–13)
> *Pompey and Plancus did not allow the Senate to be consulted about **assembling** the patricians. . . .*

As future passive participles, the gerundives **redūcendō** and **convocandīs** are future and passive: "about to be brought back," "about to be assembled." They are also adjectives, agreeing with the pronoun **eō** and the noun **patriciīs**, respectively. The literal future passive meaning of the gerundive is present in such English words as *agenda*, "things about to be done," but in translating the Latin gerundive into idiomatic English, often a verbal noun ending in -*ing* will be used, as in the examples above: "bringing . . . back" and "assembling."

Here are some examples of how gerundives are used in Latin and translated into English. Note how the gerundive and the noun it modifies can serve any of the usual constructions of nouns in the various cases.

1. The gerundive and its noun in the *genitive case* are used with **causā** or **grātiā**, "for the sake of," to express purpose, e.g.:
   Cōnsul creātus est reī pūblicae **gubernandae causā.**
   *The consul was elected for the sake of governing the state* (literally, *for the sake of the state about to be governed*).
2. The gerundive and its noun in the *genitive case* are also used with special adjectives, e.g.:
   Cōnsul erat **cupidus** reī pūblicae **gubernandae.**
   *The consul was desirous of governing the state.*
3. The *dative case* of the gerundive and its noun is used when the gerundive phrase serves as the indirect object, e.g.:
   Cōnsul multum tempus reī pūblicae **gubernandae** dedit.
   *The consul gave much time to governing the state.*
4. The gerundive and its noun are also used in the *dative case* with special adjectives, e.g.:
   Cōnsul erat **idōneus** reī pūblicae **gubernandae.**
   *The consul was suitable for governing the state.*
5. The gerundive and its noun are found in the *accusative case* with **ad**, showing purpose, e.g.:
   Cōnsul creātus est **ad** rem pūblicam **gubernandam.**
   *The consul was elected for the purpose of governing (i.e., to govern) the state.*

37

6. The *ablative case* of the gerundive and its noun is used in prepositional phrases with **dē, ex,** and **in,** e.g.:
   Cōnsul cōnsilia capiēbat **dē** rē pūblicā **gubernandā.**
   *The consul made plans concerning governing the state.*
7. The *ablative case* of the gerundive and its noun may also serve as an ablative of means, e.g.:
   Cōnsul rem pūblicam gubernāvit cōnsiliīs **capiendīs.**
   *The consul governed the state by making plans.*

Remember that in form and function the *gerundive* is an *adjective*, which means that it will modify a noun.

| 1st Conj. | parand*us*, *-a*, *-um* |
|-----------|-------------------------|
| 2nd Conj. | habend*us*, *-a*, *-um* |
| 3rd Conj. | mittend*us*, *-a*, *-um* |
|           | iaciend*us*, *-a*, *-um* |
| 4th Conj. | audiend*us*, *-a*, *-um* |

**Salūs populī suprēma lēx est.** *The safety of the people is the supreme law.*
(Cicero, *On Laws*, III.8)

## Exercise 57c

*Read aloud and translate the following sentences.*

1. Patriciī propter candidātōrum tumultūs ad interrēgēs prōdendōs convocābantur.
2. Comitia cōnsulāria cōnsulum praetōrumque creandōrum causā habita sunt.
3. Multī crēdēbant Pompēium virum Caesarī auctoritāte pārem esse idōneumque reī pūblicae gubernandae.
4. Senātōrēs Caesare necandō rem pūblicam restituere cōnātī sunt.
5. Cicerō cupidus bonae ōrātiōnis audiendae semper erat.
6. Senātūs cōnsultum ultimum ad conservandam rem pūblicam factum est.
7. Tribūnus plēbis referrī ad senātum dē lēgibus ferendīs quae factiōnibus resisterent nōn passus est.
8. Itaque Cicerōnī roganti cūr ipse cōnsul factus esset, Cn. Pompēius respondit, "Reī pūblicae conservandae grātiā."
9. Milō operam dedit redūcendō Cicerōnī.
10. Senātōrēs saepe convocātī sunt rērum tractandārum causā.

**auctoritās, auctoritātis** (*f*), influence
**gubernō** (1), to govern, rule
**cupidus, -a, -um** ( + *gen.*), desirous

**lēgem ferre,** to pass a law
**grātiā** ( + *gen.*), for the sake of

38

# Building Up the Meaning XII

## Expressions of Purpose

You have now learned several different ways to express the idea of purpose in Latin. Observe how the following sentence may be rendered in Latin:

> The Senate makes laws to govern the people.

Purpose Clause: Senātus lēgēs fert **ut** populum Rōmānum **gubernent**.
Relative Clause of Purpose: Senātus lēgēs fert **quae** populum Rōmānum **gubernent**.
Gerundive with **ad**: Senātus lēgēs fert **ad** populum Rōmānum **gubernandum**.
Gerundive with **causā**: Senātus lēgēs fert populī Rōmānī **gubernandī causā**.
Gerundive with **grātiā**: Senātus lēgēs fert populī Rōmānī **gubernandī grātiā**.

Note: the gerundive usually precedes **causā** and **grātiā**.

# Word Study XV

## Participles in the Romance Languages

In later Latin, the gerundive with the ablative singular ending came to be used as the equivalent of the present participle and, in fact, was adopted as such by Italian. Spanish preserved the function of the Latin gerundive and called it the *gerundio*. Compare the French present participle, which derives from the present participle in **-nt-**, in the chart below:

| Latin<br>Gerundive (abl. sing.) | Italian<br>Pres. Part. | Spanish<br>Gerundio | French<br>Pres. Part. |
|---|---|---|---|
| amandō | amando | amando | aimant |
| tenendō | tenendo | teniendo | tenant |
| vīvendō | vivendo | viviendo | vivant |

### Exercise 57d

Construct the Latin gerundive equivalents of the following Italian and Spanish forms. The French is given for comparison.

| Italian<br>Pres. Part. | Spanish<br>Gerundio | Latin<br>Gerundive (abl. sing.) | French<br>Pres. Part. |
|---|---|---|---|
| desiderando | desiendo | _____ | désirant |
| facendo | haciendo | _____ | faisant |
| preparando | preparando | _____ | préparant |
| scrivendo | escribiendo | _____ | écrivant |
| videndo | viendo | _____ | voyant |

1  A.D. **XV Kal. Febr.**: fifteen days before the Kalends of February = January 18.
2  **dictātor:** Milo was chief magistrate, or dictator, of Lanuvium, a small town in the Alban hills south of Rome. He was visiting for the purpose of appointing a priest, most likely for the city's famous cult of Juno Sospita.
3  **Bovillās . . . Arīciā:** Bovillae was a small but ancient town some 12 miles (7 1/2 kilometers) south of Rome. Aricia, about 4 miles (2 1/2 kilometers) further south, was the first way station on the Appian Way; Horace stopped there en route to Brundisium. See the map on page 90.
6  **ūnus, duo dē plēbe nōtī hominēs:** note the asyndeton or lack of conjunction. The verb **erant** is to be understood (an example of ellipsis).
7  **L. Sullae dictātōris:** L. Cornelius Sulla, some thirty years before this, had been the first military dictator of the late Republic. His victory in a civil war left him master of Rome and champion of the Optimate cause. Note the methodical presentation of facts throughout this first paragraph, almost as if Asconius were presenting a transcript of the trial. Notice, also, the interplay of the historical perfect tense with the imperfect.
10  **in ultimō agmine:** "at the rear of the column." The two parties were passing one another, going in opposite directions.
    **euntēs:** present participle of the irregular verb **eō.**
    **rixam commīsērunt:** this phrase makes it clear that Asconius believed the responsibility for initiating hostilities lay with Milo's men. **Rixa** is a skirmish, **pugna** (12), a pitched battle.
14  **Milō . . . exturbārī tabernam iussit:** this complex sentence may reveal the difficulty in Milo's mind of making the decision to do away with Clodius. It contrasts with the previous rather terse, simple sentences, which had given momentum to the narration.
    **vulnerātum:** another example of ellipsis, **esse** being omitted.
15  **cum . . . intellegeret:** a **cum** causal clause, as is (**cum**) . . . **esset habitūrus** (15–16).
    **vīvō eō . . . occīsō (eō):** ablative absolutes; **eō** = **Clōdiō.**
    **futūrum:** again, ellipsis of **esse;** the subject of the infinitive is **illud,** referring to the wounding of Clodius.
16  **etiamsī subeunda esset poena:** "even if he had to undergo punishment. . . .";  **esset** is subjunctive in a conditional clause.
17  **multīsque vulneribus cōnfectus:** ellipsis of **est** after **cōnfectus;** the connective **-que** binds together **extractus est** and **cōnfectus (est).**
18  **Cadāver in viā relictum:** cadāver is the object of **sustulit** and **iussit.**
21  **ante . . . hōram:** before the end of the first hour of the night, about 7 p.m.
23  **factī invidiam:** "anger at the deed. . . .";  the objective genitive **factī** denotes the object of the anger, the killing of Clodius.
26  **Eīsque hortantibus:** ablative absolute.
    **vulgus imperītum:** note **vulgus,** a rare 2nd declension neuter noun in **-us.**
27  **in rostrīs posuit:** the speaker's platform (**rostra,** literally "beaks of ships," which decorated the platform and gave it its name) was not in the same place at Asconius's writing as it was in the time of the events narrated. It was moved by Julius Caesar from just in front of the Curia to an adjacent site.

# 58
# A Political Murder

The political struggles of 53 B.C. reached a climax in January of 52, when a brawl on the Appian Way between Clodius and Milo led to Clodius's death. This homicide triggered mob riots and the subsequent burning of the Senate House in Rome.

A.d. XV Kal. Febr. Milō Lānuvium, ex quō erat mūnicipiō et ubi tum dictātor, profectus est ad flāminem prōdendum posterā diē. Occurrit eī circā hōram nōnam Clōdius paulō ultrā Bovillās, rediēns Arīciā, ubi decuriōnēs erat allocūtus. Vehēbātur Clōdius equō; servī XXX ſeɾē expedītī, ut illō tempore mōs erat iter facientibus, gladiīs cinctī sequēbantur. Erant cum  5
Clōdiō praetereā trēs comitēs eius, ex quibus eques Rōmānus ūnus, duo dē plēbe nōtī hominēs. Milō raedā vehēbātur cum uxōre Faustā, filiā L. Sullae dictātōris, et M. Fufiō familiāre suō. Sequēbātur eōs magnum servōrum agmen, inter quōs gladiātōrēs quoque erant, ex quibus duo nōtī, Eudamus et Birria. Eī in ultimō agmine tardius euntēs cum servīs P. Clōdiī rixam  10
commīsērunt. Ad quem tumultum cum respexisset Clōdius minitābundus, umerum eius Birria rumpiā trāiēcit. Inde cum orta esset pugna, plūrēs cansā adiuvandī ad Milōnem accurrērunt. Clōdius vulnerātus in tabernam proximam in Bovillānō agrō dēlātus est. Milō, cum cognōvit vulnerātum Clōdium, cum sibi perīculōsius illud vīvō eō futūrum intellegeret, occīsō autem  15
magnum solācium esset habitūrus etiamsī subeunda esset poena, exturbārī tabernam iussit. Atque ita Clōdius latēns extractus est multīsque vulneribus cōnfectus. Cadāver in viā relictum, quia servī Clōdiī aut occīsī erant aut graviter sauciī latēbant, Sex. Teidius senātor, quī forte rūre in urbem revertēbātur, sustulit et lectīcā suā Rōmam ferrī iussit.  20
Perlātum est corpus Clōdiī ante prīmam noctis hōram, īnfimaeque plēbis et servōrum maxima multitūdō magnō luctū corpus in ātriō domūs positum circumstetit. Augēbat autem factī invidiam uxor Clōdiī Fulvia, quae cum effūsā lamentātiōne vulnera eius ostendēbat. Maior posterā diē lūce prīmā multitūdō eiusdem generis cōnflūxit, complūrēsque nōtī hominēs vīsī sunt.  25
Eīsque hortantibus vulgus imperītum corpus nūdum ac lutātum, ut vulnera vidērī possent, in Forum dētulit et in rostrīs posuit. Ibi prō contiōne T. Munātius Plancus, quī competītōribus studēbat, invidiam in Milōnem invehendō fēcit. Populus, duce Sex. Clōdiō scrībā, corpus in Cūriam intulit cremāvitque subselliīs et tribūnālibus et mēnsīs et cōdicibus librāriōrum;  30
quō igne et ipsa quoque Cūria flagrāvit et item Porcia Basilica, quae erat eī iūncta, ambusta est.
— Asconius, *Commentary on Cicero's Speech for Milo* (excerpts)

41

**prō contiōne:** contiō is a technical political term meaning an open meeting of the people to discuss the issues involved in an upcoming vote for a law or magistrate. Such meetings, usually held in the Forum, were rowdy and boisterous and often resulted in violence during the late Republic.

**T. Munātius Plancus:** Plancus had supported Milo's political opponents and had interfered with the election of an **interrēx** in 52 B.C. (see 57:12–14).

29 **duce Sex. Clōdiō scrība:** an agent and probably freedman of P. Clodius.

31 **quō igne:** ablative of cause, approximating **propter** or **ob** + acc.

**Porcia Basilica:** this basilica, the earliest in Rome, was built in 184 B.C.

---

**mūnicipium, -ī** (*n*), town
**flāmen, flāminis** (*m*), priest
**ultrā** (+ *acc.*), beyond
**decuriō, decuriōnis** (*m*), town councilman
**expedītus, -a, -um,** lightly equipped
**eques, equitis** (*m*), knight, member of the equestrian order
**agmen, agminis** (*n*), column, band
**minitābundus, -a, -um,** menacing
**umerus, -ī** (*m*), upper arm
**rumpia, -ae** (*f*), pike, spear
**causā adiuvandī,** for the sake of helping
**proximus, -a, -um,** nearest
**solācium, -ī** (*n*), relief
**etiamsī,** even if, although
**exturbō** (1), to take by storm
**cadāver, cadāveris** (*n*), corpse, body
**saucius, -a, -um,** wounded, hurt
**rūre,** from the country
**īnfimus, -a, -um,** lowest, most vile
**luctus, -ūs** (*m*), mourning
**invidia, -ae** (*f*), ill will

**vulgus, -ī** (*n*), mob, rabble
**imperītus, -a, -um,** ignorant
**lutō** (1), to make grimy, soil
**rostra, -ōrum** (*n pl*), Rostra, speaker's platform in the Forum
**prō** (+ *abl.*), in front of, before
**contiō, contiōnis** (*f*), public meeting
**in** (+ *acc.*), against
**invehendō,** by assaulting with words
**dux, ducis** (*m*), leader
**scrība, -ae** (*m*), scribe, clerk
**cremō** (1), to burn
**subsellium, -ī** (*n*), bench
**cōdex, cōdicis** (*m*), ledger, tablet
**librārius, -ī** (*m*), copier, secretary
**ignis, ignis** (*m*), fire
**flagrō** (1), to blaze up, burn
**item,** likewise, also
**Porcius, -a, -um,** Porcian, of M. Porcius Cato, famous Roman censor
**basilica, -ae** (*f*), basilica, public courthall

---

**vehō, vehere** (3), **vexī, vectum,** to carry, convey
**cingō, cingere** (3), **cīnxī, cinctum,** to gird, equip
**dēferō, dēferre** (*irreg.*), **dētulī, dēlātum,** to bring down
**subeō, subīre** (*irreg.*), **subiī, subitum,** to undergo, endure
**cōnficiō, cōnficere** (3), **cōnfēcī, cōnfectum,** to finish off
**revertor, revertī** (3), **reversus sum,** to turn back, return
**perferō, perferre** (*irreg.*), **pertulī, perlātum,** to deliver, bring
**cōnfluō, cōnfluere** (3), **cōnflūxī, cōnfluctum,** to flow together
**invehō, invehere** (3), **invexī, invectum,** to speak out against
**ambūrō, ambūrere** (3), **ambussī, ambustum,** to scorch, burn

42

### Exercise 58a

Answer the following questions in English, with reference to the specified lines of the reading passage.

1. When and where did the events of the narrative take place? (1–3)
2. Why was Milo on the Appian Way? Why was Clodius? (2–4)
3. Describe the respective traveling styles of Clodius and Milo. (4–10)
4. Who began the ruckus? Describe what happened to Clodius. (10–11 and 11–12)
5. Describe how the body came to Rome and its reception on arrival. (19–21 and 22–25)
6. How did the mob come to bring the body into the Forum? What was its appearance? (26–27)
7. What finally happened to the body of Clodius and what consequences did this act have? (29–30 and 31–32)

### Exercise 58b

1. Why did Milo decide to kill Clodius? Can you think of other examples of violent acts perpetrated for political reasons?
2. Explain how Asconius's account of the events on the Appian Way makes Milo's plea of self-defense untenable.
3. What are the characteristics of Asconius's prose style? Is the narrative simple and straightforward or embroidered with supposition and personal opinion? Does the style fit the content?

### Exercise 58c

Imagine that you were traveling in Milo's party along the Appian Way. Write a descriptive and dramatic account of the events of January 18 as you witnessed them. Include a map showing the relative locations of the places referred to in the reading and the positions of Clodius and Milo.

# VERBS: The Gerund or Verbal Noun

Look at these examples from the reading:

Inde cum orta esset pugna, plūrēs causā **adiuvandī** ad Milōnem accurrērunt. (12–13)
> *Then, when an all-out battle had begun, more (slaves) ran toward Milo for the sake of **helping out**.*

Ibi prō cōntiōne T. Munātius Plancus . . . invidiam in Milōnem **invehendō** fēcit. (27–29)
> *There, before a public gathering, T. Munatius Plancus raised hatred against Milo by **assaulting him with words**.*

43

In these examples, **adiuvandī** and **invehendō** are genitive and ablative forms, respectively, of the *gerund*, or verbal noun, corresponding to the English verbal noun in *-ing*. The Latin gerund is active in meaning: "helping," "assaulting." It has the same forms as the neuter singular of the gerundive, except that the nominative is replaced by the present active infinitive. Similarly, in English we can say either *Writing well is an art* (gerund) or *To write well is an art* (infinitive). Here are the forms of the gerund:

| Nom. | (parāre) | preparing |
|------|----------|-----------|
| Gen. | habendī | of having |
| Dat. | mittendō | for sending |
| Acc. | iaciend*um* | throwing |
| Abl. | audiendō | by listening |

| The Gerundive | The Gerund |
|---------------|------------|
| is a verbal adjective; | is a verbal noun; |
| is passive in its literal sense; | is active in sense; |
| agrees with a noun or pronoun; and | is equivalent to the English verbal noun in -ing; |
| has all the case forms of the adjective **magnus, -a, -um.** | has all the case forms of the neuter singular gerundive, except the nominative; and |
| | uses the present active infinitive for the nominative case. |

The Romans preferred a gerundive to a gerund when the thought required a direct object. For example, the sentence "The boy is becoming more desirous of hearing the speech" could be translated with a gerund in the genitive case ("of hearing") and a direct object of the verbal idea contained in the gerund:

Puer **ōrātiōnem audiendī** cupidior fit.
*The boy is becoming more desirous of hearing the speech.*

The Romans, however, preferred to put the direct object of the gerund (i.e., **ōrātiōnem**) into the genitive case, dependent on "more desirous (of )," and to modify it with a gerundive:

Puer **ōrātiōnis audiendae** cupidior fit.
(literally) *The boy is becoming more desirous of the speech about to be heard.*

The following sentence from Cicero (*On the State*, III.35) shows both a gerund and a gerundive construction:

Nam extrā **ulcīscendī** aut **prōpulsandōrum hostium** causam, bellum gerī iūstum nūllum potest.

*For no war can be waged justly except for the sake of avenging (a wrong)* (**ulcīscendī**: gerund) *or repelling an enemy* (**prōpulsandōrum hostium**: gerundive).

## Exercise 58d

*Read each of the following sentences aloud and determine whether a gerund or gerundive is being used. Then translate.*

1. Praedōnibus īnsidiae sunt modus operandī.
2. Tribūnī in Milōnem dīcendō invidiam īnfimae plēbis augēre cōnātī sunt.
3. Servī praedōnum repellendōrum causā viātōrēs comitantur.
4. Gladiātōribus vīsīs, servī Clōdiī ācriōrēs ad pugnandum factī sunt.
5. Ad corpus Clōdiī cremandum scelestī hominēs Cūriam flagrāvērunt.
6. Cicerō, arbiter bibendī creātus, "Bene Clōdiō" iterum iterumque dīcēbat. Causā iocī?
7. Senātōrī Rōmānō nūllum tempus ad revertendum Rōmam erat.
8. Milō iter faciēbat Lānuvium flāminis prōdendī grātiā.
9. Complūrēs servī adiuvandī causā ad Milōnem accurrērunt.
10. Fuitne Cūria idōneus locus cremandō corporī Clōdiī?

insidiae, -ārum (*f pl*), ambush          ācer, ācris, ācre, fierce

## Exercise 58e

*Complete the thoughts of the following authors with the correct form of the gerund. The infinitive of each verb is given in parentheses.*

1. Homō ad duās rēs, ad _____, et ad _____est nātus. (intellegere) (agere)
   *Man is born for two purposes, for thinking and for doing.* (Cicero)
2. _____, _____, bene _____prospera omnia cēdunt. (vigilāre) (agere) (cōnsulere)
   *All success comes from vigilance, energy, planning.* (Sallust)
3. Studium _____voluntāte, quae cōgī nōn potest, cōnstat. (discere)
   *The eagerness of learning depends on willingness, which cannot be secured by force.* (Quintilian)
4. Hae vicissitūdinēs fortūnae, etsī nōbīs iūcundae in _____nōn fuērunt, in _____tamen erunt iūcundae. (experīrī) (legere)
   *These changes of fortune, even though they have not been pleasant for us in the experiencing, nevertheless will be pleasant in the reading.* (Cicero)

# Political Hooliganism

Here Cicero writes in a letter to his brother Quintus about what had happened in a public meeting in the Forum, prior to a trial of Milo in 56 B.C. Charges of public violence had been brought by the tribune Clodius. As you read aloud and translate, try to identify the ways in which Cicero makes his narrative more vivid and more personal. We begin **in mediās rēs,** right in the middle of things.

Milō adfuit. Dīxit Marcellus, ā mē rogātus. Eī Pompēius advocātus dīxit, sīve voluit; nam, ut surrēxit, operae Clōdiānae clāmōrem sustulērunt; idque eī perpetuā ōrātiōne contigit, nōn modo ut acclāmātiōne, sed ut convīciō et maledictīs impedīrētur.

Quī ut perōrāvit, surrēxit Clōdius. Eī tantus clāmor ā nostrīs (placuerat 5 enim referre grātiam), ut neque mente neque linguā neque ōre cōnsisteret. Ea rēs ācta est, cum hōrā sextā vix Pompēius perōrāsset, usque ad hōram octāvam, cum omnia maledicta, versūs etiam obscēnissimī in Clōdium et Clōdiam dīcerentur. Hōrā ferē nōnā, quasī signō datō, Clōdiānī nostrōs cōnspūtāre coepērunt. Exarsit dolor. Urgērunt illī, ut ē locō nōs movērent. 10 Factus est ā nostrīs impetus; fuga operārum. Ēiectus dē rostrīs Clōdius; ac nōs quoque tum fūgimus, nē quid turbā.

—Cicero, *Letters to His Brother Quintus,* II. 3

**advocātus, -ī** (*m*), supporter
**sīve,** or rather
**opera, -ae** (*f*), hooligan, ruffian
**eī . . . contigit,** it befell him, happened to him
**ut . . . impedīrētur,** result clause dependent upon **contigit**
**convīcium, -ī** (*n*), insult
**perōrō** (1), to complete a speech
**referre grātiam,** to return the favor (said with sarcasm)
**mēns, mentis** (*f*), mental faculties

**cōnsisteret,** he could continue
**ea rēs ācta est,** this went on
**hōrā sextā,** at noon
**cum,** during which time
**Clōdia,** Clodius's notorious sister
**cōnspūtō** (1), to spit on in contempt
**urgeō** (2), to press hard, push
**fuga operārum,** supply **fuit**
**ēiectus** = **ēiectus est**
**nē quid** = **nē aliquid accideret,** so that nothing might happen
**turbā** = **in turbā**

# Oratory in Republican Politics

Skill in public speaking, or rhetoric, was a requirement for political success in Rome, for all public offices required speechmaking and the ability to persuade. By Cicero's time, the final stage in the education of a Roman youth was contact with a **rhētor**, an instructor in public speaking who taught skills in debate and in advocating a particular course of action. The preparation of a speech included gathering of material and its proper arrangement, selection of appropriate language, memorization, and delivery. A good speech had a certain desirable structure to it, including a beginning (**exordium**), designed to win the favorable attention of the audience; the body (consisting of **partītiō**, "outline"; **cōnfirmātiō**, "positive arguments"; and **refūtātio**, "rebuttal"); and the conclusion (**perōrātiō**), designed to summarize and appeal to emotion. In *On the Orator*, Cicero wrote:

> Eloquence requires many things: a wide knowledge of very many subjects (verbal fluency without this being worthless and even ridiculous), a style, too, carefully formed not merely by selection, but by arrangement of words, and a thorough familiarity with all the feelings which nature has given to men, because the whole force and art of the orator must be put forth in allaying or exciting the emotions of his audience.

These figures represent typical oratorical gestures and postures of the 1st centuries B.C. and A.D. The **āctiō**, or delivery of a speech, involved theatrics such as running about, the stamping of feet, getting on one's knees, waving of arms, and a wide range of voices and expressions to play on the audience's emotions.

47

1 **Nisi Clōdius . . . occīsus esset, ille . . . fēcisset:** "If Clodius had not been killed, would he have done? . . . ." This is a *past contrary to fact condition*, where **nisi . . . occīsus esset** is the if-clause, and **ille . . . fēcisset** the main clause. Such conditions, using the pluperfect subjunctive, refer to events which could have happened in the past but, in fact, did not. Cicero uses this construction to play on the imagined fears of the jury by creating a "What if?" scenario. **Nisi . . . incenderit?:** this, and the questions which follow, are called rhetorical questions, that is, they have no answer or the answer is assumed as obvious. **ille praetor. . . .:** "would he as praetor. . . ."

2 **quī . . . incenderit:** "the type of person who burned . . . ."; this is a *relative clause of characteristic*, describing the general type of person who would do a particular thing. The thought is: what could be expected from Clodius, if he were elected, when even as a dead man he caused such destruction? **ūnō . . . duce:** ablative absolute. Sextus Clodius was the henchman of P. Clodius who instigated the burning of his corpse. See 58:29.

3 **Quō:** ablative of comparison with **miserius, acerbius**, and **luctuōsius**. The antecedent is the burning of the Senate House. Note the singsong rhythm of the adjectives and the punching repetition, or anaphora, of **quid**.

4 **Templum sanctitātis . . . ūnī ordinī:** Cicero refers to the Senate House, in all its dimensions, as the sanctuary of the senatorial order (**ūnī ordinī**) and the symbol of the Republic. This part of the conclusion is called the **indignātiō**, an emotional outburst designed to arouse the audience against the opponent.

6 **īnflammārī, exscindī, fūnestārī, . . . fierī:** these infinitives follow **vīdimus** (4), in indirect statement. "What have we seen more appalling . . . than that this precinct of holiness . . . was torched. . . ." Note the asyndeton.

7 **imperītā:** Asconius also used this word to describe the mob, in Chapter 58:26. **quamquam esset miserum id ipsum:** "although that itself would have been tragic enough. . . ."; **quamquam** is found with the subjunctive when introducing an act as conceived but not achieved.

8 **Cum . . . ausus sit:** a **cum** circumstantial or causal clause with the perfect subjunctive. Translate "when he dared" or "since he dared." **Audēre** is a semi-deponent verb, that is, its present system is in the active and its perfect system is in the passive. **ustor . . . signifer:** Sextus Clodius is characterized as a corpse burner, an attendant or assistant to the undertaker who cremated the dead, and as a soldier who carried the insignia of his unit, leading the charge. **quid signifer prō vīvō nōn esset ausus:** "what would he not have dared as a standard-bearer for the living (Clodius)?" Note the balance between **ausus sit ustor prō mortuō** and **signifer prō vīvō nōn esset ausus**.

9 **sunt quī . . . querantur:** "there are those who . . . ," a relative clause of characteristic. So also (**quī**) **taceant** and **quī . . . putent** (9–10). **querantur, (quī) taceant:** supply a connecting word, such as "but" or "yet." Cicero expresses indignation here about the alleged hypocrisy of those who complain about Milo's deed on the Appian Way, yet keep silent about such a monstrous deed as the arson of the Senate House.

# 59
# Cicero Defends Milo

In this selection from the **perōrātiō** of the speech *Pro Milone*, Cicero completes his defensive strategy—to depict Clodius as a would-be tyrant and to celebrate Milo as a tyrannicide and patriot. Note the attempts to win the sympathy of the jury by appealing to god and country and by emotional reference to the Curia as symbol of the Republic.

Nisi Clōdius pestis occīsus esset, ille praetor, ille vērō cōnsul, ille dēnique vīvus malī nihil fēcisset, quī mortuus ūnō ex suīs satellitibus Sex. Clōdiō duce Cūriam incenderit? Quō quid miserius, quid acerbius, quid luctuōsius vīdimus? Templum sanctitātis, amplitūdinis, mentis, cōnsiliī pūblicī, caput urbis, āram sociōrum, portum omnium gentium, sēdem ab ūniversō populō 5 concessam ūnī ordinī—īnflammārī, exscindī, fūnestārī, neque id fierī ā multitūdine imperītā, quamquam esset miserum id ipsum, sed ab ūnō? Cum tantum ausus sit ustor prō mortuō, quid signifer prō vīvō nōn esset ausus? Et sunt quī dē viā Appiā querantur, taceant dē Cūriā! Et quī ab eō spīrante Forum putent potuisse defendī, cuius nōn restiterit cadāverī Cūria! 10 Excitāte, excitāte ipsum, sī potestis, ā mortuīs: frangētis impetum vīvī, cuius vix sustinētis furiās īnsepultī?

Sed obstābat eī nēmō praeter Milōnem; Milō ūnus urgēbat. Haec tanta virtūs, iūdicēs, ex hāc urbe expellētur, extermiābitur, prōiciētur? Ō mē miserum! Ō mē īnfēlīcem! Revocāre tū mē in patriam, Milō, potuistī, ego 15 tē in patriā retinēre nōn poterō? Utinam dī immortālēs fēcissent—pāce tuā, patria, dīxerim—utinam P. Clōdius nōn modo vīveret, sed etiam praetor, cōnsul, dictātor esset potius quam hoc spectāculum vidērem! Ō dī immortālēs! Fortem et ā vōbīs, iūdicēs, cōnservandum virum! "Minimē, minimē," inquit, "immō vērō poenās ille dēbitās luerit: nōs subeāmus, sī ita necesse 20 est, nōn dēbitās." Hicine vir patriae nātus usquam nisi in patriā moriētur, aut, sī forte, prō patriā? Huius vōs animī monumenta retinēbitis, corporis in Italiā nūllum sepulcrum esse patiēminī? Hunc suā quisquam sententiā ex hāc urbe expellet, quem omnēs urbēs expulsum ā vōbīs ad sē vocābunt? Ō terram illam beātam, quae hunc virum excēperit, hanc ingrātam, sī 25 ēiēcerit, miseram, sī āmīserit!

—Cicero, *Pro Milone*, 90, 101–105 (excerpts)

(The verdict in Milo's trial appears on p. 54)

10. **cadāverī**: dative with **restiterit**. Subordinate clauses (here, **cuius . . . Cūria**) that follow a subjunctive clause (here, **quī . . . putent**) are sometimes attracted into the subjunctive mood themselves when they contribute to the main thought; so **restiterit** here. The antecedent of **cuius** is **eō**, Clodius.

12 **īnsepultī**: Cicero's continual comments on the power of Clodius dead as well as alive (2, 8, 9–12) reinforce in the jurors' minds what kind of man Clodius was and, therefore, the magnitude of Milo's "service" to Rome.

13 **Sed obstābat**: here begins the **conquestiō** or appeal to the jury for sympathy.

15 **tū mē in patriam . . . ego tē in patriā**: reference to Milo's assistance in Cicero's recall from exile. See 57:4. Note the balance of words here.

16 **Utinam . . . fēcissent**: "If only the gods had brought it about that. . . ."; **utinam** with a past subjunctive regularly expresses a wish incapable of fulfillment. Here, the pluperfect tense expresses a wish unfulfilled in the past.

   **pācē tuā . . . dīxerim**: "I say this with your permission," an example of the *potential* subjunctive, expressing a possibility. The perfect tense may be translated as present.

17 **utinam . . . vīveret . . . esset . . . vidērem**: the imperfect subjunctive is used to indicate a wish unfulfilled in present time. "If only Clodius were alive now (but he is not). . . ."

19 **Fortem . . . virum**: exclamatory accusatives. The gerundive **cōnservandum** here expresses obligation or necessity, "a man who must be preserved."

   **Minimē . . . nōn dēbitās**: Cicero uses this imaginary remark spoken by Milo to dramatize the latter's self-sacrifice. What happened to Clodius (**ille**) was his due (**dēbitās**); Milo (**nōs**) is prepared to face what might happen, however unjust (**nōn dēbitās**).

21 **Hicine . . . Huius . . . Hunc**: note the interplay of question and exclamation in this final paragraph, and compare this with the questions and exclamations following **ille . . . ille . . . ille** (1) in the preceding paragraph.

   **vir patriae nātus**: "a man born for his country. . . ."; **patriae** is dative of purpose.

   **patriae . . . patriā . . . patriā**: the emphasis here is on the fact that it is the jury's patriotic duty to reward Milo, as a tyrannicide, with freedom.

22 **Huius . . . animī monumenta**: the memorial to Milo is Rome's freedom from Clodius.

24 **expulsum ā vōbīs**: the traditional worst penalty for guilty members of the senatorial order was exile, here depicted as a fate worse than death (as Cicero himself well knew!) for a man as "patriotic" as Milo.

25 **Ō terram illam beātam . . . hanc ingrātam . . . miseram**: exclamatory accusatives. Note how the successively abbreviated accusative phrases bring things to a final halt. The interspersed future more vivid conditions suggest that the consequences for Rome in banishing Milo will be real ones.

**pestis, pestis** (*f*), plague, disease
**satellēs, satellitis** (*m/f*), accomplice
**acerbus, -a, -um,** hideous, appalling
**luctuōsus, -a, -um,** heartbreaking
**sanctitās, sanctitātis** (*f*), holiness

**amplitūdō, amplitūdinis** (*f*), grandeur, majesty
**socius, -ī** (*m*), ally
**portus, -ūs** (*m*), harbor, haven
**sēdēs, sēdis** (*f*), site, abode
**ordō, ordinis** (*m*), order, rank, class

inflammō (1), to kindle, set aflame
fūnestō (1), to defile or pollute with
   a corpse
ustor, ustōris (m), corpse-burner
signifer, -ī (m), standard-bearer,
   leader
spīrō (1), to breathe, be alive
sustineō (2), to withstand, check
furia, -ae (f), frenzy, madness
īnsepultus, -a, -um, unburied
iūdex, iūdicis (m), judge, juror
exterminō (1), to drive out, banish

Utinam . . . ! Would that . . . !, I
   wish that . . . !
pāce tuā, pardon me, by your leave
cōnservandum, to be preserved
poenās luere, to pay the price
hicine, emphatic form of hic +
   -ne
usquam, anywhere
monumentum, -ī (n), memorial
beātus, -a, -um, happy
ingrātus, -a, -um, ungrateful

concēdō, concēdere (3), concessī, concessum, to grant
exscindō, exscindere (3), exscidī, exscissum, to destroy utterly
queror, querī (3), questus sum, to moan, whine, complain
obstō, obstāre (1), obstitī (+ dat.), to stand against, oppose
āmittō, āmittere (3), āmīsī, āmissum, to lose

## Exercise 59a

*Answer in English the following questions on the reading passage.*

1. How does Cicero characterize Clodius in this passage? Milo? What words, images, and rhetorical techniques bring out the contrast?
2. Cicero suggests that Milo deserves acquittal for protecting Rome against Clodius. Is this a valid defense? Can illegal acts justly be defended in the interest of national security?
3. How does Cicero manipulate the fears of the jury regarding political violence? Given the facts of the case as presented by Asconius, was this a safe strategy?
4. Find examples of the following techniques of Cicero's forensic oratory. Do you think that theatrics should have a place in the courtroom?
     exaggeration    emotional appeal    suggestion    invective
       rhetorical question    exclamation    sarcasm

## Exercise 59b

Contrast Cicero's rhetoric with Asconius's careful description of Milo's shrewd political calculations prior to his decision to murder Clodius (58:14–17). Compare Asconius's version of Milo's motives with Cicero's picture of Milo as a noble, self-sacrificing patriot and savior of his country. Then choose one of these positions and prepare arguments for class debate on the question of Milo's guilt or innocence.

# VERBS: Contrary to Fact Conditions

In Chapter 55 you learned three general types of conditional sentences in Latin: simple, future more vivid, and future less vivid. There is a fourth, general type, called *contrary to fact*. Look at the following sentences:

> Sī Clōdius cōnsul **esset**, rem pūblicam **dēlēret**.
> If *Clodius* **were** *consul (now in the present, which he is not)*, **he would** *(now, in the present)* **destroy** *the state.*
> Sī Clōdius cōnsul **fuisset**, rem pūblicam **dēlēvisset**.
> If *Clodius* **had been** *consul (in the past, which he was not)*, **he would have** *(sometime in the past)* **destroyed** *the state.*

As do other conditions, the *contrary to fact*, or *unreal*, condition contains an if-clause introduced by **sī** or **nisi**, and a main clause or conclusion. The difference between contrary to fact and other conditions is that the former uses past subjunctives in both the if- and main clauses, the imperfect referring to the present and the pluperfect to past time. In meaning, contrary to fact conditions refer to hypothetical events or situations which could have or might have happened but, in fact, did not happen.

## Exercise 59c

*Read aloud and translate the following sentences.*

1. Sī Clōdius vīveret, omnēs Rōmānī facta eius timērent.
2. Sex. Clōdius sī Clōdiō mortuō Cūriam flammāre ausus esset, quid eō vīvō fēcisset?
3. Rēs pūblica dēlērētur, nisi lēgēs firmae essent.
4. Timērētisne Clōdium, iudicēs, sī vīvus esset?
5. Sī Milō per viam Appiam occīsus esset, Clōdius praetor factus esset.
6. Nisi factiōnēs perīculōsae removērentur, nūllī candidātī salvī essent.
7. Sī Milō suōs servōs Clōdium occīdisse negāvisset, errāvisset.
8. Sī tū Rōmānus essēs, peterēsne cōnsulātum?
9. Nōnne rēs pūblica conservāta esset, sī Milō cōnsul creātus esset?
10. Sī Milō līberātus esset, Plancus laetus nōn fuisset.

**nego** (1), to deny

---

**Utinam populus Rōmānus ūnam cervīcem habēret!** *If only the Roman people had but one neck!* Quoting the emperor Caligula as he raged against popular opposition to his wishes. (Suetonius, *Caligula*, XXX.2)

**Utinam lēx esset eadem quae uxōrī est virō.** *I wish that the same rules applied to both man and wife.* (Plautus, *The Merchant*, 821)

---

52

# Building Up the Meaning XIII

## Distinguishing Conditional Sentences

You have now met the four main types of conditional sentences in Latin, each characterized by a dependent if-clause introduced by **sī** or **nisi**, and a main clause or conclusion.

1. **Simple** or **factual**: corresponding indicative tenses in each clause.
   a. Sī tē **video**, laetus **sum**.    *If I see you, I am happy.*
   b. Sī tē **vidēbam**, laetus **eram**.    *If I saw you, I was happy.*
2. **Future more vivid**: future indicative in each clause.
   a. Sī tē **vidēbō**, laetus **erō**.    *If I see (will see) you, I will be happy.*
   b. Sī tē **vīderō**, laetus **erō**.    *If I see (will have seen) you, I will be happy.*
3. **Future less vivid** or **should-would**: present subjunctive in each clause.
   a. Sī tē **videam**, laetus **sim**.    *If I should see you (and I may), I would be happy.*
4. **Contrary to fact**: imperfect or pluperfect subjunctive in each clause.
   a. **Present**: imperfect subjunctive in each clause.
   Sī tē **vidērem**, laetus **essem**.    *If I were seeing you (but I'm not), I would be happy.*
   b. **Past**: pluperfect subjunctive in each clause.
   Sī tē **vīdissem**, laetus **fuissem**.    *If I had seen you (but I didn't), I would have been happy.*

Here are several things to remember when dealing with conditional sentences:
1. Simple and future more vivid conditions are real or factual and thus are found with the indicative mood. Future less vivid and contrary to fact conditions are unreal or hypothetical and are found with the subjunctive.
2. When translating future more vivid conditions, attention should be paid to translating the future or future perfect indicative as an English present indicative. The future perfect indicative, which the Romans often preferred to the simple future, appears when the action of the if-clause is seen as completed before that of the main clause, which itself is future:

     Sī Rōmam **vēnerimus**, laetī **erimus**.    *If we come (shall have come) to Rome, we will be happy.*

3. The tenses of the if- and main clauses in conditionals may be mixed as the sense requires:
     Sī tē heri **vīdissem**, laetus hodiē **essem**.    *If I had seen you yesterday, today I would be happy.*

## Exercise 59d

*Categorize each of the following conditions as simple, future more vivid, future less vivid, present contrary to fact, past contrary to fact, or mixed, and then translate.*

1. Miser sum, nisi tē videō.
2. Miser essem, nisi tē vīdissem.
3. Miser eram, nisi tē vidēbam.
4. Miser sim, nisi tē videam.
5. Miser fuissem, nisi tē vīdissem.

6. Miser fuī, nisi tē vīdī.
7. Miser erō, nisi tē vīderō.
8. Miser erō, nisi tē vidēbō.
9. Miser essem, nisi tē vidērem.

## Exercise 59e

*Repeat the previous exercise, substituting* **audīre** *for* **vidēre**. *Read each conditional sentence aloud with the correct verb form before translating.*

## The Verdict

During the first day of Milo's four-day trial, some 81 potential jurors had been selected by Pompey. After the summations and before the vote was taken on the final day, both prosecution and defense rejected five jurors from each of the three classes, 30 in all, leaving 51 to decide the verdict. Each juror erased one of the letters on his voting tablet, one side of which was marked **A** (**absolvō**) and the other **C** (**condemnō**). Here is the decision.

Senātōrēs condemnāvērunt XII, absolvērunt VI; equitēs condemnāvērunt XIII, absolvērunt IIII; tribūnī aerāriī condemnāvērunt XIII, absolvērunt III. Vidēbantur nōn ignōrāvisse iūdicēs īnsciō Milōne initiō vulnerātum esse Clōdium, sed compererant, postquam vulnerātus esset, iussū Milōnis occīsum. Milō in exsilium Massiliam intrā paucissimōs diēs profectus est. Bona eius propter aeris aliēnī magnitūdinem sēmiunciā vēniērunt.

—Asconius, *Commentary on Cicero's Speech for Milo* (excerpt)

**Massilia, -ae** (*f*), a city in Gaul
**initium, -ī** (*n*), beginning

**aes aliēnum**, debt
**sēmiuncia, -ae** (*f*), 1/24th (the value)

**comperiō, comperīre** (4), **comperī, compertum**, to find out for certain
**vēneō, vēnīre** (4), **vēniī, vēnitum**, to be sold

# PART III
## *Warfare in the Late Republic*

The supreme man of war during the late Republic was C. Julius Caesar. He fought a continuous war (58–51 B.C.) against the barbarians of Gaul, ostensibly to protect the northern frontier of Rome but in reality to win allies, increase his war chest, and build up an army personally loyal to him as commander. His achievements, which included the conquest of all Gaul, its addition to the Roman Empire, and Rome's first official contact with the far-flung shores of Britain, were chronicled in his famous *Commentarii de bello Gallico (Commentaries on the Gallic War)*. Caesar's Gallic achievements and Pompey's rise to the sole consulship of Rome precipitated a confrontation between the two generals, which erupted in 49 B.C. when Caesar led his troops out of his province of Gaul and across the Rubicon River into Italy. What followed was four years of bloody civil war between the Pompeians, representing the Republic and the interests of the Senate, and the Caesarians, who favored radical political change and the transfer of power to the middle class. Pompey, along with many senators, fled to Greece. Caesar, postponing a march on Rome itself, first protected his flank by reducing Pompeian forces in Spain and then met Pompey in Greece at the decisive battle of Pharsalus.

In his *Commentaries on the Civil War*, Caesar provides memoirs or reports of the events of 49–48 B.C., in which he attempts to present himself and his cause in the best possible light. Cicero's letters to his friends and family during this period provide a personal counterpoint to the propaganda of Caesar's writing. Upon the outbreak of hostilities, Cicero found himself caught in a dilemma: should he support Pompey, who had helped in his recall from exile and now represented the cause of the Republic, or should he support Caesar to insure his own safety and that of his family?

C. Iulius Caesar          M. Tullius Cicero          Cn. Pompeius Magnus

55

2 **S.P.D.: Salūtem plūrimam dīcit.** Note the special warmth of Cicero's greeting.
4 **quid sit vōbīs faciendum:** "what you must do."
   **ille:** Caesar, after crossing the Rubicon on the night of January 11, had postponed his entry into Rome (**urbem,** 5) to pursue Pompey to the south.
5 **dīripiendam:** "to be plundered."
6 **vereor ut . . . possit:** "I am afraid that he will not be able."
   **Dolābella:** P. Cornelius Dolabella was husband of Cicero's daughter Tullia and a supporter of Julius Caesar.
   **metuō nē. . . .:** "I fear that. . . ."
7 **ut . . . nōn liceat:** a result clause.
8 **vestrī similēs:** "like you"; **vestrī** is genitive plural of the personal pronoun **vōs.** Cicero often prefers the genitive to the dative with **similis** when referring to people.
   **sintne:** "whether or not there are. . . ."
9 **videndum est ut . . . possītis:** "you must consider whether. . . ."; **ut** sometimes means "how" or "whether" in an indirect question.
   **Quōmodo quidem nunc sē rēs habet:** "As things stand now," literally, "How the situation holds itself now."
10 **modo . . . nōbīs . . . liceat: modo** with the subjunctive means "provided that. . . ."
   **haec . . . loca:** that is, the area of Campania, centering on Capua, where Cicero was in charge.
11 **in nostrīs praediīs:** several days after this letter was written, Cicero's family left Rome for their villa at Formiae.
   **verendum est, nē. . . .:** "there should be concern that. . . ."
12 **famēs in urbe:** the dislocation and anxiety following the evacuation of the Republicans from Rome and the impending arrival of Caesar's army is described elsewhere by Cicero as **plēna timōris et errōris omnia.**
   **velim . . . consīderētis:** "I would like you to make plans. . . ."; **velim,** when followed by a verb in the present subjunctive, introduces a wish referring to the future.
   **Pompōniō . . . Camillō:** T. Pomponius Atticus was Cicero's literary advisor and confidant, to whom he addressed over 400 letters. Camillus was a friend and fellow lawyer.
13 **animō fortī:** "stout-hearted"; an ablative noun followed by an adjective is used to describe a personal quality or characteristic.
17 **Pedem:** one **pēs** or Roman foot = .97 English feet, or .29 meters.
   **istīus:** Caesar; **iste** is frequently used to show contempt. By the time of this letter, Pompey had fled to Greece, leaving all of Italy in Caesar's hands.
18 **exceptum īrī:** "going to be captured," the rare future passive infinitive.
19 **quid agam?:** "what should I do?" This use of the subjunctive expresses doubt or uncertainty in the form of an unanswered question; similarly, **persequar** (19) and **trādam** (20).
20 **Fac (mē) posse (trādere) tūtō:** "Suppose that I could do so (surrender to Caesar) safely. . . ."

# 60
# *An Eyewitness to Civil War*

These four selections from Cicero's correspondence date from the early
months of the Civil War and reveal his personal and political fears and
anxieties, as he witnessed what were to become the death throes of the
Republic.

A. Cicero is writing en route to Capua on January 22, 49 B.C., in reply to
a letter from his wife Terentia. At Pompey's request, he had taken charge
of levying troops in Campania, leaving Rome and family behind.

TULLIUS TERENTIAE ET PATER TULLIOLAE DUABUS ANIMIS
SUIS ET CICERO MATRI OPTIMAE, SUAVISS. SORORI S. P. D.

Sī vōs valētis, nōs valēmus. Vestrum iam cōnsilium est, nōn sōlum meum,
quid sit vōbīs faciendum. Sī ille Rōmam modestē ventūrus est, rēctē in
praesentiā domī esse potestis; sīn homō āmēns dīripiendam urbem datūrus   5
est, vereor ut Dolābella ipse satis nōbīs prōdesse possit. Etiam illud metuō
nē iam interclūdāmur, ut, cum velītis, exīre nōn liceat. Reliquum est, quod
ipsae optimē cōnsīderābitis, vestrī similēs fēminae sintne Rōmae. Sī enim
nōn sunt, videndum est ut honestē vōs esse possītis. Quōmodo quidem nunc
sē rēs habet, modo ut haec nōbīs loca tenēre liceat, bellissimē vel mēcum   10
vel in nostrīs praediīs esse poteritis. Etiam illud verendum est, nē brevī
tempore famēs in urbe sit. Hīs dē rēbus velim cum Pompōniō, cum Camillō,
cum quibus vōbīs vidēbitur, cōnsīderētis, ad summam, animō fortī sītis.
Vōs, meae cārissimae animae, quam saepissimē ad mē scrībite et vōs quid
agātis et quid istīc agātur. Valēte.                                        15
                    —Cicero, *Letters to His Friends*, XIV.14

B. The following letter to Atticus clearly reveals Cicero's indecision about
whether to align himself with Caesar or Pompey in the war.

CICERO ATTICO SAL.

Pedem in Italiā videō nūllum esse, quī nōn in istīus potestāte sit. Dē Pompēiō
sciō nihil, eumque, nisi in nāvem sē contulerit, exceptum īrī putō. Ego
quid agam? Quā aut terrā aut marī persequar eum, quī ubi sit, nesciō?
Trādam igitur istī mē? Fac posse tūtō (multī enim hortantur), num etiam   20
honestē? Nūllō modō. Equidem ā tē petam cōnsilium, ut soleō. Explicārī
rēs nōn potest.
                    —Cicero, *Letters to Atticus*, VII.22 (excerpt)

23 **CN. MAGNUS:** Pompey was called Magnus after 81 B.C. because of victories in Italy, Sicily, and Africa.

24 **S.V.B.: Sī valēs, bene (est).**
**Tuās litterās:** this letter is in reply to one received from Cicero several days earlier, asking whether Cicero should stay in Capua or join Pompey.

25 **Āpūliā:** Apulia is still the name of a region of southeastern Italy.

27 **commūnī cōnsiliō:** despite his reservations about Pompey's strategy against Caesar, Cicero was personally in his debt, owing to Pompey's influence in gaining his recall from exile nine years previously. Pompey also now represented the cause of the Republic and, thus, of Cicero himself.

31 **legiōnibus:** the strength of a **legiō**, the largest fighting unit of the Roman army, varied from 4000–6000 men. Although Caesar had commanded 10 legions in Gaul, he was seriously undermanned during the Civil War.

32 **nōn dubitāvī quīn:** "I did not hesitate to. . . ."; **quīn** introduces the subjunctive in a clause of doubt.

33 **saepius . . . videor:** Caesar here subtly suggests that Cicero will come over to him (but he is wrong!). Note the confident tone.
**Ita dē mē merēris:** "You deserve this from me," **ita** referring to Caesar's claim in the previous sentence (**saepius mihi factūrus videor**) that he will remain in Cicero's debt. After refusing an invitation to join the Triumvirate, Cicero had been forced to reconcile himself to the control of Pompey, Caesar, and Crassus in 56 B.C.

## Exercise 60a

*Answer the following questions on the reading selections.*

1. In what ways does Cicero reveal his affection for his family in letter A?
2. What are Cicero's fears for his family as war breaks out? Why do you suppose he left his family in Rome?
3. Under what conditions might Cicero's family leave Rome now?
4. What specific features of language reveal Cicero's sense of urgency and anxiety in this letter?
5. In B, what seems to be Cicero's attitude toward Pompey's strategy against Caesar? Who seems to have the upper hand, early in the war?
6. Discuss Cicero's options as he expresses them to Atticus. What technique of expression does he use? Does Cicero seem to be a decisive person?
7. Compare the letters of Pompey and Caesar (C and D) to Cicero. How are the content, tone, and language similar? How are they different?
8. What does each general hope to gain from Cicero? On what does each base his appeal?
9. What do letters C and D reveal about the personalities of the opponents?
10. What do all four letters tell us about Cicero as a private citizen? As a man of public affairs?

C. Pompey addresses the following letter to Cicero while retreating south to Brundisium, a port of embarkation to Greece. Cicero is greeted as a victorious general (**imperātor**) by virtue of his conquest of native bandits while governing Cilicia the previous year. Pompey is governor (**prōcōnsul**) of Spain.

## CN. MAGNUS PROCOS. S. D. M. CICERONI IMP.

S.V.B. Tuās litterās libenter lēgī. Recognōvī enim tuam pristinam virtūtem etiam in salūte commūnī. Cōnsulēs ad eum exercitum, quem in Āpūliā 25 habuī, vēnērunt. Magnōpere tē hortor prō tuō singulārī perpetuōque studiō in rem pūblicam, ut tē ad nōs cōnferās, ut commūnī cōnsiliō reī pūblicae adflictae opem atque auxilium ferāmus. Cēnseō ut viā Appiā iter faciās et celeriter Brundisium veniās.

—Cicero, *Letters to Atticus*, VIII.11c

D. Caesar, who wrote the following letter while on the march against Pompey, apologizes for his necessary brevity. He is attempting to woo Cicero as an ally.

## CAESAR IMP. S. D. CICERONI IMP. 30

Cum properārem atque essem in itinere, praemissīs iam legiōnibus, tamen nōn dubitāvī quīn et scrīberem ad tē et grātiās tibi agerem, etsi hoc et fēcī saepe et saepius mihi factūrus videor. Ita dē mē merēris. In prīmīs ā tē petō, quoniam cōnfīdō mē celeriter ad urbem ventūrum, ut tē ibi videam, ut tuō cōnsiliō, grātiā, dignitāte, ope omnium rērum ūtī possim. Festīnātiōnī meae 35 brevitātīque litterārum ignōscēs.

—Cicero, *Letters to Atticus*, IX.6a (excerpt)

**anima, -ae** (*f*), darling, heart, soul
**modestē**, under control, with restraint
**in praesentiā**, present
**sīn**, but if, on the other hand
**āmēns, āmentis**, mad, insane
**honestē**, respectably, with honor
**bellissimē**, in great comfort, elegance
**praedium, -ī** (*n*), estate, property
**famēs, famis** (*f*), hunger
**ad summam**, above all
**istīc**, over there
**pedem**, a foot (length of measure)
**potestās, potestātis** (*f*), power, control

**sē cōnferre**, to take oneself, flee
**tūtō**, safely
**equidem**, certainly, surely
**pristinus, -a, -um**, previous, former
**salūs, salūtis** (*f*), safety
**exercitus, -ūs** (*m*), army
**singulāris, -is, -e**, extraordinary, unique
**ops, opis** (*f*), aid, help
**properō** (1), to hurry, hasten
**legiō, legiōnis** (*f*), legion, military unit
**dubitō** (1), to hesitate, be in doubt
**etsi**, even if, although
**dignitās, dignitātis** (*f*), reputation

dīripiō, dīripere (3), dīripuī, dīreptum, to lay waste, plunder
prōsum, prōdesse (*irreg.*), prōfuī (+ *dat.*), to be useful, benefit, help
metuō, metuere (3), metuī, metūtum, to fear, be afraid of
interclūdō, interclūdere (3), interclūsī, interclūsum, to shut off
excipiō, excipere (3), excēpī, exceptum, to catch, capture
adflīgō, adflīgere (3), adflīxī, adflīctum, to strike down
cēnseō, cēnsēre (2), cēnsuī, cēnsum, to be of the opinion
mereor, merērī (2), meritus sum, to deserve, earn
ūtor, ūtī (3), ūsus sum (+ *abl.*), to use, take advantage of
ignōscō, ignōscere (3), ignōvī, ignōtum (+ *dat.*), to pardon, forgive

# VERBS: Clauses of Fearing

Thus far, you have learned that **ut** (or negative **nē**) introduces several different types of subjunctive clauses: indirect command, purpose, and result (negative **ut nōn**). A fourth type, clauses of *fearing*, is illustrated by the following sentences taken from the reading:

. . . vereor **ut** Dolābella ipse satis nōbīs prōdesse **possit**. (6)
*I fear that Dolabella himself cannot be of sufficient help to us.*
. . . metuō **nē** iam **interclūdāmur**. . . . (6–7)
*I am afraid that we may be cut off already. . . .*

You will note that a clause of fearing is introduced by a word of fearing and uses **ut** or **nē** and a verb in the subjunctive (usually present or imperfect), following the regular rules for sequence of tenses. The word of fearing is usually a verb such as **metuō**, **timeō**, or **vereor**, but it can be a noun such as **metus, timor,** or **perīculum**. Note in the examples above that in clauses of fearing, unlike other **ut** or **nē** clauses, **ut** is translated *that . . . not*, and **nē** is translated *that*.

As an alternative to a subjunctive clause of fearing, the verb **timeō** may be accompanied by an infinitive:

Cicerō Terentiam **relinquere** timēbat. *Cicero was afraid to leave Terentia behind.*

## Exercise 60b

*Read aloud and translate these sentences containing clauses of fearing.*

1. Pompēius veritus est nē Caesar tōtam Italiam in eius potestāte iam habēret.
2. Terentia atque Tullia Rōmae diūtius manēre timēbant.
3. Equidem Caesar nōn verēbātur ut Pompēium vinceret.
4. Cicerō verērī vidētur nē Caesar cīvibus Rōmānīs noceat.
5. Cicerō timet ut Terentia litterās herī scrīpserit.
6. Atticus semper metuēbat nē Caesar dictātor fierī vellet.

60

7. "Metuō et timeō nē hoc bellum cīvīle tandem fīat," inquit Cicerō.
8. Nē Cicerō ā Terentiā iam interclūsus esset summum perīculum fuit.
9. Rōmānī numquam veritī sunt nē bellō vincerentur.
10. Metuitne Pompēius ut omnēs legiōnēs suae essent fidēlēs?


# Building Up the Meaning XIV

## Uses of the Independent Subjunctive

In this and recent chapters, you have seen several uses of the independent subjunctive, that is, subjunctive verbs that are found in main (not subordinate) clauses. These uses may be summarized as follows:

1. **Jussive** and **hortatory** were both introduced in Chapter 56. Jussive subjunctives are found in the 3rd person, hortatory in the 1st person.

   | | | |
   |---|---|---|
   | **Discēdat.** | *Let him leave.* | (jussive) |
   | **Exeāmus** Rōmā. | *Let us leave Rome.* | (hortatory) |

2. **Deliberative** (the formal term derives from **dēlīberāre**, "to mull over" or "weigh carefully"). This subjunctive expresses doubt or uncertainty and is usually found in the 1st person singular or plural only. Deliberative questions may be introduced by a question word such as an interrogative pronoun.

   | | |
   |---|---|
   | **Discēdāmus?** | *Should we go?* |
   | **Quid facerem?** | *What was I to do?* |

   The negative is **nōn**:

   | | |
   |---|---|
   | **Nōn discēdāmus?** | *Should we not go?* |

3. **Optative** (the formal term derives from **optāre**, "to wish for"). Wishes are usually introduced by **Utinam . . .** , followed by the subjunctive. The present tense is used when the wish may be fulfilled in the future:

   | | |
   |---|---|
   | **Utinam discēdāmus.** | *I wish we would go (and we might).* |

   The imperfect tense refers to an unfulfilled wish in the present:

   | | |
   |---|---|
   | **Utinam discēderēmus.** | *I wish we were going (but we're not).* |

   The pluperfect tense refers to an unfulfilled wish in past time.

   | | |
   |---|---|
   | **Utinam discessissēmus.** | *I wish we had gone (but we hadn't).* |

   The negative of an optative subjunctive is **nē**:

   | | |
   |---|---|
   | **Utinam nē discēdāmus.** | *I wish we wouldn't go.* |

   **Velim, nōlim,** or **mālim** may replace **Utinam . . .** in introducing a wish with the present subjunctive referring to future time:

   | | |
   |---|---|
   | **Velim discēdāmus.** | *I would like us to go.* |

   This is a roundabout or polite form of command, as in the following example from the reading:

   | | |
   |---|---|
   | . . . **velim . . . cōnsīderētis.** | . . . *I would like you to make plans.* . . . |

   (12–13)

61

## Exercise 60c

*Identify the type of subjunctive construction (jussive, hortatory, deliberative, or optative) in each sentence, and read aloud and translate.*

1. Velim mihi ignōscās.
2. Spērēmus quae volumus, sed quod acciderit ferāmus.
3. Quō Pompēiānī fugere possint?
4. Quid dīcerem?
5. Utinam nē mē vīdissēs.
6. "Omnia vincit amor et nōs cēdāmus amōrī," scrīpsit Vergilius poēta.
7. Palmam quī meruit, ferat.
8. Quī beneficium dedit, taceat; narret quī accēpit.
9. "Quid agam, iūdicēs?" rogāvit Cicerō. "Ēloquar an sileam?"
10. Velim tibi persuādeās.
11. Utinam Cicerō mihi epistulam scrīpsisset!
12. Iuvenālis scrīpsit, "Quid Rōmae faciam? Mentīrī nesciō."
13. Utinam facile vēra invenīre possēmus.
14. "Cēdant arma togae" significat "lēx magis quam vīs."
15. Mīlitēs Caesaris Rōmā quam celerrimē discēdant.

**palma, -ae** (*f*), palm branch of victory

**Iuvenālis, -is** (*m*), Juvenal, a Roman poet

**cēdō, cēdere** (3), **cessī, cessum,** to yield, to submit to

# Word Study XVI

## Salutations

The salutations used by the Romans in letters reflected those used in familiar conversational speech. Epistles began with **S.V.B.E.** (**Sī valēs, bene est**) or **S.V.B.E.E.V.** (**Sī valēs, bene est, ego valeō**) and ended with **Valē** or **Avē**. Avē was often used as a morning salutation and **Valē** in the evening, whereas **Salvē** was used interchangeably. Although these words were not adopted into Romance speech for familiar salutations, Latin has had an important effect on the way people have greeted each other over the centuries.

|         | *Good Day!*     | *Good Evening!*    | *Good Night!*         | *Good-bye!* |
|---------|-----------------|--------------------|-----------------------|-------------|
| Latin   | **Bona diēs!**  | **Bonum serum!**   | **Bona nox!** (noct-) | **Ad deum!** |
| Italian | Buon giorno!    | Buona sera!        | Buona notte!          | Addio!      |
| French  | Bonjour!        | Bonsoir!           | Bonne nuit!           | Adieu!      |
| Spanish | ¡Buenos días!   | ¡Buenas tardes!    | ¡Buenas noches!       | ¡Adiós!     |

Although *jour* and *giorno* might not be obvious derivatives from **diēs**, they arrive through the intermediary Latin word **diūrnus, -a, -um**, which itself came into English as *journal* and *diary*. The Latin adjective **sērus, -a, -um**, adverb **sērō**, and noun **sērum, -ī**, all mean *late in the day*, and it is easy to see the relevance of the Spanish *tardes*. The phrase **Ad deum**, *To God*, and its Romance derivatives may be compared to the English *Goodbye*, which is a contraction of the phrase *God be with you*, the word *good* being substituted for the word *God*.

## Roman Siege Warfare

Through a combination of discipline, practical ingenuity, and technology, the Romans excelled in the art of taking walled cities and strongholds. If a city seemed vulnerable, it was surrounded by holding troops who drove the defenders from the walls using slingstones, arrows, and missile engines, such as the "wild ass" (**onager**), for hurling stones, or the various **tormenta**, such as the "hurlers" (**ballista, catapulta**), for throwing stones and darts. Roman artillery was capable of throwing a 60 pound (27 kilogram) stone or a 12 foot (3.6 meter) pike over half a mile (1 kilometer). The remaining troops attempted to scale the walls with ladders or to break open the gates using the "tortoise" (**testūdō**), a formation of soldiers with shields locked overhead in tortoiseshell fashion. If storming the walls proved unproductive or impractical, then the army began a more formal siege (**oppugnātiō**). With the legionaries working under the protection of various kinds of sheds and shelters, such as the "little mouse" (**musculus**) and "vineyard" (**vīnea**) and

under the covering fire of the various siege engines, an earthen ramp (**agger**) was built up to the point of attack on the wall. When the ramp reached the wall, movable towers (**turrēs**) were dragged to the top, from which soldiers could assault the city with siege engines, pull down the walls with large hooks on poles, breach the wall with a battering ram, or go under it with "rabbit tunnels" (**cunīculī**).

1 **illō:** Caesar promotes objectivity by referring to himself in the 3rd person. He was engaging Pompey's western forces in Spain while Trebonius was in Gaul.
**geruntur:** the historic present is used for vividness.

2 **Massiliae:** Massilia, modern Marseilles, was an important seaport in southern Gaul, founded by the Greeks (see the map on p. 90). This area had been Romanized in the 2nd century B.C.; Caesar pacified the remainder of Gaul in 58–51 B.C.

4 **prōvinciā:** Massilia was situated in Gallia Narbonensis, an area of Transalpine Gaul referred to by the Romans as "The Province." The French still call this area in southern France "Provence."

5 **vīmina māteriamque:** wicker, covered with raw hides to protect against fire, was used in the construction of **vīneae** and other sheds designed for siege.

7 **castrīs:** a Roman camp was a small, self-sustaining city, fortified by a ditch (**fossa**), an earthen wall (**agger**), and a log rampart (**vallum**).
**prōspicere . . . ut:** "to see how. . . ."; an implied indirect question, governing **tenderent, adīrent,** and **exposcerent.** The direct question in its simplest form would have been, "What's going on down there?"

8 **omnis iuventūs:** the abstract noun **iuventūs,** "youth," is used here for the concrete noun **iuvenēs,** "young men." These ranged in age from 20–45.

9 **superiōris aetātis:** the genitive, modified by an adjective, can be used to describe or characterize.

11 **Neque . . . quīn . . . exīstimāret:** "There was no one who did not think. . . .";
**quīn (quī + nē)** introduces a (negative) *relative clause of characteristic* with the subjunctive, describing a general type of person.

13 **honestī ex iuventūte:** "the best of the young men"; a part of the whole can be indicated either by **ex** + abl., as here, or by the partitive genitive, as **cuiusque aetātis amplissimī,** following.

15 **ad virtūtem: ad** + acc. indicates purpose or respect.
**hōc animō:** = **tantō animō,** introducing the result clause **ut . . . vidērentur.**

17 **nostrīs . . . nāvibus:** the Roman fleet consisted of 12 warships (**nāvēs longae**), hastily constructed nearby and manned by legionaries commanded by Decimus Brutus. The Massiliote and Pompeian fleet consisted of over 30 ships.
**artificiō . . . et mōbilitātī:** datives with **locus dabātur.**

18 **ferreīs manibus iniectīs:** these "iron hands," or grappling hooks, enabled naval warfare to be turned into land fighting.

21 **īnferēbant: īnferre** can mean "to inflict something" (acc.) "on someone" (dat.). Note how the prefixes **im-, im-, im-** emphasize the unexpected resistance.

22 **trirēmēs:** three banks of oars (**trēs rēmī**) were used to power these war galleys to ramming speed. Tactics required maneuvering an enemy vessel into a position of disadvantage, then ramming it with the **rōstrum** or bronze beak which projected from the ship's prow.

25 **graviter . . . vehementissimē:** these adverbs and the emphatic verb prefixes heighten the action and contribute to the drama of Brutus's escape.
**utraque:** singular, with **nāvis** understood. The verb is plural because two ships are involved, albeit individually.

# 61
# *The Siege of Massilia*

*In this selection from his Civil War, Caesar has left the land and naval siege of Massilia, a Gallic city loyal to Pompey, in the hands of a subordinate officer, C. Trebonius.*

Dum haec in Hispāniā ab illō geruntur, C. Trebōnius lēgātus, quī ad oppugnātiōnem Massiliae relictus erat, duābus ex partibus aggerem, vīneās turrēsque ad oppidum agere īnstituit. Ad ea perficienda opera C. Trebōnius magnam iūmentōrum atque hominum multitūdinem ex omnī prōvinciā vocat; vīmina māteriamque comportārī iubet. Quibus comparātīs rēbus, 5 aggerem in altitūdinem pedum LXXX exstruit.

*After briefly describing the preparations for the land siege, Caesar praises the enemy's courage and then turns to the fight at sea.*

Facile erat ē castrīs C. Trebōnī atque omnibus superiōribus locīs prō-spicere in urbem, ut omnis iuventus quae in oppidō remānserat omnēsque superiōris aetātis cum līberīs atque uxōribus aut in mūrō ad caelum manūs tenderent aut templa deōrum immortālium adīrent et ante simulācra prōiectī 10 victōriam ā dīs exposcerent. Neque erat quisquam omnium quīn in eius diēī cāsū suārum omnium fortūnārum ēventum cōnsistere exīstimāret. Nam et honestī ex iuventūte et cuiusque aetātis amplissimī nōminātim ēvocātī atque obsecrātī nāvēs cōnscenderant. Commissō proeliō nāvālī, Massiliēn-sibus rēs nūlla ad virtūtem dēfuit; hōc animō dēcertābant ut nūllum aliud 15 tempus ad cōnandum habitūrī vidērentur.

Dīductīsque nostrīs paulātim nāvibus et artificiō gubernātōrum et mōbi-litātī nāvium locus dabātur et sī quandō nostrī facultātem nactī ferreīs man-ibus iniectīs nāvem religāverant, undique suīs labōrantibus succurrēbant. Simul ex minōribus nāvibus magna vīs ēminus missa tēlōrum multa 20 nostrīs dē imprōvīsō imprūdentibus atque impedītīs vulnera īnferēbant. Cōn-spicātaeque nāvēs trirēmēs duae nāvem D. Brūtī, quae ex īnsignī facile agnōscī poterat, duābus ex partibus sēsē in eam incitāvērunt. Sed tantum, rē prōvīsā, Brūtus celeritāte nāvis ēnīsus est ut parvō mōmentō antecēderet. Illae adeō graviter inter sē incitātae cōnflīxērunt ut vehementissimē utraque 25 ex concursū labōrārent, altera vērō praefractō rōstrō tōta conlābefieret. Quā rē animadversā, quae proximae eī locō ex Brūtī classe nāvēs erant in eās impedītās impetum faciunt celeriterque ambās dēprimunt.

*The Caesarians routed the Massiliote fleet, sinking five ships and capturing four, while driving off the ships of Pompey.*

—Caesar, *Commentaries on the Civil War,* II.1–6 (excerpts)

lēgātus, -ī (m), 2nd in command, lieutenant
opera, operum (n pl), siege-works
iūmentum, -ī (n), work animal
vīmen, vīminis (n), wicker, reed
castra, -ōrum (n pl), camp
iuventūs, iuventūtis (f), youth, young men
aetās, aetātis (f), age, time of life
simulācrum, -ī (n), image, statue
cāsus, -ūs (m), outcome, happening
ēventus, -ūs (m), consequence, result
exīstimō (1), to think
honestus, -a, -um, respected, best
cuiusque, of every
amplus, -a, -um, eminent, important

nōminātim ēvocātī, mustered or called out by name
proelium, -ī (n), battle
dēcertō (1), to fight to the finish
gubernātor, gubernātōris (m), helmsman
mōbilitās, mōbilitātis (f), maneuverability
sī quandō, whenever
facultās, facultātis (f), opportunity
ferreus, -a, -um, made of iron
ēminus, from a distance
tēlum, -ī (n), weapon
dē imprōvīsō, unexpectedly
īnsigne, īnsignis (n), insignia, colors
parvō mōmentō, a little way
concursus, -ūs (m), collision
classis, classis (f), fleet

perficiō, perficere (3), perfēcī, perfectum, to complete, accomplish
tendō, tendere (3), tetendī, tēntum, to stretch, extend
cōnscendō, cōnscendere (3), cōnscendī, cōnscēnsum, to board ship
dēsum, dēesse (irreg.), dēfuī (+ dat.), to be lacking
dīdūcō, dīdūcere (3), dīdūxī, dīductum, to separate, draw apart
nanciscor, nanciscī (3), nactus sum, to obtain
succurrō, succurrere (3), succurrī, succursum (+ dat.), to help, aid
cōnspicor, cōnspicārī (1), cōnspicātus sum, to catch sight of
ēnītor, ēnītī (3), ēnīsus sum, to strive, make an effort
antecēdō, antecēdere (3), antecessī, antecessum, to get ahead of, precede
cōnflīgō, cōnflīgere (3), cōnflīxī, cōnflictum, to collide
conlabefīō, conlabefierī (irreg.), conlabefactus sum, to fall, collapse, break up
dēprimō, dēprimere (3), dēpressī, dēpressum, to sink, press down

## Exercise 61a

*Answer the following questions in English, with reference to the specified lines of the reading passage.*

1. Describe the siege preparations of the Romans. (1–6)
2. Pompey was in Greece at this time. Why do you suppose Caesar was attacking a city in southern Gaul? (see Section introduction)
3. As seen from the Roman camp, what was the scene inside the walls of Massilia? (7–11)
4. What was so special to the Massiliotes about this particular day? (11–12)
5. How would you characterize the people of Massilia? What Latin phrase brings out Caesar's respect for the enemy's courage? (15)

66

6. For what reason did the sailors on board the Massiliote ships fight with special determination on this day? (15–16)
7. What advantages did the enemy enjoy over the Romans and why? What enemy tactics caused the Romans special problems? (17–19 and 20–21)

### Exercise 61b

*You are a crewman aboard one of Brutus's ships and you have just witnessed the battle. Write a letter in English to your family or a friend and describe the battle and its outcome.*

## Review of Interrogative and Relative Pronouns

Remember that the function of a relative pronoun in its own clause determines its case, e.g., **Ego sum vir *quem* heri vīdistī.** The interrogative adjective has the same form as the relative pronoun.

### Exercise 61c

*In each of the following sentences, fill in the blank with the correct Latin form corresponding to the English cue, and then read the sentence aloud and translate.*

1. Trirēmēs incitāvērunt nāvem Brūtī, _____ ex īnsignī facile agnōscī poterat. (which)
2. Massiliēnsibus victīs, _____ Caesar nunc proelium committet? (with whom, pl.)
3. Omnēs Massiliēnsēs _____ templa deōrum adiērunt eō diē spem habuērunt. (who)
4. Tēla, _____ ad Rōmānōs repellendōs nactī erāmus, ferrea erant. (which)
5. _____ rēbus comparātīs, mīlitēs aggerem exstruere coepērunt. (Which)
6. Utinam lēgātus _____ oppugnātiō Massiliae cōnfīsa erat nē dēficiat. (to whom)
7. Omnēs rogābant _____ nautae optimī essent. (whose, sing.)
8. _____ cīvēs exīstimāvērunt deōs victōriam sibi datūrōs esse? (Which)
9. _____ opus iūmentum in castrīs Rōmānīs perficit? (What)
10. Vultne Caesar, _____ dictātor esse māvult quam cōnsul, rēx fierī? (who)

## Indefinite Pronouns and Adjectives

In this and recent chapters, you have seen several pronouns and adjectives related to **quis** and **quī**. These are known as *indefinites*, because they designate some person or thing without specifying which one. Observe the following:

> Neque erat **quisquam** . . . quīn . . . exīstimāret. (11–12)
> *And there was not **anyone** (i.e., no one) who did not think.* . . .
> Nam et honestī ex iuventūte et **cuiusque** aetātis amplissimī. . . . (12–13)
> *For the best of the youth and the worthiest of **every** age.* . . .

In the first example, **quisquam** is an indefinite pronoun; in the second, **cuiusque** is an indefinite adjective. Both are compound forms of the word **quis.** Some of these words, such as **quīdam** and **aliquis** and their other forms, will be familiar, since you have seen them frequently in readings. Observe the following sets of indefinite pronouns and adjectives:

| | |
|---|---|
| Servus **aliquid** portat. | *The slave is carrying **something**.* |
| Servus **aliquās** epistulās portat. | *The slave is carrying **some** letters.* |
| Exīstimō **quōsdam** bonōs nātūrā esse. | *I think that **certain** people are naturally good.* |
| **Quīdam** mīles fratrem suum necāvit. | *A **certain** soldier slew his brother.* |
| **Quisque** sē optimum esse exīstimat. | ***Everyone** thinks that he is the best.* |
| Mercātor **cuique** nautae pecūniam dedit. | *The merchant gave **each** sailor money.* |
| Iūstitia numquam nocet **cuiquam.** | *Justice never harms **anyone**.* |

The adjective form of **quisquam** is rarely found.

Here is a summary of indefinite pronouns and adjectives; for a complete list of these forms, refer to the charts at the end of this book. Remember that it is only the **quis** or **quī** part of the word that changes.

| Pronoun | | | Adjective | | |
|---|---|---|---|---|---|
| m | f | n | m | f | n |
| aliquis, | aliquis, | aliquid (*someone, something*) | aliquī, | aliqua, | aliquod (*some, any*) |
| quīdam, | quaedam, | quiddam (*a certain one*) | quīdam, | quaedam, | quoddam (*a certain*) |
| quisque, | quisque, | quidque (*each, every one*) | quisque, | quaeque, | quodque (*each, every*) |
| quisquam, | quisquam, | quidquam (*anyone, anything*) | same as pronoun but rarely found (*any*) | | |

68

# Notes

1. The feminine singular form of the adjective **aliquī** is **aliqua**, rather than **aliquae**. This is also true of the neuter nominative and accusative plural.

2. The neuter singular form of the pronoun **quīdam** is **quiddam**, of the adjective, **quoddam**.

3. Due to pronunciation, the **-m** in the accusative singular and genitive plural forms of **quīdam** changes to **-n**: quendam, quandam, quōrundam, quārundam.

4. The nominative singular masculine form of the adjective corresponding to the pronoun **quisque** is **quisque**, not **quīque**.

5. The forms of **quisquam** occur mostly with a negative, expressed or implied, as in the example above: **neque . . . quisquam.**

6. **Quidquam** has an alternative spelling, **quicquam**.

---

**Cum dēbēre carnufex cuiquam quicquam quemquam, quemque quisque conveniat, neget.** *Since the rascal denies that anyone owes anything to anyone, let whoever sue whomever.* (Ennius, fragment of a comedy)

---

## Exercise 61d

*Read aloud and translate the following sentences.*

1. Sī aliquis illud dīcit, mentītur.
2. Quīdam ē mīlitibus dīxit sē glande vulnerātum esse.
3. "Estne aliquis domī?" clāmāvit praedō.
4. Quot hominēs, tot sententiae: suus cuique mōs.
5. Iūstitia numquam nocet cuiquam.
6. Alicui rogantī melius quam iubentī parēmus.
7. Exemplum deī quisque est in imāgine parvā.
8. Nūlla causa iūsta cuiquam esse potest contrā patriam arma capiendī.
9. Aliquid bonī semper bonīs.
10. Videō quōsdam adesse quī Massiliae pugnāverint.
11. Quaedam ē mulieribus cogitābant suōs virōs eō diē nōn reditūrōs esse.
12. Neque est quisquam quī sine aliquō metū in proelium introeat.

iūstitia, -ae (*f*), justice

---

**At tuba terribilī sonitū taratantara dīxit.** *But the war trumpet spoke its frightening call: "Taratantara."* (Ennius, *Annals*, II)

# Roman Bullets

Lead shots were the projectiles used by slingers (**funditōrēs**), auxiliary soldiers who provided protection for troops during battle or construction of siege-works. The bullets, which the Romans called "acorns" (**glandēs**), were pointed ovals inscribed with the name of the commanding general, the corps of slingers, or the maker of the bullet. Often the inscription contained curses or insults directed at the enemy. The bullet with this inscription was used against Caesar in the Civil War:

Cn. Mag(nus) Imp(erātor)

In 91 B.C. Pompeius Strabo, father of Pompey the Great, laid a two-year siege against Asculum, an allied Italian city which had revolted against Roman domination. Here are inscriptions from several bullets found there:

Ferī (side 1)   Pomp(ēium) (side 2)
Asclānīs (d)ōn(um).
Fugitīvī peristis.
Em tibi malum malō.

feriō, ferīre (4), to strike

# Massilia Falls

Given the difficulties of besieging Massilia on land and the courage of its inhabitants, the Romans were forced to build a brickwork tower (**turris laterīcia**) up against their siege wall. They then constructed a 60 foot (18 meter) covered gallery (**mūsculus**) extending from the tower to the enemy's wall. Find out what finally happened by reading Caesar's narrative.

Interim sub mūsculō mīlitēs vectibus īnfima saxa turris hostium quibus fundāmenta continēbantur convellunt. Musculus ē turrī laterīciā ā nostrīs tēlīs tormentīsque dēfenditur; hostēs ē mūrō ac turribus summoventur; nōn datur lībera mūrī dēfendendī facultās. Complūribus iam lapidibus ex illīs quae suberant turrī subductīs, repentīnā ruīnā pars eius turris concidit, pars reliqua cōnsequēns prōcumbēbat, cum hostēs urbis dīreptiōne perterritī inermēs cum īnfulīs sē portīs forās ūniversī praecipitant, ad lēgātōs atque exercitum supplicēs manūs tendunt.

—Caesar, Commentaries on the Civil War, II.11 (excerpts)

| | |
|---|---|
| **vectis, vectis** (*m*), lever, crowbar | **inermis, -is, -e**, unarmed |
| **saxum, -ī** (*n*), rock, stone | **īnfula, -ae** (*f*), heavy wool band |
| **fundāmentum, -ī** (*n*), foundation | worn by suppliants |
| **repentīnus, -a, -um**, sudden | **ūniversus, -a, -um**, all together |
| **dīreptiō, dīreptiōnis** (*f*), breach | **supplex, supplicis** (*m/f*), suppliant |

**convellō, convellere** (3), **convellī, convulsum,** to tear away, weaken

**prōcumbō, prōcumbere** (3), **prōcubuī, prōcubitum,** to keel over

# A Casualty of War

This epitaph, commemorating a soldier who fell in battle, was inscribed on a cenotaph, that is, a tomb with no remains. Use a classical dictionary or other reference work on Roman history to investigate the circumstances of his death, and then write his biography, incorporating the information contained in the epitaph.

M CAELIO T F LEM BON
O LEG XIIX ANN LIII s
CECIDIT BELLO VARIANO OSSA
INFERRE LICEBIT P CAELIVS T F
LEM FRATER FECIT

**M(arcō) Caeliō T(itī) f(īliō), Lem(ōniā) (tribū), (domō) Bon(ōniā),**
**c(enturiōnī) Leg(iōnis) XIIX, ann(ōrum) LIII s(ēmissis);**
**cecidit bellō Vāriānō. Ossa**
**īnferre licēbit. P(ūblius) Caelius T(itī) f(īlius),**
**Lem(ōniā) (tribū), frāter fēcit.**

tribus, -ūs (*f*), tribe

Lemōnia, one of 16 rustic tribes near Rome

O = centum, for centuriō

XIIX = XVIII

sēmis, sēmissis (*m*), one-half

1 **equitēs ab sinistrō . . . cornū:** these **equitēs** are cavalry, which consisted of non-Roman allies from Gaul and Spain. Pompey hoped to win the day with superior cavalry, with which he had a 7 to 1 advantage. Fighting at Pharsalus took place only on Caesar's right wing, as the left wing was protected by the Enipeus River. For the location of Pharsalus, see the map on p. 90.

2 **sagittariōrum:** the auxiliary forces, called **auxilia**, consisted of archers and slingers drawn from the Romanized areas of the empire and were stationed on the wings as support artillery.

4 **turmātim: turmae** were squadrons of 30 men, ten of which made an **āla**, or cavalry wing.

6 **quartae aciēī, quam īnstituerat ex cohortium numerō:** Caesar's favorite battle formation was the **triplex aciēs**, consisting of three battle lines, one line behind the other with the legions side by side. Caesar's main force numbered 80 cohorts of 22,000, Pompey's 110 cohorts of 45,000 men. Caesar had formed a fourth line from the cohorts of the third to face Pompey's superior cavalry.
   **dedit signum:** signals in the field were given by warhorns, **cornua** and **tubae**.

7 **īnfestīs . . . signīs:** "with unit colors in battle array."

11 **pugnantibus . . . Pompēiānīs:** "of those Pompeians fighting . . ."; the dative of reference is used here where a genitive would be expected in English.

17 **Caesar . . . oppugnārent:** Pompey's army routed, Caesar turns to attack his camp, behind the lines. Caesar, who wore a red cloak (**palūdāmentum**) in battle, was often in the thick of the fighting.
   **vallum:** a wooden palisade and earthen embankment fortified a Roman camp.

18 **cohortātus est:** do not confuse **cohortor** with **cohors**.
   **beneficiō . . . ūterentur: ūtor** takes an ablative object.

21 **animō perterritī:** "broken in spirit"; **animō** is ablative of respect.

22 **signīsque mīlitāribus:** for a legion to lose its insignia or eagle (**aquila**) in battle was a disgrace and could lead to the disbandment of the unit.

25 **centuriōnibus tribūnīsque mīlitum:** centurions were the backbone of the army and usually were grizzled veterans. **Tribūnī mīlitum**, of which there were six per legion, each commanded the unit for two months of the year.

28 **quae . . . , quī . . . , cui . . . :** these relative pronouns introduce subjunctive clauses of characteristic, denoting a general type. In a previous, and perhaps biased, chapter, Caesar tells us that before the battle, Pompey's men were squabbling openly among themselves about rewards and priesthoods and were assigning consulships for years to come, while some were claiming the houses and property of the soldiers in Caesar's camp.

30 **miserrimō ac patientissimō:** this description may be exaggerated and somewhat propagandistic, although Caesar was, no doubt, short of supplies.

33 **decumānā portā:** the gate of the Roman camp farthest from the enemy, so called because the 10th cohort of each legion was stationed there.

34 **Lārīsam:** Larisa was a town in Thessaly, near Pharsalus. Pompey fled to Egypt, where he was stabbed to death by agents of King Ptolemy.

# 62
# The Battle of Pharsalus

Caesar met Pompey on the Greek plain of Pharsalus on August 9, 48 B.C. We pick up the narrative here after the initial engagement, which, in the tactics of the time, required the legionaries of the army to throw their javelins from formation and then draw their swords and charge into hand-to-hand combat.

Eōdem tempore equitēs ab sinistrō Pompēī cornū, ut erat imperātum, ūniversī prōcucurrērunt, omnisque multitūdō sagittāriōrum sē prōfūdit. Quōrum impetum noster equitātus nōn tulit sed paulātim ē locō mōtus cessit, equitēsque Pompēī hōc ācrius īnstāre et sē turmātim explicāre aciemque nostram ā latere apertō circumīre coepērunt. Quod ubi Caesar 5 animadvertit, quārtae aciēī, quam īnstituerat ex cohortium numerō, dedit signum. Illae celeriter prōcucurrērunt īnfestīsque signīs tantā vī in Pompēī equitēs impetum fēcērunt ut eōrum nēmō cōnsisteret omnēsque conversī nōn sōlum locō excēderent, sed prōtinus incitātī fugā montēs altissimōs peterent. Quibus summōtīs omnēs sagittāriī funditōrēsque dēstitūtī inermēs 10 sine praesidiō interfectī sunt. Eōdem impetū cohortēs sinistrum cornū pugnantibus etiam tum ac resistentibus in aciē Pompēiānīs circumiērunt eōsque ā tergō sunt adortae. Eōdem tempore tertiam aciem Caesar, quae quiēta fuerat et sē ad id tempus locō tenuerat, prōcurrere iussit. Ita cum recentēs atque integrī dēfessīs successissent, aliī autem ā tergō adorīrentur, sustinēre 15 Pompēiāni nōn potuērunt atque ūniversī terga vertērunt.

Caesar Pompēiānīs ex fugā intrā vallum compulsīs nūllum spatium perterritīs darī oportēre exīstimāns mīlitēs cohortātus est ut beneficiō fortunae ūterentur castraque oppugnārent. Castra ā cohortibus quae ibi praesidiō erant relictae industriē dēfendēbantur, multō etiam ācrius ā Thrācibus bar- 20 barīsque auxiliīs. Nam quī ab aciē refūgerant mīlitēs, et animō perterritī et lassitūdine cōnfectī, missīs plērīque armīs signīsque mīlitāribus magis dē reliquā fugā quam dē castrōrum dēfēnsiōne cōgitābant. Neque vērō diūtius quī in vāllō cōnstiterant multitūdinem tēlōrum sustinēre potuērunt sed cōnfectī vulneribus locum relīquērunt, prōtinusque omnēs ducibus ūsī cen- 25 turiōnibus tribūnīsque mīlitum in altissimōs montēs, quī ad castra pertinēbant, cōnfūgērunt.

In castrīs Pompēī vidēre licuit multa quae nimiam luxuriam et victōriae fīdūciam dēsignārent, ut facile exīstimārī posset nihil eōs dē ēventū eius diēī timuisse, quī nōn necessāriās conquīrerent voluptātēs. At hī miserrimō 30

ac patientissimō exercituī Caesaris luxuriam obiciēbant, cui semper omnia
ad necessārium ūsum dēfuissent. Pompēius, iam cum intrā vāllum nostrī
versārentur, equum nactus dētrāctīs īnsignibus imperātōris decumānā portā
sē ex castrīs ēiēcit prōtinusque equō citātō Lārīsam contendit.
—Caesar, *Commentaries on the Civil War*, III.93–96 (excerpts)

cornū, -ūs (*n*), end of a battle line,
~ wing
sagittārius, -ī (*m*), archer
equitātus, -ūs (*m*), cavalry
turmātim, in squadrons
explicō (1), to extend ranks
aciēs, aciēī (*f*), battle line
latus, lateris (*n*), side, flank
cohors, cohortis (*f*), cohort, 1/10th
of a legion of troops
signum, -ī (*n*), unit ensign or colors,
used for battle signals
prōtinus, immediately
funditor, funditōris (*m*), slinger
praesidium, -ī (*n*), defense, protection
etiam tum, even then

integer, -gra, -grum, whole, fresh
spatium, -ī (*n*), space
industriē, with energy
lassitūdō, lassitūdinis (*f*), exhaustion
plērīque, plēraeque, plēraque, very
many
centuriō, centuriōnis (*m*), centurion, leader of 100 men
tribūnus mīlitum, military tribune,
legionary officer
pertineō (2), to extend to, reach
nimius, -a, -um, too much, excessive
fidūcia, -ae (*f*), confidence
voluptās, voluptātis (*f*), pleasure
citō (1), to spur on, rouse up

īnstō, īnstāre (1), īnstitī, to pursue eagerly
summoveō, summovēre (2), summōvī, summōtum, to drive off
dēstituō, dēstituere (3), dēstituī, dēstitūtum, to desert, abandon
interficiō, interficere (3), interfēcī, interfectum, to kill
succēdō, succēdere (3), successī, successum ( + *dat.*), to relieve, reinforce
conquīrō, conquīrere (3), conquīsīvī, conquīsītum, to procure, obtain
obiciō, obicere (3), obiēcī, obiectum, to throw in one's face, taunt
versor, versārī (1), versātus sum, to stay, be situated in
contendō, contendere (3), contendī, contentum, to hurry, try to reach

## Exercise 62a

*Answer the following questions in English, with reference to the specified
lines of the reading passage.*

1. What initiative does Pompey take at the beginning of the passage?
   (1–2)
2. What advantage does he hope to exploit with this tactic? (1–5)
3. What unusual tactic does Caesar use to counter this maneuver? (5–7)
4. Describe how Caesar gained the upper hand in the engagement. (7–10)
5. What was the fate of Pompey's auxiliaries? How did Caesar exploit this?
   (10–11)

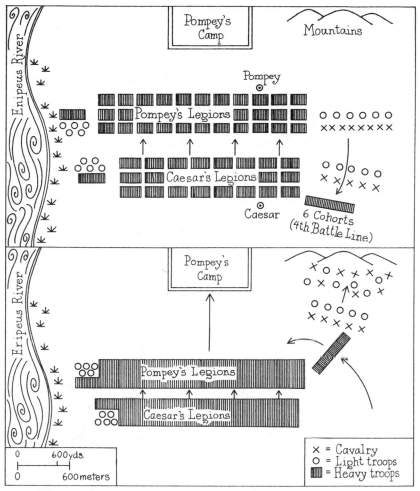

The Battle of Pharsalus 48 B.C.

6. What was Caesar's final, crushing blow? What happened to Pompey's men? (13–16)
7. Describe the resistance of the Pompeians at the camp. (19–21)
8. How did the refugees from the battle behave? What were the reasons? (21–27)
9. What did Caesar find in Pompey's camp? Why should he have derived special satisfaction from this discovery? (28–32)
10. From the last sentence, what do we learn about Pompey? (32–34)

## VERBS: Ablative with Special Verbs

Several deponent verbs and their compounds are used with the ablative case: **fruor, fungor, potior, ūtor,** and **vescor,** of which **ūtor** is the most commonly found. You met **vescor** in *Pastimes and Ceremonies,* Chapter 47:

Trēs annōs ego et leō in eādem spēluncā habitābāmus, **eōdem cibō vescentēs.**
*For three years, the lion and I lived in the same cave, eating* **the same food.**

In the current passage we have:

Caesar . . . mīlitēs cohortātus est ut **beneficiō** fortunae ūterentur. . . . (17–19)
*Caesar encouraged his men to take advantage of fortune's favor.* . . .

. . . omnēs **ducibus ūsī** centuriōnibus tribūnīsque mīlitum. . . . (25–26)
*all having made use of* the **centurions and military tribunes as leaders.** . . .

These ablatives serve as ablatives of means, as illustrated by the following:

| | |
|---|---|
| Ūtitur **gladiō.** | *He makes use of his sword.* |
| | (literally, *He benefits himself* **by his sword.**) |
| **Castrīs** potītus est. | *He took possession of the camp.* |
| | (literally, *He made himself powerful* **by the camp.**) |

Be sure you know the principal parts and meanings of these special verbs that are used with the ablative case:

**fruor, fruī** (3), **fructus sum,** to enjoy, have benefit of
**fungor, fungī** (3), **functus sum,** to perform, discharge
**potior, potīrī** (4), **potītus sum,** to get possession of, obtain
**ūtor, ūtī** (3), **ūsus sum,** to use, make use of
**vescor, vescī** (3), to eat, feed on

---

**Quō usque tandem abūtēre, Catilīna, patientiā nostrā?** *For how long will you abuse our patience, Catiline?* (Cicero, *First Oration Against Catiline,* 1)

---

## Exercise 62b

*Complete the following sentences with the correct forms of the words in parentheses, then read aloud and translate. The singular or plural nominative is provided.*

1. Fruimur atque ūtimur _____. (plūrimae maritimae rēs)
2. Leō ex manū hominis _____ vescēbātur. (cibus)
3. Nē audeat Caesar ūtī _____ rēgis nisi iussū populī. (insignia, -ium)

76

4. Ita nōbīs _____ perfruī liceat. (salva rēs pūblica)
5. Velim ē patre obtineās pecūniam _____ ūtāmur. (quae)
6. Cum _____ perfunctī essent, centuriōnēs ā Caesare laudātī sunt. (maximī labōrēs)
7. Pompēiānī _____ perfruī vīsī sunt. (voluptās)
8. In proeliō Pharsālī, Caesar quattuor _____ ūtēbātur. (aciēs)
9. Plūrimī mīlitēs _____ ūtī possunt. (gladius)
10. Diū cum esset pugnātum, _____ _____-que nostrī potītī sunt. (impedīmenta) (castra)

# Building Up the Meaning XV

## Genitive and Dative with Special Verbs

In addition to the verbs found with the ablative, you have met other special verbs, those with objects in the genitive or dative case.

1. Genitive with Special Verbs
   Oblīvīscor, meminī, and misereor all take the *genitive case*, meminī being found most often with these genitive forms of the personal pronoun:

   | Singular | meī | *of me* | tuī | *of you* |
   |---|---|---|---|---|
   | Plural | nostrī | *of us* | vestrī | *of you* |

   Thus,
   Meminit nostrī. *He remembers us. He is mindful of us.*
   Oblīvīscor and meminī may also be found with the accusative, with the same sense.
   Oblīvīscor nōmina or nōminum. *I forget names. I am forgetful of names.*

2. Dative with Special Verbs
   These verbs fall into two main groups:
   a. Certain intransitive verbs may be found with the *dative of the indirect object*. These verbs have no direct object, as in English.

   | Caesar nēminī cēdit. | *Caesar yields to no one.* |
   |---|---|
   | Bonīs nocet quī malīs parcit. | *He does harm to the good who is sparing to the bad.* |

   Among the most important of these verbs which you have seen are:

   | | | |
   |---|---|---|
   | appropinquāre, to approach | licēre, to be allowed | parēre, to obey |
   | crēdere, to believe | nocēre, to harm | persuādēre, to persuade |
   | favēre, to favor | nūbere, to marry | |
   | ignōscere, to pardon | occurrere, to meet | placēre, to please |
   | imperāre, to order | parcere, to spare | resistere, to resist |

77

b. The second group consists of verbs which are compounded with prepositions.

| | |
|---|---|
| Mīles **vulnerātō amīcō** *successit.* | The soldier *aided* **his wounded comrade.** |
| Aliquandō ducēs **virtūtī** *dēsunt.* | Sometimes leaders *lack* **courage.** |

You have seen:

| | |
|---|---|
| **dēesse,** to be lacking | **succēdere,** to relieve |
| **praecipere,** to instruct | **succurrere,** to help |
| **prōdesse,** to benefit | |

In addition, **praeficiō** and **praesum** are commonly used with the dative:

| | |
|---|---|
| Caesar Trebōnium **oppugnātiōnī** *praefēcit.* | Caesar *placed* Trebonius *in command of* **the siege.** |
| Antonius **sinistrō cornū** *praefuit.* | Antony *was in charge of* **the left wing.** |

Be sure you know the principal parts and meanings of these verbs:

**praeficiō, praeficere** (3), **praefēcī, praefectum,** to put in charge of
**praesum, praeesse** (*irreg.*), **praefuī,** to be in charge of

## Exercise 62c

*Complete each sentence with the proper form of the word in parentheses, and then read aloud and translate. The nominative singular or plural is given.*

1. Meminit _____, sed oblīvīscitur _____. (ego) (tū)
2. _____ imperābātur ut signum dārent. (Tubicinēs)
3. Centuriōnēs semper pārent _____. (imperātor)
4. Caesar praefēcit Marcum Antōnium _____. (cornū sinistrum)
5. Miserēminī _____ quī in proeliō mortuī sunt. (mīlitēs)
6. Pompēius imperāvit _____ ut _____ pārērent. (omnēs suī) (tribūnī)
7. Potestne Caesar meminisse _____ cuiusque omnium centuriōnum? (nōmen)
8. Cum Pompēiānī acerrimē pugnāvissent, Caesariānī _____ parcere voluērunt. (eī)
9. Labiēnus exīstimāvit frātrem suum _____ praefutūrum esse. (sagittāriī)
10. _____ nōn licet oblīvīscī _____. (Nōs) (Caesar)

78

# The Ides of March

On March 15, 44 B.C., Julius Caesar was murdered by a faction of the senatorial nobility because, as dictator, he threatened senatorial control of the government of the Republic. Of the events that took place on the Ides of March, no eyewitness accounts survive. Nicolaus of Damascus came to Rome sometime during Augustus's reign and had the opportunity to interview those who may have witnessed the murder.

> The Senate rose in respect for his position when they saw him entering. Those who were to have a part in the plot stood near him. Right next to him went Tullius Cimber, whose brother had been exiled by Caesar. Under pretext of a humble request on behalf of his brother, Cimber approached and grasped the mantle of his toga, seeming to want to make a more positive move with his hands upon Caesar. Caesar wanted to get up and use his hands, but was prevented by Cimber and became exceedingly annoyed. That was the moment for the men to set to work. All quickly unsheathed their daggers and rushed at him. Caesar rose to defend himself. They were just like men doing battle against him. Under the mass of wounds, he fell at the foot of Pompey's statue. Everyone wanted to seem to have had some part in the murder, and there was not one of them who failed to strike his body as it lay there, until, wounded thirty-five times, he breathed his last.
>
> Nicolaus of Damascus, *Historici Graeci Minores*, para. 24

Denarius of Greek mint, 42 B.C. This face shows the cap of liberty (**pilleus**), between two daggers, and the legend: **EID(ibus)**, **MAR(tiis)**.

## Exercise 62d

The following hasty note of congratulations to Basilus is thought to have been written by Cicero on the day of the assassination, in reply to a report received from Basilus. L. Minucius Basilus was an officer in Gaul under Caesar and was one of his assassins. Translate Cicero's message.

CICERO BASILO SAL.

Tibi grātulor, mihi gaudeō; tē amō, tua tueor; ā tē amārī et quid agās quidque agātur certior fierī volō.

—Cicero, *Letters to His Friends*, VI.15

    **tueor, tuērī** (2), **tuitus sum,** to look out for, protect
    **certior fierī,** to be informed

# The Death of Pompey

Pompey met his end on September 28, 48 B.C. as he landed in Egypt, seeking asylum after his disastrous loss at Pharsalus.

It was some distance from the trireme to (the shore of Alexandria) and Pompey, seeing that none of the company addressed a single friendly word to him, turned his eyes toward Septimius (who had been one of Pompey's officers) and said: "Surely I am not mistaken. You and I have been comrades-in-arms together." Septimius merely nodded his head, saying nothing and giving no sign of friendly feeling. Deep silence fell again, and Pompey took a small notebook in which he had written down in Greek the speech which he proposed to use in addressing King Ptolemy, and began to look through it. As they drew near the shore his wife Cornelia and his friends watched from the trireme to see what would happen. Cornelia was in a state of terrible anxiety, but she began to take heart when she saw great numbers of the King's people gathering together at the landing place, apparently to give him an honorable reception. But just then, as Pompey took Philip's hand so as to rise up more easily to his feet, Septimius ran him through the body with his sword from behind; then Salvius and then Achillas drew their daggers and stabbed him. And Pompey, drawing his toga down over his face with both hands, endured their blows; he neither said nor did anything unworthy of himself, only groaned a little, and so ended his life in his sixtieth year and only one day after his birthday.

Plutarch, *Pompey*

# The Death of Cicero

On December 7, 43 B.C., Cicero bravely faced death at the hands of assassins sent by Mark Antony, who sought to succeed Caesar as dictator of Rome.

Cicero, realizing that he could not be rescued from the hands of Antony, first made for his estate at Tusculum and, from there, by traveling crossways across the peninsula, he set out for Formiae to board a ship leaving Gaeta. There, weariness of both flight and life itself seized him, for, having set out to sea several times, contrary winds had brought him back and then the tossing of the ship had become unendurable. On returning to his villa, he exclaimed, "I will now die in the land I have so often served." It is a fact that he ordered his slaves, willing to fight bravely and loyally to the finish, to put down his litter and to endure without resistance what an unjust fate had laid upon them all. As he stretched himself out from his litter and offered his neck without hesitation, his head was cut off. Charging that his hands had written things against Antony, the assassins cut off those as well. And so the head was carried back to Antony and by his order was placed between Cicero's two hands on the Rostra where, as former consul, he had spoken out with remarkable eloquence against Antony that very year.

Livy, *Periochae*, CXX

# PART IV
## Public Life and Imperial Administration in the Early Empire

### The Roman Principate

The beginning of Roman imperial rule took place near Actium, off the western coast of Greece, for it was here that Octavian defeated the combined naval forces of Antony and Cleopatra to become master of the Mediterranean world. After his victory, Octavian gradually assumed autocratic powers under the guise of restoring the Republic and ushered in a period of **Pāx Rōmāna**. Command of the entire Roman Empire thus came into the hands of this one man, Gaius Julius Caesar Octavianus, called **Augustus** ("consecrated" or "holy"). His rule, which ended the Republic (509–27 B.C.), has come to be known as the *Principate*, from the unofficial title **prīnceps** ("first citizen"). The next 500 years of Roman history were dominated by over 95 rulers, or emperors, whose feats and follies established a cult of personality over the more than 50 million people of the Empire. The emperor, whose official title was **Imperātor**, was formally granted his powers by senatorial decree and by ratification of the people, but the real basis of his power was the allegiance of the military. The role of the Senate gradually became ceremonial, and its functions were assumed by a vast bureaucracy, mainly dependent upon the **auctōritās**, or personal prestige, of the emperor himself.

Beginning with Augustus, both the military and civilian populations of the Empire swore an oath of allegiance to the new emperor and renewed it on each anniversary of his accession. The following oath was sworn to Caligula by a community in Spain in A.D. 37:

> I solemnly swear that I will be an enemy to those who I learn are enemies to Gaius Caesar Germanicus. If anyone brings or shall bring danger to him and his welfare, I will not cease to pursue him with arms and deadly war on land and on sea until he has paid the penalty to him; I will hold neither myself nor my children dearer than his welfare; and I will regard as enemies of mine those who have hostile intentions against him. If I knowingly swear or shall swear falsely, then may Jupiter Optimus Maximus and the deified Augustus and all the other immortal gods cause me and my children to be deprived of fatherland, safety, and all good fortune.
>
> *Corpus Inscriptionum Latinarum*, II.172

Augustus

In addition to oaths of allegiance, the relationship between ruler and ruled was fostered by emperor worship, through the imperial cult established by Augustus, and by emperor deification. Julius Caesar was the first Roman ruler to be declared a god posthumously by the Senate, and emperors as early as Caligula began to seek divinity during their reigns.

## A Roman Senator of the Empire

C. Plinius Secundus, or Pliny the Younger, perhaps best known for his vivid eyewitness account of the eruption of Vesuvius in A.D. 79, was born to a prosperous landowning family at Comum, in the Cisalpine province of northern Italy. Although a lawyer by vocation, Pliny published hundreds of letters, including his official correspondence with the emperor Trajan, who ruled A.D. 98–117. These letters provide an intimate look at the personal and professional life of a member of the Roman ruling class during the reigns of the emperors Domitian and Nerva, as well as Trajan. Pliny was privileged to witness the reconciliation between Senate and emperor after Domitian and the transition of the Empire into what Gibbon called "the period in the history of the world during which the condition of the human race was most happy and prosperous." As an advocate for the Senate, Pliny prosecuted or defended a number of Roman officials accused of maladministration and embezzlement in their provinces. This, coupled with the fact that he was knowledgeable about financial affairs, having served as head

Trajan

of the state treasury, led to his commission in A.D. 110 as special envoy of the emperor Trajan, with the title lēgātus Augustī cōnsulārī potestāte, to deal with problems of inefficiency and corruption in the province of Bithynia-Pontus. The last of Pliny's ten books of epistles contains over 100 letters of correspondence to and from Trajan, in which Pliny asks for advice on such matters as procedure, law, finance, building projects, and security. It is believed that Pliny died in office in Bithynia just before A.D. 114.

Here is a translation of part of an inscription which was placed in the baths at Comum and which records details of Pliny's private life:

Gaius Plinius Caecilius Secundus, son of Lucius of the tribe Oufentina, consul, augur, praetorian commissioner with full consular power for the province of Pontus and Bithynia, sent to that province in accordance with the Senate's decree by the Emperor Nerva Trajan Augustus, curator of the bed and banks of the Tiber and the sewers of Rome, official of the Treasury of Saturn, official of the military Treasury, praetor, tribune of the people, quaestor of the Emperor, commissioner for the Roman knights, military tribune of the Third Gallic Legion, magistrate of the Board of Ten, left by will public baths at a cost of . . . and an additional 300,000 sesterces for furnishing them, with 1,866,666 sesterces to support a hundred of his freedmen, and subsequently to provide an annual dinner for the people of the city. . . . Likewise in his lifetime he gave 500,000 sesterces for the maintenance of boys and girls of the city and also 100,000 for the upkeep of the library. . . .

*Corpus Inscriptionum Latinarum*, V.5262

2  **Tua pietās . . . optāverat ut. . . . :** = **Optāverās tibi tuā pietāte ut.** . . . "You had wished, because of your devotion, that. . . ."; **optō,** is followed by an indirect command.
   **quam tardissimē:** "at the latest possible moment."

3  **dī immortālēs:** this phrase probably indicates official, or public, respect for the gods, rather than personal belief on the part of Pliny.
   **virtūtēs tuās: virtūs** here is "virtue," rather than "courage." The thought is that the gods have put Trajan at the helm of state sooner than anticipated, because of Nerva's untimely death.
   **ad gubernācula reī pūblicae:** this metaphor depicts the state as a ship, with the emperor at the helm. The "ship of state" is a common image in literature.

4  **quam suscēperās:** as Nerva's official adopted heir, or Caesar, Trajan had already begun to assume some of the duties of state.
   **Precor . . . ut . . . omnia . . . contingant:** "I pray that all things may turn out. . . ."; **ut . . . contingant** is an indirect command after **precor.**

5  **digna saeculō tuō: dignus** requires an ablative of respect, where we say "worthy of . . ."; **digna** elaborates on the meaning of **prospera.**

6  **optime:** in addressing the Emperor as **optimus,** Pliny foreshadows what will later become the extraordinary title **Optimus,** granted to Trajan alone among all Caesars. Trajan enjoyed the association with Jupiter Optimus Maximus which this title brought, even celebrating it on his coins.
   **prīvātim et pūblicē:** both as a personal individual and as a public official.

7  **Marcus Ulpius Trāiānus:** no contemporary literary account of Trajan's life survives. The surviving accounts of Suetonius, the imperial biographer who wrote chatty and anecdotal lives of the first twelve Caesars, end with Domitian. Subsequent literature omits the lives of Nerva and Trajan and resumes with Hadrian, Trajan's successor.

8  **inūsitātae cīvīlitātis et fortitūdinis:** *genitives of description,* used to denote a quality, when the quality is modified by an adjective. The *ablative of description,* much more commonly found, describes a special or physical characteristic, e.g., **puella eximiā fōrmā,** "a girl of outstanding beauty."
   **Rōmānī imperiī . . . fīnēs:** the territory of the Roman Empire reached its greatest extent under Trajan, who added Dacia, now Rumania, and Mesopotamia, now Iraq.

14  **ad augendum fiscum:** the emperor's private purse, as opposed to the **aerārium,** or State Treasury, of which Pliny had been an official.

15  **immūnitātēs cīvitātibus tribuēns:** the word **immūnitās** means exemption from **mūnera,** or public duties. Public service, an honor for citizens in the early Empire, had become a requirement of public life in provincial communities by Eutropius's day.

20  **Ossa conlāta in urnam auream in Forō:** Trajan's ashes were enshrined in the base of his column in his imperial forum, built just to the northeast of the Roman Forum. The sculpted relief which spirals up the 140-foot (43 meter) column celebrates his victory over the Dacians and tells us much about the imperial army.

# 63
# *Emperor and Empire*

A. *This letter was written by Pliny to Trajan in* A.D. *98, in celebration of the Emperor's accession upon the sudden death of his adoptive father Nerva.*

## C. PLINIUS TRAIANO IMPERATORI

Tua quidem pietās, imperātor sanctissime, optāverat ut quam tardissimē succēderēs patrī; sed dī immortālēs festīnāvērunt virtūtēs tuās ad gubernācula reī pūblicae quam suscēperās admovēre. Precor ergō ut tibi et per tē generī hūmānō prospera omnia, id est digna saeculō tuō, contingant. Fortem tē  5
et hilarem, imperātor optime, et prīvātim et pūblicē optō.

—Pliny, *Letters,* X. 1

B. *Although Eutropius, the writer of this passage, lived several hundred years after Trajan, he nonetheless preserves at least the spirit of the popular attitude toward Trajan during the emperor's lifetime.*

Marcus Ulpius Trāiānus rem pūblicam ita administrāvit ut omnibus prīncipibus meritō praeferātur, inūsitātae cīvīlitātis et fortitūdinis. Rōmānī imperiī, quod post Augustum dēfēnsum magis fuerat quam nōbiliter ampliātum, fīnēs longē lātēque diffūdit. Glōriam tamen mīlitārem cīvīlitāte et moder-  10
ātiōne superāvit, Rōmae et per prōvinciās aequālem sē omnibus exhibēns, amīcōs salūtandī causā frequentāns, vel aegrōtantēs vel cum festōs diēs habuissent, convīvia cum īsdem indiscrēta vicissim habēns, saepe in vehiculīs eōrum sedēns, nūllum senātōrem laedēns, nihil iniūstum ad augendum fiscum agēns, per orbem terrārum aedificāns multa, immūnitātēs  15
cīvitātibus tribuēns, nihil nōn tranquillum et placidum agēns. Ob haec per orbem terrārum deō proximus nihil nōn venerātiōnis meruit et vīvus et mortuus. Obiit aetātis annō LXIII, mēnse IX, diē IV; imperiī XIX, mēnse VI, diē XV. Inter dīvōs relātus est solusque omnium intrā urbem sepultus est. Ossa conlāta in urnam auream in Forō, quod aedificāvit, sub columnā  20
posita sunt, cuius altitūdō CXLIV pedēs habet. Huius tantum memoriae dēlātum est ut usque ad nostram aetātem nōn aliter in senātū prīncipibus acclāmētur nisi "Fēlīcior Augustō, melior Trāiānō."

—Eutropius, A *Short History of Rome from its Foundation,* VIII. 2–5

(excerpts)

| | |
|---|---|
| **pietās, pietātis** (*f*), devotion | **saeculum, -ī** (*n*), reign, age |
| **sanctus, -a, -um,** hallowed, august | **meritō,** deservedly |
| **gubernāculum, -ī** (*n*), rudder, helm | **inūsitātus, -a, -⋯ n** ⋯ unusual |

cīvīlitās, cīvīlitātis (f), politeness,
    courtesy
ampliō (1), to enlarge, increase
finēs, finium (m pl), territory
longē lātēque, far and wide
aequālis, -is, -e, fair, just
frequentō (1), to visit often
indiscrētus, -a, -um, without prej-
    udice or social distinction
vicissim, in turn, in exchange

iniūstus, -a, -um, improper, unjust
fiscus, -ī (m), emperor's private funds
orbis terrārum, world, earth
immūnitās, immūnitātis (f), ex-
    emption
venerātiō, venerātiōnis (f), respect
usque, up to, as far as
nōn aliter = nihil aliud
acclāmō (1), to cry out in approval

succēdō, succēdere (3), successī, successum ( + dat.), to succeed in office
suscipiō, suscipere (3), suscēpī, susceptum, to accept, begin, undertake
precor, precārī (1), precātus sum, to pray, beg, request
praeferō, praeferre (irreg.), praetulī, praelātum, to put first, prefer
diffundō, diffundere (3), diffūdī, diffūsum, to spread out, extend
obeō, obīre (irreg.), obiī, obitum, to depart, die

> **Putō deus fīō.** *I think I'm becoming a god!* Said by Vespasian, on his deathbed. (Suetonius, V*espasian,* 23)

Flattery of the emperor was a reality of imperial political life that Pliny
readily understood. In a speech thanking the Emperor for granting him the
consulship of A.D. 100, Pliny identifies Trajan as Jove on earth.

This truly is the concern of an emperor and even of a god—to restore good
feeling between rival cities, to restrain angry peoples not by force but by reason,
to correct the injustices of government officials, and to undo what should never
have been done—finally, like a shooting star, to see and hear all, and to be
present and offer assistance whenever called upon. It is in this way that I believe
the father of the universe controls all with a nod of his head, whenever he looks
down upon the earth and thinks it worthy to reckon the destinies of mortal men
among the works of the gods. He is now free of this duty and can turn his full
attention to the heavens, since he has given you to us to carry out his responsibility
toward the human race.

Pliny, *Panegyric,* 80.3–5

On coin A, Jupiter Optimus Maximus, addressed as **Cōnservātor Pater Patriae,** is shown
standing protectively over Trajan dressed in a toga. On coin B, look for the small globe just
below the bust of Trajan. This coin is about the size of an American nickel.

86

## Exercise 63a

Coins were used by Roman emperors as instruments of propaganda. Through their coins, which have been found as far away from Rome as India and China, Roman emperors were able to communicate to their subjects the virtues of Roman imperial rule. Study the coin pictured and be ready to discuss its "message" in the light of the preceding English translation of Pliny. What does this coin tell us about Trajan? What message did it send to those who possessed, used, or saw it? What kinds of "messages" do modern coins send?

## Exercise 63b

Answer in English the following questions about the reading passages.

1. What is the purpose of Pliny's letter? What is its manner and tone of address?
2. How did those in public life hope to advance themselves during the imperial period? Is there any sign of a self-serving motive on Pliny's part?
3. What characteristics of Trajan as a ruler does Eutropius emphasize?
4. What evidence do we have in this passage that Trajan was a soldier-emperor?
5. What reveals Trajan to be a man of the people? What reputation did he enjoy as a result?
6. What special honor was granted to Trajan at his death? What was his age at death? For how long had he ruled?
7. What revealed Trajan's popularity, even 200 years after his demise?
8. Is there any consistency between what Eutropius and Pliny say about Trajan and what Trajan "says" about himself on his coinage? Were emperors revered by their subjects as gods or men, or both?

# VERBS: Impersonal Verbs

You may recall the following sentences from *Pastimes and Ceremonies*:

| | |
|---|---|
| Mē **taedet** solitūdinis. | *I am tired of being alone.* |
| | (literally, *It wearies me. . . .*) |
| Festīnāre tē **oportet.** | *You must hurry.* |
| | (literally, *It is necessary for you to hurry.*) |

In each of these examples, the verb is used *impersonally*, that is, with the subject "it" implied in the 3rd person singular form of the verb. Good English often requires a transformation of the impersonal verb into a personal:

| | |
|---|---|
| **Licet** nōbīs hīc manēre? | (literally) *Is it allowed for us to stay here?* |
| | (better English) *May we stay here?* |

Most impersonal verbs belong to the 2nd conjugation, forming their tenses in regular fashion. From **licet, licēre, licuit** come **licet, licēbat, licēbit, licuerat,** and **licuerit.** Remember that *impersonal verbs are found only in the 3rd person singular.*

## The Uses of Impersonal Verbs

1. The following impersonal verbs have meanings related to feelings:

Mē **miseret** eius.          *I pity him.*
Mē **paenitet** crūdēlitātis.  *I regret (am sorry for) my cruelty.*
Mē **pudet** errōris.         *I am ashamed of my mistake.*
Mē **taedet** sermōnis.       *I am tired of conversation.*

You will note that these impersonal verbs are accompanied by the accusative of the person who feels and the genitive of the cause of the feeling. Such verbs may also be accompanied by an infinitive phrase describing the cause of the feeling, e.g.:

Nōs **pudet** *male fēcisse.*     *We are ashamed of having done poorly.*

2. The following impersonal verbs are found with either the infinitive or the subjunctive.

| Infinitive | Subjunctive | |
|---|---|---|
| Tē *festīnāre* **oportet.** | **Oportet** *festīnēs.* | *You ought to hurry.* |
| Tibi *manēre* **licet.** | **Licet** *maneās.* | *You may stay.* |
| Tibi *exīre* **necesse est.** | **Necesse est** *exeās.* | *You must leave.* |

Note: **Licet** and **necesse est** can be used with either the dative, as above, or the accusative, e.g.:

Tē manēre **licet.**     *You may stay.*

Other common verbs of this type are **decet,** "it is right" or "it is proper," and **libet,** "it is pleasing" or "it is agreeable."

3. Some ordinary verbs may be used impersonally.

Mihi manēre **placet.**     *I am happy to stay.* (literally, *It pleases me to stay.*)
Nōs īre **iuvat.**          *We are pleased to go.*

---

**Cui peccāre licet, peccat minus.** *The one who is allowed to make mistakes makes fewer of them.* (Ovid, *Loves,* III.iv.9)

**Miseret tē aliōrum; tuī nec miseret nec pudet.** *You take pity on others; but you feel no pity or shame for yourself.* (Plautus, *Trinummus,* 431)

---

## Exercise 63c

*Read aloud and translate the following sentences into idiomatic English.*

1. Senātuī placuit lēgātōs mittere ad Dāciōs.
2. Nervā mortuō, Trāiānum necesse erat imperātōrem fierī.
3. Decet Trāiānō amīcōs salūtandī causā frequentāre.
4. Oportet epistulam ad imperātōrem scrībās ut eī grātūlēris.
5. Mē nōn sōlum paenitet stultitiae meae sed etiam pudet.
6. Multīs epistulīs scrīptīs, Plīniō festīs diēbus fruī licēbit.
7. Taedet imperātōrem audīre eadem semper.
8. Trāiānus amīcīs aegrōtantibus auxilium dabat quod sē miserēbat eōrum.
9. Nec mē pudet concēdere nescīre quod nesciam.
10. Licuit Trāiānō imperātōrī ossa sua intrā urbem sepelīrī.
11. Optimī imperātōrēs nōn agunt quod libet, sed quod decet.
12. Plīnium laudāvisse Trāiānum nōn paenitet.

## Exercise 63d

*Translate the following into Latin.*

1. I am weary of life.
2. We will be sorry that we did this.
3. Pliny took pity on his slaves.
4. It is proper for a senator to praise the emperor.
5. Trajan must leave Rome at once.

# Passive Verbs Used Impersonally

Look at the following sentences:

| | |
|---|---|
| **Pugnātum est** ācriter. | *The fight was fierce.*<br>(literally, *It was fought fiercely.*) |
| Ad summum collem **perventum est.** | *The top of the hill was reached.* |
| Mihi ab eō **persuadēbātur.** | *He persuaded me.* |

The passive of intransitive verbs may be used in the 3rd person singular with an implied subject "it," that is, impersonally, when the writer wishes to emphasize the *action* rather than the person or persons performing the action. English tends to express the same idea either by using a noun or by changing the verb to the active voice.

## Exercise 63e

*Translate the following into good English.*

1. Ad Forum imperātōris salūtandī causā concurritur.
2. Senātōribus ab imperātōre saepe parcitur.

3. Nervā mortuō, vehementer dolēbātur.
4. Cum ventum esset ad domum Plīniī, convīvae intrāvērunt.
5. Dē imperātōre bene narrātur.
6. Cum Dāciīs usque ad noctem pugnābitur.
7. Mox ad Forum Trāiānum perventum est.
8. Plīniō ab amīcō epistulam scrībere persuādēbātur.
9. Quibus senātōribus ab imperātōre favēbitur?
10. Dāciīs persuādērī nōn poterat ut pācem facerent.

> Tū regere imperiō populōs, Rōmāne, mementō
> (hae tibi erunt artēs) pācīque impōnere mōrem,
> parcere subiectīs et dēbellāre superbōs.
>                                    Vergil, *Aeneid*, VI.851–853

## Exercise 63f

*Make a list of all the modern countries wholly or partly contained
within the boundaries of the Roman Empire during the time of Trajan,
as illustrated by the map below. Consult a modern atlas for assistance,
as necessary.*

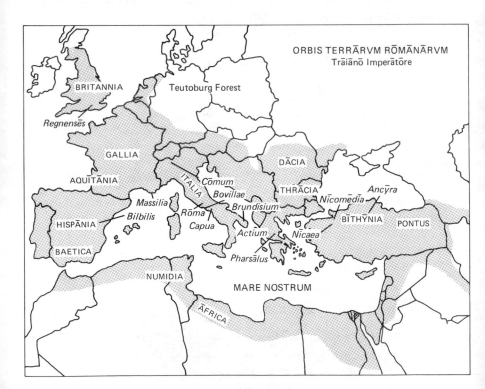

# An Imperial Building Program

Trajan extended the boundaries of the Roman Empire to the limits of the civilized world, with the exception of India and China. The wealth that poured into Rome from these imperial territories enabled Trajan to undertake a massive building program, to the extent that the Emperor Constantine later called him **Parietāria**, "Wallflower," because his name was inscribed on so many walls. He built baths, aqueducts, roads, and bridges at home and abroad, and, in keeping with his imperial vision of Rome as a cosmopolis, he constructed a huge market, which was supplied by his new harbor at Ostia. His crowning achievement was the last and greatest of the imperial **fora**, Trajan's Forum, where the Emperor's remains were laid to rest at the foot of his column celebrating the defeat of the Dacians. It was the Emperor's hope that Rome would become the architectural showpiece of the world, much as the Athens of Pericles had been, and his coins often boast of this intention. In general, Roman rulers used their buildings as architectural propaganda, to symbolize the material rewards of prosperity under imperial rule and to portray such imperial virtues as **concordia**, **abundantia**, **fēlīcitās**, and **aeternitās**. Provincial municipalities often competed for imperial favor by constructing baths, **fora**, theaters, and aqueducts in the image of Rome herself. Pliny, in writing to Trajan of the public works in Bithynia, several times refers to those "whose utility and beauty will be most worthy of your age."

Trajan's Column

2  **Lēx Pompēia:** after conquering the Greek East, Pompey established by edict in
65 B.C. the law under which the new Roman province of Bithynia would be
governed.

   **būlēn:** Greek *boulê* = Roman **senātus** or, more properly, a **decuriō** or "town
council." The language and culture of Bithynia were mainly Greek. For the
places mentioned in this reading, refer to the map on p. 90.

   **ā cēnsōribus leguntur:** municipal censors, on the Roman model, selected from
ex-magistrates the **decuriōnēs,** or those who would serve for life on the town
council. Later in the Empire, councilmen were chosen from the wealthier
property owners, who then went on to hold magistracies.

3  **dare pecūniam:** in the more Romanized western provinces, an honorary fee,
the **honōrārium decuriōnātūs,** was generally paid by those selected to local
senates by the censor of the town.

   **indulgentia tua:** with the special permission of the emperor a local town council
could appoint to its own body a person of special distinction as a civic honor.
In certain cities of Bithynia, these honorary councilmen had begun to pay
the **honōrārium,** perhaps as a source of municipal income.

4  **super lēgitimum numerum:** usually several hundred, but this varied.

5  **Anicius . . . iussit īnferre:** Anicius, a previous governor, had established the
**honōrārium decuriōnātūs** for all councilmen in a few cities.

7  **aliud aliīs, . . . īnferre:** "to make a payment . . . which varied from one city
to another."

   **Superest . . . ut . . . dispiciās:** "it remains for you to consider. . . ."; the result
clause serves as the subject of **superest,** used impersonally.

9  **ā tē cōnstituī decet:** the subject is the previous **quod**-clause, the ruling that will
result from Trajan's consideration of the matter (**dispiciās,** 7).

13  **dēbeant necne:** "whether or not they ought. . . ."; **dēbeant** is subjunctive in a
double indirect question with **necne.** This indirect question serves as the
subject of **nōn potest statuī,** following.

14  **sequendam . . . putō:** supply **esse,** "in my opinion, must be followed. . . .";
the omission of **esse** is very common in Pliny.

17  **Nīcomēdīae et Nīcaeae:** Nicomedia was the provincial capital of Bithynia and
Nicaea its chief rival. Both were self-governing cities under the general control
of the Roman governor.

   **quīdam . . . in opus damnātī:** these were non-Roman provincial subjects who
were sentenced **in opus,** to the mines or quarries, or **in lūdum,** to serve at
or in the games. Convicted criminals lost freedom and citizenship and were
reduced to the status of slaves. Crimes warranting such punishment were
theft, forgery, arson, and sacrilege.

18  **pūblicōrum servōrum:** the **pūblicī servī** were a privileged class of slaves who
earned a salary by assisting municipal officials as clerks and by serving the
state in other menial capacities. Pliny states elsewhere that public slaves were
even used to guard prisoners, evidently an impropriety. Communities were
apparently either using convicts to perform public work in order to avoid the
costly purchase of slaves or the public slaves themselves were using convicts
for their own work.

# 64
# *Local Government and Security in the Provinces*

Pliny's correspondence with Trajan during his tenure as imperial legate of Bithynia-Pontus reveals much about how the Romans governed their empire. The following selections deal with problems of provincial government and security that are typical of an empire whose size and diversity demanded an ever-increasing centralization of government in the hands of the emperor in Rome.

A. Pliny consults Trajan on a matter of municipal government.

## C. PLINIUS TRAIANO IMPERATORI

Lēx Pompēia, domine, quā Bīthȳnī et Ponticī ūtuntur, eōs quī in būlēn ā cēnsōribus leguntur, dare pecūniam nōn iubet; sed eī quōs indulgentia tua quibusdam cīvitātibus super lēgitimum numerum adicere permīsit et singula mīlia dēnāriōrum et bīna intulērunt. Anicius deinde Maximus prōcōnsul 5 eōs etiam quī ā cēnsōribus legerentur, dumtaxat in paucissimīs cīvitātibus, aliud aliīs, iussit īnferre. Superest ergo, ut ipse dispiciās, an in omnibus cīvitātibus certum aliquid omnēs quī deinde būleutae legentur dēbeant prō introitū dare. Nam, quod in perpetuum mānsūrum est, ā tē cōnstituī decet, cuius factīs dictīsque dēbētur aeternitās. 10

—Pliny, *Letters*, X.112

B. Trajan gives his reply.

## TRAIANUS PLINIO

Honōrārium decuriōnātūs omnēs, quī in quāque cīvitāte Bīthȳniae decuriōnēs fiunt, īnferre dēbeant necne, in ūniversum ā mē nōn potest statuī. Id ergō, quod semper tūtissimum est, sequendam cuiusque cīvitātis lēgem putō. 15

—Pliny, *Letters*, X.113

C. In this letter, Pliny asks Trajan what to do about condemned criminals who have been found performing the duties of public slaves.

## C. PLINIUS TRAIANO IMPERATORI

In plērīsque cīvitātibus, domine, maximē Nīcomēdīae et Nīcaeae, quīdam vel in opus damnātī vel in lūdum similiaque hīs genera poenārum pūbli-

cōrum servōrum officiō ministeriōque funguntur atque etiam ut pūblicī
servī annua accipiunt. Quod ego cum audīssem, diū multumque haesitāvī, 20
quid facere dēbērem. Nam et reddere poenae post longum tempus plērōsque
iam senēs, et, quantum adfirmātur, frūgāliter modestēque vīventēs nimis
sevērum arbitrābar, et in pūblicīs officiīs retinēre damnātōs nōn satis honestum putābam; eōsdem rursus ā rē pūblicā pascī ōtiōsōs inūtile, nōn pascī
etiam perīculōsum exīstimābam. Necessāriō ergō rem tōtam, dum tē cōn- 25
sulerem in suspēnsō relīquī.

—Pliny, Letters, X.31

20 **audīssem:** = **audīvissem.**
21 Note the parallel indirect statements: **reddere** . . . **sevērum arbitrābar** and **retinēre** . . . **honestum putābam** and **pascī** . . . **inūtile** . . . **perīculōsum exīstimābam.** The infinitives each act as the subject of an understood verb, **esse,**
which completes its clause. The first clause means, then, "I decided that
restoring . . . was heartless."
23 **nōn satis honestum:** "not appropriate to public service (**honōs**)." The use of
convicts might compromise the confidential nature of some duties performed
by public slaves, such as record-keeping or guarding prisoners.
25 **perīculōsum:** some of these prisoners could be trained gladiators who might
cause serious trouble.
 **dum tē cōnsulerem:** "until I could consult you. . . ."; **dum** is found with the
present or imperfect subjunctive when denoting expectancy.

**Bīthynī et Ponticī,** the people of
 Bithynia and Pontus
**būlē, būlēs** (*f*) (Greek word, usually
 spelled *boulê*), senate or town
 council in a Greek city
**cēnsor, cēnsōris** (*m*), censor, one who
 enrolls senators
**dumtaxat,** at most, not more than
**būleuta, -ae** (*m*) (Greek word, usually spelled **bouleutês**), senator
 or councilman in a Greek city
**introitus, -ūs** (*m*), entrance, admission
**honōrārium decuriōnātūs,** admission fee for the senate

**in ūniversum,** in general
**maximē,** especially, notably
**damnō** (1), to condemn, sentence
**ministerium, -ī** (*n*), service, employment
**annuum, -ī** (*n*), yearly salary
**quantum adfirmātur,** by all accounts
**frūgāliter,** with thrift, restraint
**sevērus, -a, -um,** heartless
**ōtiōsus, -a, -um,** free from public
 duty, not working
**necessāriō** (*adverb*), necessarily,
 unavoidably

**legō, legere** (3), **lēgī, lēctum,** to choose, select
**īnferō, īnferre** (*irreg.*), **intulī, illātum,** to pay
**supersum, superesse** (*irreg.*), **superfuī,** to remain, be left
**dispiciō, dispicere** (3), **dispexī, dispectum,** to consider, reflect on
**statuō, statuere** (3), **statuī, statūtum,** to lay down a rule, establish

## Exercise 64a

Answer the following questions in English with reference to the specified lines of the reading passage.

1. Does provincial law provide for payment of a fee by newly-enrolled town councilmen? (A.2–3)
2. What particular new councilmen have paid a fee? (A.3–5)
3. What decision did Anicius make that has caused confusion? (A.5–7)
4. What does Pliny want Trajan to decide? (A.7–9)
5. What is the emperor's response to Pliny? (B.14–15)
6. What different problem does Pliny explain in the third passage? (C.16–20)
7. What extenuating circumstances cause Pliny's hesitation? (C.21–23)
8. What dilemma does he face regarding the criminals? (C.24–25)

## Exercise 64b

1. To what extent have the cities of Bithynia-Pontus, an area of Greek culture, adopted institutions of Roman government? How did Rome insure its political control over the government of provincial communities?
2. Did communities of Bithynia-Pontus have any local autonomy? What is the evidence for this?
3. In passage C, what do we learn about Pliny as a person? As an administrator?

## Exercise 64c

After reading passage C above, imagine that you are the Emperor Trajan. Write in English a letter of reply to Pliny, outlining your proposed solution to the problem and the reasons behind your decision.

# A Town Councilman from Pompeii

The following inscription commemorates the civic generosity of Numerius Popidius Celsinus, who rebuilt the Temple of Isis, which had been totally destroyed by earthquake. Celsinus was elected to the city council of Pompeii at the age of six out of gratitude to the real donor, Numerius Popidius Ampliatus, his father, who was ineligible for election to the council of decurions because he had been born a slave.

N(umerius) Popidius N(umeriī) f(īlius) Celsinus
aedem Īsidis terrae mōtū conlāpsam
ā fundāmentō p(ecūniā) s(uā) restituit. Hunc decuriōnēs ob līberālitātem
cum esset annōrum sex ōrdinī suō grātīs adlēgērunt.

*Corpus Inscriptionum Latinarum,* X.846

# VERBS: Relative Clause of Characteristic

For some time now, you have seen examples of the following type of subjunctive clause:

Et sunt **quī** dē viā Appiā **querantur, taceant** dē Cūriā! (59:9)
*And there are those* **who complain** *about the Appian Way (affair), (yet)* **keep silent** *about the Curia!* (Speaking of unnamed persons)

Neque erat quisquam omnium **quīn** ( = **quī nē**) in eius diēī cāsū suārum omnium fortūnārum ēventum cōnsistere **exīstimāret.** (61:11–12)
*Nor was there anyone* **who did not think** *that the outcome of all his fortunes rested on the events of that day.*

Each of these sentences has a dependent clause introduced by a relative pronoun and containing a verb or verbs in the subjunctive. This type of clause is called a *relative clause of characteristic,* because it characterizes or describes an antecedent as a general or indefinite type, rather than as a specific and definite person or thing. Observe the following examples:

| | |
|---|---|
| Iste est vir **quem** omnēs **timent.** | *He is (in fact) the man* **whom** *everyone* **fears.** |
| Iste est vir **quem** omnēs **timeant.** | *He is the (type of) man* **whom** *everyone* **fears (would fear).** |

The relative clause of characteristic is especially common after such expressions as **est quī, sunt quī, nēmō est quī,** and **quis est quī,** and it is usually translated with phrases such as "of the sort that . . . ," "the kind of . . . ," or "of such a kind. . . ." Here are some examples:

| | |
|---|---|
| Quis est **quī** hoc **faciat?** | *Who is there* **of the sort who would do** *this?* |
| Sunt **quī** **dīcant.** . . . | *There are those* **who say.** . . . |
| Is nōn est **quī** hoc **dīcat.** | *He is* **not** *the* **kind of person who says (would say)** *this.* |
| Nēmō est **quīn sciat.** . . . | *There is* **no one who does not know.** . . . ( = *Everyone knows.* . . .) |

## *Exercise 64d*

*Read aloud and translate the following sentences.*

1. Quae cīvitās est quae nōn dēlērī possit?
2. Is erat Augustus quī iniūriae ignōsceret.
3. Nēmō fuit omnium pūblicōrum servōrum quīn damnātus esset.
4. Quid est quod in hāc prōvinciā Plīnium nōn vexet?
5. Nōn is sum quī scelestōs laudem.
6. Nūllus imperātor tam sapiēns est quīn aliquandō erret.

7. Plērīque decuriōnēs fuērunt quī honōrārium nōn intulerant.
8. Plīnius multa scrībit quae sentiat.
9. Quis est cui possessiō lībertātis nōn sit cāra?
10. Numquam cognōvī imperātōrem quī sibi nōn optimus vidērētur.
11. Plīnius multa scrīpsit quae Trāiānus vix intellēxit.
12. Sunt quī putent Bīthȳniam molestissimam omnium prōvinciārum esse.

---

**Difficilius est prōvinciās obtinēre quam facere; vīribus parantur, iūre retinentur.** *It is harder to hold onto provinces than to acquire them; they are obtained by might but retained by justice.* (Florus, *Epitome*, II.II.30)

---

## Trajan's Reply

*Translate Trajan's reply to Pliny about the convicts who were serving as public slaves. Can you locate the relative clause of characteristic? Compare Trajan's reply with your own.*

Meminerimus idcircō tē in istam prōvinciam missum, quoniam multa in eā ēmendanda appāruerint. Erit autem hoc maximē corrigendum. Quī igitur intrā hōs proximōs decem annōs damnātī nec ūllō idōneō auctōre līberātī sunt, hōs oportēbit poenae suae reddī; sī quī vetustiōrēs invenientur et senēs ante annōs decem damnātī, distribuāmus illōs in ea ministeria, quae nōn longē ā poenā sint. Solent enim    5
eiusmodī hominēs ad balineum, ad purgātiōnēs cloācārum, item mūnītiōnēs viārum et vīcōrum darī.

—Pliny, *Letters*, X.32

| | |
|---|---|
| **meminerimus,** let us remember | **vetustus, -a, -um,** of long standing |
| **idcircō,** for that reason | **eiusmodī,** of this kind |
| **ēmendanda,** to be in need of reform | **balineum, -ī** (*n*), public bath |
| **erit . . . corrigendum,** will have to be corrected | **purgātiō, purgātiōnis** (*f*), a cleaning |
| **hoc** = the use of prisoners as public slaves | **cloāca, -ae** (*f*), sewer, drain |
| **ūllus, -a, -um,** any | **mūnītiō, mūnītiōnis** (*f*), construction, repair |
| **auctor, auctōris** (*m*), authority | **vīcus, -ī** (*m*), side street |

## Building Up the Meaning XVI

### Clauses of Doubt, Causal Clauses, and Relative Clauses of Purpose

Here is a summary of several new types of subjunctive clauses which you have seen in recent readings:

1. Clause of Doubt
   Nōn dubitāvī **quīn** et **scrīberem** ad tē et grātiās tibi **agerem**. (60:32)
   *I did not doubt* **that I would write** *to you and* **thank** *you*.

   Sentences showing doubt or hesitation consist of the following pattern:

   **Dubitō.** . . . *I doubt.* . . .
   **Nōn dubitō.** . . . *I have no doubt.* . . .
   **Quis dubitat** . . . ? *Who would doubt* . . . ? $\Big\}$ + **quīn** + subjunctive
   **Nōn dubium est.** . . . *There is no doubt.* . . .

   Thus,

   > Quis dubitat **quīn** Trāiānus optimus imperātor **fuerit?**
   > *Who doubts that Trajan was the best of emperors?*

2. Causal Clauses
   **Quoniam** multa in eā ēmendanda **appāruerint.** . . . ("Trajan's Reply," p. 97, lines 1–2)
   *Since many things seemed in need of reform there.* . . .
   **Quoniam cōnfīdō** mē celeriter ad urbem ventūrum esse. . . . (60:34)
   *Since I am confident that I will return quickly to Rome.* . . .

A clause introduced by **quod, quoniam,** or **quia,** meaning "since" or "because," is found with the subjunctive when *it gives a reason as viewed by someone other than the writer,* as in the first sentence below. When the reason given *is that of the writer,* the indicative is used, as in the second sentence below.

   Meus pater mē pūnīvit **quod** domum sērius **redierim.**
   *My father punished me* **because I came** *home too late.* (his alleged reason, which may or may not be the true reason)
   Meus pater mē pūnīvit **quod** domum sērius **rediī.**
   *My father punished me* **because I came** *home too late.* (a fact, as I maintain)

3. Relative Clause of Purpose
   Scīpiō et Plancus . . . referrī ad senātum dē patriciīs convocandīs, **quī** interrēgem **prōderent,** nōn sunt passī. (57:11–13)
   *Scipio and Plancus did not allow the Senate to be consulted concerning assembling the patricians* **to elect** *an interrex.*

The relative pronoun **quī, quae, quod** is often used as the equivalent of **ut** in introducing a purpose clause. The relative ties the purpose clause more directly to a specific person or thing: in the sentence above, the antecedent of **quī** is **patriciīs.** Any case may be used, e.g.:

   Plīnius epistulās scrīpsit **quibus** nōtissimus **fieret.**
   *Pliny wrote letters* **in order to become** *famous.*

## Exercise 64e

*In each sentence below, identify the type of indicative or subjunctive clause as causal, doubt, characteristic, purpose, or regular relative, and then read the sentence aloud and translate it.*

1. Fīēbant tandem aliī ex aliīs interrēgēs quia comitia cōnsulāria habērī nōn poterant.
2. In castrīs Pompeī vidēre licuit multa quae victōriae fidūciam dēsignārent.
3. Cicerō, quod ēloquentissimus ōrātor esset, lēctus est quī ad plēbem ōrātiōnem habēret.
4. Plīnius damnātōs pūnīvit quod sine auctōre līberātī essent.
5. Caesar equitēs praemittit quī cornū sinistrum hostis circumveniant.
6. Quod ubi Caesar animadvertit, quartae aciēī, quam īnstituerat ex cohortium numerō, dedit signum.
7. Pūblicī servī annuum accipiunt quō cibum sibi emant.
8. Nōn dubium erat quīn aliquī būleutārum honōrārium decuriōnātūs īnferrent.
9. Duae trirēmēs in nāvem D. Brūtī, quae ex īnsignī facile agnōscī poterat, sē incitāvērunt.
10. Neque erat quisquam omnium quīn in eius diēī cāsū suārum omnium fortūnārum ēventum cōnsistere exīstimāret.
11. Bīthȳnī lēgātōs Rōmam mīsērunt quī auxilium ab imperātōre peterent.
12. Plīnius nōn dubitāvit quīn Trāiānus senibus lībertātem datūrus esset.

# Word Study XVII

Here are some **sententiae** written in French, Italian, and Spanish, together with their English translations. Using the related Romance words, write the same **sententiae** in Latin, using a separate sheet of paper.

1. O Liberté, O Liberté, que de crimes on commet on ton nom! (French)
   *O Liberty, O Liberty, how many crimes are committed in your name!*

   **crīmen, crīminis** (n)  **lībertās, lībertātis** (f)

2. Non ogni fiore fa buon odore. (Italian)
   *Not every flower makes a sweet smell.*

   **odor, odōris** (m)

3. Rey nuevo, ley nueva. (Spanish)
   *New king, new law.*

2 **dēferēbantur:** Christians were identified by informers, presumably fellow provincials. **Dēlātōrēs** (the term is derived from the 4th principal part of **dēferō**), "informers," were common and notorious during the Empire.

3 **an essent:** "whether or not they were. . . ."; understand **utrum** in a double indirect question.

4 **dūcī:** "led to execution." Organized persecution of Christians did not begin until the 3rd century A.D., but provincial governors, under imperial mandate to keep the peace, often used summary police powers to suppress Christians charged with disobedience, immorality, or treason.

    **Neque . . . dubitābam . . . dēbēre:** "I had no doubt that. . . ."; **dubitō** is found with an infinitive in writers of the Empire.

6 **inflexibilem obstinātiōnem:** there had been no formal edict of Trajan to suppress Christians; Pliny was acting on his own authority in punishing them for their obstinate rejection of his authority. During the Republic and Empire, certain cults were banned owing to criminal or scandalous behavior of their members, rather than because of religious prejudice. The Romans were generally tolerant of religious diversity and allowed the survival of various gods alongside those of the state religion but were annoyed at Christians who refused to recognize the validity of other gods and forms of worship and who actively solicited converts.

7 **adnotāvī in urbem remittendōs:** "I ruled that they should be sent back to Rome"; **quōs** is the subject of **remittendōs** (**esse**). Roman citizens could appeal to Caesar for trial in Rome, as did St. Paul to Nero.

8 **diffundente sē crīmine plūrēs speciēs incidērunt:** "as the accusations spread, more cases came to light."

10 **cum:** introducing **appellārent** (10), **supplicārent** (12), and **maledīcerent** (12).
    **praeeunte mē:** Pliny dictated the formula of the oath or prayer.

11 **imāginī tuae:** dative with **supplicārent** and antecedent of **quam**. Emperor worship was not compulsory, but there was a cult of the emperor established in each province as a focus of political loyalty to Rome. Adoration of the emperor's statue, as a pledge of allegiance, was rejected by Christians as a form of idolatry. Later in the 2nd century, this rejection became the basis for a charge of **maiestās**, or treason.

12 **maledīcerent Chrīstō: maledīcere** means "to curse," with the curse itself serving as the direct object and the recipient the indirect object.

18 **Adfirmābant:** the subject is those Christians who had been accused but were no longer participating and were being held for Trajan's judgment. Pliny here begins a description of the main elements in Christian liturgy.

19 **quod essent solitī:** "because they had been accustomed. . . ."; why is the verb subjunctive here? What preceding word reveals that this is not Pliny's opinion?

20 **statō diē:** Sunday, the day after the Jewish Sabbath.
    **sēcum invicem:** chanting back and forth, in alternate verses.

21 **nē fūrta . . . abnegārent:** indirect commands after **sacrāmentō . . . obstringere** (parallel to **nōn in scelus aliquod**). Some scholars think that this list is a reference to the Ten Commandments.

100

# 65

# Religion and the State during the Empire

This letter of Pliny contains the earliest and most complete pagan account of the official Roman attitude toward Christians. Pliny asks Trajan for guidance in dealing with the Christians in his province and relates what initiative he has taken thus far.

At the beginning of his letter Pliny confesses, "I am not at all sure whether a pardon ought to be granted to anyone retracting his beliefs, or if he has once professed Christianity he shall gain nothing by renouncing it; and whether it is the mere name of Christian which is punishable, even if innocent of the crime, or rather the crimes associated with the name." He continues:

## C. PLINIUS TRAIANO IMPERATORI

Interim, in eīs quī ad mē tamquam Chrīstiānī dēferēbantur, hunc sum secūtus modum. Interrogāvī ipsōs an essent Chrīstiānī. Cōnfitentēs iterum ac tertiō interrogāvī supplicium minātus: persevērantēs dūcī iussī. Neque enim dubitābam quālecumque esset quod fatērentur, pertināciam certē et 5 inflexibilem obstinātiōnem dēbēre pūnīrī. Fuērunt aliī similis āmentiae, quōs, quia cīvēs Rōmānī erant, adnotāvī in urbem remittendōs.

Mox ipsō trāctātū, ut fierī solet, diffundente sē crīmine plūrēs speciēs incidērunt. Prōpositus est libellus sine auctōre multōrum nōmina continēns. Quī negābant esse sē Chrīstiānōs aut fuisse, cum praeeunte mē deōs ap- 10 pellārent et imāginī tuae, quam propter hoc iusseram cum simulācrīs nū- minum adferrī, tūre ac vīnō supplicārent, praetereā maledīcerent Chrīstō, quōrum nihil cōgī posse dicuntur quī sunt rē vērā Chrīstiānī, dīmittendōs putāvī.

Aliī ab indice nōminātī esse sē Chrīstiānōs dīxērunt et mox negāvērunt; 15 fuisse quidem sed dēsiisse, quīdam ante triennium, quīdam ante plūrēs annōs, nōn nēmō etiam ante vīgintī. Hī quoque omnēs et imāginem tuam deōrumque simulācra venerātī sunt et Chrīstō maledīxērunt. Adfirmābant autem hanc fuisse summam vel culpae suae vel errōris, quod essent solitī statō diē ante lūcem convenīre, carmenque Chrīstō quasi deō dīcere sēcum 20 invicem sēque sacrāmentō nōn in scelus aliquod obstringere, sed nē fūrta, nē latrōcinia, nē adulteria committerent, nē fidem fallerent, nē dēpositum appellātī abnegārent. Quibus perāctīs mōrem sibi discēdendī fuisse rūrsusque coeundī ad capiendum cibum, prōmiscuum tamen et innoxium; quod ipsum facere dēsiisse post ēdictum meum, quō secundum mandāta tua hetaeriās 25 esse vetueram. Quō magis necessārium crēdidī ex duābus ancillīs, quae ministrae dicēbantur, quid esset vērī, et per tormenta quaerere. Nihil aliud invēnī quam superstitiōnem prāvam et immodicam.

—Pliny, *Letters*, X.96 (excerpts)

(Trajan's reply appears on p. 106)

22  **nē dēpositum appellātī abnegārent:** a **dēpositum** is something entrusted. In the absence of banks, property could be left with friends for safekeeping to be returned on demand, a trust apparently commonly abused.

23  **mōrem . . . fuisse** and **quod . . . dēsiisse** (24–25): continuation of the indirect statement after **adfirmābant** (18).

    **discēdendī . . . coeundī ad capiendum cibum:** note the use of gerunds and gerundives here.

24  **cibum, prōmiscuum tamen et innoxium:** Christians were suspected of ritual murder, cannibalism, and the drinking of blood, all associated with the Eucharist.

25  **secundum mandāta tua hetaeriās esse vetueram:** these **hetaeriae** (Greek) or **collēgia** (Latin) were political and social clubs with a long history of political disruption dating back to the Republic. Members of **hetaeriae** enjoyed meals in common, thus the Christian *agapê* or fellowship meal.

26  **quae ministrae dīcēbantur: ministra** is the Latin translation of the feminine form of *diakonos*, the Greek word for servant (cf. **ancilla**), which gives the English word *deacon(ess)*. Slaves could be tortured to give evidence.

**supplicium, -ī** (*n*), punishment
**quāliscumque, quāliscumque, quālecumque,** of whatever kind
**pertinācia, -ae** (*f*), stubbornness
**obstinātiō, obstinātiōnis** (*f*), determination
**āmentia, -ae** (*f*), madness
**adnotō** (1), to make a ruling
**trāctātus, -ūs** (*m*), investigation
**speciēs, speciēī** (*f*), example, case
**libellus, -ī** (*m*), notice, poster
**nūmen, nūminis** (*n*), divine power, god
**tūs, tūris** (*n*), incense
**supplicō** (1) ( + *dat.*), to offer worship to
**index, indicis** (*m*), spy, informer
**triennium, -ī** (*n*), three-year period

**carmen, carminis** (*n*), song, hymn
**invicem,** back and forth
**sacrāmentum, -ī** (*n*), oath
**fūrtum, -ī** (*n*), theft, fraud
**latrōcinium, -ī** (*n*), robbery
**adulterium, -ī** (*n*), adultery
**appellō** (1), to call by name
**abnegō** (1), to refuse, deny
**prōmiscuus, -a, -um,** common, ordinary
**innoxius, -a, -um,** harmless
**secundum** ( + *acc.*), according to
**hetaeria, -ae** (*f*), political club or association
**ministra, -ae** (*f*), attendant
**prāvus, -a, -um,** depraved, perverse
**immodicus, -a, -um,** excessive

dēferrō, dēferre (*irreg.*), dētulī, dēlātum, to inform against, accuse
cōnfiteor, cōnfitērī (2), cōnfessus sum, to confess
minor, minārī (1), minātus sum, to threaten
fateor, fatērī (2), fassus sum, to admit, confess
prōpōnō, prōpōnere (3), prōposuī, prōpositum, to put forth
dēsinō, dēsinere (3), dēsiī, to stop, cease
veneror, venerārī (1), venerātus sum, to worship
sistō, sistere (3), stitī, statum, to establish
obstringō, obstringere (3), obstrinxī, obstrictum, to bind up, tie to
fallō, fallere (3), fefellī, falsum, to betray, falsify
peragō, peragere (3), perēgī, perāctum, to carry through, complete

## Exercise 65a

*Answer the following questions in English with reference to the specified lines of the reading passage.*

1. How were Christians identified in Bithynia? (2)
2. What were Pliny's investigative procedures? (3–4)
3. Why did Pliny think that Christians were deserving of punishment? What Latin words did he use to characterize their attitude? (5–6)
4. What was the penalty for refusal to deny being a Christian? What happened to Christians who were Roman citizens? (4 and 6–7)
5. What was the reason for the sharp increase in accusations? (8–9)
6. What tests were suspects required to pass in order to prove their "innocence"? (10–14)
7. From where did Pliny get his information? What were the summae culpae of the Christians? (15–17 and 18–23)
8. What Roman misconception about Christian beliefs do the words prōmiscuus and innoxius reveal? (24)
9. What concession did the Christians make to Roman law? (25–26)
10. How did Pliny attempt to confirm what he had heard about Christians? (26–27)

## Exercise 65b

1. What seems to have been Pliny's attitude toward Christians? Apathy? Fear? Hatred? Amazement? Do you think his treatment of them was just?
2. What were the dangers inherent in the Roman method of identifying Christians? Can you think of similar circumstances in modern history?
3. For what political reasons might the emperor have been suspicious of Christians?
4. Did Roman citizens and provincial subjects receive equal treatment under the law?
5. How did the average imperial Roman view the gods? Recall what Petronius wrote on the subject (54:24–30).

# Religion in the Provinces

Roman gods were sometimes adopted wholesale in the provinces and fused with local deities. This can be seen clearly in Britain, where the Roman army was the main vehicle of Romanization. Here is an inscription from a small altar dedicated by a soldier in payment of a vow to **Mars Brāciāca**, "Mars in Pants." The word **brācae** refers to the trousers or breeches worn by Gallic barbarians, but never by Greeks or Romans. Although this altar was found in Britain, the soldier was serving in a unit of provincial auxiliaries from Aquitania, in southwestern Gaul (see the map on p. 90).

**Deō Martī Brāciācae**
**Q. Sittius Caeciliān(us) Praef(ectus) Coh(ortī) I. Aquītānō**
**V(ōtum) S(olvit)**

# VERBS: Gerundive of Obligation

| | |
|---|---|
| Scelestī pūniendī sunt. | *Criminals* **must be punished.** |
| Epistula **erat scrībenda.** | *A* **letter had to be written.** |
| Sacrāmentum **dīcendum erit.** | *The oath* **will have to be sworn.** |

You will recognize the forms **pūniendī, scrībenda,** and **dīcendum** as gerundives, verbal adjectives characterized by **-nd-** and translated in the passive. When used with a form of **esse,** provided or understood, the gerundive is known as a *gerundive of obligation* and is translated "must be . . . ," "should be . . . ," "has to be. . . ." This use of the gerundive is commonly called the *passive periphrastic*, the term *periphrastic* meaning "roundabout" and referring to the use of a helping or auxiliary verb, such as **sunt, erat,** or **erit,** as above.

Compare the following two sentences:

| | |
|---|---|
| Crūdēlitās vītanda est. | *Cruelty must be avoided.* |
| Crūdēlitās **tibi** vītanda est. | *Cruelty must be avoided* **by you.** |

In English, the second sentence may also be translated

*You must avoid cruelty.*

The dative has become the subject in English and the verb is now translated as active. Consider the following sentences:

| | |
|---|---|
| Nōbīs eundum est Rōmam. | *We must go to Rome.* |
| | (literally, *It must be gone by us to Rome.*) |
| Fūrī fugiendum erat. | *The thief had to run away.* |
| Mihi statim ēgrediendum erit. | *I will have to leave at once.* |

104

Unlike the previous examples, in these sentences the gerundive is used *impersonally*, that is, with the neuter singular ending -um together with a 3rd person singular form of the verb **esse** and is translated literally by the word "it." These sentences must be transformed into the active in English translation with the dative supplying the subject. With the impersonal use of the gerundive of obligation, the dative expresses the agent by whom the action is to be carried out rather than a prepositional phrase with **ā** or **ab**, as is usual with passive verbs. This use of the dative is commonly called the *dative of agent*. Observe the following examples:

**Omnibus Chrīstiānīs** ē Bithȳniā discēdendum erat. (dative of agent)
*All Christians had to leave Bithynia.*
Bīthȳnia **ab omnibus Chrīstiānīs** relinquēbātur. (ā/ab + abl.)
*Bithynia was being abandoned by all Christians.*

---

**Carthāgō dēlenda est!** *Carthage must be destroyed!* Exclaimed by Cato the Elder at Senate meetings during the Punic Wars.

---

## Exercise 65c

*Read aloud and translate each of the following sentences.*

1. Lēgēs omnibus cīvibus observandae sunt.
2. Plīnius ā Trāiānō quaerēbat quae cōnsilia capienda essent dē Chrīstiānīs.
3. Quī negābant sē Chrīstiānōs esse dīmittendī erant.
4. Dī immortālēs cīvibus Rōmānīs semper venerandī sunt.
5. Plīnius putāvit eōs quī cīvēs Rōmānī erant Rōmam remittendōs esse.
6. Ā Plīniō Chrīstiānīs persuādendum erat ut simulācrum Trāiānī venerārentur.
7. Ūniversus hic mundus ūna cīvitās commūnis deōrum atque hominum exīstimanda sit.
8. Vigilandum erit semper; multae īnsidiae sunt bonīs.
9. Fallendī cupiditās nōbīs vītanda erit.
10. Plīnius adnotāvit Chrīstiānōs propter pertinaciam pūniendōs esse.

## Exercise 65d

*Complete the following sentences by supplying the appropriate form from the pool on page 106, and then translate the completed sentences.*

1. Sī nōbīscum venīre nōn vīs, _____ domī manendum est.
2. Cum Plīnius revocātus esset, _____ Rōmam erat regrediendum.
3. Hic puer _____ est laudandus quod mē maximē adiūvit.

105

4. Fātum est suum _____ ferendum.
5. Ubi Rōmam perveniētis, ad Circum Maximum _____ eundum erit.

| nōbīs | vōs | mihi | ego | tibi | cuique | nōs | tū | vōbīs | eī | quisque |

## Trajan on the Christians

*Read Trajan's reply to Pliny's letter concerning the Christians, and then answer in English the following questions. Note the use of gerunds and gerundives.*

Āctum quem dēbuistī, mī Secunde, in excutiendīs causīs eōrum, quī Chrīstiānī ad tē dēlātī fuerant, secūtus es. Neque enim in ūniversum aliquid, quod quasi certam fōrmam habeat, cōnstituī potest. Conquīrendī nōn sunt; sī dēferantur et arguantur, pūniendī sunt, ita tamen ut, quī negāverit sē Chrīstiānum esse idque rē ipsā manifestum fēcerit, id est supplicandō dīs nostrīs, quamvīs suspectus in praeteritum, 5 veniam ex paenitentiā impetret. Sine auctōre vērō prōpositī libellī in nūllō crīmine locum habēre dēbent. Nam et pessimī exemplī nec nostrī saeculī est.

—Pliny, *Letters*, X.97

 āctum, -ī (*n*), procedure
causa, -ae (*f*), case
certam fōrmam, a fixed rule
manifestus, -a, -um, clear, evident
quamvīs, although
in praeteritum, formerly

venia, -ae (*f*), pardon
paenitentia, -ae (*f*), repentance
impetrō (1), to obtain, secure
pessimī exemplī, the worst sort of precedent (genitive of description)

excutiō, excutere (3), excussī, excussum, to examine, inspect
conquīrō, conquīrere (3), conquīsīvī, conquīsītum, to hunt down, seek out
arguō, arguere (3), arguī, argūtum, to accuse, denounce

## Exercise 65e

1. How does Trajan feel about the way in which Pliny has been handling the situation thus far?
2. Is Pliny to seek out Christians? How does the construction **conquīrendī nōn sunt** (3) reinforce Trajan's wishes?
3. What is to happen to the Christians who are accused? Is there any contradiction between the fact that Christians are not to be hunted down but are to be punished, if found?
4. How does Trajan address Pliny's uncertainty about Christians who deny their beliefs?
5. What previous practice described by Pliny will Trajan not tolerate?

The abbreviation Q.E.D., for **quod erat dēmōnstrandum,** *which was to be shown,* is often found following mathematical proofs and solutions to problems.

# PART V
## Daily Life in the Early Empire

The last three chapters of this book deal with aspects of Roman private life: the settings in which Romans lived in city and country, the everyday activities of rich and poor, and their relationships with members of their **familia**, which included slaves and freedmen as well as blood relatives.

Most of the texts you are about to read were written by Pliny the Younger, whom you have already met in some of his more public roles, and his older contemporary, the poet Martial (A.D. c. 40–104). Martial was a native of the village of Bilbilis in northeastern Spain but came to Rome as a young man and lived there for thirty-five years; he achieved considerable fame (though not much fortune) as a writer of epigrams, short poems that made witty comments on the passing scene. When he finally retired to Bilbilis shortly before A.D. 100, a generous and cultured woman named Marcella seems to have acted as his patron, providing him with a small estate and also with the stimulating conversation he sorely missed after he left Rome. The exact date of his death is unknown, but he seems to have lived only a few years after returning to Spain.

In addition to these literary texts you will also read some documents written by or for ordinary Romans without much pretension to advanced education or culture: epitaphs expressing the grief and affection family members felt for one another, inscriptions on the iron collars of runaway slaves (which incidentally show us what Romans used for "street addresses"), and some of the signs and notices that met their eyes as they walked down the street.

---

### SOME ROMAN STREET SIGNS

NO LOITERING: **Ōtiōsīs locus hīc nōn est. Discēde, morātor.** *This is no place for idlers. Go away, loiterer.*

POST NO BILLS: **Quis hīc ūlla scrīpserit, tābēscat neque nōminētur.** *Whoever writes anything here, may he waste away and never be spoken of.*

LOST PROPERTY: **Urna aēnea periit dē tabernā. Sīquis rettulerit, dabuntur H-S LXV. Sī fūrem dabit unde rem servāre possīmus, H-S XX.** *A copper pot has disappeared from this shop. If someone returns it, 65 sesterces will be paid him. If he hands over the thief, from whom we can recover the article, 20 sesterces.*

---

2 **inque . . . erat:** i.e., the shopkeepers' activities, the effective **līmen** of their establishments, extended beyond the architectural **līmen** and into the streets. This encroachment was halted by the emperor Domitian in an edict of A.D. 92; in this sense he "ordered the streets to grow wider" (3).

5 **catēnātīs . . . lagōnīs:** a form of advertising for a wineshop.

6 **mediō . . . lutō:** ablative of place where without a preposition (common in poetry).

7 **caeca novācula:** the street-corner barber's razor (or the cutpurse's knife?) is "unseen" because of the milling crowd, and hence more dangerous.

8 **nigra:** from the smoke of the cooking-fire.

9 **servant:** "are keeping to," "are staying inside."

10 **magna:** "just one big."

---

**Quid Rōmae faciam? Mentīrī nesciō.** *What am I to do in Rome? I don't know how to lie.* (Juvenal III.41)

---

1 **cōgitandī . . . quiēscendī:** genitives dependent on **locus** in the next line.
   **Sparse:** a friend of Martial, protected by his wealth from urban discomfort.

2 **Negant vītam:** i.e., they make city life unbearable; the rest of the poem illustrates what Martial means by this.

3 **pistōrēs:** with the noise of their heavy millstones, grinding the flour for the next morning's baking.

5 **ōtiōsus:** while waiting for customers.
   **quatit mēnsam:** to attract the attention of potential customers by rattling the heap of coins on it.

6 **Nerōniānā . . . massā:** "with his heap (of coins minted in the reign) of Nero" (A.D. 54–68), who debased the currency.

7 **palūcis malleātor Hispānae:** "the hammerer of Spanish gold dust," perhaps a maker of gold leaf for gilding.

8 **nitentī:** with specks of gold embedded in it after long use.

9 **turba . . . entheāta Bellōnae:** "Bellona's raving mob," a reference to the Eastern cult of Ma-Bellona, introduced to Rome in the early first century B.C. and characterized by frenzied dancing and loud music.

10 **fasciātō . . . truncō:** "his body swathed (in bandages)," descriptive ablative. A beggar, mutilated in a shipwreck, has worked up a convincing line of patter (**loquāx**) describing the catastrophe and his desperate need of alms.

11 **sulpurātae . . . mercis:** "of sulfured merchandise," either sulfur-tipped sticks used as matches or glassware repaired with sulfur, used like glue. Perhaps the peddler's eye condition was caused by his contact with the chemical.

14 **ad cubīle est Rōma:** to the tired poet who can't get to sleep, it is as if the city's entire population were standing beside his bed, making a racket and keeping him awake.
   **Taediō fessīs:** taediō is ablative of cause with **fessīs**; fessīs is dative with **libuit** (15); with **fessīs** supply **nōbīs** ( = **mihi**).

# 66
# *Environments*

A. Martial rejoices at the solving of an urban traffic problem.

### The Streets of Rome

Abstulerat tōtam temerārius īnstitor urbem
inque suō nūllum līmine līmen erat.
Iussistī tenuīs, Germānice, crēscere vīcōs,
et modo quae fuerat sēmita, facta via est.
Nūlla catēnātīs pīla est praecincta lagōnīs     5
nec praetor mediō cōgitur īre lutō,
stringitur in dēnsā nec caeca novācula turbā,
occupat aut tōtās nigra popīna viās.
Tōnsor, caupo, coquus, lanius sua līmina servant.
Nunc Rōma est, nūper magna taberna fuit.    10
       —Martial, *Epigrams* VII.61

īnstitor, īnstitōris (*m*), shopkeeper
tenuis, -is, -e, slender, narrow
modo (*adverb*), recently
sēmita, -ae (*f*), path
catēnō (1), to chain

pīla, -ae (*f*), pillar
lagōna, -ae (*f*), bottle
caecus, -a, -um, blind, unseen
tōnsor, tōnsōris (*m*), barber

praecingō, praecingere (3), praecinxī, praecinctum, to gird, wrap around

B. Amidst the noises of a great city, Martial "can't hear himself think."

### The Sounds of Rome

Nec cōgitandī, Sparse, nec quiēscendī
in urbe locus est pauperī. Negant vītam
lūdī magistrī māne, nocte pistōrēs,
aerāriōrum marculī diē tōtō;
hinc ōtiōsus sordidam quatit mēnsam     5
Nerōniānā nummulārius massā,
illinc palūcis malleātor Hispānae
trītum nitentī fūste verberat saxum;
nec turba cessat entheāta Bellōnae,
nec fasciātō naufragus loquāx truncō,    10
nec sulpurātae lippus īnstitor mercis.
Tū, Sparse, nescīs ista nec potēs scīre.
Nōs trānseuntis rīsus excitat turbae,
et ad cubīle est Rōma. Taediō fessīs
dormīre quotiēns libuit, īmus ad vīllam.    15
       —Martial, *Epigrams* XII.57 (abridged)

aerārius, -ī (m), coppersmith
marculus, -ī (m), hammer
hinc, from this place, here
nummulārius, -ī (m), moneychanger
massa, -ae (f), mass, heap
illinc, from that place, there
nitēns, -ntis, shining, glittering
naufragus, -ī (m), shipwrecked man

loquāx, loquācis, talkative
truncus, -ī (m), trunk, body
lippus, -a, -um, bleary-eyed
cubīle, cubīlis (n), bed
taedium, -ī (n), annoyance
fessus, -a, -um, weary
quotiēns, as often as, whenever

quatiō, quatere (3), ——, quassum, to shake
terō, terere (3), trīvī, trītum, to rub, wear away

---

## SOME ROMAN "STREET ADDRESSES"
(inscribed on runaway slaves' collars)

Tenē mē quia fūgī. Redūc mē ad Flōram ad tōnsōrēs. *Detain me, because I have run away. Return me to Barbers' Street near (the temple of) Flora.*

Tenē mē, nē fugiam, et revocā mē in Forō Trāiānī in purpurēticā ad Pacasium dominum meum. *Detain me so that I do not escape, and return me to my master Pacasius in Dyers' Street in the Forum of Trajan.*

---

1 **nemus:** the first of a long series of subjects of the verb **sunt** (7).
  **textilis:** "woven"; because the shoots of the grapevine that casts the shade are intertwined.
  **supīnī:** "low-lying," probably because these vines are supported by poles or low arbors and hence are closer to the ground than those trained on trees, as the Romans sometimes did.
2 **ductile:** "channeled"; Martial's vineyard is artificially irrigated.
3 **biferō . . . Paestō:** "rose gardens not about to yield (i.e., not inferior) to twice-bearing Paestum." This town on the coast south of Naples was famous for its commercial rose plantations, which produced two crops a year.
4 **quod . . . holus:** having lived thirty-five years (7) in the mild Italian climate, Martial regards as a special blessing a kitchen-garden that produces winter vegetables even in northeastern Spain; **holus** is the antecedent of **quod**, as **turris** of **quae** (6).
5 **anguilla:** "eel(s)," singular used collectively; they were kept live in a tank or fishpond, for food.
6 **similēs . . . avēs:** i.e., doves white like the dovecote they inhabit.
7 **dominae:** this word is the ancestor of It. *donna*, Sp. *doña*, and Fr. *dame*, and has much the same meaning here, "(my) lady."
  **reversō:** supply **mihi**.
8 **Marcella:** though she is otherwise unknown, Martial refers to this woman in several poems with gratitude and admiration; she was evidently a native of Bilbilis and a generous benefactor to the poet.
  **rēgna:** poetic plural for singular.
9 **Nausicaā** (*nom.*): a princess, daughter of King Alcinoös, encountered by Odysseus as he was returning home from the Trojan War (*Odyssey*, Books VI–VIII).

110

## Exercise 66a

*Using reading passages A–C as guides, give the Latin for:*

1. It pleased the emperor to order all shopkeepers to remain in their shops. (A.1–4)
2. Consuls were forced to walk in the middle of the street. (A.6)
3. Barbers, cooks, (and) butchers had to stay inside their own thresholds. (A.9; use gerundive of obligation.)
4. What had recently been (one) big shop was becoming a city again. (A.10)
5. There was opportunity at Rome for neither writing nor sleeping. (B.1–2)
6. Rome was full of noise which (was such that it) woke the poet up. (B.13) (Use a relative clause of characteristic.)
7. Whenever it pleases him to go to Rome, the passing crowds deny (him) sleep. (B.15)
8. A villa was given to the poet (after he) returned home. (C.7–8)
9. If a king had granted him his kingdom, the poet would have refused. (C.9–10)
10. He preferred his own wooded pastures, fountains, (and) meadows to ("than") the most magnificent gardens. (C.10)

C. Martial describes the Spanish farm where he spent his last years.

**A Poet's Country "Estate"**
Hoc nemus, hī fontēs, haec textilis umbra supīnī
    palmitis, hoc riguae ductile flūmen aquae,
prātaque, nec biferō cessūra rosāria Paestō,
    quodque virct lānī mēnse nec alget holus,
quaeque natat clausīs anguilla domestica lymphīs,    5
    quaeque gerit similēs candida turris avēs,
mūnera sunt dominae: post septima lūstra reversō
    hās Marcella domōs parvaque rēgna dedit.
Sī mihi Nausicaā patriōs concēderet hortōs,
    Alcinoō possem dīcere, "Mālō meōs."    10
        —Martial, *Epigrams* XII.31

nemus, nemoris (n), wooded pasture
fōns, fontis (m), fountain, spring
palmes, palmitis (m), vine-branch
riguus, -a, -um, watering, irrigating
flūmen, flūminis (n), river, stream
prātum, -ī (n), meadow, grass
vireō (2), to be green, flourish

domesticus, -a, -um, tame
lympha, -ae (f), water
candidus, -a, -um, white
turris, turris (f), tower, dovecote
lūstrum, -ī (n), five-year period
patrius, -a, -um, of a father, ancestral

1 **Lāriī lacūs:** now Lake Como, in the far north of Italy above Milan.
 **plūrēs vīllae:** supply **sunt.**
 **ut . . . ita:** "as they . . . so (also) they . . . ," or "they both . . . and. . . ."
2 **exercent:** "keep (me) busy."
 **saxīs:** dative with a compound verb (**impōnō**), "set on the rocks," i.e., on cliffs
   along the lakeshore.
 **mōre Bāiānō:** "in the style of Baiae."
3 **illam . . . hanc:** "the former . . . the latter"; the two pronouns (and their derivatives **illīc** and **hīc,** 7–8) are used in this sense throughout this letter.
4 **cothurnīs . . . socculīs:** the **cothurnus** was a high-heeled, thick-soled boot worn
   by tragic actors to give extra height and dignity; the **socculus** was a low shoe
   worn by comic actors; Pliny whimsically compares them to the elevated and
   water-level situations of his two villas.
5 **utrīque:** dative of possession; supply **est.**
 **dīversitāte:** ablative of cause (not comparison) with **iūcundior;** translate with
   "by" or "because of."
6 **lacū:** ablative with **ūtitur,** which here means "commands a view of."
7 **duōs:** supply **sinūs** from the preceding line.
 **illīc:** i.e., at "Tragedy"; **hīc** in the next line refers to "Comedy."
 **gestātiō:** "promenade," for riding (in a litter or on horseback).
8 **longō līmite:** "in a long line."
 **xystō . . . īnflectitur:** "it (the **gestātiō** at "Comedy") curves gently in a walkway."
   The **xystus** was lined with shade trees and was intended for recreational
   walking, as the **gestātiō** for riding.
9 **haec frangit:** supply **fluctūs** from the preceding clause. At "Comedy" the waves
   of the lake break against the foundations of the villa.
 **possīs:** potential subjunctive, "you would be able to," "you could."
10 **piscārī:** with this infinitive, and **iacere** in the next line, supply **possīs** from the
   preceding line.

Two villas with colonnades and gardens (from a Pompeian mural).

112

D. Pliny describes the attractions of two of his many villas.

## A Rich Man's Country Estates

Lāriī lacūs in lītore plūrēs vīllae meae, sed duae ut maximē dēlectant ita exercent. Altera imposita saxīs mōre Bāiānō lacum prōspicit, altera aequē mōre Bāiānō lacum tangit. Itaque illam "Tragoediam," hanc appellāre "Cōmoediam" soleō; illam, quod quasi cothurnīs, hanc quod quasi socculīs, sustinētur. Sua utrīque amoenitās, et utraque possidentī ipsā dīversitāte 5 iūcundior. Haec lacū propius, illa lātius ūtitur; haec ūnum sinum mollī curvāmine amplectitur, illa ēditissimō dorsō duōs dirimit; illīc rēcta gestātiō longō līmite super lītus extenditur, hīc spatiōsissimō xystō leviter īnflectitur; illa fluctūs nōn sentit, haec frangit; ex illā possīs dēspicere piscantēs, ex hāc ipse piscārī hāmumque dē cubiculō ac paene etiam dē lectulō ut ē nāviculā 10 iacere.

—Pliny, *Letters* IX.7 (abridged)

| | |
|---|---|
| lacus, -ūs (*m*), lake | rēctus, -a, -um, straight |
| amoenitās, amoenitātis (*f*), charm, pleasantness | līmes, līmitis (*m*), path, line |
| sinus, -ūs (*m*), curve, bay | spatiōsus, -a, -um, spacious |
| mollis, -is, -e, soft, gentle | leviter, lightly, slightly |
| ēditus, -a, -um, raised, high | fluctus, -ūs (*m*), wave |
| dorsum, -ī (*n*), back, ridge | hāmus, -ī (*m*), hook |
| illīc, in that place, there | lectulus, -ī (*m*), bed |

prōspiciō, prōspicere (3), prōspēxī, prōspectum, to look out (over)
sustineō, sustinēre (2), sustinuī, sustentum, to hold up, support
possideō, possidēre (2), possēdī, possessum, to possess, own
dirimō, dirimere (3), dirēmī, dirēmptum, to separate, divide
īnflectō, īnflectere (3), īnflexī, īnflexum, to bend, curve
dēspiciō, dēspicere (3), dēspēxī, dēspectum, to look down on
piscor, piscārī (1), piscātus sum, to fish

## Summary of Case Usages

### Genitive

1. Possessive: **Servī baculum vīlicī** timent. (11:10)
2. Objective: **Augēbat factī invidiam** uxor Clōdiī. (58:23)
3. Subjective: **Mūnera sunt dominae.** (66C:7)
4. Partitive: **Quid ille nōbīs bonī fēcit?** (55:21)
5. With **causā/grātiā**: Ardeat **amōris et dēsīderī meī** causā. (56c:5)
6. Descriptive: **Ūnus (gladiātor) alicuius flātūrae** fuit. (55:25)
7. With impersonal verbs: **Mē taedet sōlitūdinis.** (49:3)
8. With special verbs: **Diī eius colōniae** miserentur. (54:23–24)
9. With special adjectives: **Immemor terrōris nocturnī**, fābulam nārrābat. (21:4)

**Dative**
1. Indirect object: Eucleidēs mandāta servīs dabat. (21:4–5)
2. Possessive: Sua utrīque amoenitās (est). (66D:5)
3. Of agent: Crūdēlitās tibi vītanda est. (Chapter 65, page 104)
4. Of reference: Spectātōribus admīrātiōnī fuērunt leōnēs. (47:1–2)
5. Of purpose: Spectātōribus admīrātiōnī fuērunt leōnēs. (When these two usages occur together, they are called the double dative.)
6. Of separation: Arma nōbīs adēmērunt. (40:20)
7. With compound verbs: Sī pīrātīs resistēmus, necābimur. (40:19)
8. With special verbs: Servō illī parvō numquam parcet. (48:11)
9. With special adjectives: puer . . . parentibus cārissimus. (Chapter 52, page 101)

**Ablative** (a conflation of three separate cases in primitive Latin)
  I. Separative Uses (the true ablative)
    1. Place from which (with ab, dē, ex): (Possīs) hāmum dē lectulō ut ē nāviculā iacere. (66D:10–11)
      Without preposition (names of towns, small islands): Brundisiō profectus est.
    2. Of separation: Fīet vir vīnō abstinentissimus. (32e:28)
    3. Of respect: Erant uterque audāciā pārēs. (57:8)
    4. Of comparison: Quis est mē miserior? (35:3)
  II. Local Uses (of a "place," locus, in space or time)
    1. Place where (with in, sub): Lacūs in lītore plūrēs vīllae (sunt). (66D:1)
      Without preposition: Sōl caelō serēnō lūcēbat. (49:1)
    2. Time when: Illō tempore annōna prō lutō erat. (54:15)
  III. Instrumental Uses
    1. Means: Thisbē amōre capta est. (43:3–4)
    2. Agent: Rīma ab amantibus inventa est. (43:7–8)
    3. Accompaniment: Cum patre filiōque suō nāvigāvit. (36:6)
    4. Manner: Līberōs maximō cum gaudiō salūtāvit. (22:9)
    5. Description: Puer eximiā pulchritūdine (fuit). (Chapter 52, page 101)
    6. With certain deponents: In spēluncā habitābāmus, eōdem cibō vescentēs. (47:20–21)
    7. Degree of difference: Multō libentius tē vidēbō. (34:10)
    8. Ablative absolute: Pýramō vīsō, amōre capta est. (43:3–4)

---

PLINY ON THE DEATH OF MARTIAL: Audiō Valerium Martiālem dēcessisse et molestē ferō. Erat homō ingeniōsus, acūtus, ācer, et quī plūrimum in scrībendō et salis habēret et fellis nec candōris minus. *I hear that Valerius Martial has died and I am grieved by the news. He was a man of great talent, clever and lively, one who had in his writing both wit and venom, and frankness as well.* (Pliny, *Letters* III.21)

## Exercise 66b

Complete the Latin sentences, identify the usage of each word that you supply, and translate the sentences.

1. Uxōrī _____ (Clodius') nūllus _____ (of death) metus erat.
2. Illum paenitet _____ _____ (his crimes).
3. Oblīvīscēbātur _____ _____ (her friends).
4. Ars _____ _____ (for art's sake). (Motto of MGM Films)
5. Hic liber nōn est _____ (for students) idōneus.
6. Milō bonōrum _____ (in the support) cōnfidēbat.
7. Rēs pūblica _____ (to Cicero) _____ _____ (a cause of the greatest concern) fuit.
8. Aurum _____ (by you) tangendum nōn est.
9. Clōdius et Milō _____ (in crime) pārēs erant.
10. Poēta dōnum _____ _____ (his lady's) _____ _____ (with great joy) accēpit.
11. Mārtiālis poēta _____ (much) melior _____ (than Cicero) fuit.
12. Cicerō _____ _____ (Greek literature) ūtēbātur.


## Exercise 66c

1. Roman poets liked to "bracket" a line with two closely related words such as verb and object or noun and modifier, set at beginning and end. Find four examples in passages A and B.
2. What is the effect of repeating the demonstrative **hic** four times at the beginning of passage C? (Hint: "demonstrative" is a derivative of **dēmōn-strāre**, "to show," "to point out.") Why would **ille** have been less effective here? How does Pliny's repetition of **hic** in passage D differ from Martial's?
3. Judging from passages A, B, and C, did Martial prefer city life or country life? Where did he actually live for most of his life? Do you find his attitude inconsistent or insincere? Does anyone in our own society have a similar ambivalence about urban living?
4. Pliny's description of "Tragedy" and "Comedy" (passage D) is a kind of stylistic balancing act, each feature of one villa carefully contrasted with a corresponding feature of the other, expressed in syntactically parallel clauses. Identify eight examples of such parallels. How does Pliny introduce variety into these parallels? Does the artificiality of Pliny's style make you doubt the sincerity of his affection for the villas, or does the care he takes with his writing express his sincere affection?

115

# 67
# The Daily Round

1 **Erret:** jussive, here and throughout. The object of Martial's curse is a rival poet who writes libelous verse against respectable people.
   **pontis . . . et clīvī:** translate with *from* rather than *of*; these were favorite haunts of beggars, probably because they slowed down traffic.
2 **ultimus:** i.e., the most wretched of all.
3 **canīnās:** i.e., fit only for dogs.
4 **Illī:** dative of reference.
5 **fornix:** often the only shelter the urban poor could find; they could not be "closed." Martial in his anger is wishing for the impossible.
7 **Orcīniānā . . . spondā:** "the couch of Orcus" (the underworld), i.e., a bier.
8 **fīla:** of the man's life, spun and eventually cut by the three Fates.
9 **sentiat . . . lītem:** i.e., remain conscious to the very end, so that as he dies he will see dogs already beginning to squabble over his body.
10 **mōtō . . . pannō:** "by shaking his ragged garment."

2 **ille . . . ille . . . ille:** "one man . . . another . . . another."
3 **diē:** antecedent of the relative pronoun **quō.**
4 **necessāria:** supply **videntur** from the following clause.
5 **sēcesseris:** i.e., from the city to the country.
6 **in Laurentīnō meō:** for Pliny's Laurentine villa, see Chapter 7, pp. 37–38.
7 **corporī:** i.e., for physical exercise, meals, baths, etc.
8 **audīsse:** supply **paeniteat** from the following phrase, "it is a matter of regret (to me) to. . . ."
9 **strepitum . . . discursum . . . labōrēs:** i.e., of the city (Rome); objects of **relinque** (10); **multum** is adverbial with **ineptōs.**
   **ut prīmum:** "as soon as."

## Exercise 67a

*Using readings A and B as guides, give the Latin for:*

1. The beggar has become hoarse from ("by") begging for bread. (A.1–3)
2. If his final hour comes soon, he will be very fortunate. (A.6–8)
3. Dogs and rapacious birds will feed on his body. (A.9–10)
4. Pliny had to attend a wedding. (Use gerundive of obligation.) (B.2)
5. He said he had used up so many days in trivial matters. (B.5–6)
6. Pliny is urging his friend to abandon city life. (B.8–10)

A.

## A Beggar's Life in the City

Erret per urbem pontis exul et clīvī,
interque raucōs ultimus rogātōrēs
ōret canīnās pānis improbī buccās.
Illī December longus et madēns brūma
claususque fornix trīste frīgus extendat:          5
vocet beātōs clāmitetque fēlīcēs
Orcīniānā quī feruntur in spondā.
At cum suprēmae fīla vēnerint hōrae
diēsque tardus, sentiat canum lītem
abigatque mōtō noxiās avēs pannō.          10

—Martial, *Epigrams* X.5 (abridged)

exul, exulis (*m*), exile, outcast
raucus, -a, -um, hoarse
rogātor, rogātōris (*m*), beggar
improbus, -a, -um, bad, vile
madēns, madentis, wet, moist
brūma, -ae (*f*), winter

fornix, fornicis (*m*), arch
frīgus, frīgoris (*n*), cold
suprēmus, -a, -um, last, final
fīlum, -ī (*n*), thread
līs, lītis (*f*), quarrel, dispute
noxius, -a, -um, harmful, rapacious

abigō, abigere (3), abēgī, abāctum, to drive away

B. ## A Gentleman's Life in the City

Sī quem interrogēs, "Hodiē quid ēgistī?" respondeat: "Officiō togae virīlis
interfuī; spōnsālia aut nūptiās frequentāvī; ille mē ad signandum testāmentum, ille in advocātiōnem, ille in cōnsilium rogāvit." Haec quō diē fēceris,
necessāria; eadem, si cotīdiē fēcisse tē reputēs, inānia videntur, multō magis,
cum sēcesseris. Tunc enim subit recordātiō: "Quot diēs quam frīgidīs rēbus    5
absūmpsī!" Quod ēvenit mihi, postquam in Laurentīnō meō aut legō aliquid
aut scrībō aut etiam corporī vacō, cuius fultūrīs animus sustinētur. Nihil
audiō quod audīsse, nihil dīcō, quod dīxisse paeniteat. Proinde tū quoque
strepitum istum inānemque discursum et multum ineptōs labōrēs, ut prīmum fuerit occāsiō, relinque tēque studiīs vel ōtiō trāde. Valē.          10

—Pliny, *Letters* 1.9 (abridged)

nūptiae, -ārum (*f pl*), wedding
advocātiō, advocātiōnis (*f*), (legal)
          counsel
inānis, -is, -e, empty, pointless
recordātiō, recordātiōnis (*f*), rec-
          ollection
frīgidus, -a, -um, cold, trivial

fultūra, -ae (*f*), support
proinde, therefore
discursus, -ūs (*m*), a running back
          and forth or around
ineptus, -a, -um, silly, foolish
ōtium, -ī (*n*), leisure

intersum, interesse (*irreg.*), interfuī (+ *dat.*), to be present, attend
sēcēdō, sēcēdere (3), sēcessī, sēcessum, to withdraw, retire
subeō, subīre (*irreg.*), subiī, subitum, to come up, occur
absūmō, absūmere (3), absūmpsī, absūmptum, to consume, use up

117

1 **Mē**: in the opening lines, here omitted, Martial describes the hectic life being led in Rome by his friend Juvenal, the satirist; the rest of the poem contrasts Martial's simple existence in rural Spain, hence the emphatic position of the pronoun at the beginning of this line.

**repetīta**: this word and **mea** (2) modify **Bilbilis** (3).

2 **rūsticum**: supply **mē** from line 1.

3 **aurō . . . et superba ferrō**: there were gold and iron mines nearby.

5 **Boterdum Plateamque**: nearby villages whose names sounded "rather uncouth" (**crassiōra**, 6) to the ears of citified Romans.

**Celtibērīs . . . terrīs**: i.e., in that part of Spain where the native (Iberian) population had received an admixture of Celtic blood from the north.

7 **improbōque somnō**: ironic; "sleeping in," as Martial does now, is "shameless" from the point of view of a hard-driving city dweller like Juvenal.

9 **tōtum . . . quidquid . . . vigilāveram**: "all the staying-up I did."

10 **ter dēnōs**: "thrice ten."

11 **petentī**: supply **mihi**.

12 **proxima**: i.e., the first that comes to hand.

13 **Surgentem**: supply **mē**.

**superbā . . . strue cultus**: "graced with a magnificent pile."

15 **quem**: the antecedent is **focus** (13).

## Roman Timekeeping

The Roman **hōra** was not a fixed period of time like the modern hour, but a fraction (one twelfth) of the daylight of a given day. Since days and nights are not of equal length throughout the year, the length of a **hōra** varied: on the longest day (June 21), when there are about fifteen hours of daylight, the **hōra** was about 1¼ hours long; on the shortest day (December 21), only about 45 minutes. After-dark hours (**hōrae noctis**) were reckoned in the same way but were less important due to the expense and inefficiency of artificial lighting. The fixed points in this system were noon and midnight, which in all seasons occurred at the end of the sixth **hōra**.

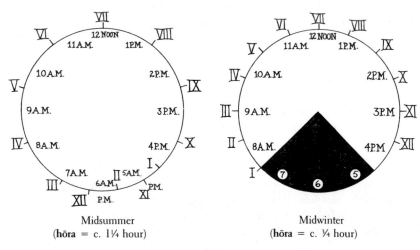

Midsummer
(**hōra** = c. 1¼ hour)

Midwinter
(**hōra** = c. ¾ hour)

118

C.

## A Poet's Life in the Country

Mē multōs repetīta post Decembrēs
accēpit mea rūsticumque fēcit
aurō Bilbilis et superba ferrō.
Hīc pigrī colimus labōre dulcī
Boterdum Plateamque (Celtibērīs      5
haec sunt nōmina crassiōra terrīs):
ingentī fruor improbōque somnō
quem nec tertia saepe rumpit hōra,
et tōtum mihi nunc repōnō quidquid
ter dēnōs vigilāveram per annōs.      10
Ignōta est toga, sed datur petentī
ruptā proxima vestis ā cathēdrā.
Surgentem focus excipit superbā
vīcīnī strue cultus īlicētī,
multā vīlica quem corōnat ōllā.      15
Sīc mē vīvere, sīc iuvat perīre.

—Martial, *Epigrams* XII. 18 (abridged)

piger, -gra, -grum, lazy, indolent
dulcis, -is, -e, sweet, pleasant
ignōtus, -a, -um, unknown
cathēdra, -ae (f), chair

focus, -ī (m), fireplace
struēs, struis (f), heap, pile
īlicētum, -ī (n), oak-grove
ōlla, -ae (f), pot

repetō, repetere (3), repetīvī, repetītum, to seek again, return to
repōnō, repōnere (3), reposuī, repositum, to put back, repay

---

**Pars magna Ītaliae est, sī vērum admittimus, in quā nēmō togam sūmit nisi mortuus.** *There's a large part of Italy (if we admit the truth) in which no one wears a toga unless he's dead.* (Juvenal III. 171–172)

---

Martial's retirement from the stress of urban living was permanent and occurred near the end of his life. Pliny, like other wealthy Romans, could "retire" whenever he wished to one of his seven villas (cf. Chapter 7, pages 37–38, and reading passage 66D). His favorite of them all was in the foothills of the Apennines, north of Rome in Tuscany. In a letter he describes his daily routine when he was in residence there during the summer.

You ask how I organize my day in summertime at my Tuscan villa. I wake up when I please, usually about the first hour, often earlier, rarely later. The window-shutters remain closed, for in silence and darkness I am wonderfully free and removed from all distractions, and left to myself; I do not follow my eyes with my mind, but rather my mind with my eyes, which see only what the mind sees so long as they see nothing else. If I have work in progress, I think; I think like one actually writing and revising, sometimes only short

119

passages, sometimes longer ones, so that they can be composed and remembered whether the subject is difficult or easy. I call in my stenographer and, letting in the daylight, I dictate what I have composed. He goes away, is called back again, and again dismissed.

At the fourth or fifth hour (for I have no fixed and precise schedule), as the weather suggests, I go to the terrace or the covered portico, work out the rest, and dictate it. I get into my carriage, and there I do the same thing I did while lying in bed or walking; my concentration lasts longer when refreshed by this change of scene. I take another short nap, then go for a walk; after that I read, aloud and with concentration, a Greek or Latin speech, not so much for the sake of my voice as for my digestion; though the voice too is strengthened. I take another walk, oil myself and take some exercise, and bathe. While I dine a book is read to me if I am with my wife or only a few friends; after dinner we have a comic actor or a lyre-player. Then I take a walk with members of my household, some of whom are quite well educated. Thus the evening is passed in various kinds of conversation, and even the longest day is quickly laid to rest.

Sometimes certain details of this routine are modified. For instance, if I have stayed in bed or walked longer than usual, after the nap and the reading I go for a ride, not in my carriage but on horseback, which is briefer because faster. Friends from nearby towns sometimes interrupt me and appropriate part of my day; sometimes, too, by this timely interruption they come to my rescue when I am tired. Occasionally I go hunting, but never without my notebooks, so that even if I catch nothing I don't come back empty-handed. Some time is also devoted to my tenants—not enough, as it seems to them; their farmers' complaints enhance my literary studies and citified pursuits. Farewell.

—Pliny, *Letters* IX.36

1 **litterās meās:** the letter you have just read in translation.
2 **exigerem . . . permūtem:** what tenses of the subjunctive, and why?
   **hōc:** Pliny's daily schedule in summertime.
3 **Nihil:** supply **permūtō** from the preceding sentence.
   **multumque . . . sūmitur:** i.e., he either goes to bed later or gets up earlier.
4 **agendī:** "of pleading (a case in court)."
5 **frequēns:** supply **est.**
   **cōmoedō vel lyristae:** "for a comic actor (to give readings) or a lyre-player."
   **locus:** supply **est.**
6 **memoriae . . . prōficitur:** "(my) memory benefits" (literally, "benefit is done to my memory").
7 **addās . . . licet:** = **licet (tibi) addere,** "you may add to this."
8 **media:** supply **sunt.**
   **ut . . . acquīrunt:** i.e., his working-days are no shorter, and a little of the night is put to use as well. Supply **sīc** before **dē,** to balance **ut:** "as (on the one hand), so (on the other). . . ."

## Exercise 67b

Using the "clocks" on page 118, answer the following questions with full Latin sentences:

1. Quotā hōrā surgere solēs aestāte? Hieme?
2. Quotā hōrā cubitum īvistī proximā nocte?
3. Quota hōra nunc est? 
4. Quotā hōrā cēnāre solet familia tua?
5. Quotā hōrā ad lūdum hodiē vēnistī?
6. Quotā hōrā surgis Sāturnī diē? Sōlis diē?

## Exercise 67c

Answer in English the following questions:

1. How late does Martial sleep in the country? Why? (C.8–10)
2. What is the implication of **Ignōta est toga?** (C.11)
3. What details suggest that Bilbilis is an unsophisticated, backwoods kind of place? (C.2, 6, 12, 15)
4. How does Pliny's routine change in winter? (D.3–4, 5–6)
5. Why do you think Pliny makes these adjustments? (D.4)

## D.  A Gentleman's Life in the Country

Scrībis pergrātās tibi fuisse littcrās meās, quibus cognōvistī quemadmodum in Tuscīs ōtium aestātis exigerem; requīris quid ex hōc in Laurentīnō hieme permūtem. Nihil, nisi quod merīdiānus somnus eximitur, multumque dē nocte vel ante vel post diem sūmitur, et sī agendī necessitās īnstat, quae frequēns hieme, nōn iam cōmoedō vel lyristae post cēnam locus, sed  5 illa quae dictāvī identidem retractantur, ac simul memoriae frequentī ēmen-dātiōne prōficitur. Habēs aestāte hieme cōnsuētūdincm, addās hūc licet vēr et autumnum, quae inter hiemem aestātemque media, ut nihil dē diē perdunt, dē nocte parvulum acquīrunt. Valē.

—Pliny, *Letters* IX.40

| | |
|---|---|
| **pergrātus, -a, -um**, very welcome | **ēmendātiō, ēmendātiōnis** (*f*), |
| **permūtō** (1), to change, modify | emendation, correction |
| **merīdiānus, -a, -um**, of noon, mid-day | **cōnsuētūdō, cōnsuētūdinis** (*f*), custom, habit |
| **retractō** (1), to rework, revise | **vēr, vēris** (*n*), spring |

**exigō, exigere** (3), **exēgī, exāctum**, to spend (time)
**requīrō, requīrere** (3), **requīsīvī, requīsītum**, to ask, inquire

# Word Study XVIII
## Latin Suffixes in the Romance Languages

You have learned some of the ways in which words are formed from other words in Latin by the addition of prefixes and suffixes. Knowing the principles of word-formation, as you have discovered, makes it possible to increase your Latin vocabulary with a minimum of memorizing. These same principles will also enable you to recognize hundreds of words in the Romance languages. Some of the Latin suffixes you have already learned, and their Romance equivalents, are shown below.

| LATIN | ITALIAN | SPANISH | FRENCH |
|---|---|---|---|
| -tās, -tātis (*f*) | -tà (*f*) | -dad (*f*) | -té (*f*) |
| ūnitās | unità | unidad | unité |
| -tiō, -tiōnis (*f*) | -zione (*f*) | -ción (*f*) | -tion (*f*) |
| nātiō | nazione | nación | nation |
| -tor, -tōris (*m*) | -tore (*m*) | -dor (*m*) | -teur (*m*) |
| ōrātor | oratore | orador | orateur |
| -entia, -ae (*f*) | -enza (*f*) | -encia (*f*) | -ence (*f*) |
| scientia | scienza | ciencia | science |
| -ōsus, -a, -um | -oso, -a | -oso, -a | -eux, euse |
| verbōsus | verboso | verboso | verbeux |

The adverb in the Romance languages is an interesting special case: it derives from Latin phrases of the type _(adjective)_ **mente**, e.g., **firmā mente**, "with a firm mind," "firmly." This type of ablative of manner was used so extensively that **mente** eventually lost most of its original meaning and became a suffix changing the preceding adjective into an adverb.

| LATIN | ITALIAN | SPANISH | FRENCH |
|---|---|---|---|
| _____ mente | -mente | -mente | -ment |
| firmā mente | fermamente | firmemente | fermement |

# 68
# *Familia*

The Romans were a strongly family-oriented people, as is abundantly attested not only in their literature but also in the visual arts and in subliterary texts such as epitaphs and letters. Even so undomestic a soul as the philosopher-poet Lucretius, a contemporary of Cicero, could paint a touching picture of the **praemia vītae**, "life's prizes": a happy home, a good wife, and "sweet children who run to meet you and snatch a kiss, touching your heart with unspoken delight." There is an element of idealization in this, of course, as there is in the conventional phrase often found in the epitaphs of Roman spouses, "they lived together so many years **sine ūllā querēlā**," "without a single complaint." So conventional was this sentiment, in fact, that it was frequently reduced to the mere abbreviation **s.u.q.** Yet genuine feeling sometimes seems to break through formula and rhetoric, in the epitaphs as in literature, in unpretentious phrases like "I put these words on her tomb so that people reading them would know how much we loved each other." Another Roman husband put it even more simply and briefly: "we worked well together." The small jet engagement medallions illustrated here symbolize the hope for this kind of enduring loyalty and affection in marriage. As the readings in this chapter show, the strong sense of responsibility and affection summed up in the word **pietās** often extended to the family slaves and freedmen as well as spouse and children.

2 **tuī:** genitive of **tū**; objective genitive with **dēsīderiō.**
  **In causā (est):** "is responsible."
3 **quod:** "the fact that . . ." (as also in 3 and 4).
  **abesse:** i.e., from each other.
  **Inde est:** "Hence. . . ." or "This is the reason for. . . ."
4 **in imāgine tuā:** "in imagining you," "dreaming of you."
  **quibus:** the antecedent is **hōrīs.**
5 **diaetam:** a Greek word meaning "apartment" or "living quarters," i.e., a suite
  of rooms for Calpurnia's personal use.
  **ipsī:** with **pedēs,** "of their own accord."
6 **aeger:** "sick (at heart)," "dejected."
  **līmine:** what kind of ablative?
7 **quō:** the antecedent is **tempus.**
  **lītibus:** "lawsuits"; Pliny was a prominent lawyer.
8 **requiēs:** supply **est.**

---

Uxor, vīvāmusque ut vīximus et teneāmus
nōmina, quae prīmō sūmpsimus in thalamō,
nec ferat ūlla diēs, ut commūtēmur in aevō,
quīn tibi sim iuvenis tūque puella mihi.

*Wife, let us live as we have lived and let us keep the names we gave each
other on our wedding night; may the day never come when we change in old
age, but let me be forever your young lover and you my girl.*

Ausonius, c. A.D. 350

---

1 **mihi:** dative of separation, with the three verbs compounded with **ex.**
3 **oculīs:** dative with the compound **obversantur.**
  **labōrēs . . . precēs . . . honor:** all in reference to Avitus' abortive political career:
  "exertions . . . campaigning . . . office."
  **meruit tantum:** "only earned (but never held)"; Avitus was elected to an
  aedileship (9) but died before taking office.
4 **animō:** supply **meō;** dative with the compound **redit.**
  **lātus clāvus:** the "broad (purple) stripe" of the senatorial tunic. Under the Empire, the privilege of wearing it was granted to senators' sons who, though not
  yet senators themselves, were about to begin their political careers.
5 **suffrāgia mea:** i.e., occasions on which I "got out the vote" for you.
6 **adulēscentiā:** like us, the Romans were especially grieved at the death of a child
  or young person with most of his life ahead of him.
  **grandis nātū:** "elderly." The gender of **parēns** is ambiguous, but it is clear from
  line 10 that Avitus' mother is meant.
7 **ante:** adverbial, "(only) a year ago."
8 **sustulerat:** a Roman husband "picked up" his wife's newborn child from the
  ground to symbolize his acceptance of it as his own and his willingness to
  raise it, which he was not otherwise obligated to do.

124

## A. A Husband in Love

### C. PLINIUS CALPURNIAE SUAE S.

Incrēdibile est, quantō dēsīderiō tuī tenear. In causā amor prīmum, deinde quod nōn cōnsuēvimus abesse. Inde est, quod magnam partem noctium in imāgine tuā vigil exigō, inde, quod interdiū, quibus hōrīs tē vīsere solēbam, ad diaetam tuam ipsī mē, ut vērissimē dīcitur, pedēs dūcunt; quod dēnique 5 aeger et maestus ac similis exclūsō, vacuō līmine recēdō. Ūnum tempus hīs tormentīs caret, quō in forō et amīcōrum lītibus conteror. Aestimā tū, quae vīta mea sit, cui requiēs in labōre, in miseriā cūrīsque sōlācium. Valē.

—Pliny, *Letters* VII.5

vigil, vigilis, awake, sleepless
maestus, -a, -um, sad
vacuus, -a, -um, empty

aestimō (1), to estimate, judge
requiēs, requiētis (f), rest

cōnsuēscō, cōnsuēscere (3), cōnsuēvī, cōnsuētum, to be accustomed
vīsō, vīsere (3), vīsī, vīsum, to go to see, visit
exclūdō, exclūdere (3), exclūsī, exclūsum, to shut out, exclude
recēdō, recēdere (3), recessī, recessum, to withdraw, retire
careō, carēre (2), caruī, caritum ( + *abl.*), to be without, lack
conterō, conterere (3), contrīvī, contrītum, to wear out, exhaust

## B. Death of a Young Husband and Father

Omnia mihi studia, omnēs cūrās, omnia āvocāmenta exēmit, excussit, ēripuit dolor, quem ex morte Iūnī Avītī gravissimum cēpī. Obversantur oculīs cassī labōrēs et īnfructuōsae precēs et honor, quem meruit tantum. Redit animō ille lātus clāvus in penātibus meīs sūmptus; redeunt illa prīma, illa postrēma suffrāgia mea, illī sermōnēs, illae cōnsultātiōnēs. Adficior 5 adulēscentiā ipsīus, adficior necessitūdinum cāsū. Erat illī grandis nātū parēns, erat uxor, quam ante annum virginem accēperat; erat filia, quam paulō ante sustulerat. Tot spēs, tot gaudia diēs ūnus in adversa convertit. Modo dēsignātus aedīlis, recēns marītus, recēns pater intāctum honōrem, orbam mātrem, viduam uxōrem, filiam pupillam īgnāramque patris relīquit. 10

—Pliny, *Letters* VIII.23 (abridged)

āvocāmentum, -ī (n), diversion, recreation
cassus, -a, -um, empty, useless
īnfructuōsus, -a, -um, fruitless
prex, precis (f), prayer, request
penātēs, penātium (m pl), household
   gods, home
suffrāgium, -ī (n), vote

necessitūdō, necessitūdinis (f), necessity, (personal) connection, relative
adversum, -ī (n), calamity
orbus, -a, -um, bereaved
viduus, -a, -um, deprived, widowed
pūpilla, -ae (f), orphan
īgnārus, -a, -um, ignorant of, not
   knowing ( + *gen.*)

125

excutiō, excutere (3), excussī, excussum, to shake out, drive out
obversor, obversārī (1), obversātus sum ( + dat.), to hover before, appear to
adficiō, adficere (3), adfēcī, adfectum, to affect, afflict
sufferō, sufferre (irreg.), sustulī, sublātum, to take up

## Pliny on Disciplining Children

A man was scolding his son because the boy was spending rather lavishly on horses and dogs. I said to him, after the young man had left, "See here, did you never do anything your father could object to? Have you never done—indeed, do you not even now do, things that your son would blame you for just as severely, if suddenly he were the father and you the son? Don't we all make mistakes of one kind or another? One man is self-indulgent in one thing, others in another, isn't that so?"

Because of our affection for each other, I am sending you this example of exaggerated severity by way of a warning not to treat your own son too strictly and harshly. Remember that he is a child and that you used to be one too, and therefore exercise your parental authority in such a way as never to forget that you are a man and the father of a man. Farewell.

—Pliny, *Letters* IX.12

1 **fuerās:** translate as simple past.
  **Charidēme:** vocative of **Charidēmus**, Latinized form of a Greek name; slaves in responsible positions such as that of **paedagōgus**, in which a good education was necessary or desirable, were often of Greek origin.
2 **puerī:** supply **meī** (genitive of **ego**), "of (me as a) boy."
3 **mihi:** dative of reference; may be translated as a possessive with **barbā**.
  **sūdāria:** "towels," placed around Martial's neck when his beard is trimmed.
4 **labrīs:** i.e., with his beard or mustache when he kisses her.
5 **tibi:** dative of reference, here (as often) indicating the person in whose eyes the statement is true.
  **Tē . . . pavet:** Charidemus is a household tyrant!
8 **mihi:** with **licēre**, parallel to **tibi**.
9 **Corripis, observās:** supply **mē** as direct object; **corripis** = "scold."
  **dūcis:** we say "heave" rather than "draw."
10 **ferulīs:** which he no doubt used on Martial as a child.
11 **Tyriōs . . . capillōs:** to wear "Tyrian-purple clothes" and use scented hair oil were marks of the fashionable Roman dandy and regarded as decadent by the conservative older generation.
12 **fēcerat:** here = **fēcisset**.
13 **nostrōs . . . trientēs:** "the cups (of wine) I drink." The **triēns** was equivalent to about five ounces.
15 **lībertum Catōnem:** both Cato the Elder (234–149 B.C.) and his great-grandson Cato the Younger (95–46 B.C.) had long been bywords for uncompromising integrity and puritanical conservatism; Martial may have either or both in mind.

## Exercise 68a

*Answer in English the following questions on readings A and B.*

1. In his wife's absence, how does Pliny spend his nights? His days? (A.2–5)
2. What does the phrase **ut vērissimē dīcitur** imply? (A.4)
3. What gives Pliny some relief from his longing for his wife? (A.6)
4. What was the nature of Pliny's friendship with Avitus? What did Pliny do with and for the young man that he remembers now with sorrow? (B.4–5)
5. What three unusual circumstances make Avitus' death particularly sad? (B.3, 6, 10)
6. Judging from reading B, what were the most important things in life to a young Roman aristocrat? (B.9–10)

C. For this **paedagōgus**, the boy he raised will never grow up.

### Martial's Old Tutor

Cūnārum fuerās mōtor, Charidēme, meārum
   et puerī custōs adsiduusque comes.
Iam mihi nigrēscunt tōnsā sūdāria barbā
   et queritur labrīs puncta puella meīs,
sed tibi nōn crēvī. Tē noster vīlicus horret,   5
   tē dispēnsātor, tē domus ipsa pavet:
lūdere nec nōbīs nec tū permittis amāre,
   nīl mihi vīs et vīs cuncta licēre tibi.
Corripis, observās, quereris, suspīria dūcis,
   et vix ā ferulīs temperat īra tua.   10
Sī Tyriōs sūmpsī cultūs unxīve capillōs,
   exclāmās, "Numquam fēcerat ista pater!"
et numerās nostrōs adstrictā fronte trientēs,
   tamquam dē cellā sit cadus ille tuā.
Dēsine: nōn possum lībertum ferre Catōnem.   15
   Esse virum iam mē dīcet amīca tibi.

—Martial, *Epigrams* XI.39

| | |
|---|---|
| **cūnae, -ārum** (*f pl*), cradle | **suspīrium, -ī** (*n*), sigh |
| **adsiduus, -a, -um,** constant | **adstrictus, -a, -um,** drawn together |
| **barba, -ae** (*f*), beard | **cella, -ae** (*f*), storeroom, cellar |
| **labrum, -ī** (*n*), lip | **cadus, -ī** (*m*), (wine-)jar |
| **horreō** (2), to tremble at, dread | |

**tondeō, tondēre** (2), **totondī, tōnsum,** to shave, trim
**pungō, pungere** (3), **pupugī, punctum,** to prick
**paveō, pavēre** (2), **pāvī,** to be terrified of

127

1 **D.M.S.**: **Dīs Mānibus Sacrum**, "sacred to the deified spirits," a common formula
  in Roman epitaphs. Sometimes, as here, it is syntactically independent of the
  rest of the inscription; sometimes, as in the next epitaph, it is followed by a
  dependent genitive, "sacred to the . . . spirits *of* so-and-so."
  **cuius**: a Greek genitive of comparison, "than whom"; such Grecisms are common in subliterary texts, which were often written by people from the Greek-
  speaking East, who had learned Latin rather imperfectly.
2 **certus**: supply **sum**, governing an indirect statement.
  **ita**: the writer apparently anticipates a result clause but never gets around to it;
  omit in translating.
3 **in diem**: "every day."
4 **quam . . . tam**: "both . . . and."
  **mōrum**: "character," a common meaning of **mōs** in the plural.
  **ideō**: anticipating **ut**, "for this reason, . . . that. . . ."; omit in translating.
5 **b(ene) m(erentī) f(ēcit)**: supply **hoc monumentum** as direct object.

7 **iam**: an important adverb here: the parents are proud of her precocity.
8 **f(ēcērunt) d(ē) s(uō)**: "made (this monument) at their own expense."

11 **maledīxit**: this verb commonly means "to curse," but here it may have its root
   sense, "spoke ill of" or "spoke a harsh word to."
12 **multum ponderis aurī**: two partitive genitives strung together rather awkwardly;
   **magnum pondus** would be better, and you may so translate it.
13 **caelātūrae Clōdiānae**: "of Clodian engraving," a technique for engraving on
   precious metals; this explains why Zosimus was entrusted with quantities of
   gold and silver.

---

**Dē mortuīs nīl nisi bonum.** *Of the dead, (speak) nothing but good.*

---

## Exercise 68b

*Answer in English the following questions on readings C and D:*

1. What, specifically, does Charidemus do that proves Martial is still a child
   to him? (C.7, 11–12, 13–14)
2. In what ways was Zosimus an ideal slave? (D.11–14)
3. Charidemus (C) and Zosimus (D) are examples of skilled slaves (later
   freed) employed in positions of considerable responsibility. Compare the
   two men in the following respects: 1) kind of responsibility, 2) personality,
   3) relationship to the author, 4) nature of the document, and the effect
   this has on the portrayal of the man.
4. What were Urbana's virtues as a wife? (D.1, 3, 4)
5. To whom does **legentēs** (D.5) refer?
6. How many months old was Cornelia Anniana when she died? (D.8)

## D. Epitaphs for Family Members

### A Well-Loved Wife

D.M.S. Urbānae coniugī dulcissimae et castissimae ac rārissimae, cuius praeclārius nihil fuisse certus. Hōc etiam titulō honōrārī meruit, quae ita mēcum cum summā iūcunditāte atque simplicitāte in diem vītae suae ēgit quam affectiōnī coniugālī tam industriā mōrum suōrum. Haec ideō adiēcī, ut legentēs intellegant, quantum nōs dīlēxerimus. Paternus b(ene) m(erentī) 5 f(ēcit).

castus, -a, -um, chaste
titulus, -ī (m), inscription
iūcunditās, iūcunditātis (f), pleasantness

simplicitās, simplicitātis (f), frankness

### A Baby Just Learning to Talk

D(īs) m(ānibus) Cornēliae Anniānae fīliae iam garrulae, bīmulae nōndum, quae vīxit annum ūnum m(ēnsēs) III d(iēs) X; dulcissim(ae) parentēs f(ēcērunt) d(ē) s(uō).

garrulus, -a, -um, prattling

bīmulus, -a, -um, two years old

### A Trustworthy Freedman

D(īs) m(ānibus) M(arcī) Canuleī Zōsimī, vīx(it) ann(ōs) XXVIII, fēcit 10 patrōnus līb(ertō) bene merentī. Hic in vītā suā nūllī maledīxit, sine volun-tāte patrōnī nihil fēcit, multum ponderis aurī arg(entīque) penes eum semper fuit, concupīvit ex cō nihil umquam. Hic arte caelātūrae Clōdiānae ēvīcit omnēs.

pondus, ponderis (n), weight,
quantity

argentum, -ī (n), silver
penes ( + acc.), in the possession of

ēvincō, ēvincere (3), ēvīcī, ēvictum, to conquer, surpass

---

## ON TOMBS

**Aedēs aedificat dīves, sapiēns monumentum. Hospitium est illud corporis, hic domus est.** *The rich man builds himself a mansion, the wise man a tomb. The former is a mere inn for the body, the latter a true home.*

**Homō es: resiste et tumulum contemplā meum.** *You are mortal: stop, and consider my tomb.*

**Carpis sī quī viās, paulum hīc dēpōne labōrem. Cūr tantum properās? Nōn est mora dum legis, audī.** *You who are traveling this road, lay down your burden here for a moment. Why are you hurrying so? It doesn't take long to read (this). Listen!*

---

# FORMS

## I. Nouns

| Number / Case | 1st Declension Fem. | 2nd Declension Masc. | 2nd Declension Masc. | 2nd Declension Neut. | 3rd Declension Masc. | 3rd Declension Fem. | 3rd Declension Neut. | 4th Declension Fem. | 4th Declension Neut. | 5th Declension Masc. |
|---|---|---|---|---|---|---|---|---|---|---|
| *Singular* | | | | | | | | | | |
| Nom. | puélla | sérvus | púer | báculum | páter | vōx | nōmen | mánus | génū | diēs |
| Gen. | puéllae | sérvī | púerī | báculī | pátris | vōcis | nōminis | mánūs | génūs | diḗī |
| Dat. | puéllae | sérvō | púerō | báculō | pátrī | vōcī | nōminī | mánuī | génū | diḗī |
| Acc. | puéllam | sérvum | púerum | báculum | pátrem | vōcem | nōmen | mánum | génū | diem |
| Abl. | puéllā | sérvō | púerō | báculō | pátre | vōce | nōmine | mánū | génū | diē |
| *Plural* | | | | | | | | | | |
| Nom. | puéllae | sérvī | púerī | bácula | pátrēs | vōcēs | nōmina | mánūs | génua | diēs |
| Gen. | puellárum | servórum | puerórum | baculórum | pátrum | vōcum | nōminum | mánuum | génuum | diḗrum |
| Dat. | puéllīs | sérvīs | púerīs | báculīs | pátribus | vōcibus | nōminibus | mánibus | génibus | diḗbus |
| Acc. | puéllās | sérvōs | púerōs | bácula | pátrēs | vōcēs | nōmina | mánūs | génua | diēs |
| Abl. | puéllīs | sérvīs | púerīs | báculīs | pátribus | vōcibus | nōminibus | mánibus | génibus | diḗbus |

## II. Adjectives

| Number<br>Case | 1st and 2nd Declension | | | 3rd Declension | | |
|---|---|---|---|---|---|---|
| | Masc. | Fem. | Neut. | Masc. | Fem. | Neut. |
| **Singular** | | | | | | |
| Nominative | mágnus | mágna | mágnum | ómnis | ómnis | ómne |
| Genitive | mágnī | mágnae | mágnī | ómnis | ómnis | ómnis |
| Dative | mágnō | mágnae | mágnō | ómnī | ómnī | ómnī |
| Accusative | mágnum | mágnam | mágnum | ómnem | ómnem | ómne |
| Ablative | mágnō | mágnā | mágnō | ómnī | ómnī | ómnī |
| **Plural** | | | | | | |
| Nominative | mágnī | mágnae | mágna | ómnēs | ómnēs | ómnia |
| Genitive | magnōrum | magnárum | magnōrum | ómnium | ómnium | ómnium |
| Dative | mágnīs | mágnīs | mágnīs | ómnibus | ómnibus | ómnibus |
| Accusative | mágnōs | mágnās | mágna | ómnēs | ómnēs | ómnia |
| Ablative | mágnīs | mágnīs | mágnīs | ómnibus | ómnibus | ómnibus |

# II. Adjectives (continued)

Adjectives have *positive*, *comparative*, and *superlative* forms. You can usually recognize the comparative by the letters -ior(-) and the superlative by *-issimus, -errimus,* or *-illimus,* e.g.:

| | | |
|---|---|---|
| ignāvus, *lazy* | ignāvior | ignāvissimus, -a, -um |
| pulcher, *beautiful* | pulchrior | pulcherrimus, -a, -um |
| facilis, *easy* | facilior | facillimus, -a, -um |

The comparative form uses the endings of 3rd declension adjectives, except for the ablative singular, which ends in **-e**, the genitive plural, which ends in **-um**, and the nominative and accusative plural, neuter, which end in **-a**.

Some adjectives are irregular in the comparative and superlative, e.g.:

| | | |
|---|---|---|
| bonus, *good* | melior, *better* | optimus, *best* |
| malus, *bad* | peior, *worse* | pessimus, *worst* |
| magnus, *big* | maior, *bigger* | maximus, *biggest* |
| parvus, *small* | minor, *smaller* | minimus, *smallest* |
| multus, *much* | plūs, *more* | plūrimus, *most, very much* |
| multī, *many* | plūrēs, *more* | plūrimī, *most, very many* |

# III. Demonstrative Adjectives and Pronouns

| Number<br>Case | Masc. | Fem. | Neut. | Masc. | Fem. | Neut. |
|---|---|---|---|---|---|---|
| **Singular** | | | | | | |
| Nom. | hic | haec | hoc | ílle | ílla | íllud |
| Gen. | húius | húius | húius | illíus | illíus | illíus |
| Dat. | húic | húic | húic | íllī | íllī | íllī |
| Acc. | hunc | hanc | hoc | íllum | íllam | íllud |
| Abl. | hōc | hāc | hōc | íllō | íllā | íllō |
| **Plural** | | | | | | |
| Nom. | hī | hae | haec | íllī | íllae | ílla |
| Gen. | hórum | hárum | hórum | illórum | illárum | illórum |
| Dat. | hīs | hīs | hīs | íllīs | íllīs | íllīs |
| Acc. | hōs | hās | haec | íllōs | íllās | ílla |
| Abl. | hīs | hīs | hīs | íllīs | íllīs | íllīs |

The intensive adjective **ipse, ipsa, ipsum** has the same endings as **ille, illa, illud** except **ipsum** in neuter nominative and accusative singular. The demonstrative **iste, ista, istud** has the same endings as **ille, illa, illud**.

| Number<br>Case | Masc. | Fem. | Neut. | Masc. | Fem. | Neut. |
|---|---|---|---|---|---|---|
| **Singular** | | | | | | |
| Nom. | is | éa | id | ídem | éadem | ídem |
| Gen. | éius | éius | éius | eiúsdem | eiúsdem | eiúsdem |
| Dat. | éī | éī | éī | eídem | eídem | eídem |
| Acc. | éum | éam | id | eúndem | eándem | ídem |
| Abl. | éō | éā | éō | eódem | eádem | eódem |
| **Plural** | | | | | | |
| Nom. | éī | éae | éa | eídem | eaédem | éadem |
| Gen. | eórum | eárum | eórum | eōrúndem | eārúndem | eōrúndem |
| Dat. | éīs | éīs | éīs | eísdem | eísdem | eísdem |
| Acc. | éōs | éās | éa | eósdem | eásdem | éadem |
| Abl. | éīs | éīs | éīs | eísdem | eísdem | eísdem |

# IV. Indefinite Adjectives and Pronouns

| Number / Case | Masc. | Fem. | Neut. | Masc. | Fem. | Neut. |
|---|---|---|---|---|---|---|
| *Singular* | | | | | | |
| Nom. | quídam | quaédam | quóddam | áliquī | áliqua | áliquod |
| Gen. | cuiúsdam | cuiúsdam | cuiúsdam | alicuius | alicuius | alicuius |
| Dat. | cuídam | cuídam | cuídam | alicui | alicui | alicui |
| Acc. | quéndam | quándam | quóddam | áliquem | áliquam | áliquod |
| Abl. | quódam | quádam | quódam | áliquō | áliquā | áliquō |
| *Plural* | | | | | | |
| Nom. | quídam | quaédam | quaédam | áliquī | áliquae | áliqua |
| Gen. | quorúndam | quarúndam | quorúndam | aliquórum | aliquárum | aliquórum |
| Dat. | quibúsdam | quibúsdam | quibúsdam | alíquibus | alíquibus | alíquibus |
| Acc. | quósdam | quásdam | quaédam | áliquōs | áliquās | áliqua |
| Abl. | quibúsdam | quibúsdam | quibúsdam | alíquibus | alíquibus | alíquibus |

The indefinite pronoun **quīdam, quaedam, quiddam** has the same forms as the indefinite adjective, except for **quiddam** in the neuter nominative and accusative singular. The indefinite pronoun **aliquis, aliquis, aliquid** has the regular forms of the interrogative adjective **quis, quis, quid**, as do the indefinite pronouns **quisque, quisque, quidque** and **quisquam, quisquam, quidquam (quicquam)**. The indefinite adjective **quisque, quaeque, quodque** has the same forms as the relative pronoun **quī, quae, quod** except for **quis-** in the masculine nominative singular.

# V. Adverbs

Latin adverbs may be formed from adjectives of the 1st and 2nd declensions by adding -ē to the base of the adjective, e.g., strēnuē, "strenuously," from strēnuus, -a, -um. To form an adverb from a 3rd declension adjective, add -iter to the base of the adjective or -ter to bases ending in -nt-, e.g., breviter, "briefly," from brevis, -is, -e, and prūdenter, "wisely," from prūdēns, prūdentis.

The comparative ends in -ius.
The superlative ends in -issimē, -errimē, or -illimē, e.g.:

| | | |
|---|---|---|
| lentē, *slowly* | lentius | lentissimē |
| fēlīciter, *luckily* | fēlīcius | fēlīcissimē |
| dīligenter, *carefully* | dīligentius | dīligentissimē |
| celeriter, *quickly* | celerius | celerrimē |
| facile, *easily* | facilius | facillimē |

Some adverbs are irregular:

| | | |
|---|---|---|
| bene, *well* | melius, *better* | optimē, *best* |
| male, *badly* | peius, *worse* | pessimē, *worst* |
| magnopere, *greatly* | magis, *more* | maximē, *most* |
| paulum, *little* | minus, *less* | minimē, *least* |
| multum, *much* | plūs, *more* | plūrimum, *most* |

Some adverbs are not formed from adjectives:

| | | |
|---|---|---|
| diū, *for a long time* | diūtius | diūtissimē |
| saepe, *often* | saepius | saepissimē |
| sērō, *late* | sērius | sērissimē |

135

# VI. Personal and Demonstrative Pronouns

| Case | 1st | 2nd | 3rd Masc. | 3rd Fem. | 3rd Neut. | 1st | 2nd | 3rd Masc. | 3rd Fem. | 3rd Neut. |
|------|-----|-----|------|------|-------|-----|-----|------|------|-------|
| | | | *Singular* | | | | | *Plural* | | |
| Nom. | égo | tū | is | éa | id | nōs | vōs | éī | éae | éa |
| Gen. | méī | túī | éius | éius | éius | nóstrī | véstrī | eórum | eárum | eórum |
| Dat. | míhi | tíbi | éī | éī | éī | nóbīs | vóbīs | éīs | éīs | éīs |
| Acc. | mē | tē | éum | éam | id | nōs | vōs | éōs | éās | éa |
| Abl. | mē | tē | éō | éā | éō | nóbīs | vóbīs | éīs | éīs | éīs |

# VII. Reflexive Pronoun

| Case | Singular | Plural |
|------|----------|--------|
| Nom. | — | — |
| Gen. | súī | súī |
| Dat. | síbi | síbi |
| Acc. | sē | sē |
| Abl. | sē | sē |

# VIII. Relative and Interrogative Pronouns and Adjectives

| Case | Singular Masc. | Singular Fem. | Singular Neut. | Plural Masc. | Plural Fem. | Plural Neut. |
|------|------|------|-------|------|------|-------|
| Nom. | quī | quae | quod | quī | quae | quae |
| Gen. | cúius | cúius | cúius | quórum | quárum | quórum |
| Dat. | cúi | cúi | cúi | quíbus | quíbus | quíbus |
| Acc. | quem | quam | quod | quōs | quās | quae |
| Abl. | quō | quā | quō | quíbus | quíbus | quíbus |

The interrogative pronoun **Quis . . . ?** has the same forms as the relative pronoun except for the nominative masculine singular **Quis . . . ?** and the nominative and accusative neuter singular **Quid . . . ?** In the singular, the feminine has the same forms as the masculine. In the plural, all forms are the same as those of the relative pronoun.

# IX. Regular Verbs Active: Infinitive, Imperative, Indicative

| | | | 1st Conjugation | 2nd Conjugation | 3rd Conjugation | 3rd Conjugation | 4th Conjugation |
|---|---|---|---|---|---|---|---|
| Present Infinitive | | | paráre | habére | míttere | iácere (-iō) | audíre |
| Present | Imperative | Singular 2 | párā | hábē | mítte | iáce | aúdī |
| | | Plural 2 | paráte | habéte | míttite | iácite | audíte |
| | Singular | 1 | párō | hábeō | míttō | iáciō | aúdiō |
| | | 2 | párās | hábēs | míttis | iácis | aúdīs |
| | | 3 | párat | hábet | míttit | iácit | aúdit |
| | Plural | 1 | parámus | habémus | míttimus | iácimus | audímus |
| | | 2 | parátis | habétis | míttitis | iácitis | audítis |
| | | 3 | párant | hábent | míttunt | iáciunt | aúdiunt |
| Imperfect | Singular | 1 | parábam | habébam | mittébam | iaciébam | audiébam |
| | | 2 | parábās | habébās | mittébās | iaciébās | audiébās |
| | | 3 | parábat | habébat | mittébat | iaciébat | audiébat |
| | Plural | 1 | parabámus | habēbámus | mittēbámus | iaciēbámus | audiēbámus |
| | | 2 | parabátis | habēbátis | mittēbátis | iaciēbátis | audiēbátis |
| | | 3 | parábant | habébant | mittébant | iaciébant | audiébant |

|  |  | parō | habeō | mittō | iaciō | audiō |
|---|---|---|---|---|---|---|
| **Future** | **Singular** 1 | parábō | habébō | míttam | iáciam | aúdiam |
|  | 2 | parábis | habébis | míttēs | iáciēs | aúdiēs |
|  | 3 | parábit | habébit | míttet | iáciet | aúdiet |
|  | **Plural** 1 | parábimus | habébimus | mittémus | iaciémus | audiémus |
|  | 2 | parábitis | habébitis | mittétis | iaciétis | audiétis |
|  | 3 | parábunt | habébunt | míttent | iácient | aúdient |
| **Perfect Infinitive** |  | parāvísse | habuísse | mīsísse | iēcísse | audīvísse |
| **Perfect** | **Singular** 1 | parávī | hábuī | mîsī | iếcī | audîvī |
|  | 2 | parāvístī | habuístī | mīsístī | iēcístī | audīvístī |
|  | 3 | parávit | hábuit | mîsit | iếcit | audîvit |
|  | **Plural** 1 | parávimus | habuímus | mîsimus | iécimus | audîvimus |
|  | 2 | parāvístis | habuístis | mīsístis | iēcístis | audīvístis |
|  | 3 | parāvêrunt | habuêrunt | mīsêrunt | iēcêrunt | audīvêrunt |

138

# IX. Regular Verbs Active: Indicative (continued)

|  |  |  | paráveram | habúeram | míseram | iéceram | audíveram |
|---|---|---|---|---|---|---|---|
| *Pluperfect* | *Singular* | 1 | paráveram | habúeram | míseram | iéceram | audíveram |
|  |  | 2 | paráverās | habúerās | míserās | iécerās | audíverās |
|  |  | 3 | paráverat | habúerat | míserat | iécerat | audíverat |
|  | *Plural* | 1 | paráverāmus | habuerāmus | mīserāmus | iēcerāmus | audīverāmus |
|  |  | 2 | paráverātis | habuerātis | mīserātis | iēcerātis | audīverātis |
|  |  | 3 | paráverant | habúerant | míserant | iécerant | audíverant |
| *Future Perfect* | *Singular* | 1 | paráverō | habúerō | míserō | iécerō | audíverō |
|  |  | 2 | paráveris | habúeris | míseris | iéceris | audíveris |
|  |  | 3 | paráverit | habúerit | míserit | iécerit | audíverit |
|  | *Plural* | 1 | paráverimus | habuérimus | mīsérimus | iēcérimus | audīvérimus |
|  |  | 2 | paráveritis | habuéritis | mīséritis | iēcéritis | audīvéritis |
|  |  | 3 | paráverint | habúerint | míserint | iécerint | audíverint |

# X. Regular Verbs Passive: Indicative

| | | | 1st Conjugation | 2nd Conjugation | 3rd Conjugation | | 4th Conjugation |
|---|---|---|---|---|---|---|---|
| **Present** | *Singular* | 1 | pórtor | móveor | míttor | iácior | aúdior |
| | | 2 | portáris | movéris | mítteris | iáceris | audíris |
| | | 3 | portátur | movétur | míttitur | iácitur | audítur |
| | *Plural* | 1 | portámur | movémur | míttimur | iácimur | audímur |
| | | 2 | portáminī | movéminī | mittíminī | iacíminī | audíminī |
| | | 3 | portántur | movéntur | mittúntur | iaciúntur | audiúntur |
| **Imperfect** | *Singular* | 1 | portábar | movḗbar | mittḗbar | iaciḗbar | audiḗbar |
| | | 2 | portābáris | movēbáris | mittēbáris | iaciēbáris | audiēbáris |
| | | 3 | portābátur | movēbátur | mittēbátur | iaciēbátur | audiēbátur |
| | *Plural* | 1 | portābámur | movēbámur | mittēbámur | iaciēbámur | audiēbámur |
| | | 2 | portābáminī | movēbáminī | mittēbáminī | iaciēbáminī | audiēbáminī |
| | | 3 | portābántur | movēbántur | mittēbántur | iaciēbántur | audiēbántur |

# X. Regular Verbs Passive: Indicative (continued)

## Future

| | | | | | | |
|---|---|---|---|---|---|---|
| Singular | 1 | portábor | movébor | míttar | iáciar | aúdiar |
| | 2 | portáberis | movéberis | mittéris | aciéris | audiéris |
| | 3 | portábitur | movébitur | mittétur | iaciétur | audiétur |
| Plural | 1 | portábimur | movébimur | mittémur | iaciémur | audiémur |
| | 2 | portábiminí | movébíminí | mittéminí | iaciéminí | audiéminí |
| | 3 | portábúntur | movébúntur | mitténtur | iaciéntur | audiéntur |

| | | PERFECT PASSIVE | | PLUPERFECT PASSIVE | | FUTURE PERFECT PASSIVE | |
|---|---|---|---|---|---|---|---|
| Singular | 1 | portátus, -a | sum | portátus, -a | éram | portátus, -a | érō |
| | 2 | portátus, -a | es | portátus, -a | érās | portátus, -a | éris |
| | 3 | portátus, -a, -um | est | portátus, -a, -um | érat | portátus, -a, -um | érit |
| Plural | 1 | portátī, -ae | súmus | portátī, -ae | erámus | portátī, -ae | érimus |
| | 2 | portátī, -ae | éstis | portátī, -ae | erátis | portátī, -ae | éritis |
| | 3 | portátī, -ae, -a | sunt | portátī, -ae, -a | érant | portátī, -ae, -a | érunt |

# XI. Regular Verbs Active: Subjunctive

| | | | 1st Conjugation | 2nd Conjugation | 3rd Conjugation | | 4th Conjugation |
|---|---|---|---|---|---|---|---|
| **Present** | *Singular* | 1 | párem | hábeam | míttam | iáciam | aúdiam |
| | | 2 | párēs | hábeās | míttās | iáciās | aúdiās |
| | | 3 | páret | hábeat | míttat | iáciat | aúdiat |
| | *Plural* | 1 | parémus | habeámus | mittámus | iaciámus | audiámus |
| | | 2 | parétis | habeátis | mittátis | iaciátis | audiátis |
| | | 3 | párent | hábeant | míttant | iáciant | aúdiant |
| **Imperfect** | *Singular* | 1 | parárem | habḗrem | mítterem | iácerem | audírem |
| | | 2 | parárēs | habḗrēs | mítterēs | iácerēs | audírēs |
| | | 3 | paráret | habḗret | mítteret | iáceret | audíret |
| | *Plural* | 1 | parárḗmus | habērḗmus | mitterḗmus | iacerḗmus | audīrḗmus |
| | | 2 | parárḗtis | habērḗtis | mitterḗtis | iacerḗtis | audīrḗtis |
| | | 3 | parárent | habḗrent | mítterent | iácerent | audírent |

# XI. Regular Verbs Active: Subjunctive (continued)

| | | | | 1st Conjugation | 2nd Conjugation | 3rd Conjugation | | 4th Conjugation |
|---|---|---|---|---|---|---|---|---|
| **Perfect** | Singular | 1 | | parāverim | habúerim | mīserim | iēcerim | audíverim |
| | | 2 | | parāveris | habúeris | mīseris | iēceris | audíveris |
| | | 3 | | parāverit | habúerit | mīserit | iēcerit | audíverit |
| | Plural | 1 | | parāvérimus | habuérimus | mīsérimus | iēcérimus | audīvérimus |
| | | 2 | | parāvéritis | habuéritis | mīséritis | iēcéritis | audīvéritis |
| | | 3 | | parāverint | habúerint | mīserint | iēcerint | audíverint |
| **Pluperfect** | Singular | 1 | | parāvissem | habuíssem | mīsíssem | iēcíssem | audīvíssem |
| | | 2 | | parāvissēs | habuíssēs | mīsíssēs | iēcíssēs | audīvíssēs |
| | | 3 | | parāvisset | habuísset | mīsísset | iēcísset | audīvísset |
| | Plural | 1 | | parāvissémus | habuissémus | mīsissémus | iēcissémus | audīvissémus |
| | | 2 | | parāvissétis | habuissétis | mīsissétis | iēcissétis | audīvissétis |
| | | 3 | | parāvissent | habuíssent | mīsíssent | iēcíssent | audīvíssent |

# XII. Regular Verbs Passive: Subjunctive

| | | | 1st Conjugation | 2nd Conjugation | 3rd Conjugation | | 4th Conjugation |
|---|---|---|---|---|---|---|---|
| **Present** | *Singular* | 1 | párer | hábear | míttar | iáciar | aúdiar |
| | | 2 | paréris | habeáris | mittáris | iaciáris | audiáris |
| | | 3 | parétur | habeátur | mittátur | iaciátur | audiátur |
| | *Plural* | 1 | parémur | habeámur | mittámur | iaciámur | audiámur |
| | | 2 | parémini | habeámini | mittámini | iaciámini | audiámini |
| | | 3 | paréntur | habeántur | mittántur | iaciántur | audiántur |
| **Imperfect** | *Singular* | 1 | pararer | habérer | mítterer | iácerer | audírer |
| | | 2 | pararéris | habéréris | mitteréris | iaceréris | audiréris |
| | | 3 | pararétur | haberétur | mitterétur | iacerétur | audirétur |
| | *Plural* | 1 | pararémur | haberémur | mitterémur | iacerémur | audirémur |
| | | 2 | pararémini | haberémini | mitterémini | iacerémini | audirémini |
| | | 3 | pararéntur | haberéntur | mitteréntur | iaceréntur | audiréntur |

The perfect passive subjunctive consists of the perfect passive participle plus the present subjunctive of the verb **esse** (see p. 147), e.g., **parātus sim**. The pluperfect passive subjunctive consists of the perfect passive participle plus the imperfect subjunctive of the verb **esse** (see p. 147), e.g., **parātus essem**.

# XIII. Irregular Verbs: Infinitive, Imperative, Indicative

| Infinitive | | | ésse | pósse | vélle | nólle |
|---|---|---|---|---|---|---|
| Imperative | | | es | — | — | nólī |
| | | | éste | — | — | nolíte |
| *Present* | *Singular* | 1 | sum | póssum | vólō | nólō |
| | | 2 | es | pótes | vīs | nōn vīs |
| | | 3 | est | pótest | vult | nōn vult |
| | *Plural* | 1 | súmus | póssumus | vólumus | nólumus |
| | | 2 | éstis | potéstis | vúltis | nōn vúltis |
| | | 3 | sunt | póssunt | vólunt | nólunt |
| *Imperfect* | *Singular* | 1 | éram | póteram | volébam | nōlébam |
| | | 2 | érās | póterās | volébās | nōlébās |
| | | 3 | érat | póterat | volébat | nōlébat |
| | *Plural* | 1 | erámus | poterámus | volēbámus | nōlēbámus |
| | | 2 | erátis | poterátis | volēbátis | nōlēbátis |
| | | 3 | érant | póterant | volébant | nōlébant |
| *Future* | *Singular* | 1 | érō | póterō | vólam | nólam |
| | | 2 | éris | póteris | vólēs | nólēs |
| | | 3 | érit | póterit | vólet | nólet |
| | *Plural* | 1 | érimus | potérimus | volémus | nōlémus |
| | | 2 | éritis | potéritis | volétis | nōlétis |
| | | 3 | érunt | póterunt | vólent | nólent |

| Infinitive | | | málle | íre | férre | férrī | fíerī |
|---|---|---|---|---|---|---|---|
| Imperative | | | — | ī | fer | férre | — |
| | | | — | íte | férte | feríminī | — |
| Present | Singular | 1 | málō | éō | férō | féror | fíō |
| | | 2 | mávīs | īs | fers | férris | fīs |
| | | 3 | mávult | it | fert | fértur | fit |
| | Plural | 1 | málumus | ímus | férimus | férimur | fímus |
| | | 2 | māvúltis | ítis | fértis | feríminī | fítis |
| | | 3 | málunt | éunt | férunt | ferúntur | fíunt |
| Imperfect | Singular | 1 | mālébam | íbam | ferébam | ferébar | fiébam |
| | | 2 | mālébās | íbās | ferébās | ferēbáris | fiébās |
| | | 3 | mālébat | íbat | ferébat | ferēbátur | fiébat |
| | Plural | 1 | mālēbámus | ībámus | ferēbámus | ferēbámur | fiēbámus |
| | | 2 | mālēbátis | ībátis | ferēbátis | ferēbáminī | fiēbátis |
| | | 3 | mālébant | íbant | ferébant | ferēbántur | fiébant |
| Future | Singular | 1 | málam | íbō | féram | férar | fíam |
| | | 2 | málēs | ībis | férēs | feréris | fíēs |
| | | 3 | málet | ībit | féret | ferétur | fíet |
| | Plural | 1 | mālémus | ībimus | ferémus | ferémur | fiémus |
| | | 2 | mālétis | ībitis | ferétis | feréminī | fiétis |
| | | 3 | málent | íbunt | férent | feréntur | fíent |

Note: perfect, pluperfect, and future perfect tenses are formed regularly from the perfect stem plus the regular endings for each tense. These tenses of **fīō** are made up of the participle **factus, -a, -um** plus **sum**, **eram**, and **erō** respectively.

# XIV. Irregular Verbs: Subjunctive

| | | | | | | |
|---|---|---|---|---|---|---|
| **Present** | *Singular* | 1 | sim | póssim | vélim | nólim |
| | | 2 | sīs | póssīs | vélīs | nólīs |
| | | 3 | sit | póssit | vélit | nólit |
| | *Plural* | 1 | símus | possímus | velímus | nōlímus |
| | | 2 | sītis | possítis | velítis | nōlítis |
| | | 3 | sint | póssint | vélint | nólint |
| **Imperfect** | *Singular* | 1 | éssem | póssem | véllem | nóllem |
| | | 2 | éssēs | póssēs | véllēs | nóllēs |
| | | 3 | ésset | pósset | véllet | nóllet |
| | *Plural* | 1 | essémus | possémus | vellémus | nōllémus |
| | | 2 | essétis | possétis | vellétis | nōllétis |
| | | 3 | éssent | póssent | véllent | nóllent |
| **Perfect** | *Singular* | 1 | fúerim | potúerim | volúerim | nōlúerim |
| | | 2 | fúeris | potúeris | volúeris | nōlúeris |
| | | 3 | fúerit | potúerit | volúerit | nōlúerit |
| | *Plural* | 1 | fuérimus | potuérimus | voluérimus | nōluérimus |
| | | 2 | fuéritis | potuéritis | voluéritis | nōluéritis |
| | | 3 | fúerint | potúerint | volúerint | nōlúerint |
| **Pluperfect** | *Singular* | 1 | fuíssem | potuíssem | voluíssem | nōluíssem |
| | | 2 | fuíssēs | potuíssēs | voluíssēs | nōluíssēs |
| | | 3 | fuísset | potuísset | voluísset | nōluísset |
| | *Plural* | 1 | fuissémus | potuissémus | voluissémus | nōluissémus |
| | | 2 | fuissétis | potuissétis | voluissétis | nōluissétis |
| | | 3 | fuíssent | potuíssent | voluíssent | nōluíssent |

147

# XIV. Irregular Verbs: Subjunctive (continued)

| | | | | | | | |
|---|---|---|---|---|---|---|---|
| **Present** | **Singular** | 1 | málim | éam | féram | férar | fíam |
| | | 2 | málīs | éās | férās | feráris | fíās |
| | | 3 | málit | éat | férat | ferátur | fíat |
| | **Plural** | 1 | mālímus | eámus | ferámus | ferámur | fiámus |
| | | 2 | mālítis | eátis | ferátis | feráminī | fiátis |
| | | 3 | málint | éant | férant | ferántur | fíant |
| **Imperfect** | **Singular** | 1 | mállem | írem | férrem | férrer | fíerem |
| | | 2 | mállēs | írēs | férrēs | ferréris | fíerēs |
| | | 3 | mállet | íret | férret | ferrétur | fíeret |
| | **Plural** | 1 | mállémus | īrémus | ferrémus | ferrémur | fierémus |
| | | 2 | mállétis | īrétis | ferrétis | ferréminī | fierétis |
| | | 3 | mállent | írent | férrent | ferréntur | fíerent |
| **Perfect** | **Singular** | 1 | mālúerim | íverim | túlerim | látus sim | fáctus sim |
| | | 2 | mālúeris | íveris | túleris | látus sīs | fáctus sīs |
| | | 3 | mālúerit | íverit | túlerit | látus sit | fáctus sit |
| | **Plural** | 1 | māluérimus | īvérimus | tulérimus | látī símus | fáctī símus |
| | | 2 | māluéritis | īvéritis | tuléritis | látī sítis | fáctī sítis |
| | | 3 | mālúerint | íverint | túlerint | látī sint | fáctī sint |
| **Pluperfect** | **Singular** | 1 | māluíssem | īvíssem | tulíssem | látus éssem | fáctus éssem |
| | | 2 | māluíssēs | īvíssēs | tulíssēs | látus éssēs | fáctus éssēs |
| | | 3 | māluísset | īvísset | tulísset | látus ésset | fáctus ésset |
| | **Plural** | 1 | māluissémus | īvissémus | tulissémus | látī essémus | fáctī essémus |
| | | 2 | māluissétis | īvissétis | tulissétis | látī essétis | fáctī essétis |
| | | 3 | māluíssent | īvíssent | tulíssent | látī éssent | fáctī éssent |

## XV. Infinitives

| Present | | | Perfect |
|---|---|---|---|
| Active | Passive | Active | Passive |
| 1 paráre | parárī | parāvísse | parátus, -a, -um ésse |
| 2 habére | habérī | habuísse | hábitus, -a, -um ésse |
| 3 míttere | míttī | mīsísse | míssus, -a, -um ésse |
| 4 audíre | audírī | audīvísse | audítus, -a, -um ésse |

| Future |
|---|
| Active |
| 1 parātúrus, -a, -um ésse<br>2 habitúrus, -a, -um ésse<br>3 missúrus, -a, -um ésse<br>4 audītúrus, -a, -um ésse |

## XVI. Participles

| Present | | Perfect | |
|---|---|---|---|
| Active | Passive | Active | Passive |
| 1 párāns, parántis | | | parátus, -a, -um |
| 2 hábēns, habéntis | | | hábitus, -a, -um |
| 3 míttēns, mitténtis | | | míssus, -a, -um |
| 4 aúdiēns, audiéntis | | | audítus, -a, -um |

| Future |
|---|
| Active |
| 1 parātúrus, -a, -um<br>2 habitúrus, -a, -um<br>3 missúrus, -a, -um<br>4 audītúrus, -a, -um |

# VOCABULARY

## A

ā, ab (+ *abl.*), by, from, away from
67 ábigō, -ígere (3), -égī, -áctum, to drive away
65 ábnegō (1), to refuse, deny
56 ábsēns, -ntis, absent
ábstinēns, -ntis, refraining from
ábsum, abésse (*irreg.*), áfuī, to be away, be distant from
67 absū́mō, -ere (3), -psī, -ptum, to consume, use up
ac, and
áccidō, -ere (3), -ī, to happen
accípiō, -ípere (3), -épī, -éptum, to receive, get
58 acclāmā́tiō, -ónis (*f*), loud outcry
63 acclámō (1), to cry out in approval
accúrrō, -rrere (3), -rrī, -rsum, to run towards, up to
58 ácer, ácris, ácre, fierce
62 ācérrimē, very fiercely
62 ácrius, more fiercely
59 acérbus, -a, -um, bitter, hideous, appalling
62 aciḗs, -éī (*f*), battle line
58 acquírō, -rere (3), -sívī, -sítum, to acquire, gain
65 áctum, -ī (*n*), procedure
58 ácta, -órum (*n pl*), public records
ad (+ *acc.*), to, towards, at, near
áddō, -ere (3), -idī, -itum, to add
ádeō, so much, to such an extent
68 adfíciō, -ícere (3), -écī, -éctum, to affect, move
64 adfírmō (1), to affirm, assert, swear
60 adflígō, -gere (3), -xī, -ctum, to strike down
55 adhíbeō, -ére (2), -uī, -itum, to offer, give to
adhúc, still, as yet
56 adíciō, -ícere (3), -iécī, -iéctum, to add
ádimō, -ímere (3), -émī, -émptum (+ *dat.*), to take away (from)
ádiuvō, -iuváre (1), -iúvī, -iútum, to help
63 adminístrō (1), to administer
admīrā́tiō, -ónis (*f*), amazement, wonder
admóveō, -movére (2), -móvī, -mótum, to move towards, bring to
65 ádnotō (1), to make a ruling
adórior, -īrī (4), -tus sum, to attack

68 adsíduus, -a, -um, constant
63 adsístō, -ere (3), ádstitī, to stand by, help
68 adstríctus, -a, -um, drawn together, contracted
ádsum, -ésse (*irreg.*), -fuī, to be present, near
68 adulēscéntia, -ae (*f*), youth
65 adultérium, -ī (*n*), adultery
54 adū́rō, -úrere (3), -ússī, -ústum, to set on fire, burn, scorch
68 advérsum, -ī (*n*), calamity, misfortune
67 advocā́tiō, -ónis (*f*), (legal) counsel
58 advocátus, -ī (*m*), supporter
aedifícium, -ī (*n*), building
aedíficō (1), to build
54 aedílis, -is (*m*), aedile
68 aéger, -gra, -grum, ill, disturbed
aegrótō (1), to be ill
63 aémulus, -a, -um, rivalling, vying
63 aequā́lis, -is, -e, fair, just
56 aéquē, equally
66 aerárius, -ī (*m*), coppersmith
59 aes, aéris (*n*), copper; money
aes aliénum, debt ("another's money")
aéstās, -átis (*f*), summer
68 aéstimō (1), to estimate, judge
61 aétās, -átis (*f*), age, time of life, old age
64 aetérnitās, -átis (*f*), eternity
68 afféctiō, -ónis (*f*), affection
áfferō, -rre (*irreg.*), áttulī, allátum, to bring, bring to, bring in
áger, ágrī (*m*), field, land
in ágrum, in depth (as opposed to frontage)
61 ágger, -eris (*m*), earthen wall, earthwork
58 ágmen, -inis (*n*), column, band
agnóscō, -óscere (3), -óvī, -itum, to recognize
ágō, ágere (3), égī, áctum, to do; speak (publicly), plead (a case); celebrate (a holiday)
grā́tiās ágere (+ *dat.*), to thank
60 ála, -ae (*f*), wing
66 álgeō, -gére (2), -sī, to be cold, feel the cold
63 aliquándō, sometimes
áliquī, áliqua, áliquod, some (or other), any
áliquis, áliquid, someone, something
sī quis (quis = áliquis), if anyone
55 áliquot (*indeclinable*), some, a few

150

áliter, otherwise
alíubī, elsewhere, somewhere else 64
álius, ália, áliud, other, another
álligō (1), to tie
álloquor, -quī (3), -cútus sum, to speak
  to, address
álter, áltera, álterum, the one, the other 68
  (of two), the second 65
altitúdō, -inis (f), height
áltus, -a, -um, tall, high
ámbō, ámbae, ámbō, both
ambítiō, -ónis (f), ambition, political
  campaigning (57) 61
ámbulō (1), to walk, walk around 54
ambúrō, -úrere (3), -ússī, -ústum, to
  scorch, burn near 55
āmēns, -ntis, mad, insane
āméntia, -ae (f), madness 58
amíca, -ae (f), girlfriend
amícus, -ī (m), friend 54
amícus, -a, -um, friendly 64
āmíttō, -íttere (3), -ísī, -íssum, to lose 57
ámō (1), to like, love 57
amoénitās, -átis (f), pleasantness, charm 54
ámor, -óris (m), love 54
amphitheátrum (also amphitheáter), -ī
  (n), amphitheater
ámphora, -ae (f), amphora, large two-
  handled earthenware jar
ampléctor, -ctī (3), -xus sum, to embrace
ampléxō (1), to embrace
ámpliō (l), to enlarge, increase
amplitúdō, -inis (f), grandeur, majesty
ámplus, -a, -um, eminent, important 67
an, or, whether
ancílla, -ae (f), slave woman
anguílla, -ae (f), eel 68
ánima, -ae (f), soul, darling
animadvértō, -tere (3), -tī, -sum, to notice
ánimus, -ī (m), mind, spirit, heart
annóna, -ae (f), price of grain
ánnus, -ī (m), year 64
ánnuum, -ī (n), yearly salary 68
ánte (+ acc.), before, in front of 62
ánte (adverb), before, previously 55
ánteā, before, previously 58
antecédō, -dere (3), -ssī, -ssum, to an-
  ticipate, precede 59
ánulus, -ī (m), ring 60
apériō, -íre (4), -uī, -tum, to open
appáreō, -ére (2), -uī, -itum, to appear 61
appéllō (1), to call, call on, invoke
appropínquō (1), (+ dat.), to approach, 56
  draw near to 54
áqua, -ae (f), water 55
áquila, -ae (f), eagle, insignia of a legion

ára, -ae (f), altar
árbitror, -árī (1), -átus sum, to think
árcus, -ūs (m), arch
árdeō, -dére (2), -sī, to burn, blaze
área, -ae (f), open space, site, (city)
  square
argéntum, -ī (n), silver
árguō, -úere (3), -uī, -útum, to accuse,
  denounce
árma, -órum (n pl), arms, weapons
armátus, -a, -um, armed
ars, -tis (f), skill, art
artifícium, -ī (n), skill
as, ássis (m), as, a small coin compara-
  ble to a penny
ásinus, -ī (m), ass, donkey
átque, and, also
átrium, -ī (n), atrium, main room of a
  Roman house
attíneō, -ére (2), -uī, to concern
aúctor, -óris (m), author, authority
auctóritās, -átis (f), authority, influence
audácia, -ae (f), daring, recklessness
audácter, boldly, with confidence
audáculus, -a, -um, bold, courageous
aúdeō, -dére (2), -sus sum, to dare
aúdiō (4), to hear, listen to
aúferō, -rre (irreg.), ábstulī, ablátum, to
  carry away, take away
aúgeō, -gére (2), -xī, -ctum, to increase
aúreus, -a, -um, golden
aúrum, -ī (n), gold
aut, or
aútem, however, but, moreover
autúmnus, -ī (m), autumn
auxílium, -ī (n), help
ávis, -is (m/f), bird
āvocāméntum, -ī (n), diversion, recreation


# B

báculum, -ī (n), stick
balíneum, -ī (n), public bath
bárba, -ae (f), beard
bárbarus, -a, -um, barbarian, foreign
bárō, -ónis (m), lout
basílica, -ae (f), public courthall
beátus, -a, -um, happy
bellíssimē, most comfortably, elegantly
béllum, -ī (n), war
béne, well
benefáciō, -fácere (3), -fécī, -fáctum, to
  do a service (to), benefit
benefícium, -ī (n), kindness, favor
benígnus, -a, -um, kind, friendly
bēstiárius, -ī (m), animal fighter (in the
  arena)
bíbō, -ere (3), -ī, to drink

151

66 **bífer, -era, -erum**, that bears (fruit or flowers) twice (a year)
68 **bímulus, -a, -um**, two years old
55 **bínī, -ae, -a**, two each
**bónus, -a, -um**, good
54 **bóna, -órum** (*n pl*), goods, material possessions
**bōs, bóvis** (*m/f*), ox, cow
**brévis, -is, -e**, short, brief
60 **brévitās, -átis** (*f*), brevity, shortness
67 **brúma, -ae** (*f*), winter
54 **búb(u)lus, -a, -um**, of or belonging to an ox
54 **búcca, -ae** (*f*), cheek, mouthful
64 **búlē, -ēs** (*f*), senate or town council in a Greek city
64 **būleúta, -ae** (*m*), senator or councilor in a Greek city
55 **burdubásta, -ae** (*m*), stick (?) (as an insult to a feeble gladiator)

## C

58 **cadáver, -eris** (*n*), corpse
**cádō, -ere** (3), **cécidī, cásum**, to fall
68 **cádus, -ī** (*m*), (wine)jar
66 **caécus, -a, -um**, blind, hidden, unseen
55 **caédō, -dere** (3), **cecídī, -sum**, to cut, beat, cut down, kill
68 **caelātúra, -ae** (*f*), engraving
**caélum, -ī** (*n*), the sky, heaven
55 **caldicerébrius, -a, -um**, hotheaded, impulsive
56 **candēlábrum, -ī** (*n*), candelabrum, candle- or lampstand
57 **candidátus, -ī** (*m*), candidate
66 **cándidus, -a, -um**, white
67 **canínus, -a, -um**, of or belonging to a dog
**cánis, -is** (*m/f*), dog
**capillátus, -a, -um**, with long hair
**capíllī, -órum** (*m pl*), hair
**cápiō, -ere** (3), **cépī, -tum**, to take, capture
**cáput, -itis** (*n*), head
68 **cáreō, -ére** (2), **-uī, -itum** (+ *abl.*), to be without, lack
65 **cármen, -inis** (*n*), song, hymn
55 **carnárium, -ī** (*n*), butcher-shop, slaughterhouse
**cárus, -a, -um**, dear, beloved
68 **cássus, -a, -um**, empty, useless
61 **cástra, -órum** (*n pl*), camp
68 **cástus, -a, -um**, chaste
54 **cásula, -ae** (*f*), little house, hut
61 **cásus, -ūs** (*m*), fall, outcome, happening, misfortune
56 **catélla, -ae** (*f*), puppy
66 **caténō** (1), to chain
67 **cathédra, -ae** (*f*), chair

**caúda, -ae** (*f*), tail
54 **caúniae, -árum** (*f pl*), figs from Caunus (in Asia Minor)
**caúpō, -ónis** (*m*), innkeeper
**caúsa, -ae** (*f*), cause, reason, case
genitive + **caúsā**, for the sake of
60 **cédō, -dere** (3), **-ssī, -ssum**, to retreat, yield, be inferior to
**celéritās, -átis** (*f*), speed
**celériter**, quickly
68 **célla, -ae** (*f*), storeroom, cellar
**céna, -ae** (*f*), dinner
**cénō** (1), to dine, eat dinner
60 **cénseō, -ére** (2), **-uī, -um**, to be of the opinion, think
64 **cénsor, -óris** (*m*), censor, one who enrolls senators
54 **centénī, -ae, -a**, a hundred each
56 **céntiēs**, a hundred times
55 **centōnárius, -ī** (*m*), maker of patchwork, rag dealer
**céntum**, a hundred
62 **centúriō, -ónis** (*m*), centurion, leader of 100 men
56 **cerebéllum, -ī** (*n*), brain, heart
**cértus, -a, -um**, certain
**cértē**, certainly, at least
55 **céterum**, for the rest, moreover
**cíbus, -ī** (*m*), food
56 **cícarō, -ónis** (*m*), small boy, pet
58 **cíngō, -gere** (3), **-xī, -ctum**, to equip, strap on
56 **cíngulum, -ī** (*n*), belt, leash
56 **cínis, -eris** (*m*), ashes
56 **círcā** (+ *acc.*), around, near
**circúmeō, -míre** (*irreg.*), **-miī, -mitum**, to go around, surround
59 **circumscríbō, -bere** (3), **-psī, -ptum**, to confine, keep in bounds
58 **circúmstō, -áre, -etī**, to stand around
64 **circumvéniō, -eníre, -énī, -éntum**, to surround
56 **cítō**, quickly, soon
62 **cítō** (1), to spur on, rouse up
60 **cívílis, -is, -e**, civil
63 **cívílitās, -átis** (*f*), politeness, courtesy
**cívis, -is** (*m*), citizen
**cívitās, -átis** (*f*), state
57 **clámitō** (1), to call
67 **clámō**, (1), to shout
67 **clámor, -óris** (*m*), shout, shouting
61 **clássis, -is** (*f*), fleet
**claúdō (clúdō), -dere** (3), **-sī, -sum**, to shut, close
68 **clávus, -ī** (*m*), stripe
**lātus clávus**, a broad purple stripe on a senator's tunic, one of the insignia of his rank
54 **clívus, -ī** (*m*), slope, hill

64 cloáca, -ae (*f*), sewer, drain
58 códex, -icis (*m*), ledger, tablet
65 cóeō, -íre (*irreg.*), -iī, -itum, to come together, meet
coépī, -ísse, -tum, to begin (perfect system only used)
59 coérceō (2), to check, restrain
cógitō (1), to think, consider
58 cognátus, -ī (*m*), relative, kinsman
cognóscō, -óscere (3), -óvī, -itum, to find out, learn, hear of
cógō, -ere (3), coégī, coáctum, to compel, force
56 cohérēs, -édis (*m*), joint heir
62 cóhors, -rtis (*f*), cohort, one-tenth of a legion
62 cohórtor, -árī (1), -átus sum, to encourage
57 colléga, -ae (*m*), colleague, partner
65 collégium, -ī (*n*), club, association
54 collúdō, -dere (3), -sī, -sum, to act in collusion (with)
cólō, -ere (3), -uī, cúltum, to cultivate, inhabit
54 colónia, -ae (*f*), colony, town
55 cólor, -óris (*m*), color, complexion
55 cólubra, -ae (*f*), snake
56 colúmba, -ae (*f*), dove
63 colúmna, -ae (*f*), column, pillar
54 comédō, -ésse (*irreg.*), -édī, -ésum, to eat up, eat
cómes, -itis (*m/f*), companion
57 comítia, -órum (*n pl*), electoral assembly of the people
61 cómminus (*adverb*), at close quarters, hand to hand
committō, -íttere (3), -ísī, -íssum, to bring together; entrust
púgnam (ríxam) committere, to join battle, start a fight
commúnis, -is, -e, common, joint
66 comoédia, -ae (*f*), comedy
67 comoédus, -ī (*m*), comic actor, comedian
cómparō (1), to buy, obtain, get ready
62 compéllō, -éllere (3), -ulī, -úlsum, to force, drive
59 compériō, -íre, -ī, -tum, to find out for certain
63 compéscō, -ere (3), -uī, to check, curb, restrain
57 competítor, -óris (*m*), fellow candidate, opponent
complúrēs, -ēs, -a, several
61 compórtō (1), to bring together, collect
54 cómputō (1), to add up, count, figure out
59 concédō, -dere (3), -ssī, -sum, to grant
cóncidō, -ere (3), -ī, to fall down

56 concupíscō, -íscere (3), ívī, -ítum, to long for
61 concúrsus, -ūs (*m*), a running together, collision
64 condíciō, -ónis (*f*), situation, position, status
60 (sē) cónferō, -rre (*irreg.*), cóntulī, collátum, to take oneself, flee
confíciō, -ícere (3), -écī, -éctum, to accomplish, finish, overwhelm
65 confíteor, -fitérī (2), -féssus sum, to confess, admit
61 conflígō, -gere (3), -xī, -ctum, to collide
58 confluō, -ere (3), -xī, to flow together
confúgiō, -úgere (3), -úgī, to flee for refuge
58 cóngruō, -ere (3), -uī, to agree with
68 coniugális, -is, -e, belonging to marriage, conjugal
61 coniúngō, -gere (3), -xī, -ctum (+ *dat.*), to join
68 cóniūnx, -ugis (*m/f*), spouse, husband, wife
61 conlabefíō, -fíerī (*irreg.*), -fáctus sum, to fall in, collapse, break up
cónor, -árī (1), -átus sum, to try
62 conquírō, -rere (3), -sívī, -sítum, to procure, obtain, seek out
61 cōnscéndō, -dere (3), -dī, -sum, to board ship
61 cónsequor, -quī (3), -cútus sum, to follow, catch up to, overtake
59 cōnsérvō (1), to preserve
60 cōnsíderō (1), to consider, think about, make plans
cōnsílium, -ī (*n*), plan, deliberation, advice
61 cónspicor, -árī (1), -átus sum, to catch sight of
58 cōnspútō (1), to spit on (in contempt)
cōnstítuō, -úere (3), -uī, -útum, to decide, determine
58 cónstō, -áre (1), -itī (+ *abl.*), to depend on, be based on
68 cōnsuéscō, -escere (3), -évī, -étum, to be accustomed
67 cōnsuētúdō, -inis (*f*), custom, habit
cónsul, -lis (*m*), consul
57 cōnsuláris, -is, -e, belonging to a consul, consular
57 cōnsulátus, -ūs (*m*), consulship
cónsulō, -ere (3), -uī, -tum, to consult, decide
68 cōnsultátiō, -ónis (*f*), consultation, discussion
62 conténdō, -dere (3), -dī, -tum, to hurry, try to reach
68 cónterō, -térere (3), -trívī, -trítum, to wear out, exhaust

153

**contíneō, -inére** (2), -ínuī, -éntum, to hold together, hold in position, contain

56 **contíngō, -íngere** (3), -igī, -áctum, to befall, happen to

58 **cóntiō, -ónis** (f), public meeting

**cóntrā** (+ acc.), opposite, in front of, facing; equivalent to, worth its weight in

65 **contrárius, -a, -um,** contrary, opposite

61 **convéllō, -éllere** (3), -éllī, -úlsum, to tear away, weaken

**convéniō, -eníre** (4), -énī, -éntum, to come together, meet, assemble

**convértō, -tere** (3), -tī, -sum, to turn (around)

58 **convícium, -ī** (n), insult

**convíva, -ae** (m), guest (at a banquet)

**convívium, -ī** (n), feast, banquet

**cónvocō** (1), to call together, assemble

56 **cōpiósus, -a, -um,** capacious, large

**cóquō, -quere** (3), -xī, -ctum, to cook

**cóquus, -ī** (m), cook

**cor, córdis** (n), heart

62 **córnū, -ūs** (n), horn; end of a battle line, wing

**coróna, -ae** (f), garland, crown

**corónō** (1), to crown, form a ring around, encircle

**córpus, -oris** (n) body

64 **córrigō, -ígere** (3), -éxī, -éctum, to correct

**corrípiō, -ípere** (3), -ípuī, éptum, to seize, scold

56 **corrotúndō** (1), to round off, "clear" (a profit)

66 **cothúrnus, -ī** (m), raised boot worn by tragic actors

**cotídiē,** daily, every day

**crās,** tomorrow

67 **crássus, -a, -um,** thick, coarse, uncouth

57 **crēbréscō, -éscere** (3), -uī, to increase, gather strength

**crédō, -ere** (3), -idī, -itum, to trust, believe

58 **crémō** (1), to burn

**créō** (1), to elect, create

54 **créscō, -ere** (3), crévī, crétum, to rise, grow, swell

64 **crímen, -inis** (n), accusation, indictment, crime

**crūdélis, -is, -e,** cruel

**crūdélitās, -átis** (f), cruelty

**cubículum, -ī** (n), bedroom

66 **cubíle, -is** (n), bed

**cúbitum íre,** to go to bed

**cúlpa, -ae** (f), fault, blame

56 **cúltus, -a, -um,** cultivated, elegant, adorned

68 **cúltus, -ūs** (m), adornment, finery, (fancy) clothing

**cum** (+ abl.), with

**cum,** when, since, whenever, although

68 **cúnae, -árum** (f pl), cradle

**cúnctī, -ae, -a,** all

65 **cupíditās, -átis** (f), desire, greed

57 **cúpidus, -a, -um** (+ gen.), desirous, eager

**cúra, -ae** (f), care, anxiety

**cúria, -ae** (f), senate house

54 **cūriósē,** carefully

**cúrō** (1), take care of, care about

56 **cúrsus, -ūs** (m), run, course, voyage

66 **curvámen, -inis** (n), curve

**cústōs, -ódis** (m), guard, guardian

# D

64 **dámnō** (1), to condemn, sentence

**dē** (+ abl.), down from, concerning, about

**débeō** (2), to owe, (one) ought

57 **débilis, -is, -e,** feeble, powerless

**dēcédō, -dere** (3), -ssī, -ssum, to die

**décem,** ten

56 **dēcérnō, -érnere** (3), -révī, -rétum, to decide, decree

61 **dēcértō** (1), to fight to the finish, fight it out

63 **décet, -ére** (2), -uit (+ acc.), it is right or fitting for (one to . . . ), one ought

55 **dēcrépitus, -a, -um,** decrepit, feeble

62 **decumánus, -a, -um,** related to the tenth (legion, e.g.)

56 **decúria, -ae** (f), group, panel, board, guild

58 **decúriō, -ónis** (m), town councilman

64 **decuriōnátus, -ūs** (m), decurionate, office of decurion

**dēféndō, -dere** (3), -dī, -sum, to defend

62 **dēfénsiō, -ónis** (f), defense

58 **défero, -rre** (irreg.), détulī, delátum, to bring down

**dēféssus, -a, -um,** weary, tired

61 **dēfíciō, -ícere** (3), -écī, -éctum, to lack, fail

**deínde,** then

65 **dēlátor, -óris** (m), informer, accuser

**dēléctō** (1), to delight

55 **dēléctor, -árī** (1), -átus sum, to please, amuse

**déleō, -ére** (2), -évī, -étum, to destroy

55 **dēlicátus, -a, -um,** spoiled, fussy, fastidious

54 **dēlicátus, -ī** (m), favorite, pet

154

63 dēmíttō, -íttere (3), -īsī, -íssum, to send down, cast down

dēnárius, -ī (m), denarius, silver coin

67 dénī, -ae, -a, ten each, ten

56 dénique, at last, finally

66 dénsus, -a, -um, dense

55 deórsum (adverb), down

65 dēpósitum, -ī (n), deposit (of money or valuables, for safekeeping)

55 dēprehéndō, -dere (3), -dī, -sum, to seize, catch

61 dēprimō, -ímere (3), -éssī, -éssum, to sink, press down

57 dēpúgnō (1), to fight it out

56 dēsīdérium, -ī (n), desire, longing

dēsíderō (1), to desire, wish

62 dēsígnō (1), to mark, indicate

65 dēsinō, -ínere (3), -iī, -itum, to stop, cease

66 dēspíciō, -ícere (3), -éxī, -éctum, to look down on

62 dēstítuō, -úere (3), -uī, -útum, to desert, abandon

61 dēsum, -ésse (irreg.), -fuī, to be lacking

62 détrahō, -here (3), -xī, -ctum, to drag from, strip off

57 dētrīméntum, -ī (n), damage, harm

déus, déī (m), (dat. and abl. pl. dīs), god

dévorō (1), to devour, eat

déxt(c)ra, -ae (f), right hand

68 diaéta, -ae (f) (Greek), room, private apartment

dícō, -cere (3), -xī, -ctum, to say, tell

65 mále dícere ( + dat.), to speak ill of, insult, curse

57 dictátor, -óris (m), dictator, magistrate with absolute power in emergencies

67 dictō (1), to dictate

55 dictáta, -órum (n pl), dictated lessons, rules

64 díctum, -ī (n), thing spoken, word

61 dīdúcō, -cere (3), -xī, -ctum, to separate, draw apart

díēs, -éī (m), day

63 diffúndō, -úndere (3), -údī, -úsum, to spread out, extend

60 dígnitās, -átis (f), reputation

63 dígnor, -árī (1), -átus sum, to consider worthy

55 dígnus, -a, -um, worthy, deserving

57 dīléctus, -ūs (m), draft of troops, levy

dīligénter, carefully

díligō, -ígere (3), -éxī, -éctum, to love, care for

dīmíttō, -íttere (3), -īsī, -íssum, to send away, let go

54 dīréctum (adverb), directly, simply, straightforwardly

61 dīréptiō, -ónis (f), breach

66 dīrimō, -ímere (3), -émī, -émptum, to separate, divide

60 dīrípiō, -ípere (3), -ípuī, -éptum, to lay waste, plunder

discédō, -dere (3), -ssī, -ssum, to depart, leave, go away

64 discéssus, -ūs (m), separation, departure

díscō, -ere (3), dídicī, to learn

67 discúrsus, -ūs (m), a running back and forth or around

55 dispēnsátor, -óris (m), steward, household manager

64 dīspíciō, -ícere (3), -éxī, -éctum, to consider, reflect on

65 dísputō (1), to dispute, argue

64 distríbuō, -úere, -uī, -útum, to distribute

díū, for a long time

56 diútius (adverb), longer

66 dīvérsitās, -átis (f), diversity, difference

63 dīvínus, -a, -um, divine

63 dívus, -ī (m), god

dō, dáre (1), dédī, dátum, to give

dólor, -óris (m), grief, pain, resentment

55 domésticus, -a, -um, of the house or family, close, intimate, tame

dómina, -ae (f), mistress, lady of the house

dóminus, -ī (m), master, owner

dómus, -ūs (f), house

dómī, at home

65 dónō (1), to present, give, donate

dórmiō (4), to sleep

66 dórsum, -ī (n), back, ridge

60 dúbitō (1), to hesitate, be in doubt

64 dúbius, -a, -um, doubtful

56 ducéntī, -ae, -a, two hundred

dúcō, -cere (3), -xī, -ctum, to lead

66 dúctilis, -is, -e, led, channeled

67 dúlcis, -is, -e, sweet, pleasant

dum, while, as long as

64 dumtáxat, at most, not more than

dúo, dúae, dúo, two

58 dux, -cis (m), leader, general

# E

Écce! Look at . . . ! Look!

65 ēdíctum, -ī (n), edict, proclamation

66 éditus, -a, -um, raised, high

56 éffluō, -úere (3), -úxī, to flow out, spill

56 effúndō, -úndere (3), -údī, -úsum, to pour out

égo, I

58 ēíciō, ēícere (3), ēiécī, ēiéctum, to throw out

64 eiúsmodī: see modus

64 éloquēns, -ntis, eloquent

155

60 **éloquor, -quī** (3), **-cútus sum**, to speak, speak out

67 **ēmendátiō, -ónis** (*f*), emendation, correction

64 **ēméndō** (1), to correct, reform

61 **ēminus** (*adverb*), at long range, from a distance

**émō, émere** (3), **ēmī, émptum**, to buy

**énim** (*postpositive*), for

61 **ēnítor, -tī** (3), **-sus sum**, to strive, make an effort

57 **ēníxē**, eagerly

66 **entheátus, -a, -um**, frenzied, raving

**éō, íre** (*irreg.*), **īvī, ítum**, to go

**epístula, -ae** (*f*), letter

55 **épulum, -ī** (*n*), (public) feast, banquet

55 **éques, -itis** (*m*), horseman, knight; a member of the equestrian class at Rome

60 **équidem**, certainly, surely

62 **equitátus, -ūs** (*m*), cavalry

**équus, -ī** (*m*), horse

**érgā** (+ *acc.*), towards

54 **érgō**, therefore, so

**ērípiō, -ípere** (3), **-ípuī, -éptum**, to snatch from, take away

**érrō** (1), to wander

55 **ésseda, -ae** (*f*), Celtic war-chariot

55 **essedárius, -a, -um**, fighting from a chariot

54 **ēsurítiō, -ónis** (*f*), famine

**et**, and, also, too

**étiam**, also, even

58 **etiámsī**, even if, although

60 **étsī**, even if, although

54 **ēvéniō, -eníre** (4), **-ḗnī, -éntum**, to happen, turn out

61 **ēvéntus, -ūs** (*m*), outcome, consequence, result

68 **ēvíncō, -íncere** (3), **-ícī, -íctum**, to conquer, surpass

61 **évocō** (1), to call out, summon

**ex, ē** (+ *abl.*), from, out of

58 **exardéscō, -déscere** (3), **-sī**, to catch fire, blaze up

**excédō, -dere** (3), **-ssī, -ssum**, to go out, leave

55 **excéllēns, -ntis**, excellent, outstanding

60 **excípiō, -ípere** (3), **-ḗpī, -éptum**, to take in, receive, catch

**éxcitō** (1), to stir up, excite, rouse, wake up

**exclámō** (1), to cry out, exclaim

68 **exclúdō, -dere** (3), **-sī, -sum**, to shut out, exclude

65 **excútiō, -tere** (3), **-ssī, -ssum**, to examine, inspect, shake out

56 **exémplar, -áris** (*n*), copy, transcript

61 **exémplum, -ī** (*n*), example, copy, precedent

**éxeō, -íre** (*irreg.*), **-iī, -itum**, to go out, get out, escape

**exérceō** (2), to exercise, occupy, keep busy

60 **exércitus, -ūs** (*m*), army

63 **exhíbeō** (2), to present, show

67 **éxigō, -ígere** (3), **-ḗgī, -áctum**, to spend (time)

**exímius, -a, -um**, outstanding

**éximō, -ímere** (3), **-ḗmī, -émptum**, to remove, omit

61 **exístimō** (1), to think, suppose

55 **éxitus, -ūs** (*m*), outcome, end

54 **exórō** (1), to pray for (with the implication that your prayer will be answered)

58 **expedítus, -a, -um**, lightly equipped

**expéllō, -éllere** (3), **-ulī, -úlsum**, to drive out, expel

**expérior, -írī** (4), **-tus sum**, to test, try, experience, undergo

**explicō** (1), to unfold, disentangle, explain

61 **expóscō, -ere** (3), **expopóscī**, to ask for, beg

54 **éxpuō, -úere** (3), **-uī, -útum**, to spit out, spit

59 **exscíndō, -ndere** (3), **-dī, -ssum**, to destroy utterly

59 **exsílium, -ī** (*n*), exile

61 **éxstruō, -ere** (3), **-xī, -ctum**, to pile up, build

**exténdō, -dere** (3), **-dī, -tum**, to stretch out, extend

59 **extérminō** (1), to drive out, banish

**éxtrā** (+ *acc.*), outside, out

**éxtrahō, -here** (3), **-xī, -ctum**, to pull out, drag out

58 **extúrbō** (1), to take by storm

67 **éxul, -lis** (*m*), exile, outcast

# F

65 **fáber, -brī** (*m*), craftsman, workman

**fábula, -ae** (*f*), story, fable, fiction

**fácilis, -is, -e**, easy

**fácile**, easily

**fáciō, -ere** (3), **fḗcī, fáctum**, to make, do

56 **fáctum, -ī** (*n*), thing done, deed, fact

57 **fáctiō, -ónis** (*f*), gang, political partisans

61 **facúltās, -átis** (*f*), opportunity

65 **fállō, -lere** (3), **feféllī, -sum**, to betray, falsify

56 **fálsus, -a, -um**, false, wrong

58 **fáma, -ae** (*f*), rumor, reputation

60 **fámes, -is** (*f*), hunger

156

família, -ae (f), family, household, troupe — 55
familiáris, -is (m/f), close friend — 67
56 fáscio (1), to bandage, swathe — 63
55 fáteor, -ērī (3), fassus sum, to admit, confess — 63
56 fátum, -ī (n), fate, destiny — 56
fáveō, -ére (2), fávī, faútum (+ dat.), to favor, support — 67 67
55 fávor, -óris (m), support, popularity
56 fávus, -ī (m), honeycomb
félix, -ícis, happy, lucky, fortunate
fémina, -ae (f), woman — 56
fére, almost, approximately — 64
51 feriō, ferīre (4), to strike — 54
férō, -rre (irreg.), túlī, látum, to carry, bring, bear — 62
51 férreus, -a, -um, made of iron — 55
55 férrum, -ī (n), iron, steel
férula, -ae (f), cane — 67
56 féssus, -a, -um, weary, tired — 61
50 festīnátiō, -ónis (f), haste — 62
festīnō (1), to hurry — 59
55 féstus, -a, -um, pertaining to a holiday, festive — 62
fidélis, -is, -e, faithful
fidēs, -éī (f), good faith, reliability, trust
52 fidúcia, -ae (f), confidence — 59
fília, -ae (f), daughter — 65
fílius, -ī (m), son
55 fílix, -icis (f), a fern, weed, worthless person
57 fílum, -ī (n), thread
fínis, -is (m), end — 55
53 fínēs, fínium (m pl), territory
fíō, fíerī (irreg.), fáctus sum, to become, be made, be done, happen — 55
53 físcus, -ī (m), emperor's private funds — 68
55 flagéllum, -ī (n), whip
58 flágrō (1), to blaze, flame
58 flámen, -inis (m), priest (of a particular god or deified emperor) — 54
55 flātúra, -ae (f), breath, fighting spirit — 57
56 fléō, -ére (2), -évī, -étum, to weep
56 flúctus, -ūs (m), wave
56 flúmen, -inis (n), river, stream
57 fócus, -ī (m), fireplace
56 fóns, -ntis (m), fountain, spring — 66
fórās (adverb), out of doors, in public
55 fórma, -ae (f), rule, formula
57 fórnix, -icis (m), arch
fórte (adverb), by chance — 61
fórtis, -is, -e, brave, strong
53 fortitúdō, -inis (f), courage
56 fortúna, -ae (f), fortune, good fortune, prosperity — 68
fórum, -ī (n), forum, marketplace
frángō, -ngere (3), frégī, -ctum, to break — 57

fráter, -tris (m), brother
frenéticus, -a, -um, raving mad
fréquēns, -ntis, frequent
frequénter, frequently
frequéntō (1), to frequent, attend, visit frequently
frígeō, -ére (2), to freeze, be cold
frígidus, -a, -um, cold, trivial
frígus, -oris (n), cold
fróns, -ntis (f), forehead, front
in frónte, frontage, length of the side of a property fronting on a road
frūgálitās, -átis (f), frugality, sober habits
frūgáliter, with thrift, with restraint
frūníscor, -íscī (3), -ítus sum, to enjoy
frúor, -ī (3), -ctus sum (+ abl.), to enjoy, have benefit of
fúga, -ae (f), a fleeing, rout, escape
fúgiō, -ere (3), fúgī, to flee
fultúra, -ae (f), support
fundāméntum, -ī (n), foundation
fúnditor, -óris (m), slinger
fūnéstō (1), to pollute with murder
fúngor, -gī (3), -ctus sum (+ abl.), to perform, discharge
fúnus, -eris (n), funeral
fūr, -ris (m), thief
fúria, -ae (f), frenzy, madness
fúrtum, -ī (n), theft, fraud
fústis, -is (m), club, stick

# G

gallīnáceus, -a, -um, belonging to domestic poultry
gallus gallīnáceus, poultry-cock, barnyard rooster
gárrulus, -a, -um, talkative, prattling
gaúdeō, -ére (2), gavísus sum, to rejoice, enjoy oneself
gaúdium, -ī (n), joy
gémitus, -ūs (m), groan
géner, -rī (m), son-in-law
gēns, -tis (f), family, clan, nation
génus, -eris (n), kind, race
gérō, -rere (3), -ssī, -stum, to wear, carry on, lead (a life)
gestátiō, -ónis (f), a place for riding, promenade
gladiátor, -óris (m), gladiator
gládius, -ī (m), sword
glāns, -ndis (f), acorn, acorn-shaped missile shot from a sling
glória, -ae (f), fame, glory
grándis, -is, -e, grown, mature, large
grándis nátū, advanced in years, elderly
grátiā (+ gen.), for the sake of

grátia, -iae (f), favor, kindness, gratitude
  grátiās ágere (+ dat.), to thank
gráviter, seriously
63 gubernáculum, -ī (n), rudder, helm
61 gubernátor, -ốris (m), helmsman
57 gubérnō (1), to govern, rule
56 gústō (1), to taste
56 gypsấtus, -a, -um, sealed with gypsum
  (plaster of Paris)

# H

  hábeō (2), to have, hold
60 hábet sē rēs, the situation is, things
  are
  hábitō (1), to live, dwell
64 haésitō (1), to hesitate, be undecided
66 hámus, -ī (m), hook
56 hérēs, -édis (m), heir
  héri, yesterday
65 hetaéria, -ae (f), political club or association
54 Heu! Alas! Ah me!
  hic, haec, hoc, this
  hīc (adverb), here
59 hícine = hic + -ne
67 híems, -mis (f), winter
  hílaris, -is, -e, cheerful
66 hinc, from here, over here
  hódiē, today
66 hólus, -eris (n), vegetables
  hómō, -inis (m), man, fellow
61 honéstus, -a, -um, respected, best
60   honéstē, respectably, honorably
68 hónor, -ốris (m), honor, (political) office
64 honōrárium, -ī (n), admission fee
68 honốrō (1), to honor
  hóra, -ae (f), hour
56 hōrológium, -ī (n), clock, sundial
68 hórreō (2), to tremble at, dread
54 horríbilis, -is, -e, horrible
  hórtor, -árī (1), -átus sum, to encourage,
  urge
  hórtus, -ī (m), garden
  hóstis, -is (m), enemy
  hūc, here, to here
65 hūmánitās, -átis (f), humanity, human
  kindness
  hūmánus, -a, -um, human

# I

  iáceō (2), to lie, be lying down, be at
  rest, be idle
  iáciō, -ere (3), iếcī, -tum, to throw
  iáctō (1), to toss
  iam, now, already
  íbi, there

64 idcírcō, for that reason
  ídem, éadem, ídem, the same
  idéntidem, again and again, repeatedly
56 ídeō, for this reason, therefore
56 idốneus, -a, -um, suitable, appropriate
54 iēiúnium, -ī (n), a fast, fast-day
  ígitur, therefore
68 ignárus, -a, -um, ignorant of, not knowing
58 ígnis, -is (m), fire
60 ignóscō, -óscere (3), -ốvī, -ốtum
  (+ dat.), to forgive, excuse
67 ignốtus, -a, -um, unknown
67 īlicétum, -ī (n), oak-grove
  ílle, ílla, íllud, that, he, she, it
66 íllīc, in that place, there
66 íllinc, from there, over there
  imágō, -inis (f), likeness, image, mental
  picture
  ímmemor, -ris (+ gen.), forgetful
  ímmō, rather, on the contrary
  ímmō vếrō, on the contrary, in fact
65 immódicus, -a, -um, excessive
  immortális, -is, -e, immortal
63 immūnitās, -átis (f), immunity, exemption
62 impedīméntum, -ī (n), baggage
  impédiō (4), to hinder, prevent, obstruct
55 impéndō, -dere (3), -dī, -sum, to spend,
  pay out
60 imperátor, -ốris (m), commander, general, emperor
58 imperítus, -a, -um, ignorant, unskilled
63 impérium, -ī (n), power, supreme authority, empire
  ímperō (1) (+ dat.), to order, command
65 ímpetrō (1), to obtain, secure by entreaty
  ímpetus, -ūs (m), attack
56 ímpleō, -ếre (2), -ếvī, -ếtum, to fill
  impốnō, -ónere (3), -ósuī, -situm, to
  place on, set on
67 ímprobus, -a, -um, bad, vile, shameless
61 (dē) imprōvīsō, unexpectedly
61 imprúdens, -ntis, ignorant, not expecting, not foreseeing
  in (+ abl.), in, on, among
  in (+ acc.), into, towards, until, against
67 inánis, -is, -e, empty, worthless, pointless
  incéndō, -dere (3), -dī, -sum, to burn,
  set on fire
  íncidō, -ere (3), -ī, incásum, to fall into,
  occur, turn up
62 incitátus, -a, -um, fast-moving, rapid
68 incrēdíbilis, -is, -e, incredible
  índe, from there, then, in consequence
  of that

65 índex, -icis (*m*), spy, informer
63 indiscrétus, -a, -um, without prejudice
　　or social distinction
56 indulgéntia, -ae (*f*), indulgence, kindness
68 indústria, -ae (*f*), industry, diligence
62 indústriē, with energy
　　íneō, -íre (*irreg.*), -iī, -itum, to go in,
　　enter
67 inéptus, -a, -um, silly, foolish
61 inérmis, -is, -e, unarmed
59 īnfélīx, -ícis, unhappy, unfortunate
58 ínferō, -re (*irreg.*), íntulī, illátum, to
　　bring in, carry in, inflict on
57 īnféstus, -a, -um, hostile
63 īnféctus, -a, -um, not done, undone
58 ínfimus, -a, -um, lowest, most vile
59 īnflámmō (1), to kindle, set aflame
66 īnfléctō, -ctere (3), -xī, -xum, to bend,
　　curve
65 īnflexíbilis, -is, -e, inflexible, stubborn
68 īnfructuósus, -a, um, fruitless
61 ínfula, -ae (*f*), wool headband worn by
　　suppliants
56 ingemḗscō, -éscere (3), -uī, to (begin to)
　　groan
　　íngēns, -ntis, huge, big, long
59 ingrátus, -a, -um, ungrateful
　　iníciō, -ícere (3), -iécī, -iéctum, to
　　throw in or on
57 inimīcítia, -ae (*f*), hostility
63 iníquitās, -átis (*f*), injustice, unfairness
59 inítium, -ī (*n*), beginning
64 iniúria, -ae (*f*), injury, injustice, wrong
63 iniústus, -a, -um, unjust, improper
65 innóxius, -a, -um, innocuous, harmless
　　ínquit, he (she) says, said
63 īnsániō (4), to act crazy
56 īnscríptiō, -ónis (*f*), inscription
59 īnsepúltus, -a, -um, unburied
58 īnsídiae, -árum (*f pl*), ambush
61 īnsígne, -is (*n*), badge, token, insignia
　　īnspíciō, -ícere (3), -éxī, -éctum, to examine, look at
66 ínstitor, -óris (*m*), shopkeeper
　　īnstítuō, -úere (3), -uī, -útum, to establish, set up, organize
62 īnstō, -áre (1), -itī, to pursue eagerly, be
　　at hand, be impending
68 intáctus, -a, -um, untouched, unused
62 ínteger, -gra, -grum, whole, fresh
　　intéllegō, -gere (3), -xī, -ctum, to understand, realize
　　ínter (+ *acc.*), between, among
63 intercédō, -dere (3), -ssī, -ssum, to intervene, oppose
60 interclúdō, -dere (3), -sī, -sum, to shut
　　off

　　intérdiū, during the day, by day
62 interfíciō, -fícere (3), -fécī, -féctum, to
　　kill
54 ínterim, meanwhile
57 intérrēx, -égis (*m*), temporary chief magistrate
　　intérrogō (1), to ask, question, interrogate
67 intérsum, -ésse (*irreg.*), -fuī (+ *dat.*), to
　　be present, attend
55 intestína, -órum (*n pl*), intestines
　　íntrā (+ *acc.*), inside, within
　　intróeō, -íre (*irreg.*), -iī, -itum, to enter,
　　go into
64 intróitus, -ūs (*m*), entrance, admission
55 intrōvérsus (*adverb*), indoors
63 inūsitátus, -a, -um, unusual
64 inútilis, -is, -e, useless, undesirable
58 ínvehō, -here (3), -xī, -ctum, to speak
　　out against, attack with words
　　invéniō, -eníre (4), -énī, -éntum, to
　　come upon, find
65 ínvicem, back and forth, in turn, responsively
58 invídia, -ae (*f*), anger, hatred
63 invísō, -ere (3), -ī, -um, to go to see, inspect
55 ínvolō (1), to fly at, attack, carry off
54 invólvo, -vere (3), -vī, -útum, to wrap
　　in, wrap up
　　ípse, ípsa, ípsum, himself, herself, itself
54 ípsimus, -ī (*m*), master of a household
　　íra, -ae (*f*), anger
　　īrátus, -a, -um, angry
　　is, éa, id, he, she, it, this, that
54 íste, -a, -ud, this, that (of yours) (often
　　disparaging)
60 ístīc, there (where you are)
　　íta, thus, in this way
　　ítaque, and so, therefore
58 ítem, likewise, also
　　íter, -íneris (*n*), journey, road
　　íterum, again, a second time
　　iúbeō, -bḗre (2), -ssī, -ssum, to order
68 iucúnditās, -átis (*f*), pleasantness, charm
　　iucúndus, -a, -um, pleasant, enjoyable
59 iúdex, -icis (*m*), judge, juror
61 iūméntum, -ī (*n*), work animal
　　iúngō, -gere (3), -xī, -ctum, to join, attach
58 iūs, -iúris (*n*), law, right
62 iússum, -ī (*n*), command, bidding
61 iūstítia, -ae (*f*), justice
61 iústus, -a, -um, just, legitimate
61 iuvéntūs, -útis (*f*), youth, young men
　　(of military age)
63 iúvō, -áre (1), iúvī, iútum, to delight,
　　please, help

159

# L

lábor, -óris (m), work, toil
labốrō (1), to work, toil, suffer, be in
   distress

68 lábrum, -ī (n), lip
56 lāc, láctis (n), milk
66 lácus, -ūs (m), lake
   laédō, -dere (3), -sī, -sum, to harm, in-
     jure
66 lagốna, -ae (f), bottle
56 lāmentátiō, -ốnis (f), lamentation,
   weeping
54 lānátus, -a, -um, covered with wool
   lanísta, -ae (m) trainer (of gladiators)
55 lanistícius, -a, -um, owned and man-
   aged by a lanista
   lánius, -ī (m), butcher
   lápis, -idis (m), stone
56 lárgiter, abundantly, in abundance,
   ( + gen.) plenty (of )
57 largítiō, -ốnis (f), bribery, bribe
62 lassitúdō, -inis (f), exhaustion, weariness
   láteō (2), to lie in hiding, hide
61 laterícius, -a, -um, made of brick
56 lāticlávius, -a, -um, fit for a senator,
   princely
65 latrōcínium, -ī (n), robbery
63 látus, -a, -um, wide, broad
62 látus, -eris (n), side, flank
   laúdō (1), to praise
   lávō, -áre (1), lávī, -átum or lótum, to
   wash
   lectíca, -ae (f), litter
66 léctulus, -ī (m), bed
   léctus, -ī (m), bed, couch
61 lēgátus, -ī (m), second in command
60 légiō, -ốnis (f), legion, military unit
64 lēgítimus, -a, -um, legal, lawful, pre-
   scribed
56 légō, -ere (3), légī, léctum, to read,
   choose
   léō, -ốnis (m), lion
   lépus, -oris (m), rabbit
66 léviter, lightly, slightly
57 lēx, légis (f), law
65 libéllus, -ī (m), notice, poster
   libénter, gladly
56 líber, -era, -erum, free, belonging to
   freedom
   líberī, -ốrum (m pl), children
   líberō (1), to set free
64 libértās, -átis (f), liberty, freedom
   lībértus, -ī (m), freedman
63 líbet, -ére (2), -uit ( + dat.), it is pleasing, agreeable
58 librárius, -ī (m), copier, secretary
   lícet, -ére (2), -uit ( + dat.), it is allowed

---

   límen, -inis (n), threshold, doorway
66 límes, -itis (m), path, line
   língua, -ae (f), tongue, speech
66 líppus, -a, -um, bleary-eyed
67 līs, lítis (f), quarrel, dispute
   líttera, -ae (f), letter (of the alphabet)
   lítterae, -árum (f pl), letter, epistle,
   literature
   lítus, -oris (n), shore
55 lívidus, -a, -um, black and blue (as by
   bruising)
   lócus, -ī (m; n in pl), place
   lóngus, -a, -um, long, tall
   lóngē, far
66 lóquāx, -ácis, talkative
   lóquor, -ī (3), locútus sum, to speak,
   talk
55 lóripēs, -edis, clubfooted
   lúcet, -ére (2), lúxit, to be light, to be
   day, to shine
   lucérna, -ae (f), lamp
59 lūctuốsus, -a, -um, distressing, heartbreaking
58 lúctus, -ūs (m), mourning, grief
   lúdō, -dere (3), -sī, -sum, to play, have
   fun
   lúdus, ī (m), game, school
58 lúgeō, -ére (2), lúxī, lúctum, to grieve,
   mourn, lament
59 lúō, -ere (3), to pay, suffer, atone for
   poénās lúere, to pay the price, suffer
   punishment
66 lústrum, -ī (n), a five-year period
58 lútō (1), to cover with mud, make dirty
   lútum, -ī (n), mud
   lūx, lúcis (f), light, daylight, dawn
62 luxúria, -ae (f), luxury
66 lýmpha, -ae (f), water
67 lyrístēs, -ae (m), lyre-player

# M

67 mádēns, -ntis, wet, moist
68 maéstus, -a, -um, sad
   mágis, more, rather
   magistrátus, -ūs (m), magistrate, magis-
   tracy
59 magnitúdō, -inis (f), magnitude, size
   magnópere, greatly
   mágnus, -a, -um, great, big, large, loud
   (voice)
   maíor, -ốris, greater, bigger
58 maledíctum, -ī (n), insult, taunt
66 malleátor, -ốris (m), hammerer, beater
   mấlō, -lle (irreg.), -luī, to prefer
   málus, -a, -um, bad, evil
   mále (adverb), badly
   mandátum, -ī (n), order, instruction

mā́ne, early in the day, in the morning 64

mā́neō, -ére (2), -sī, -sum, to remain, stay 65

manifḗstus, -a, -um, clear, evident 58

manucíolum, -ī (n), handful, small bundle 65

manūmíttō, -míttere (3), -mī́sī, -míssum, to manumit, set (a slave) free 54

mā́nus, -ūs (f), hand, band (of men) 55

márculus, -ī (m), small hammer, mallet 54

mā́re, -is (n), sea

margarī́tum, -ī (n), pearl

marítimus, -a, -um, belonging to the sea, maritime 54

marī́tus, -ī (m), husband

mássa, -ae (f), mass, heap 63

matélla, -ae (f), vessel, chamber pot 68

mā́ter, -tris (f), mother

mātéria, -ae (f), timber, matter

māxílla, -ae (f), jaw 61

máximus, -a, -um, very great, greatest, very large 63

médius, -a, -um, mid-, middle of

Mehércule! or Mehérculēs! By Hercules! Indeed! 60

mélior, meliṓris, better 59

méminī, -inísse (perfect with present meaning) (+ gen. or acc.), to remember 55

mémor, -oris (+ gen.), remembering, mindful of

memória, -ae (f), memory 64

mēns, -tis (f), mind, heart, reason, sanity 60, 66

ménsa, -ae (f), table 61

ménsis, -is (m), month

méntior, -ī́rī (4), -ī́tus sum, to lie

méreō (2) (sometimes deponent), to deserve, earn

merīdiā́nus, -a, -um, of noon, midday 54

mérítō, deservedly

mérus, -a, -um, pure, undiluted, nothing but

merx, -cis (f), merchandise, goods

métuō, -ere (3), -ī, metū́tum, to fear, be afraid of 63

métus, -ūs (m), fear

méus, -a, -um, my, mine

mícō, -áre (1), -uī, to move quickly to and fro, flash; to play morra 68

mī́les, -itis (m), soldier

mīlitáris, -is, -e, military

mílle, a thousand

mílvus, -ī (m), kite (a bird of prey)

mínimē, least, not at all, by no means, no

miníster, -trī (m), subordinate official, attendant

ministérium, -ī (n), service, employment

miní́stra, -ae (f), attendant

minitābúndus, -a, -um, menacing

mínor, -ā́rī (1), -ā́tus sum, to threaten

mínor, -ṓris, smaller

minū́tus, -a, -um, small, little

mī́rus, -a, -um, wonderful, marvelous, strange

miscix (spelling and meaning uncertain), mixed, diluted, wishy-washy

miséllus, -a, -um (diminutive of míser), poor little

míser, -era, -erum, unhappy, miserable, wretched

miséreor, -érī (2), -itus sum (+ gen.), to pity, take pity on

míseret (mē) (impersonal + gen.), I pity

miséria, -ae (f), affliction, trouble

míttō, -ere (3), mī́sī, míssum, to send, let go

mōbílitās, -ā́tis (f), quickness, mobility, maneuverability

moderátiō, -ṓnis (f), moderation, restraint

modéstē, with restraint, under control

módo, only, only recently, just now
  nōn módo . . . sed étiam, not only . . . but also
  módo . . . módo, now . . . now, sometimes . . . sometimes

módus, -ī (m), way, method
  eiúsmodī, of this kind, this sort of
  núllō módō, in no way, not at all

móllis, -is, -e, soft, gentle

mōméntum, -ī (n), a short period of time, a (short) distance

móneō (2), to advise, warn

mōns, -tis (m), mountain, hill

monuméntum, -ī (n), monument, tomb, reminder, token

mórdeō, -dére (2), momórdī, -sum, to bite

mórior, -ī (3), -tuus sum, to die

móror, -ā́rī (1), -ā́tus sum, to delay, remain, stay

mors, -tis (f), death

mortā́lis, -is, -e, mortal, human

mórtuus, -a, -um, dead

mōs, mṓris (m), custom, (pl) habits, ways, character (of a person)

mótor, -ṓris (m), one who moves, shakes, rocks

móveō, -ére (2), mṓvī, mṓtum, to move, remove, shake

mox, soon, presently

múlier, -eris (f), woman

multitū́dō, -inis (f), crowd, mob

múltus, -a, -um, much, (pl) many
  múltum (adverb), much, greatly, very

63 múndus, -ī (m), world, universe
58 mūnicípium, -ī (n), town
64 mūnítiō, -ónis (f), construction, repair
múnus, -eris (n), duty, gift, (gladiatorial)
show
múrus, -ī (m), wall
mūs, múris (m), mouse
61 músculus, -ī (m), covered gallery used in
siege warfare

# N

nam, for
61 nancíscor, -ī (3), náctus sum, to gain
possession of, acquire, get
55 nánnus, -ī (m), dwarf
nárrō (1), to tell (a story)
náscor, -ī (3), nátus sum, to be born
nátō (1), to swim
nātúra, -ae (f), nature
56 naúfragō (1), to be wrecked
66 naúfragus, -ī (m), a shipwrecked person
61 naúta, -ae (m), sailor
66 nāvícula, -ae (f), small ship, boat
návigō (1), to sail
56 návis, -is (f), ship
-ne, (indicates a question)
nē (+ subjunctive), in order to prevent,
not to
nec, and . . . not
nec . . . nec . . . , neither . . . nor
64 necessáriō (adverb), necessarily, unavoidably
62 necessárius, -a, -um, necessary
necésse, necessary
67 necéssitās, -átis (f), necessity, necessary
duty, obligation
68 necessitúdō, -inis (f), (personal) connection, relative
nécō (1), to kill
59 négō (1), to say that . . . not, deny, refuse, decline
56 negōtiátiō, -ónis (f), business
56 negótior, -árī (1), -átus sum, to do business, be a businessman
némō, -inis (m), no one
66 némus, -oris (n), wooded pasture, grove
neque, and . . . not
55 nérvia, -órum (n pl), sinews, tendons
nésciō (4), to be ignorant, not know
54 nésciō quid, something or other
níger, -gra, -grum, black
68 nigréscō, -éscere (3), -uī, to grow black
níhil, nothing
nímis, too much, too
62 nímius, -a, -um, excessive, too much
nísi, unless, if . . . not, except

66 nítēns, -ntis, shining, glittering
63 nōbíliter, with distinction, splendidly
nóceō (2) (+ dat.), to harm
noctúrnus, -a, -um, occurring at night
55 noctúrnae, -árum (f pl), Nocturnal
Ones, witches
nólō, -lle, -luī, to be unwilling, not
wish, refuse
nómen, -inis (n), name
61 nōminátim (adverb), by name
nóminō (1), to name, mention by name,
speak of
nōn, not
nóndum, not yet
nónus, -a, -um, ninth
nōs, we, us
nóster, -tra, -trum, our
nótus, -a, -um, known, well-known
66 novácula, -ae (f), razor
nox, -ctis (f), night
67 nóxius, -a, -um, harmful, dangerous,
rapacious
núbō, -bere (3), -psī, -ptum (+ dat.),
to marry
54 núdus, -a, -um, naked, bare
56 núgae, -árum (f pl), trifles, jokes
núllus, -a, -um, no, none
Num . . . ? Surely . . . not . . . ? (introduces a question that expects the
answer "no")
65 númen, -inis (n), divine power, divinity,
god
númerō (1), to count
númerus, -ī (m), number
66 nummulárius, -ī (m), money-changer
54 númmus, -ī (m) (irreg. gen. pl. núm-
mūm), coin, money
númquam, never
nunc, now
núper, recently
67 núptiae, -árum (f pl), wedding
63 nútus, -ūs (m), nod, divine will

# O

54 Ō! Oh! (expressing a wish)
63 ob (+ acc.), because of, on account of
63 óbeō, -íre (irreg.), -iī, -itum, to meet
(death), die
62 obíciō, -ícere (3), -iécī, -iéctum, to
throw in one's face, taunt
56 oblīvíscor, -víscī (3), -tus sum (+ gen.),
to forget
58 obscénus, -a, -um, obscene
óbsecrō (1), to beseech, beg
obsérvō (1), to watch, pay attention to,
comply with

162

65 **obstinátiō, -ónis** (f), obstinacy, stubbornness
59 **óbstō, -áre** (1), **-itī** (+ *dat.*), to stand against, oppose
65 **obstríngō, -ngere** (3), **-nxī, -ctum,** to bind up, tie to
68 **obvérsor, -árī** (1), **-átus sum,** to appear before (in thought or imagination)
67 **occásiō, -ónis** (f), opportunity
**occídō, -dere** (3), **-dī, -sum,** to kill
**óccupō** (1), to seize, occupy, take over
**occúrrō, -rrere** (3), **-rrī, -rsum** ( + *dat.*), to meet
54 **óculus, -ī** (m), eye
64 **ódor, odóris** (m), scent, odor
**offícium, -ī** (n), duty, job
67 **ólla, -ae** (f), pot
**ómnis, -is, -e,** all, the whole, every, each
56 **ónerō** (1), to load
57 **ópera, -ae** (f), effort, work, (political) henchman, ruffian
57    **óperam dáre,** to give attention to, work hard
**opériō, -íre** (4), **-uī, -tum,** to hide, cover
**opórtet, -ére** (2), **-uit** (+ *infin.*), it is proper, right, one must
**óppidum, -ī** (n), town
**ópprimō, -ímere** (3), **-éssī, -éssum,** to overwhelm
51 **oppugnátiō, -ónis** (f), attack, assault
52 **oppúgnō** (1), to attack, assault
50 **óps, ópis** (f), aid, help
57 **optimátēs, -átium** (m pl), the "best men," the senatorial party at Rome
**óptimus, -a, -um,** best, very good, excellent
   **óptimē,** best, very well, very carefully
**óptō** (1), to wish
**ópus, -eris** (n), work, effort, (penal) labor
57    **ópus est,** it is necessary, there is need of
58 **ōrátiō, -ónis** (f), speech, oration
**ōrátor, -óris** (m), orator, speaker
53 **órbis, -is** (m), circle
53    **órbis terrárum,** the world
58 **órbus, -a, -um,** bereaved
59 **órdō, -inis** (m), order, rank, class
**órior, -írī** (4), **-tus sum,** to rise, arise, begin
**órō** (1), to beg, entreat
**ōs, óris** (n), mouth, face, expression
**os, óssis** (n), bone
**osténdō, -dere** (3), **-dī, -tum,** to show, point out
54 **óstium, -ī** (n), door
54 **ōtiósus, -a, -um,** at leisure, idle, free from public duty, not working
67 **ótium, -ī** (n), leisure

# P

**paedagógus, -ī** (m), tutor
**paéne,** almost
65 **paeniténtia, -ae** (f), regret, repentance
63 **paénitet, -ére** (2), **-uit,** it causes one (*acc.*) to regret something (*gen.*), one regrets
57 **pálam,** openly, publicly
60 **pálma, -ae** (f), palm branch of victory
66 **pálmes, -itis** (m), vine-branch, vine
62 **palūdáméntum, -ī** (n), cloak worn by high-ranking military officers
66 **pálux, -ucis** (f), gold dust
**pánis, -is** (m), bread, food
54 **pánnus, -ī** (m), cloth, rag, garment
57 **pār, páris,** equal
**párcō, -cere** (3), **pepércī** (+ *dat.*), to spare
**párēns, -ntis** (m/f), parent, father, mother
**páreō** (2) (+ *dat.*), to obey
55 **páriō, -ere** (3), **péperī, -tum,** to bear, give birth to
**pars, -tis** (f), part, (political) party
**párvulus, -a, -um,** small, little, baby
**párvus, -a, -um,** small
**páscō, -cere** (3), **pávī, pástum,** to feed
54 **pássus, -a, -um,** dishevelled
**páter, -tris** (m), father
**pátior, -tī** (3), **-ssus sum,** to suffer, endure, permit
**pátiēns, -ntis,** (long-)suffering, patient
**pátria, -ae** (f), native land, home-town, town
57 **patrícius, -ī** (m), patrician, aristocrat
54 **patrimónium, -ī** (n), patrimony
66 **pátrius, -a, -um,** belonging to a father, father's
**patrónus, -ī** (m), patron, former master of a freed slave
59 **paúcī, -ae, -a,** few
   **paucíssimī, -ae, -a,** a very few
**paulátim,** gradually, little by little
58 **paúlō,** (by) a little
**paúper, -eris,** poor
**páveō, -ére** (2), **pávī,** to be frightened or terrified at
**pāx, pácis** (f), peace
**pecúnia, -ae** (f), money
**peíor, -óris,** worse
**penátēs, -ium** (m pl), household gods, home
**pénes** (+ *acc.*), in the possession of
**péragō, -ágere** (3), **-égī, -áctum,** to carry through, complete
**pérdō, -ere** (3), **-idī, -itum,** to destroy, lose
**perdúcō, -cere** (3), **-xī, -ctum,** to lead to, bring to

163

55   **péreō, -íre** (*irreg.*), **-iī, -itum,** to perish, die

    **pérferō, -rre** (*irreg.*), **pértulī, perlátum,** to bring to (a destination), deliver, report

61   **perfíciō, -ícere** (3), **-écī, -éctum,** to complete, finish

62   **pérfruor, -ī** (3), **-ūctus sum,** to enjoy

62   **perfúngor, -gī** (3), **-ctus sum,** to perform (a task), finish

67   **pergrátus, -a, -um,** very pleasing, very popular

    **perīculōsus, -a, -um,** dangerous

    **perículum, -ī** (*n*), danger

68   **permíttō, -íttere** (3), **-īsī, -íssum,** to permit, allow

67   **permūtō** (1), to change, modify

58   **perórō** (1), to complete a speech

58   **perpétuus, -a, -um,** continuous, complete, entire

54   **pérsequor, -quī** (3), **-cūtus sum,** to pursue, chase

54   **persevérō** (1), to persevere, continue, persist, last

    **persuádeō, -dére** (2), **-sī, -sum** ( + *dat.*), to persuade

62   **pertérreō, -ére** (2), **-uī, -itum,** to frighten, terrify

65   **pertinácia, -ae** (*f*), stubbornness

54   **pertíneō, -ére** (2), **-uī,** to pertain to, relate to, reach to, lie near

    **pervéniō, -eníre** (4), **-énī, -éntum,** to come through to, arrive at, reach

    **pēs, pédis** (*m*), foot

    **péssimus, -a, -um,** worst, very bad

59   **péstis, -is** (*f*), plague, disease

    **pétō, -ere** (3), **-īvī, -ītum,** to seek, aim at, attack

56   **philósophus, -ī** (*m*), philosopher

63   **píetās, -átis** (*f*), devotion (to duty)

67   **píger, -gra, -grum,** lazy, indolent

66   **píla, -ae** (*f*), pillar, column

54   **pílō** (1), to remove the hair from

54   **pílus, -ī** (*m*), a hair

56   **píngō, -ngere** (3), **-nxī, -ctum,** to paint, depict

54   **píper, -ris** (*n*), pepper

    **pīráta, -ae** (*m*), pirate

66   **píscor, -árī** (1), **-átus sum,** to fish

    **pístor, -óris** (*m*), miller, baker

56   **píus, -a, -um,** devoted to duty, loyal

    **pláceō, -ére** (2), **-uī** ( + *dat.*), to please

63   **plácidus, -a, -um,** kindly, indulgent, calm

54   **plánē,** wholly, absolutely, nothing but

54   **plángō, -gere** (3), **-xī, -ctum,** to beat, strike, mourn for

55   **plaúdō, -dere** (3), **-sī, -sum,** to applaud, clap the hands

57   **plēbs, -ébis** (*f*), plebeians, common people

    **plḗnus, -a, -um,** full

62   **plērúsque, -aque, -úmque,** most of, (*pl.*) very many

56   **plōrō** (1), to weep

    **plúit, -úere** (3), **plúit,** it is raining

    **plúrimus, -a, -um,** most, very much

    **plūs, plúris,** more

55   **plússcius, -a, -um,** knowing more than others, skilled (in witchcraft)

    **poéna, -ae** (*f*), punishment, penalty

    **poéta, -ae** (*m*), poet

56   **pōmum, -ī** (*n*), fruit, fruit tree

68   **póndus, -eris** (*n*), weight, quantity

    **pōnō, pónere** (3), **pósuī, pósitum,** to put, place

    **pōns, -ntis** (*m*), bridge

    **popína, -ae** (*f*), eating house, bar, cookshop

    **pópulus, -ī** (*m*), people

    **pórcus, -ī** (*m*), pig

54   **pórrō,** then, furthermore

    **pórta, -ae** (*f*), gate

59   **pórtus, -ūs** (*m*), harbor, haven

64   **posséssiō, -ónis** (*f*), possession

66   **possídeō, -idére** (2), **-édī, -éssum,** to take possession of

    **póssum, pósse** (*irreg.*), **pótuī,** to be able

    **post** ( + *acc.*), after

    **pósteā,** afterwards

    **pósterus, -a, -um,** next, following

    **póstquam,** after

    **postrḗmō,** finally

    **postrḗmus, -a, -um,** last

60   **potéstās, -átis** (*f*), power, opportunity

62   **pótior, -īrī** (4), **-ītus sum** ( + *abl.*), to get possession of, obtain

    **pótius,** rather, more (than)

61   **praecéptum, -ī** (*n*), command

55   **praecídō, -dere** (3), **-dī, -sum,** to cut off, cut through

66   **praecíngō, -gere** (3), **-xī, -ctum,** to gird, wrap around

    **praecípiō, -ípere** (3), **-épī, -éptum** ( + *dat.*), to instruct, order

    **praecipitáre** (sē), to hurl oneself, rush

    **praeclárus, -a, -um,** distinguished, famous

60   **praédium, -ī** (*n*), landed property, estate

    **praédō, -ónis** (*m*), robber

65   **praéeō, -íre** (*irreg.*), **-iī, -itum,** to go before, lead the way

    **praéferō, -férre** (*irreg.*), **-tulī, -látum,** to carry in front, give precedence to, prefer

62   **praefíciō, -ícere, -écī, -éctum** ( + *dat.*), to put in charge of

164

praefríngō, -íngere (3), -ḗgī, -áctum, to break off in front — 65

praemíttō, -íttere (3), īsī, -íssum, to send ahead — 58

praeséntia, -ae (f), presence

praesídium, -ī (n), defense, protection — 61

praésum, -ésse (irreg.), -fuī (+ dat.), to be in charge of — 60

praetéreā, besides, moreover

praetéreō, -íre (irreg.), -iī, -itum, to go past — 62

in praetéritum, in the past, formerly — 61

praetextátus, -a, -um, wearing the tóga praetéxta — 61

praétor, -óris (m), praetor — 58

praetúra, -ae (f), praetorship, office of praetor — 56

prátum, -ī (n), meadow, grass

právus, -a, -um, depraved, perverse

précor, -árī (1), -átus sum, to pray, beg, request — 63

prex, -écis (f), prayer, request

prímus, -a, -um, first

in prímīs, in particular

prímō, at first, first

prímum (adverb), first, at first

quam prímum, as soon as possible

ut prímum, when first, as soon as

prínceps, -cipis (m), emperor, leader, leading citizen

prístinus, -a, -um, previous, former

prīvátim, privately, in private

(in) prīvátō, in private, privately

prō (+ abl.), in front of, before, on behalf of, for, in place of, equivalent to

prō cónsule, proconsul

próbus, -a, -um, honest, upright

prōcónsul, -lis (m), proconsul — 54

prōcúmbo, -mbere (3), -buī, -bitum, to keel over — 55

prōcúrrō, -cúrrere (3), -cucúrrī, -cúrsum, to run forth, rush out

pródō, -ere (3), -idī, -itum, to give rise to, produce, appoint

proélium, -ī (n), battle

prōfíciō, -ícere (3), -écī, -éctum, to accomplish, gain

proficíscor, -icíscī (3), -éctus sum, to set out — 63

prōfúndō, -úndere (3), -údī, -úsum, to pour forth — 65

prohíbeō (2), to prohibit, forbid, prevent — 61

prōíciō, -ícere (3), -iécī, -iéctum, to throw forward or headlong — 64

proínde, therefore — 54

prōmíscuus, -a, -um, common, ordinary

próperō (1), to hurry, hasten

propínquus, -ī (m), relative

própius (adverb), nearer — 66

prōpónō, -ónere (3), -ósuī, -ósitum, to put forth — 65

própter (+ acc.), on account of

prósperus, -a, -um, prosperous, successful, favorable — 58

prōspíciō, -ícere (3), -éxī, -éctum, to see before one, to look out over — 61

prósum, -désse (irreg.), -fuī (+ dat.), to be useful, benefit, help — 60

prótinus, immediately

prōvídeō, -idére (2), -ídī, -ísum, to foresee, expect

prōvíncia, -ae (f), province

próximus, -a, -um, nearest, next

públicō (1), to publish, make public

públicus, -a, -um, public

in públicō, in public, publicly

púdet, -ére (2), -itum, it makes one (acc.) ashamed of something (gen.), one is ashamed

puélla, -ae (f), girl, girlfriend

púer, -erī (m), boy

púgna, -ae (f), battle, fight

púgnō (1), to fight

púlcher, -chra, -chrum, beautiful, handsome

pulchritúdō, -inis (f), beauty

púngō, -gere (3), púpugī, -ctum, to prick — 68

púniō (4), to punish

pūpílla, -ae (f), orphan — 68

purgátiō, -ónis (f), a cleaning — 64

púrus, -a, -um, pure, spotless, clean

pútō (1), to think, consider

## Q

quācúmque, wherever — 54

quadringentī, -ae, -a, four hundred — 55

quaérō, -rere (3), -sívī, -sítum, to seek, look for, ask (for) — 65

quáliscúmque, -iscúmque, -ecúmque, of whatever kind

Quam . . . ! How . . . !

quam, than

quam (+ superlative), as . . . as possible

quam tardíssimē, as late as possible — 63

quámquam, although

quámvīs, although

quándō, when

sī quándō, whenever

quántus, -a, -um, how big, how much

quántum (adverb), to what extent, to the extent to which

Quárē . . . ? For what reason . . . ? Why . . . ?

quártus, -a, -um, fourth

quási, as if

quátiō, -tere (3), -ssum, to shake — 66

quáttuor, four
56 quemadmodum, in what way, as
59 quéror, -rī (3), -stus sum, to moan,
    whine, complain
    quī, quae, quod, who, which, that
    Quī . . . ? Quae . . . ? Quod . . . ?
    What . . . ? Which . . . ?
54 quía, because, that
56 quīcúmque, quaecúmque, quod-
    cúmque, whoever, whatever
    quídam, quaédam, quóddam, a certain,
    (pl) some
    quídem, indeed
    nē . . . quídem, not even
    quiéscō, -ere (3), quiévī, quiétum, to
    rest
62 quiétus, -a, -um, at rest, inactive
60 quīn, (but) that, who . . . not
    quīnque, five
    Quis . . . ? Quid . . . ? Who . . . ?
    What . . . ? Which . . . ?
67 (sī) quis: see áliquis
55 quísquam, quícquam, anyone, anything
61 quísque, quaéque, quídque, each
56 quísquis, quícquid, whoever, whatever
    quō, there, to that place
    Quō . . . ? Where . . . to?
55 quod, because, that
    quóniam, since
    quóque, also
    quot, as many as
    Quot . . . ? How many . . . ?
66 quótiēns, as often as, whenever
    Quótus, -a, -um . . . ? Which (in nu-
    merical order) . . . ?

## R

    raéda, -ae (f), traveling carriage, coach
56 rána, -ae (f), frog
68 rárus, -a, -um, rare
63 rátiō, -ónis (f), reason
67 raúcus, -a, -um, hoarse
68 recédō, -dere (3), -ssī, -ssum, to with-
    draw, retire
62 récēns, -ntis, recent, fresh, untired
    récitō (1), to read aloud, recite
60 recognóscō, -óscere (3), -óvī, -itum, to
    recognize
63 reconcíliō (1), to reconcile, bring into
    harmony
67 recordátiō, -ónis (f), recollection
    réctus, -a, -um, right, proper, upright,
    honest, straight
60 récte ésse, to be all right
    réddō, -ere (3), -idī, -itum, to give back,
    return
    rédeō, -íre (irreg.), -iī, -itum, to return,
    go back

    redúcō, -cere (3), -xī, -ctum, to lead
    back, take back, bring back
    réferō, -rre (irreg.), réttulī, relátum, to
    bring back
57 reférre ad senátum, to put a motion
    before the senate
62 refúgiō, -úgere (3), -úgī, to turn and run
    away, flee for safety
65 régnō (1), to rule as king, reign
    régnum, -ī (n), kingdom
    regrédior, -dī (3), -ssus sum, to go back,
    return
54 religiósus, -a, -um, religious
61 réligō (1), to hold in place, make fast,
    secure
    relínquō, -ínquere (3), -íquī, -íctum, to
    leave, leave behind
60 relíquus, -a, -um, the rest of, the re-
    maining
60 relíquum est, it remains (to do some-
    thing)
61 remáneō, -ére (2), -sī, to remain
65 remíttō, -íttere (3), -īsī, -íssum, to send
    back
    repéllō, -ere (3), réppulī, repúlsum, to
    drive off, drive back, beat back
61 repentínus, -a, -um, sudden
    répetō, -ere (3), -ívī, -ítum, to seek
    again, return to
67 repónō, -ónere (3), -ósuī, -ósitum, to
    put back, repay
67 repútō (1), to think over, bear in mind,
    consider
68 réquiēs, -étis (f), rest
56 requiéscō, -éscere (3), -évī, -étum, to
    rest
67 requírō, -rere (3), -sívī, -sítum, to ask,
    inquire
    rēs, réī (f), thing, matter, affair, situa-
    tion
56 rēs géstae, deeds, exploits, history
57 rēs pública, republic, state
    rē vérā, really, actually
54 resalútō (1), to greet in return, return a
    greeting
55 résecō, -cáre (1), -cuī, -ctum, to cut off,
    clip
    resístō, -ístere (3), -titī (+ dat.), to re-
    sist, stand up to
56 respíciō, -ícere (3), -éxī, -éctum, to look
    round at
    respóndeō, -dére (2), -dī, -sum, to an-
    swer, reply
55 réstis, -is (f), rope
57 restítuō, -úere (3), -uī, -útum, to re-
    store, reinstate
59 retíneō, -ére (2), -uī, reténtum, to hold
    back, keep
67 retráctō (1), to rework, revise

166

rétrahō, -here (3), -xī, -ctum, to pull back, bring back, restore    58

retrōvérsus (*adverb*), backwards    56

revértor, -tī (3), -sus sum, to turn back, return, come home

révocō (1), to recall, call back

rēx, régis (*m*), king    67

ríguus, -a, -um, watering, irrigating

rīma, -ae (*f*), crack    55

rīsus, -ūs (*m*), laughter, laugh, smile

ríxa, -ae (*f*), quarrel, brawl    56

rogātor, -óris (*m*), beggar

rógō (1), to ask

rosārium, -ī (*n*), rose garden, rose plantation    59

róstrum, -ī (*n*), beak, a ship's ramming-beak    57, 61

    róstra, -órum (*n pl*), speaker's platform in the Forum, adorned with the beaks of captured enemy ships    66, 55

ruīna, -ae (*f*), ruin, collapse    59

rūmor, -óris (*m*), rumor

rúmpia, -ae (*f*), pike, spear

rúmpō, rúmpere (3), rúpī, rúptum, to burst, break    57

rúrsus, again

rūs, rúris (*n*), country (as opposed to city)    57

rústicus, -a, -um, of or belonging to the country or farm

rústicus, -ī (*m*), peasant, farmer

# S

sácculus, -ī (*m*), little sack, bag

sacrāméntum, -ī (*n*), oath    64

saéculum, -ī (*n*), reign, age

saépe, often

    quam saepíssimē, as often as possible

sagittárius, -ī (*m*), archer, bowman

sálūs, -útis (*f*), greetings, safety    55

salútō (1), to greet, welcome

sálvus, -a, -um, undamaged, all right, safe    55

sánctitās, -átis (*f*), holiness, sanctity    64

sánctus, -a, -um, hallowed, august    56

sápiēns, -ntis, wise    56

satélles, -itis (*m*), follower, henchman, accomplice

sátis, enough    56

saúcius, -a, -um, wounded

sáxum, -ī (*n*), rock, stone

sceléstus, -a, -um, wicked    54

scélus, -eris (*n*), crime    63

schéma, -atis (*n*) (Greek), figure of speech    59, 67

scílicet, obviously, of course, no doubt (sometimes ironic)

scíō (4), to know    60

scríba, -ae (*m*), scribe, clerk

scríbō, -bere (3), -psī, -ptum, to write

scúlpō, -pere (3), -psī, -ptum, to sculpt, carve

sē, himself, herself, oneself, itself, themselves

sēcédō, -dere (3), -ssī, -ssum, to withdraw, retire

sécō, -áre (1), -uī, -tum, to cut, beat, flog

secúndum ( + *acc.*), beside, next to, according to

sed, but

sédeō, -ére (2), sédī, séssum, to sit

sédēs, -is (*f*), site, abode

sédō (1), to settle, calm

sémis, -íssis (*m*), a half

sémita, -ae (*f*), path

sémper, always

sempitérnō, forever

semúncia, -ae (*f*), one twenty-fourth

senātor, -óris (*m*), senator

senátus, -ūs (*m*), senate

    senātūs cōnsúltum, decree of the senate

sénex, -is (*m*), old man

senténtia, -ae (*f*), motion, feeling, opinion

séntiō, -tíre (4), -sī, -sum, to feel, notice, realize

sepéliō, -elíre (4), -elívī, -últum, to bury

séptimus, -a, -um, seventh

sepúlc(h)rum, -ī (*n*), tomb

séquor, -quī (3), -cútus sum, to follow

serénus, -a, -um, clear, bright

sérius (*adverb*), too late

sérmō, -ónis (*m*), conversation, talk

sérvō (1), to save, keep, protect, take care of

sérvus, -ī (*m*), slave

sēstertiárius, -a, -um, worth one sēstértius, i.e., worthless

sēstértius, -ī (*m*) (*gen pl*, sēstértium), sestertius, coin worth four ásses

sevérus, -a, -um, severe, harsh, heartless

sévir, -irī (*m*), member of a board of six

    sévir Augustális, a priest in charge of the worship of the emperor in provincial towns

sēvirátus, -ūs (*m*), the office of sévir

sī, if

sīc, thus, in this way

síccitās, -átis (*f*), dryness, drought

sídus, -eris (*n*), star

sígnifer, -erī (*m*), standard-bearer, leader

sígnō (1), to affix a seal to, attest by affixing a seal to

sígnum, -ī (*n*), signal, sign

síleō (2), to be silent

símilis, -is, -e (+ dat.), like, similar (to)
68 simplícitās, -átis (f), frankness, honesty
símul, together, at the same time
61 simulácrum, -ī (n), image, statue
60 sīn (sī + -ne), but if, on the other hand
síne (+ abl.), without
60 singuláris, -is, -e, extraordinary, unique
54 síngulī, -ae, -a, single, individual, each
and every one
siníster, -tra, -trum, left
66 sínus, -ūs (m), curve, bay
65 sístō, -ere (3), stítī, státum, to set up,
establish
58 síve, or rather
66 sócculus, -ī (m), low-heeled shoe worn
by comic actors
59 sócius, -ī (m), ally
sōl, sólis (m), sun
58 sōlácium, -ī (n), comfort, consolation,
relief
sóleō, -ére (2), -itus sum, to be accustomed, in the habit
sōlitúdō, -inis (f), loneliness, solitude
57 sólum (adverb), only
57 nōn sólum . . . sed étiam, not
only . . . but also
sólus, -a, -um, alone
63 sólvō, -vere (3), -vī, -útum, to release,
set free
sómnus, -ī (m), sleep
sórdidus, -a, -um, dirty
66 spatiósus, -a, -um, spacious
62 spátium, -ī (n), space
65 spéciēs, -éī (f), appearance, kind, type
59 spectáculum, -ī (n), sight, spectacle
spectátor, -óris (m), spectator, onlooker
spēlúnca, -ae (f), cave
61 spérō (1), to hope
61 spēs, -éī (f), hope
59 spírō (1), to breathe, be alive
67 spónda, -ae (f), bed, couch
spōnsália, -ium (n pl), betrothal
státim, immediately
státua, -ae (f), statue
64 státuō, -úere (3), -uī, -útum, to lay
down a rule, establish
57 státus, -ūs (m), state, condition, situation
stō, stáre (1), stétī, státum, to stand
54 stoláta, -ae (f), woman dressed in a stóla
(long robe)
55 strāmentícius, -a, -um, of straw
55 strāméntum, -ī (n), straw
55 strátum, -ī (n), blanket, saddlecloth,
saddle
strépitus, -ūs (m), noise, din
54 strídeō, -ére (2), -ī, to shriek, howl
54 strídor, -óris (m), a shrieking, howling
54 stríga, -ae (f), witch

stríngō, -ngere (3), -nxī, -ctum, to draw
(a sword)
67 strúēs, -is (f), heap, pile
stúdeō (2) (+ dat.), to study, favor, support
63 stultítia, -ae (f), foolishness, folly
56 suávis, -is, -e, sweet, delightful
61 subdúcō, -cere (3), -xī, -ctum, to pull
from under, remove
58 súbeō, -íre (irreg.), -iī, -itum, to go under, undergo, endure, occur
súbitō, suddenly
55 subolfáciō, -ere (3), to perceive as if by
smell, suspect
58 subséllium, -ī (n), bench
61 súbsum, -ésse, súffuī (+ dat.), to be
under
62 succédō, -dere (3), -ssī, -ssum (+ dat.),
to relieve, reinforce
57 succíngō, -gere (3), -xī, -ctum, to equip
61 succúrrō, -rrere (3), -rrī, -rsum (+ dat.),
to help, aid
68 sūdárium, ī (n), towel
54 súdō (1), to sweat
68 súfferō, súfferre (irreg.), sústulī,
sublátum, to take up
55 súfflō (1), to blow on, breathe on
68 suffrágium, -ī (n), vote, influence ex-
erted on behalf of a candidate
66 sulpurátus, -a, -um, sulfured
sum, ésse (irreg.), fúī, to be
65 súmma, -ae (f), sum, total, full extent
55 ad súmmam, in sum, in short
57 súmmē, in the highest degree, very vig-
orously
62 summóveō, -ovére (2), -óvī, -ótum, to
drive off, remove
súmmus, -a, -um, very great, the greatest, the top of . . .
súmō, -mere (3), -mpsī, -mptum, to
take
56 súper (+ acc.), over, above
supérbus, -a, -um, proud, arrogant,
magnificent
61 supérior, -or, -us, higher, more advanced (in age)
63 súperō (1), to overcome, defeat
65 superstítiō, -ónis (f), superstition
64 supérsum, -ésse (irreg.), -fuī, to remain,
be left, survive
66 supínus, -a, -um, low-lying
61 súpplex, -icis (m/f), suppliant
65 supplícium, -ī (n), punishment
65 súpplicō (1), to offer worship to
55 suppónō, -ónere (3), -ósuī, -ósitum, to
put in place of, substitute
67 suprémus, -a, -um, last, final, highest
súrgō, -rgere (3), -rréxī, -rréctum, to get
up, rise

168

55 **súrsum** (*adverb*), up, high
63 **suscípiō, -ípere** (3), **-épī, -éptum,** to accept, begin, undertake
65 **suspéctus, -a, -um,** suspect, suspected
64 **(in) suspénsō,** undecided, in suspense
68 **suspírium, -ī** (*n*), sigh
59 **sustíneō** (2), to withstand, check, support
**súus, -a, -um,** his, hers, one's, its, their (-own)

# T

**tabellárius, -ī** (*m*), courier
**tabérna, -ae** (*f*), shop, tavern
56 **tábula, -ae** (*f*), board, tablet, gameboard
**táceō** (2), to be quiet, say nothing
63 **taédet, -dére** (2), **-sum est,** it makes one (*acc.*) tired of something (*gen.*)
66 **taédium, -ī** (*n*), weariness, boredom, annoyance
**tális, -is, -e,** such, of this kind
**tam,** so
**támen,** however, nevertheless
54 **támquam,** like, as if, as
**tándem,** at last, at length
54 **tángō, -ere** (3), **tétigī, táctum,** to touch
**tántus, -a, -um,** so great, so much
**tántum** (*adverb*), to such an extent, so much, only
**tárdus, -a, -um,** slow, late in coming
63 **quam tardíssimē,** as late as possible
58 **tárdius** (*adverb*), more slowly
55 **taúrus, -ī** (*m*), bull
61 **télum, -ī** (*n*), weapon
**temerárius, -a, -um,** rash, reckless, bold
63 **témperō** (1), to control, rule, abstain, refrain
**témplum, -ī** (*n*), temple
**témpus, -oris** (*n*), time
61 **téndō, -dere** (3), **teténdī, -tum,** to stretch, extend
54 **ténebrae, -árum** (*f pl*), darkness
**téneō, -ére** (2), **-uī, -tum,** to hold
66 **ténuis, -is, -e,** slender, narrow
67 **ter,** three times, thrice
**térgum, -ī** (*n*), back, rear
62 **ā térgō,** (from) behind
62 **térga vértere,** to turn tail, flee
66 **térō, -ere** (3), **trívī, trítum,** to rub, wear away
**térra, -ae** (*f*), earth, land
**térror, -óris** (*m*), terror, fear
55 **tertiárius, -ī** (*m*), gladiator substituted for one who has been killed
**tértius, -a, -um,** third
65 **tértiō,** (for) the third time
**testaméntum, -ī** (*n*), testament, will

66 **téxtilis, -is, -e,** woven
**tímeō** (2), to fear
**tímor, -óris** (*m*), fear
68 **títulus, -ī** (*m*), inscription
**tóga, -ae** (*f*), toga; sometimes symbolic of life in peacetime as opposed to war, of civil as opposed to military life, or of a formal as opposed to an informal life style
**tóga virílis,** plain white toga worn by adult men; its assumption at puberty was celebrated by a coming-of-age ceremony
**tóllō, -ere** (3), **sústulī, sublátum,** to lift, raise, pick up
68 **tóndeō, -dére** (2), **totóndī, -sum,** to shave
66 **tónsor, -óris** (*m*), barber
61 **torméntum, -ī** (*n*), torment, torture; war-machine for hurling missiles
**tot,** so many
**tótus, -a, -um,** all, the whole
65 **tractátus, -ūs** (*m*), investigation
57 **tracto** (1), to discuss, handle
**trádō, -ere** (3), **-idī, -itum,** to hand over, pass on (information), report
66 **tragoédia, -ae** (*f*), tragedy
**tráhō, -here** (3), **-xī, -ctum,** to drag, pull, draw out, prolong
54 **trāíciō, -ícere** (3), **-iécī, -iéctum,** to stab through, pierce
63 **tranquíllus, -a, -um,** tranquil, peaceful
**tráns** (+ *acc.*), across
66 **tránseō, -íre** (*irreg.*), **-iī, -itum,** to go across, go past, pass
55 **trecéntiēs,** three hundred times
**trēs, trēs, tría,** three
56 **tribúnal, -ális** (*n*), tribunal, magistrate's raised platform
57 **tribúnus, -ī** (*m*), tribune
57 **tribúnus plébis,** magistrate elected to protect the interests of the lower classes at Rome
62 **tribúnus mílitum,** one of the six senior officers of a Roman legion
61 **tríbuō, -úere** (3), **-uī, -útum,** to allot, grant
61 **tríbus, -ūs** (*f*), tribe
**triclínium, -ī** (*n*), dining room
55 **tríduum, -ī** (*n*), three-day period
65 **triénnium, -ī** (*n*), three-year period
68 **tríēns, -ntis** (*m*), drinking cup holding one-third of a sextarius, or about five ounces
62 **tríplex, -icis,** triple
61 **trirémis, -is, -e,** having three oars to a bench
54 **trīstimónium, -ī** (*n*), sadness, sorrow
**trístis, -is, -e,** sad, gloomy, harsh

55   **trū́dō, -dere** (3), **-sī, -sum,** to push, shove (along)

66   **trúncus, -ī** (m), trunk (of the body), body

    **tū,** you (sing.)

54   **tū́ba, -ae** (f), trumpet

    **tū́bicen, -inis** (m), trumpeter

62 ·  **tū́eor, tuérī** (2), **tū́itus sum,** to look out for, protect

54   **tum,** at that moment, then

63   **tū́meō** (2), to swell with anger

    **tumúltus, -ūs** (m), uproar, din, commotion

54   **tunc,** then, at that time, in those days

    **tū́rba, -ae** (f), crowd, mob

62   **tū́rma, -ae** (f), cavalry squadron of thirty men

62   **turmā́tim,** in squadrons

61   **tū́rris, -is** (f), tower, siege tower, dovecote

65   **tūs, tū́ris** (n), incense

57   **tū́tus, -a, -um,** safe

60     **tū́tō,** safely

    **tū́us, -a, -um,** your (sing.)

# U

56   **ūbértim,** abundantly, copiously

    **ū́bi,** where, when

55   **ubī́que,** everywhere

54   **ū́dus, -a, -um,** wet, soaked

59   **ulcī́scor, -cī́scī, -tus sum,** to take revenge on, punish

64   **ū́llus, -a, -um,** any

    **ū́ltimus, -a, -um,** last, least, most wretched

58   **ū́ltrā** ( + acc.), beyond

    **úmbra, -ae** (f), shadow, shade

58   **úmerus, -ī** (m), upper arm

    **úmquam,** ever

    **Únde . . . ?** Where . . . from?

    **úndique,** on all sides, from all sides

    **unguéntum, -ī** (n), ointment, perfume, oil

55   **únguis, -is** (m), nail (of the hand or foot), claw

    **únguō, -guere** (3), **-xī, -ctum,** to anoint, smear with oil

59   **ūnivérsus, -a, -um,** whole, entire

64     **in ūnivérsum,** in general

    **ū́nus, -a, -um,** one

    **urbs, -bis** (f), city

54   **urceātim,** by the pitcher, in buckets

58   **ū́rgeō, -ére** (2), **úrsī,** to press, insist

56   **úrna, -ae** (f), urn

56   **ū́rō, -ere** (3), **ússī, ústum,** to burn

59   **úsquam,** anywhere

63   **úsque,** up to, as far as

59   **ū́stor, -ṓris** (m), corpse burner

62   **ū́sus, -ūs** (m), use, need, requirement

    **ut** ( + indicative), when, as

    **ut** ( + subjunctive), so that, that, to

    **utérque, útraque, utrúmque,** each (of two), both

59   **útinam,** would that, I wish that

55   **ū́tique,** at any rate, at least

60   **ū́tor, -ī** (3), **ū́sus sum** ( + abl.), to use, take advantage of

    **úxor, -ṓris** (f), wife

# V

63   **vácō** (1), to be empty, free, have time

68   **vácuus, -a, -um,** empty

    **váldē,** very, very much

    **váleō** (2), to be strong, be well

62   **vállum, -ī** (n), palisade, stockade of wooden stakes

55   **várius, -a, -um,** particolored, spotted

55   **vávatō, -ónis** (m), doll

61   **véctis, -is** (m), lever, crowbar

    **veheménter,** violently, vigorously, immensely, greatly

    **vehículum, -ī** (n), (wheeled) vehicle

58   **véhō, -here** (3), **-xī, -ctum,** to carry, convey

63   **vélōx, -ócis,** swift, rapid

55   **vélum, -ī** (n), sail

    **véndō, -ere** (3), **-idī, -itum,** to sell

59   **véneō, -íre** (4), **-iī, -itum,** to be sold

63   **venerā́tiō, -ónis** (f), veneration, homage

65   **véneror, -ā́rī** (1), **-ā́tus sum,** to venerate, worship

65   **vénia, -ae** (f), pardon

    **véniō, venī́re** (4), **vḗnī, véntum,** to come

67   **vēr, -ris** (n), spring (the season)

    **vérberō** (1), to beat

    **véreor, - érī** (2), **-itus sum,** to be afraid, fear

62   **vérsor, -ári** (1), **-átus sum,** to stay

    **vérsus, -ūs** (m), verse, line (of poetry)

60   **vértō, -tere** (3), **-tī, -sum,** to turn

    **vérus, -a, -um,** true

    **vḗrō,** truly, indeed

    **rē vḗrā,** really, actually

    **véscor, -ī** (3) ( + abl.), to feed (on)

    **véster, -tra, -trum,** your (pl.)

    **véstis, -is** (f), clothing, garment

    **vétō, -áre** (1), **-uī, -itum,** to forbid, prohibit

    **vétus, -eris,** old

64   **vetústus, -a, -um,** of long standing

    **véxō** (1), to annoy, harass

    **vía, -ae** (f), road, street

    **viā́tor, -óris** (m), traveler

63   **více** (abl., irreg.), place, role, duty

    **vīcī́nus, -a, -um,** neighboring, nearby

63 vicíssim, in turn, in exchange
58 vicissitúdō, -inis (f), change, vicissitude
victória, -ae (f), victory
64 vícus, -ī (m), side street, alley
vídeō, vidére (2), vídī, vísum, to see
víduus, -a, -um, deprived, widowed
68 vígil, -ilis, awake, sleepless.
vígilō (1), to be watchful, stay awake
vīgíntī, twenty
67 vílica, -ae (f), overseer's wife
vílicus, -ī (m), overseer, farm manager
vílla, -ae (f), farmhouse, country house, villa
61 vímen, -inis (n), wicker, reed
víncō, -ere (3), vīcī, víctum, to win, conquer, overcome
vínea, -ae (f), vines, vineyard, movable shelter for siege-workers
vínum, -ī (n), wine
víolō (1), to harm, violate
vir, vírī (m), man, grown man
66 víreō (2), to be green, flourish
vírgō, -inis (f), maiden
virílis, -is, -e, a man's, of a man
tóga virílis: see tóga
59 vírtūs, -útis (f), courage, determination, strength
vīs, vim (acc.), vī (abl.) (f), force, (pl) strength

68 vísō, -ere (3), -ī, to go to see, visit
víta, -ae (f), life
63 vítium, -ī (n), fault, vice
vítō (1), to avoid
54 vítulus, -ī (m), calf
vívō, -vere (3), -xī, -ctum, to live
56 vívus, -a, -um, alive, living
vix, scarcely, with difficulty, only just
vócō (1), to call
55 vólō (1), to fly
vólō, vélle (irreg.), vóluī, to wish, want, be willing
58 volúntās, -átis (f), will, willingness, consent
62 volúptās, -átis (f), pleasure
vōs, you (pl.)
vōx, vócis (f), voice
65 vótum, -ī (n), vow
58 vúlgus, -ī (n), the common people, mob, rabble
vúlnerō (1), to wound
vúlnus, -eris (n), wound
54 vúlpēs, -is (f), fox

# X

66 xýstum, -ī (n), (Greek word) shaded walkway

171

# PROPER NAMES

**Alcínous, -ī** (*m*), legendary king encountered by Odysseus (*Od.* VI–VIII) (66C:10)
**Anícius Máximus,** Roman governor of Bithynia before Pliny (64:5)
**Antónius, M.** (Marc Antony), member of second Triumvirate and paramour of Cleopatra (Ex. 62c)
**(Vía) Áppia,** Rome's first great highway, built by Appius Claudius Caecus (312 B.C.), from Rome to the end of the Italian peninsula at Brundisium (58 *passim*)
**Apúlia,** modern Puglia, province of SE Italy, just above the "heel" of the Italian "boot" (60:25)
**Arícia,** town 16 miles S. of Rome on the Appian Way (58:3)
**Asc(u)lánus, -ī** (*m*), a resident of Asculum (61, p. 70)
**Ásia,** Asia Minor, modern Turkey (54:7)
**Átticus, T. Pompónius,** close friend and correspondent of Cicero (60:12)
**Augústus,** first emperor of Rome (27 B.C.–A.D. 14) (63)
**Avītus, Iūnius,** young friend of Pliny (68B:2)
**Bāiánus, -a, -um,** belonging to the resort town of Baiae near Naples (66D:2)
**Básilus, L. Minúcius,** officer under Caesar in Gaul and one of his assassins (Ex. 62d)
**Bíbulus, M.,** Caesar's colleague in the consulship of 59 B.C., proposer of Pompey's sole consulship in 52 B.C. (57:23)
**Bílbilis,** home town of the poet Martial in NE Spain (67C:3)
**Bírria, -ae** (*m*), a gladiator and henchman of Milo (58:10)
**Bīthŷnus, -ī** (*m*), a Bithynian, inhabitant of Bithynia in Asia Minor (64:2)
**Bonônia,** modern Bologna, city in Italy (61, p. 71)
**Bōtérdum,** an unsophisticated village in NE Spain (67C:5)
**Bovíllae, -árum** (*f pl*), a town S. of Rome on the Appian Way (58:3)
**Bovillánus, -a, -um,** of or belonging to Bovillae (58:14)
**Brundísium,** modern Brindisi, town in the "heel" of the Italian peninsula, port of embarkation to Greece (60:29)
**Brútus, D. Iúnius,** one of Caesar's officers in Gaul (61:22)
**Caésar, -aris,** used generically of "the Emperor" (56S:4)
**Caésar, C. Iúlius** (100–44 B.C.), general, statesman, author of commentaries on the Gallic and civil wars, cos. 59 B.C. (62 *passim*)
**Caesariánus, -ī** (*m*), a soldier or supporter of C. Iulius Caesar (Ex. 62c)
**Camíllus,** a friend of Cicero (60:12)
**Cáppadox, -ocis** (*m*), a Cappadocian, inhabitant of Cappadocia in Asia Minor (54S:5)
**Céltibēr, -rī** (*m*), inhabitant of Celtiberia (region of NE Spain) (67C:5)
**Charidémus,** Greek freedman, **paedagōgus** to the poet Martial (68C:1)
**Chíus, -a, -um,** Chian, of Chios (island off coast of Asia Minor), famous for luxurious living (54S:2)
**Cícerō, M. Túllius** (106–43 B.C.), statesman, orator, author of philosophical and rhetorical works and over 900 letters, cos. 63 B.C. (Part II *passim*)
**Clódia,** sister of P. Clodius and mistress of the poet Catullus (58S:9)
**Clōdiánus, -ī** (*m*), a supporter of P. Clodius (58S:9)
**Clódius (P. Clódius Púlcher),** political strongman for the Caesarian faction, brother of the notorious Clodia; as tribune of the plebs in 58 B.C., responsible for Cicero's exile (Part II *passim*)
**Clódius, Sex.,** agent of P. Clodius, probably his freedman (58:29)
**Dácius, -ī** (*m*), inhabitant of Dacia (modern Rumania) (Ex.63c)
**Dolābélla, P. Cornélius,** a Caesarian, Cicero's son-in-law (60:6)
**Échion, -ōnis** (*m*), a rag dealer, one of Trimalchio's guests (55:1)
**Eudámus,** a gladiator and henchman of Milo (58:9)
**Faústa,** wife of Milo (58:7)
**Fortūnáta,** a freedwoman, wife of Trimalchio (56:21)
**Fúfius, M.,** a friend of Milo (58:8)
**Fúlvia,** wife of Clodius (58:23)

172

**Ganymédēs, -is** (*m*), one of Trimalchio's guests in the *Cena* (54:1)
**Germánicus**, a surname of (among others) the emperor Domitian (66A:3)
**Glýcō, -ōnis** (*m*), a deceived husband, gossiped about by Trimalchio's guests (55:14)
**Habínnas, -ae** (*m*), a stonemason, one of Trimalchio's guests (56:8)
**Hermógenēs, -is** (*m*), father-in-law of Glyco (55:17)
**Hispánia, -ae** (*f*), Spain (61:1)
**Hispánus, -a, -um**, Spanish (66B:7)
**Hypsaéus, P. Plaútius**, candidate for consul, 53 B.C. (57:1)
**Iắnus, -ī** (*m*), patron god of gates, doors, and the month of January (66C:4)
**Ísis, -idis** (*f*), Egyptian goddess worshiped in the Greco-Roman world (64, p. 95)
**Iúppiter, Ióvis** (*m*), king of the gods (54:25)
**Labiénus, T.**, principal lieutenant of Caesar in Gaul (Ex. 62c)
**Lānúvium**, Milo's home town, about 20 miles S. of Rome (58:1)
**Lārísa**, town in N. Greece near Pharsalus (62:34)
**Lárius (lácus)**, modern Lake Como in N. Italy (66D-1)
**Laurentínum, -ī** (*n*), a country estate near Laurentum (67D:2)
**Mammaéa, -ae** (*m*), popular small-town politician discussed in the *Cena* (55:19)
**Mánēs, -ium** (*m pl*), the deified spirits of the dead (68D:1)
**Marcélla**, a Spanish woman, friend and patron of the poet Martial (66C:8)
**Marcéllus, M. Claúdius**, cos. 51 B.C., a prominent Optimate (58S:1)
**Martialis, M. Valerius**, Roman writer of epigrams, from Spain (A.D. 40–104) (Ex. 66b)
**Massília**, modern Marseilles, on the Mediterranean coast of France (59S:5)
**Massiliénsis, -is** (*m/f*), a Massiliote, resident of Massilia (61:14)
**Mílō, T. Ánnius**, political strongman for the Optimates, rival and murderer of the Caesarian Clodius (Part II *passim*)
**Nausícaā**, daughter of King Alcinous (66C:9)
**Nerōniánus, -a, -um**, belonging to Nero, Roman emperor A.D. 54–68 (66B:6)
**Nérva**, Roman emperor A.D. 96–98 (Ex. 63e)
**Nīcaéa**, city in Bithynia (in Asia Minor) (64:17)
**Nīcomḗdia**, capital of Bithynia (in Asia Minor) (64:17)
**Norbánus**, unpopular small-town politician discussed in the *Cena* (55:20)
**Orcīniánus, -a, -um**, belonging to Orcus (the underworld), pertaining to death (67A:7)
**Paéstum**, town on the Italian coast south of Naples (66C:3)
**Petraítēs, -is** (*m*), a famous gladiator of the 1st century A.D. (56:11)
**Pharsálus, -ī** (*f*), town in N. Greece, site of the final defeat of Pompey by Caesar in 48 B.C. (Ex. 62b)
**Pláncus, T. Munátius**, tribune of the plebs 53 B.C., a partisan of Pompey (57:12)
**Plátea**, an unsophisticated village in NE Spain (67C:5)
**Plínius (C. Plínius Caecílius Secúndus)**, lawyer, statesman, and writer of the Imperial period (A.D. 62–114) (Part IV *passim*)
**Pompēiánus, -ī** (*m*), a Pompeian, partisan of Pompey the Great (Ex. 60c)
**Pompéius (C. Pompéius Mágnus)**, general and statesman of the late Republic, Caesar's most powerful rival (57 *passim* and Part III *passim*)
**Pompónius** (60:12), (see Atticus)
**Pónticus, -ī** (*m*), an inhabitant of Pontus in Asia Minor (64:2)
**(Basílica) Pórcia**, Rome's oldest basilica, built by the censor M. Porcius Cato in 184 B.C. (58:31)
**Safínius**, a small-town politician mentioned in the *Cena* (54:7)
**Scīpiō, Q. Metéllus**, candidate for consul in 53 B.C., father-in-law of Pompey (57:1)
**Spársus**, a wealthy friend of Martial (66B:1)
**Súlla, L. Cornélius**, dictator 81–79 B.C., an extreme Optimate and father-in-law of Milo (58:7)
**Sulpícius, Sérvius**, interrex who appointed Pompey sole consul in 52 (57:24)
**Teídius, Sex.**, Roman senator who brought Clodius's corpse back to Rome (58:19)
**Teréntia**, wife of Cicero (60:1)
**Thraex (Thrax), -cis** (*m*), Thracian, inhabitant of Thrace in N. Greece; also a gladiator with Thracian-style equipment (62:20; 55:25)
**Títus**, aedile of the town where the *Cena* takes place (55:8)
**Trāiánus, M. Úlpius**, Roman emperor A.D. 98–117 (Part IV *passim*)

**Trebónius, C.**, Caesar's lieutenant (later one of his assassins) who conducted the siege of Massilia in 49 B.C. (61:1)

**Trimálchiō (C. Pompéius Trimálchiō Maecēnātiánus)**, nouveau-riche freedman, host of the banquet described in the *Cena Trimalchionis* (56:1)

**Tullíola** (diminutive of Tullia), daughter of Cicero (60:1 )

**Týrius, -a, -um,** pertaining to Tyre, center of the purple-dye industry; hence, purple, luxurious, extravagant (68C:11)

**Vāriánus, -a, -um,** pertaining to P. Quintilius Varus, Roman general who suffered a disastrous defeat in Germany in A.D. 9 (61s, p. 71)

# ACKNOWLEDGMENTS

The authors and publisher are grateful to the following for permission to reproduce photographs: Alinari/Art Resource, New York, for pages 23, 47, 55a, 82, 91, 112; The Bettman Archive, New York, for page 55c; the Trustees of the British Museum for pages 15, 79, 86; the Vindolanda Trust, the Chesterholm Museum for page 123a; Frederick Lewis, New York, for page 83; Ron Palma for page 55b; the Romisch-Germanisches Museum, Cologne, for page 123c; the Royal Commission on Historical Monuments, London, for page 123b.

The drawings that appear on pages 6, 63, 70, 71, 75, and 118 of this book were done by Claudia Karabaic Sargent.

For literary extracts we would like to credit the following individuals and/or sources:

pages 33, 41, and 54: Professor James S. Ruebel, Iowa State University; page 36: Casson, "And Never Say No—Politics as usual in Ancient Rome," Smithsonian, Oct. 1984; page 79: Workman, *They Saw It Happen in Classical Times*, Basil Blackwell, Oxford, 1965; page 80: Warner, *Fall of the Roman Republic: Plutarch's Life of Pompey*, Penguin, Baltimore, 1964; page 81: Lewis and Reinhold, *Roman Civilization, Sourcebook II; The Empire*, Harper & Row, 1966; pages 83 and 101: Radice, *Pliny, Letters and Panegyricus*, Harvard University Press, Cambridge, 1975.